D1217624

FOURTEENTH CENTURY ENGLAND

III

The essays in this volume present new research on aspects of the politics and culture of fourteenth-century England, including close studies of political events such as the quarrel of Edward II and Thomas of Lancaster and Bishop Despenser's Crusade, fresh considerations of the political and cultural context of English royal tombs and the Wilton Diptych, a number of important analyses of regional politics and regional culture in Bristol, East Anglia and Winchester – all with implications for the bigger picture – and a discussion of late medieval French attitudes to the deposition of Richard II; that and studies of the war with France and the Bishop of Norwich's attack on Flanders carry the focus beyond the shores of England.

W. M. ORMROD is Professor of Medieval History at the University of York.

Fourteenth Century England

ISSN 1471–3020

General Editors
Chris Given-Wilson
J. S. Hamilton
W. M. Ormrod
Nigel Saul

The series aims to provide a forum for the most recent research into the political, social, economic, ecclesiastical and cultural history of the fourteenth century in England. Contributions are currently invited for the next volume, which will appear in 2006; draft submissions should be sent by June 2005 to Professor J. S. Hamilton at the following address:

Department of History
Baylor University
Waco
Texas 76798–7306
USA

FOURTEENTH CENTURY ENGLAND

III

Edited by W. M. Ormrod

THE BOYDELL PRESS

© Contributors 2004

All Rights Reserved. Except as permitted under current legislation
no part of this work may be photocopied, stored in a retrieval system,
published, performed in public, adapted, broadcast,
transmitted, recorded or reproduced in any form or by any means,
without the prior permission of the copyright owner

First published 2004
The Boydell Press, Woodbridge

ISBN 1 84383 046 9

The Boydell Press is an imprint of Boydell & Brewer Ltd
PO Box 9, Woodbridge, Suffolk IP12 3DF, UK
and of Boydell & Brewer Inc.
PO Box 41026, Rochester, NY 14604–4126, USA
website: www.boydellandbrewer.com

A catalogue record for this book is available
from the British Library

This publication is printed on acid-free paper

Printed in Great Britain by
Antony Rowe Ltd., Chippenham, Wiltshire

CONTENTS

ILLUSTRATIONS

CONTRIBUTORS

Mark Arvanigian	California State University, Fresno
Jane Beal	University of California, Davis
Kelly DeVries	Loyola College in Maryland
Alastair Dunn	Oakham School
David Green	Trinity College, Dublin
Andy King	University of Durham
Christian D. Liddy	University of Durham
Lisa Monnas	London
Anthony Musson	University of Exeter
W. M. Ormrod	University of York
Mark Page	University of Leicester
D. M. Palliser	University of Leeds
Craig Taylor	University of York
Kris Towson	University of St Andrews

PREFACE

Fourteenth Century England, now in its third volume, exists to publish, biennially, a representative sample of recent and innovative work on the history of the fourteenth century, with particular emphasis on the politics and political culture of England. It is organised under the co-editorship of Nigel Saul (Royal Holloway, University of London), Chris Given-Wilson (University of St Andrews) and Mark Ormrod (University of York); J. S. Hamilton (Baylor University) has recently joined the editorial group.

Fourteenth Century England does not publish the proceedings of a conference, although some of the contributions naturally arise from conference papers. In particular, a number of the articles published here were first aired in 2002 in sessions sponsored by the Society of the White Hart at the International Congress on Medieval Studies, Western Michigan University, and at sessions organised by the Society for Fourteenth-Century Studies at the International Medieval Congress, University of Leeds. Between them, these two conferences now provide the main regular venue for the presentation and discussion of new research in the field. The editors of *Fourteenth Century England*, who organise the Society for Fourteenth-Century Studies, are especially grateful to the Society of the White Hart for its continued patronage of international research on later medieval English history.

Rather than following a single theme, then, the contributions to this volume represent a cross-section of recent research in fourteenth-century studies and reflect the concerns and trends of current scholarship on the field. The articles by Andy King, Christian D. Liddy, Kris Towson and Kelly DeVries indicate the considerable potential that still exists for close work on the problems of evidence and interpretation relating to discrete episodes in the political history of the period: such revisionism itself reflects the complexity and breadth of the primary sources relating to the fourteenth century. It might be pointed out in particular that a number of those and other studies in this volume demonstrate the 'return to the chronicles' that has been a feature of political history over the last decade or so: no longer merely a last refuge when the documentary sources dry up, the chronicles – as Andy King, Jane Beal, Kelly DeVries and Craig Taylor remind us – can provide compelling evidence of political motivations and cultural phenomena alike. Another strand of scholarship represented here is the biographical and prosopographical approach: the articles by Anthony Musson, David Green, Mark Arvanigian and Alastair Dunn indicate a powerful tradition in fourteenth-century studies, whose approach has been particularly evident in the work of the Society of the White Hart and which finds fruition elsewhere in *Medieval Prosopography* and (soon to come) in contributions to the *Oxford Dictionary of National Biography*. Mark Page's article speaks to an equally powerful tradition of meticulous and systematic research in the manorial records of the period to reveal trends in the economic life (in this case) of large-scale estates. Finally, David Palliser, Anthony Musson and Lisa Monnas all reveal new aspects of the political and material culture generated and 'lived' by royal and other high-status patrons. In these three works, as in the articles by Jane Beal, David Green and Craig Taylor, we can see how scholars rooted in the traditional and valued methodology of documentary analysis can find new perspectives on their subjects by considering the intellectual and material cultures in which fourteenth-century people operated and by being alive and receptive to the interdisciplinary methodologies that have become so integral to medieval studies in recent generations.

It remains for me to thank the Board and staff of Boydell & Brewer, especially Richard Barber and Caroline Palmer, for their continued support for *Fourteenth Century England*, my fellow editors Nigel Saul and Chris Given-Wilson for their experienced guidance, and the contributors to Volume III for their scholarship, professionalism and good humour. The first cycle of editorship having been completed with this volume, the responsibility for *Fourteenth Century England IV* will be taken by J. S. Hamilton and potential contributors may contact him at the Department of History, Baylor University, Waco, Texas 76798–7306, USA.

W. M. Ormrod
May 2003

ABBREVIATIONS

BIHR	*Bulletin of the Institute of Historical Research*
BL	British Library, London
BPR	*Register of Edward the Black Prince* (4 vols, London, 1930–33)
BRO	Bristol Record Office, Bristol
CChR	*Calendar of Charter Rolls*
CCR	*Calendar of Close Rolls*
CCW	*Calendar of Chancery Warrants*
CFR	*Calendar of Fine Rolls*
CIM	*Calendar of Inquisitions Miscellaneous*
CIPM	*Calendar of Inquisitions Post Mortem*
Complete Peerage	G. E. Cokayne, *The Complete Peerage*, new edn (13 vols, London, 1910–59)
CPR	*Calendar of Patent Rolls*
DNB	*Dictionary of National Biography*, ed. L. Stephen and S. Lee (63 vols, London, 1885–1903)
EHR	*English Historical Review*
Foedera	*Foedera, conventions, literae et cujuscunque generis acta publica*, ed. T. Rymer, various editions (as individually specified)
HRO	Hampshire Record Office, Winchester
JGR 1379–83	*John of Gaunt's Register, 1379–1383*, ed. Eleanor C. Lodge and Robert Somerville (2 vols, Camden Society, 3rd ser. lvi–lvii, London, 1937)
NRO	Norfolk Record Office, Norwich
PW	*Parliamentary Writs*, ed. F. Palgrave (2 vols in 4 parts, London, 1827–34)
PRO	The National Archives: Public Record Office, Kew
RCHM	Royal Commission on Historical Monuments
Royal Wills	*A Collection of All the Wills now known to be extant of all the Kings and Queens of England, Princes and Princesses of Wales and every Branch of the Blood Royal from the Reign of William the Conqueror to that of Henry VII*, ed. J. Nichols (London, 1780)
RP	*Rotuli Parliamentorum* (6 vols, London, 1783)
RS	*Rotuli Scotiae*, ed. D. MacPherson (2 vols, London, 1814–19)
SR	*Statutes of the Realm* (11 vols, London, 1810–28)
TRHS	*Transactions of the Royal Historical Society*
VCH	*Victoria County History of England*
WAM	Westminster Abbey Muniments, London

ROYAL MAUSOLEA IN THE LONG FOURTEENTH CENTURY
(1272–1422)

D. M. Palliser

In the fourteenth century Westminster Abbey fulfilled the double function of coronation church and mausoleum for the kings of England, a combination rare among the royal churches of medieval Europe. By tradition, the two functions had been combined from a very early period, even from the Abbey's distant origins. 'From the era of its first foundation', claimed Prior John Flete in the fifteenth century, 'this has been the place of royal consecration, the burial place of kings [*regum sepultura*], and the repository of the royal insignia.'[1] In fact, however, the systematic combination of functions came much later than Flete implied. Coronations were held there almost without exception from 1066, but it was not until the thirteenth and fourteenth centuries that it became the usual regum sepultura. Why was this? How far did it represent a royal cult of the Confessor, and how far the growing importance of London-Westminster as a capital? And once the tradition was established, why were some monarchs buried elsewhere, whether through choice or circumstance? The royal connections with the Abbey have been extensively discussed, most recently and helpfully by Emma Mason, Paul Binski and David Carpenter,[2] but there is more to be said on the wider issues raised by royal choices of burial places.

Between 1066 and 1216 there was apparently no close relationship between Abbey and monarchy, despite the fact that the Confessor had rebuilt it as his mausoleum church.[3] The successive coronations of Harold II (probably) and William I in the newly completed Abbey were surely intended to emphasise their respective legitimacy as heirs to the Confessor's throne rather than any special regard for his cult or foundation; and both kings chose to be buried elsewhere in churches they had founded or patronised. This was, indeed, the pattern with all the Anglo-Norman kings: 'each founder intended to be buried alone or, at most, with the immediate members of his family, perhaps in order to ensure an exclusive concentration of

---

[1] *The History of Westminster Abbey by John Flete*, ed. J. A. Robinson (Cambridge, 1909), p. 63; Emma Mason, *Westminster Abbey and its People c.1050–c.1216* (Woodbridge, 1996), pp. 288, 305. Throughout this essay, 'the Abbey' means Westminster.

[2] Mason, *Westminster Abbey*, esp. pp. 269–305; Paul Binski, *Westminster Abbey and the Plantagenets: Kingship and the Representation of Power 1200–1400* (London, 1995), passim; D. A. Carpenter, *The Reign of Henry III* (London, 1996), esp. pp. 409–61; D. A. Carpenter, 'Westminster Abbey in Politics, 1258–1269', *Thirteenth Century England VIII*, ed. Michael Prestwich, R. H. Britnell and Robin Frame (Woodbridge, 2001), pp. 49–58. See also *The Cloister and the World: Essays in Medieval History in Honour of Barbara Harvey*, ed. John Blair and Brian Golding (Oxford, 1996). An exception to the neglect of the wider perspectives is John Steane, *The Archaeology of the Medieval English Monarchy*, 2nd edn (London, 1999), pp. 41–70.

[3] Mason, *Westminster Abbey*, pp. 269–87. No monarch after the Confessor was buried there until Henry III; and none before him except Harold I (1040), unless there is truth in the tradition that King Saeberht (d.616/17) was the first founder and was buried there.

monastic intercessions'.[4] No members of the royal family seem to have copied Edward in being buried at Westminster except for his widow Edith and Henry I's first queen, Matilda, neither of whom may have intended burial there.[5]

Nor was it only that Westminster was not yet a royal mausoleum: there was simply no special relationship between Abbey and crown other than at coronations, despite frequent assertions to the contrary. On the one hand, 'it is the monastery's slowness in exploiting Edward which is remarkable': the Confessor was canonised in 1161, but even that failed to spark a royal or popular cult. And on the crown's part, Dr Mason sees antipathy rather than indifference. 'The Norman and Angevin kings appear almost to have had a grudge against the abbey, perhaps because it was too close to the palace or because its claims were unacceptable.'[6]

Whether that is so or not, the Angevins maintained a special relationship instead with Fontevraud, a double monastery in the Loire Valley. Henry II was buried there in 1189, and his son Richard I ten years later. The loss of Anjou to the French crown in 1203–04 prevented the continuation of this tradition, and King John opted for burial in his Cistercian foundation of Beaulieu, later choosing instead Worcester cathedral because of his veneration for St Wulfstan.[7] Nevertheless, John's widow Isabella was permitted burial at Fontevraud in 1246, and although John and Henry III both had to be buried in England, their hearts were successively donated to Fontevraud, that of Henry as late as 1291.[8]

Henry III

'Fiction and Invention', says Dr Mason, echoing an eighteenth-century historian of the Abbey, 'played no small part in creating the image, and hence the political potential, of Westminster as perceived in turn by Henry III and Richard II.'[9] Both were devoted to the cult of their canonised predecessor, and both forged close royal links with the Abbey. The origins of Henry's devotion to St Edward are obscure, but he certainly signalled it as early as 1228 in a petition to the pope.[10] In 1239 he named his first-born son after the Confessor; in 1241 he began a new shrine for the saint; and in 1245 he started to replace the Confessor's abbey church by a magnificent new one. His principal aim, as attested by Matthew Paris, was to honour St Edward, and he signalled the completion of the eastern parts of the church on 13 October 1269 by a solemn dedication service, coupled with the translation of Edward's remains from his tomb north of the high altar to a new and lavish shrine in his own chapel of St Edward. The shrine base, together with the base of Henry's own intended tomb and the presbytery pavement, were all apparently made by the Cosmati firm for Henry in the 1260s, though the chronology is not free of prob-

---

4   Mason, *Westminster Abbey*, p. 271.
5   Ibid., pp. 270–92.
6   Frank Barlow, *Edward the Confessor* (London, 1970), p. 266; Mason, *Westminster Abbey*, p. 287.
7   *Royal Wills*, pp. 13–14; *Foedera*, Record Commission edn (4 vols in 7 parts, London, 1816–69), I, p. 144.
8   1291 writ: WAM, 6318B, printed in A. P. Stanley, *Historical Memorials of Westminster Abbey*, 1st edn (London, 1868), p. 505. Cf. J. C. Wall, *The Tombs of the Kings of England* (London, 1891), pp. 242, 249; Binski, *Westminster Abbey*, pp. 92, 102.
9   Mason, *Westminster Abbey*, p. 305.
10 Binski, *Westminster Abbey*, p. 52.

lems.[11] And finally, when Henry died in 1272, he was given temporary burial in the very tomb from which the Confessor's remains had been moved three years before.[12]

The sheer scale of Henry's achievement has not always been sufficiently emphasised. Colvin has calculated that he spent in all well over £40,000 on Abbey and shrine, at a time when his average annual income was some £34,000. This puts into perspective Louis IX's contemporary building of the Ste Chapelle (for the equivalent of some £10,000), which has been claimed as 'perhaps the most ambitious of all the buildings constructed in the Middle Ages by sovereigns'.[13] The parallel with the Ste Chapelle is an apt one; it has been argued convincingly that it was, together with Reims, Amiens and St Denis, one of the models that Henry III and his master mason, Henry of Reyns, had most in mind in designing Westminster. Furthermore Louis built the Ste Chapelle specifically to house relics of the Passion, and at least one of Henry's purposes was to make Westminster a worthy home for precious relics.

Clearly, therefore, Henry had more than one purpose in rebuilding Westminster. He wished to honour St Edward and his shrine; to house other relics; and to enhance the Abbey's coronation role by providing in its new crossing 'a worthier theatre for coronations' where 'the sacrality of kingship . . . could be proclaimed, celebrated, and enhanced'.[14] Christopher Wilson goes further, suggesting that the new Abbey was

> to combine in a single building the functions of Reims, St-Denis and the Sainte-Chapelle. To the established roles of coronation church, shrine and repository for the regalia, Henry added two more. By 1246 he had decided to be buried near St Edward rather than in the choir of the London Temple Church: the intention was clearly to inaugurate an English royal pantheon comparable to that which had long existed at St-Denis. In 1247 Henry obtained from the Patriarch of Jerusalem the relic of the Precious Blood of Christ, which he bore to the Abbey in a solemn procession intended to recall those which had marked Louis' reception of the Crown of Thorns and other relics of Christ's Passion in 1239 and 1241.[15]

With the argument for a multi-purpose royal church owing much to foreign models there is no problem, but two qualifications will be suggested to Wilson's summary. It is not clear that Henry intended 'to inaugurate an English royal pantheon'; and nor is it certain that, once such a pantheon was established, St Denis was the only continental model which English kings had in mind.

[11] D. A. Carpenter, 'King Henry III and the Cosmati Work at Westminster Abbey', *The Cloister and the World*, ed. Blair and Golding, pp. 178–95; reprinted in Carpenter, *Reign of Henry III*, pp. 409–25. For the suggestion that Henry had long planned 13 October 1269 as an appropriate 'symmetrical' date, see Carpenter, 'Westminster Abbey in Politics', pp. 54–5.

[12] R. A. Brown, H. M. Colvin and A. J. Taylor, *The History of the King's Works: The Middle Ages* (2 vols, London, 1963), I, p. 479.

[13] Ibid., I, pp. 155–7; Binski, *Westminster Abbey*, p. 207 n. 3, citing Kimpel and Suckale; *Age of Chivalry: Art in Plantagenet England 1200–1400*, ed. Jonathan Alexander and Paul Binski (London, 1987), p. 77.

[14] Henrietta Leyser, 'Cultural Affinities', *The Short Oxford History of the British Isles: The Twelfth and Thirteenth Centuries, 1066–c.1280*, ed. Barbara Harvey (Oxford, 2001), p. 189.

[15] Christopher Wilson, Pamela Tudor-Craig, John Physick and Richard Gem, *The New Bell's Cathedral Guides: Westminster Abbey* (London, 1986), p. 25.

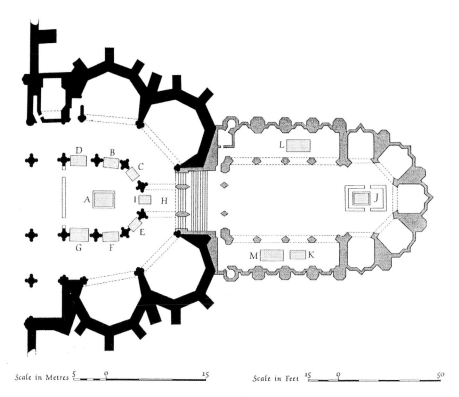

Figure 1. Westminster Abbey: the east end and Henry VII's Chapel, showing the royal tombs. A: shrine of Edward the Confessor. B: Henry III. C: Eleanor of Castile. D: Edward I. E: Philippa of Hainault. F: Edward III. G: Richard II and Anne of Bohemia. H: Henry V's chapel. I: Henry V's tomb. J: Henry VII and Elizabeth of York. K: Lady Margaret Beaufort. L: Elizabeth I. M: Mary, Queen of Scots

Unquestionably, Henry had a long-standing wish for burial in his new Abbey, and that was due to his devotion to the cult of St Edward – rather than, say, to the proximity of his palace, or the fact that London-Westminster was becoming effectively a twin capital city. By a writ of 23 October 1246 he announced his intention to be buried there, while his surviving will of 1253 confirmed his choice, 'not withstanding that I previously chose burial at the New Temple in London'. The writ gave as his motive 'reverence for the most glorious King Edward', while in his will he called the Abbey 'the church of Blessed Edward of Westminster', rather than by its dedication to St Peter.[16]

In the event, Henry's decision set a precedent. Until 1471, all his successors but three were buried in St Edward's Chapel, and even of those three, two (Edward II and Henry VI) may have intended to follow suit (Figure 1). How far, however, did Henry consciously plan 'an English royal pantheon'? That has often been assumed;

[16] Writ: WAM, 6318ᴬ; copy in WAM, 'Domesday', fol. 62r; printed by Stanley, *Historical Memorials*, 1st edn, p. 504; 3rd edn (London, 1869), p. 599. Will: *Royal Wills*, p. 15.

but it may be that all he intended was a mausoleum for himself and, at most, his immediate family. There was no special architectural provision for the royal tombs, which simply ringed the shrine, horseshoe-fashion, between the columns; the space is surprisingly cramped for a dedicated and permanent mausoleum.[17]

Even Henry's immediate family were not all buried in the Abbey. In 1287 his widow Eleanor took the veil at Amesbury (Wiltshire); she was buried there in 1291, but her heart was buried separately in the London Greyfriars, where one of her daughters was already buried.[18] Richard, earl of Cornwall, Henry's brother, was interred in his foundation of Hailes (Gloucestershire), together with his second wife and son, while his first wife was buried at Beaulieu (Hampshire). Edward I's daughter Eleanor was also buried at Beaulieu, while another of Edward's daughters, Mary, retired to Amesbury at her grandmother's prompting, and was buried there.[19] It is true that Henry III buried the heart of his murdered nephew, Henry of Almayne, close to the Confessor's shrine; and he also buried four of his own children, who had died young, in a collective tomb, possibly where Richard II's tomb was later built, and later moved to its present position just south of the Confessor's chapel, where they were subsequently joined by five infant children of Edward I. Two children of William de Valence who died in 1276–7 were also buried by Edward under grave slabs still surviving in the Confessor's chapel. These, however, were not normal royal burials, and both kings may have been entrusting those who died prematurely to the special protection of the saint.[20]

There is no evidence that, with these exceptions, Edward I took any special interest in the Abbey – whether as a mausoleum or otherwise – until halfway through his long reign. Instead, from 1277, he patronised lavishly his new Cistercian abbey of Vale Royal (Cheshire), which he regarded as his special foundation in rather the way his father had regarded Westminster, and where he may conceivably have planned to be buried.[21] In 1272 he did have his father buried in Westminster Abbey in the tomb now vacated by the Confessor, but that was only a temporary solution. Not until 1280 did Edward import precious stones for Henry's permanent tomb, and not until 1291 did he have it completed.[22]

Edward I

1290 seems, in fact, to mark a real turning point in the establishment of a permanent royal mausoleum at Westminster. Three things came together in quick succession: Edward's removal of his father's body to its new tomb; the sudden death of his

---

[17] H. M. Colvin, *Architecture and the After-Life* (London, 1991), p. 139; Binski, *Westminster Abbey*, pp. 91–2.

[18] Brown, Colvin and Taylor, *King's Works*, I, p. 486.

[19] Binski, *Westminster Abbey*, p. 92.

[20] *Westminster Abbey: Official Guide*, ed. T. Trowles (London, 2002), pp. 45, 85; Wilson et al., *Westminster Abbey*, pp. 118, 125. Cf. Brown, Colvin and Taylor, *King's Works*, I, pp. 478–9; Joan Tanner, 'Tombs of Royal Babies in Westminster Abbey', *Journal of the British Archaeological Association* 3rd ser. xvi (1953), pp. 26–32; Elizabeth M. Hallam, 'Introduction: The Eleanor Crosses and Royal Burial Customs', *Eleanor of Castile 1290–1990*, ed. David Parsons (Stamford, 1991), p. 15. There is some disagreement about whether the royal children's collective tomb was later moved: see below, n. 61.

[21] Brown, Colvin and Taylor, *King's Works*, I, pp. 248–57; Binski, *Westminster Abbey*, pp. 3, 8–9, 12; J. Denton, 'From the Foundation of Vale Royal Abbey to the Statute of Carlisle', *Thirteenth Century England IV*, ed. P. R. Coss and S. D. Lloyd (Woodbridge, 1992), pp. 123–37.

[22] Brown, Colvin and Taylor, *King's Works*, I, p. 479.

beloved queen Eleanor; and the king's sudden abandonment of interest in Vale Royal at the end of that year. The keeper of the works there was informed flatly that 'the king has ceased to concern himself with the works of that church, and henceforth will have nothing more to do with them'. Edward's reasons were not given; Colvin speculates that the monks had in some way displeased him, but Binski plausibly links it to the death of Eleanor.[23]

The reburial of Henry III should be considered first. His permanent tomb has a base produced by the same Cosmati team whom Henry had employed since the 1260s, which may well have been begun, if not completed, before his death. Yet it was not until 11 May 1290 that Edward 'suddenly and unexpectedly' (as the Bury Chronicle puts it) moved his father's body into the tomb,[24] and not until 1291 that he commissioned William Torel to design the existing bronze effigy. The delay is indeed puzzling, as Carpenter has noted; and there is much to be said for his suggestion that in the 1270s and 1280s Edward was hoping for a cult of his father (similar to that then growing around Louis IX), the Cosmati tomb being intended as a shrine. There are indeed records of miracles, and of royal encouragement of the cult, while the tomb incorporates recesses of a kind usually associated with shrines. If so, it may well be that the unceremonious reburial of Henry by night in 1290 was carried out by a disappointed son once the cult had flickered out.[25]

What was more decisive for Edward's developing ideas was the death of Queen Eleanor at Harby (Nottinghamshire) on 28 November 1290, followed by the king's decision to commemorate her by the most lavish series of monuments ever accorded to an English king or queen: three separate tombs and twelve memorial crosses, all erected between 1291 and 1294. The full scope of the programme is beyond the present purpose; but most relevant is the fact that there were three elaborate tombs, housing respectively her entrails (Lincoln), her heart (London Blackfriars) and her embalmed body (Westminster Abbey). Those at Lincoln and Westminster, complete by 1293, were each surmounted by a gilt-bronze effigy by William Torel.[26] With Henry's tomb in the place of honour immediately north of St Edward's shrine, and his daughter-in-law between the next pair of pillars to the east, the horseshoe of royal tombs was beginning to form.

Henry's and Eleanor's tombs, with their very similar effigies, must surely be seen not only as gestures of familial devotion, but also, as Colvin puts it, of Edward's desire to enhance the prestige of the monarchy through 'visible symbols of its piety and power'. Colvin also adds that the idea of a mausoleum around the Confessor's shrine may have been inspired by the example of Louis IX, who in 1263–4 had commissioned a set of sixteen effigies of his ancestors for St Denis.[27] That need not, however, have provided the only model. Edward and Eleanor had married in 1254 in the Cistercian monastery of Las Huelgas near Burgos, which had been founded specifically as the Castilian dynastic mausoleum and coronation church; and in

---

[23] Ibid., I, p. 252; Binski, *Westminster Abbey*, p. 3.

[24] *The Chronicle of Bury St Edmunds 1212–1301*, ed. Antonia Gransden (London, 1964), p. 94.

[25] Wilson et al., *Westminster Abbey*, p. 119; Carpenter, *Reign of Henry III*, pp. 423–4.

[26] Joan Evans, *English Art 1307–1461* (Oxford, 1949), pp. 1–5; Brown, Colvin and Taylor, *King's Works*, I, pp. 479–85; *Age of Chivalry*, ed. Alexander and Binski, pp. 361–6; *Eleanor of Castile*, ed. Parsons, passim. For drawings of the Lincoln monument before its destruction, see Brown, Colvin and Taylor, *King's Works*, I, pl. 35; *Age of Chivalry*, ed. Alexander and Binski, p. 366.

[27] Brown, Colvin and Taylor, *King's Works*, I, p. 485.

1270 they had visited Palermo, where the cathedral had served as the mausoleum of the Staufen dynasty. Hallam is surely right that it was Edward I who, whatever his model, set out to turn Westminster into 'an English royal mausoleum and major focus of the cult of kingship'.[28]

After 1291 Edward continued to bury royal relatives both in and close to St Edward's Chapel, including two who both died in 1296: his brother Edmund, earl of Lancaster, and his father's half-brother William de Valence, earl of Pembroke. Edmund was buried in the presbytery, north of the high altar, with his first wife Aveline two places to the west. Though the countess had died in 1272, both tombs are stylistically of about 1297–1300, and were presumably commissioned together by Edward; that of Edmund has been described by Wilson as 'the most ambitious canopy tomb of its date in Europe'.[29] William de Valence was buried in St Edmund's chapel, in a fine tomb of Limoges workmanship which was, after the gift of Henry III's heart to Fontevraud, 'the last physical manifestation of the Plantagenet dynasty's political and territorial links in western France'.[30]

Edward I, therefore, was probably the conscious creator of a permanent royal mausoleum at Westminster, and when he died at Burgh-by-Sands (Cumberland) in 1307 it was doubtless his intention to be buried in Westminster Abbey. Unfortunately, he left no extant will after 1272, when he had dictated one on crusade, specifying no burial place; and some later colourful stories about his deathbed intentions, recorded by Froissart and Walsingham, have sometimes been taken too seriously.[31] Edward II may be criticised for giving his father only a plain tomb in the Abbey, and never adding an effigy, but to accuse him of 'non-compliance' with his father's wishes, as is still sometimes done, is to go beyond the evidence.[32] Had Edward I not come, by the 1290s, to plan for his own burial at Westminster, it is hard to explain why he should have left space west of his father's and wife's tombs, and his placing of other family tombs further away.

If, however, it was Edward I rather than Henry III who settled on the Abbey as a permanent royal mausoleum, why did he do so? Colvin's view that he wished to enhance the prestige of the monarchy with major 'visible symbols' explains the purpose, but not the location; and some of the usual explanations will not do. There was no necessary link between a coronation church and a royal mausoleum, a connection made only after Edward united the two. Edward did not share his father's attachment either to Abbey or to shrine. Henry's death had brought the rebuilding of the Abbey church to a halt, and Edward felt no obligation to continue funding it, despite his father's explicit testamentary injunction to him.[33] Nor is the

---

28 Hallam, 'Introduction', p. 15; Binski, *Westminster Abbey*, pp. 92, 103, 120.
29 *Age of Chivalry*, ed. Alexander and Binski, p. 339. The positioning of the two – now separated by Aymer de Valence's tomb of the 1320s – may reflect an original intention to have placed between them Edmund's second wife Blanche: Binski, *Westminster Abbey*, p. 113 (with 'Edward' for 'Edmund').
30 Binski, *Westminster Abbey*, p. 113.
31 *Royal Wills*, p. 18; *Foedera*, Record Commission edn, I, p. 495; Michael Prestwich, *Edward I* (London, 1988), p. 557.
32 E.g., Christopher Daniell, *Death and Burial in Medieval England 1066–1550* (London, 1997), pp. 87–8; Steane, *Archaeology of the Medieval English Monarchy*, p. 55. Prestwich, *Edward I*, p. 566, suggests that the tomb was surmounted by a temporary effigy pending the making of a permanent one, but there is no evidence for it: Phillip Lindley, *Gothic to Renaissance: Essays on Sculpture in England* (Stamford, 1995), p. 102.
33 *Royal Wills*, pp. 15, 16.

proximity of Westminster Palace, another object of Henry's lavish building programme, a sufficient explanation. Instead of funding the Abbey fabric, Edward turned in 1292 to rebuilding St Stephen's Chapel, probably 'to rival the lavish elegance of the Sainte-Chapelle in which the King's cousin worshipped in Paris'.[34] Despite that, after Eleanor's death Edward seems to have disliked staying at the palace, preferring instead the house of the archbishop of York further downstream; and in 1298, after a serious fire, the palace was left half-ruined with St Stephen's Chapel incomplete.[35]

The true explanation is probably a broader one: that a royal focus on the Abbey fitted with Edward I's development of London-Westminster as the normal centre of government. It was Edward who abandoned the traditional royal attachment to Winchester, and who spent much more time than his predecessors in or close to London; and it was during his reign that London 'came fully to be established as a capital city in the modern sense of the term'.[36] It would be all of a piece with such a policy that he should turn the major royal church in this developing capital into 'a St-Denis, Sainte-Chapelle and Rheims all rolled into one'.[37]

Edward II, Edward III and Richard II

From 1307 the Abbey was for over a century the almost invariable choice of burial place for sovereigns, and usually for their consorts and close family members. That was perhaps signalled as early as 1308, when Edward II, having buried his father in the Confessor's chapel the year before, translated the remains of King Saeberht of the East Saxons, then believed to be the founder of the first Abbey church, to a place of honour south of the high altar.[38] In 1318 Edward II's stepmother Margaret opted for burial in the church of the London Greyfriars, which had been rebuilt at her expense; but in 1324 Aymer de Valence, earl of Pembroke, was buried in the Abbey. Edward II himself, though he left no extant will, presumably intended his own burial in St Edward's Chapel, for after he died on 21 September 1327 the Abbey paid for two monks to travel to Nottingham 'to ask [the new regime] for the body of the dead king'.[39]

That, of course, did not happen: Edward II was buried instead in St Peter's Abbey, Gloucester, on 20 December, but the circumstances are usually misunderstood. Much weight has been put on a history of St Peter's stressing the initiative of its abbot, John Thokey. Thokey was said to have accepted the body after other neighbouring houses (St Augustine's, Bristol, Kingswood and Malmesbury) had all refused it 'because of fear of Roger de Mortimer and Queen Isabella'.[40] It is clear

---

[34] Brown, Colvin and Taylor, *King's Works*, I, p. 510.

[35] Ibid., I, pp. 505, 512–13.

[36] Derek Keene, 'London from the Post-Roman Period to 1300', *The Cambridge Urban History of Britain I: 600–1540*, ed. D. M. Palliser (Cambridge, 2000), p. 215.

[37] Hallam, 'Introduction', p. 15.

[38] Wilson et al., *Westminster Abbey*, p. 106; and cf. above, n. 3.

[39] WAM, 20344. T. F. Tout, 'The Captivity and Death of Edward of Carnarvon', *The Collected Papers of T. F. Tout* (3 vols, Manchester, 1932–4), III, p. 169 n. 1, who had the reference at second hand, asked if the date could be narrowed to before or after the burial at Gloucester. Unfortunately, it cannot be dated more precisely than the year starting Michaelmas 1327.

[40] *Historia et cartularium monasterii Sancti Petri Gloucestriae*, I, ed. W. H. Hart (Rolls Series, London, 1863), pp. 44–5.

from the royal archives, however, that Gloucester was the deliberate choice of Isabella and Mortimer, who presumably did not want an accessible tomb at Westminster to become a potential focus for an opposition cult of the murdered king.[41]

Yet as soon as the young Edward III took personal rule and overthrew Mortimer, that was what happened. The rebuilding of St Peter's Abbey, begun in 1331, is often said to have been funded by offerings at Edward's tomb, unlikely though he may seem as a candidate for royal sainthood; and the abbey history claims that oblations there paid for the choir vault and some of the stalls.[42] The shrine-like tomb with its superb effigy is usually dated to the early 1330s, and there can be little doubt that the initiative for the shrine and the rebuilding came from Edward III. And gifts continued to be made by the royal family for many years, including a gold ship donated by the king in 1341, a heart and urn of gold by Queen Philippa, and a gold crucifix by their son Edward prince of Wales.[43]

Even if Edward III was content to honour his father's memory at a distance, he certainly determined fairly early to endorse the use of Westminster Abbey as the normal royal burial place. That is made quite clear by Edward's remarkable writ of 24 August 1339 about his brother John of Eltham, earl of Cornwall. John had died young some two years earlier, and had been buried somewhere in the Abbey. Edward now asked the abbot and monks, on behalf of his mother Isabella, to translate John's remains to 'a more suitable position among the royals' (*a autre plus convenable place entre les Roials*), while reserving 'the most honourable positions for the repose and burial of us and of our heirs'.[44] The location chosen for John's new tomb was the Chapel of Sts Edmund and Thomas the Martyr, in which a diminutive tomb was later built close to it for two of Edward's own children who died young.[45] Queen Isabella, however, chose to be buried (1358) in the Franciscan Priory in Newgate, despite her intervention to secure an appropriately royal position in the Abbey for her son John; and her daughter, Joan, queen of Scotland, followed her example in 1362.[46]

There is some suggestion that in 1338 Edward might have promised to be buried in Cologne, but if so, the 1339 writ clearly shows he already had Westminster in mind; and in 1359, according to John of Reading, he re-emphasised his preference for the Abbey, so as to lie near his grandfather, 'that most illustrious and courageous

---

[41] Tout, 'Captivity and Death', pp. 168–9. Cf. David Verey and Alan Brooks, *Gloucestershire 2: the Vale and the Forest of Dean* (The Buildings of England, London, 2002), p. 397, published as this essay was completed, and coming independently to the same view.

[42] *Historia . . . Gloucestriae*, I, p. 47.

[43] Ibid., I, p. 48; Evans, *English Art 1307–1461*, pp. 153, 164–5; Brown, Colvin and Taylor, *King's Works*, I, p. 486; Verey and Brooks, *Gloucestershire 2*, pp. 397, 420.

[44] WAM, 6300*, printed in the appendix to Stanley, *Historical Memorials*, first 3 edns (1868–9), various pagination, in Binski, *Westminster Abbey*, pp. 177, 218 n. 14 (misnumbering the writ as 6300**), and in W. M. Ormrod, 'The Personal Religion of Edward III', *Speculum* lxiv (1989), p. 868 n. 109.

[45] Blanche of the Tower (d.1342) and William of Windsor (d.1348). The tomb is given the impossibly early date of 1340 in Royal Commission on Historical Monuments (hereafter RCHM), *An Inventory of the Historical Monuments in London, I: Westminster Abbey* (London, 1924), p. 42; pls 74, 75. It was probably created for Blanche in 1343, and the miniature effigies added in 1376: Brown, Colvin and Taylor, *King's Works*, I, p. 486 and n. 5.

[46] Brown, Colvin and Taylor, *King's Works*, I, p. 486; F. D. Blackley, 'The Tomb of Isabella of France, Wife of Edward II of England', *Bulletin of the International Society for the Study of Church Monuments* viii (1983), pp. 161–4.

soldier'.[47] Queen Philippa, who predeceased him in 1369, was buried on the south-east side of the chapel, in a tomb already finished, since in 1367 Jean de Liège was paid for her effigy.[48] According to Froissart, she had begged the king on her deathbed that he would share her tomb; but, whether this is true or not, when Edward died in 1377, he was buried in the next bay west. By then, however, he had outlived his son and heir Edward, prince of Wales (the 'Black Prince'), who chose burial instead at Canterbury, where he and his wife had founded chantries as early as 1361–3, and to which cathedral he made lavish legacies.

The Black Prince, making his will on 7 June 1376, asked for burial 'in the cathedral church of the Trinity of Canterbury, where the body of the true martyr, my lord St Thomas, rests in the centre of the chapel of our Lady Undercroft'. That suggests a devotion both to the Trinity and to Becket; the very different lives of archbishop and prince were both rich in Trinitarian associations.[49] In contrast, Edward III's will, made on 7 October 1376, asked for 'a royal tomb in the church of St Peter of Westminster among our ancestors the kings of England of famous memory'.[50] By expressing himself thus, Edward was in fact inventing as much as reinforcing a tradition, since he was only the third sovereign since the Conquest to be buried in the Abbey.

This 'invention of tradition' was taken further by Richard II, the first monarch since Henry III with a deep devotion to the Confessor. The roots of his devotion – as with Henry – are unclear, but they might have stemmed from the accident that his birthday (6 January) coincided with the anniversary of the Confessor's burial at Westminster.[51] Certainly Richard turned to St Edward's tomb for reassurance in the crisis of the Peasants' Revolt, when he was only fourteen.[52] He was also the first since Henry to continue the lavish rebuilding of the Abbey church. Yet he equally saw himself as heir to the tradition of the Plantagenet mausoleum, so that he was to copy Edward III word for word in his own will (16 April 1399), emphasising burial 'among our ancestors the kings of England of famous memory' rather than proximity to the saint's shrine.[53]

The sense of dynastic continuity, indeed, goes back to the early years of his reign. The bronze effigies of both the Black Prince and Edward III are identical in style, and were probably made at the same time and in the same workshop, some years after their deaths. Neither tomb is well documented, but one entry in the patent rolls shows that marble for Edward III's tomb was being shipped from Dorset as late as

---

[47] Ormrod, 'Personal Religion of Edward III', p. 860 and n. 68, p. 872; Binski, *Westminster Abbey*, p. 195 (misciting Ormrod on p. 219 n. 154).
[48] Brown, Colvin and Taylor, *King's Works*, I, pp. 486–7; Lawrence Stone, *Sculpture in Britain: the Middle Ages*, 2nd edn (Harmondsworth, 1972), p. 192; Binski, *Westminster Abbey*, pp. 179–80.
[49] London, Lambeth Palace Library, Reg. Sudbury, fol. 90v, printed in *Royal Wills*, pp. 66–7; Christopher Wilson, 'The Medieval Monuments', *A History of Canterbury Cathedral*, ed. Patrick Collinson, Nigel Ramsay and Margaret Sparks (Oxford, 1995), pp. 494–5.
[50] Lambeth Palace Library, Reg. Sudbury, fol. 97v, printed in *Royal Wills*, p. 60.
[51] Eleanor Scheifele, 'Richard II and the Visual Arts', *Richard II: The Art of Kingship*, ed. Anthony Goodman and James Gillespie (Oxford, 1999), p. 262.
[52] *The Westminster Chronicle 1381–1394*, ed. L. C. Hector and B. F. Harvey (Oxford, 1982), pp. 8–11. The following section draws heavily on Nigel Saul, 'Richard II and Westminster Abbey', *The Cloister and the World*, ed. Blair and Golding, pp. 196–218, and Nigel Saul, *Richard II* (London, 1997), pp. 311–16.
[53] *Foedera*, ed. G. Holmes (20 vols, London, 1727–9), VIII, p. 75; *Royal Wills*, p. 192; translation in John Harvey, *The Plantagenets*, 2nd edn (London, 1959), p. 222.

1386.[54] Binski has plausibly suggested that it was Richard and his advisers who completed the tombs of both his father and grandfather in the mid-1380s, in each case with imagery and epitaphs with a consciously commemorative programme. In particular, Edward III's tomb was designed to hark back to the culture and mythology of the court of Edward I, and to look forward to the future of his prolific family. 'Edward III's tomb is, in short, the most roundly dynastic of any in the church.'[55]

By the 1380s Richard was demonstrating his affection for Abbey and shrine with lavish offerings and gifts, and he also undertook generous funding of the nave, the rebuilding of which had been restarted by the abbot in 1376. In 1386 Richard granted the abbot and convent £100 a year 'in aid of the *novum opus* [the nave] of the monastery out of devotion to the shrine of St Edward the Confessor', and in 1389 (since the regime of 1386–9 had apparently nullified the grant) he put his financial support on a firmer footing. In all, he may have spent between £10,000 and £12,000 on the Abbey and its furnishings, including his own tomb, before his deposition brought work to a halt.[56]

Naturally, Richard had other considerations in mind than devotion to the Confessor and his church, including the enhancing of the crown's image and prestige. Not only did he continue the use of the Abbey for royal burials, but he was the first Plantagenet to make it also a curial mausoleum. As Dean Stanley justly observed, 'his courtiers and officers were the first magnates not of royal blood who reached the heart of the Abbey'.[57] He may have been influenced by the example of Charles V of France, who had lately begun to extend the privilege of burial in St Denis to distinguished courtiers such as Bertrand du Guesclin. Richard followed suit in 1388, ordering burial in the Abbey for two of his chamber knights (Berners and Salisbury) who had been executed by the Lords Appellant; they were buried in the Chapel of St John the Baptist. In 1395 he had Queen Anne's chamberlain interred in St Edmund's Chapel, in 1396 another chamber knight (Golafre) in the south ambulatory, and in 1398 Archbishop Waldby, one of his most senior clerks, also in St Edmund's Chapel.[58] Most controversially, in 1395 he insisted on burying his treasurer, Bishop John Waltham, in the Confessor's chapel. According to Walsingham, the monks protested that previously only kings had been buried there, but Richard overrode them, arguing that Waltham was 'deserving of burial among kings'.[59]

There was, of course, no such dispute when Queen Anne had died on 7 June 1394, after which Richard commissioned a double tomb for them both. Though his surviving will requesting an Abbey burial dates from 1399, his intentions were made clear on Anne's death; and the will he gave the Abbey for safekeeping in 1394

[54] *CPR 1385–9*, p. 127; Brown, Colvin and Taylor, *King's Works*, I, p. 487; John Blair, 'Purbeck Marble', *English Medieval Industries*, ed. John Blair and Nigel Ramsay (London, 1991), p. 43.

[55] Binski, *Westminster Abbey*, pp. 195–9 (quotation from p. 198).

[56] Saul, 'Richard II and Westminster Abbey', pp. 200–4.

[57] Stanley, *Historical Memorials*, 3rd edn (1869), p. 212.

[58] Saul, 'Richard II and Westminster Abbey', pp. 210–12.

[59] Thomas Walsingham, *Historia Anglicana*, ed. H. T. Riley (2 vols, Rolls Series, London, 1863–4), II, p. 218. The monks protested too much: previous interments had included, besides other royal kin, abbots, benefactors and corrodians: Saul, 'Richard II and Westminster Abbey', p. 212 n. 70.

(not known to survive) presumably specified burial at Westminster.[60] The space, the most south-westerly in the horseshoe, was apparently occupied by another royal tomb which was moved to make room, though it is, surprisingly, uncertain whose tomb it was.[61] Two surviving contracts of 1395, for the marble chest and for the metal work, specified completion within two years; the effigies were probably cast by 1396, but the final payment for gilding was made in 1398–9; and the striking epitaph was probably composed in that year. The total cost was nearly £1,000.[62] The special bond between Richard and Anne was signalled by their joint burial, since no previous English king and queen are known to have shared the same tomb; and his choice of their joint resting place was surely intended, as Saul says, 'to emphasize his place in the dynastic succession'. Their tomb completed the series round the Confessor's shrine, and in Binski's view its design reflected self-consciously upon the mausolea of both Westminster and St Denis. It concluded Richard's promotion of the Abbey as a focus for royal power and royal lineage, ironically since he was the last of his direct line.[63] Certainly, Richard was very conscious of his royal ancestry, and although he was only the fourth post-Conquest monarch buried in the Abbey, his intention to be buried 'among our ancestors the kings of England' may refer as much to the royal statues he had erected in Westminster Hall as to the Abbey tombs.[64]

Richard was not, however to be placed by Anne's side for many years. When he died at Pontefract in February 1400, Henry IV had the corpse brought to London for requiem masses at St Paul's, but it was then taken to King's Langley for burial in the Dominican priory there.[65] Adam Usk commented drily on 'how many thousands of marks did he spend on vainglorious tombs for himself and his wives amidst the kings at Westminster, only for fortune to foil his plans!'[66] King's Langley was perhaps chosen as being out of the way (to minimise the risk of an unofficial cult), and yet a favourite royal manor. Edward II had had Gaveston interred there, while Edward III's fifth son – Edmund de Langley, duke of York – had been born there. It is ironic that Richard may himself have set a precedent of honourable but out-of-the-way burial there: when in 1388–9 he had brought back from Bordeaux the body of his elder brother Edward (d.1371), he had had it reinterred at King's Langley, perhaps because of his sensitivity about being a younger son.[67]

Oddly, there survives in King's Langley parish church a tomb from the priory which may have been originally intended for Richard II. Its heraldry suggests this,

[60] Binski, *Westminster Abbey*, p. 200; A. K. McHardy, 'Richard II: A Personal Portrait', *The Reign of Richard II*, ed. Gwilym Dodd (Stroud, 2000), pp. 11, 155.

[61] Saul, 'Richard II and Westminster Abbey', p. 210 n.

[62] *Foedera*, ed. Holmes, VII, pp. 795–8; Stone, *Sculpture in Britain*, pp. 193–4; Brown, Colvin and Taylor, *King's Works*, I, pp. 487–8; *Age of Chivalry*, ed. Alexander and Binski, pp. 393–4; Phillip Lindley, 'Absolutism and Regal Image in Ricardian Sculpture', *The Regal Image of Richard II and the Wilton Diptych*, ed. Dillian Gordon, Lisa Monnas and Caroline Elam (London, 1997), pp. 61–74.

[63] Saul, *Richard II*, p. 429; Binski, *Westminster Abbey*, p. 202.

[64] W. M. Ormrod, 'Richard II's Sense of English History', *Reign of Richard II*, ed. Dodd, p. 108.

[65] Joel Burden, 'How do You Bury a Deposed King? The Funeral of Richard II and the Establishment of Lancastrian Royal Authority in 1400', *Henry IV: The Establishment of the Regime, 1399–1406*, ed. Gwilym Dodd and Douglas Biggs (Woodbridge, 2003), pp. 39–43.

[66] *The Chronicle of Adam Usk 1377–1421*, ed. C. Given-Wilson (Oxford, 1997), pp. 94–5; Saul, *Richard II*, pp. 427–8.

[67] Ormrod, 'Richard II's Sense of English History', p. 105.

though it became instead a tomb for Edmund de Langley and his wife Isabel. J. E. Powell thought that Richard originally intended his own burial at Langley, only to change his mind when Queen Anne died; but that is unlikely. The tomb-chest could well have been commissioned for Westminster, and then made available after 1394 to Duke Edmund as workshop waste.[68] Certainly Richard's body was to lie at Langley throughout the reign of his successor, and not until 1413 did Henry V make amends by reburying it with great ceremony alongside Anne of Bohemia at Westminster.[69]

Henry IV, Henry V and Henry VI

Henry IV not only kept his cousin's body at a distance from the Abbey, but showed no interest in burial there himself. By his will, drawn up on 21 January 1409, he asked for burial 'in the chirch at Caunterbury, aftyr the descrecion of my cousin the archbyshcopp' (that is, Thomas Arundel, who had crowned him), but this was probably a polite fiction concealing a decision already made, since in 1410 Henry's half-brother, John Beaufort, was interred immediately east of where Henry himself was to be buried in 1413.[70] Henry's alabaster tomb stands immediately north of Becket's shrine, in a corresponding position to that of his uncle the Black Prince to the south. It is surmounted by effigies of himself and Queen Joan, who long survived him and was buried there in 1437. And about 1437–9 a new chapel of St Michael was added nearby to house the triple tomb of Lady Margaret Beaufort (d.1439) and her two royal husbands, Henry's half-brother John Beaufort, earl of Somerset (d.1410), and Henry's second son Thomas, duke of Clarence (d.1421): in 1440 Henry VI granted permission for the removal of Beaufort's and Clarence's bodies to it.[71]

Henry IV's will did not explain his choice of Canterbury, but reasons can be suggested. He may have considered the Confessor's chapel overcrowded, and he lacked Richard's attachment to the Abbey. He had close ties to the Beauchamp family, earls of Warwick, who had been involved in lawsuits against the Abbey; Richard II had imposed a settlement in the Abbey's favour, but significantly, when the dispute was renewed in 1403, the decision went the other way. Henry may also have wished to follow the precedent of his uncle the Black Prince. He was the first monarch anointed at his coronation with oil which – so legend asserted – had been given by the Virgin to St Thomas. Walsingham reported a version of the story by which the oil had been given to the Black Prince in anticipation of his coronation, but which could not be found when Richard II was crowned. The story proved highly satisfactory in linking Henry both to his uncle and to St Thomas.[72] And Henry's motives must surely have included – like the Black Prince's – proximity to Becket's shrine. Only three and a half years before making his will, Henry had

---

68 J. Enoch Powell, 'A King's Tomb', *History Today*, October 1965, pp. 713–17; Saul, 'Richard II and Westminster Abbey', p. 209 n. 60.

69 Saul, *Richard II*, p. 428.

70 *Royal Wills*, p. 203; Wilson, 'Medieval Monuments', p. 498.

71 Wilson, 'Medieval Monuments', pp. 503–6.

72 C. Wilson, 'The Tomb of Henry IV and the Holy Oil of St Thomas of Canterbury', *Medieval Architecture in its Intellectual Context*, ed. E. Fernie and P. Crossley (London, 1990), pp. 181–90; Wilson, 'Medieval Monuments', pp. 498–9; Burden, 'How do You Bury a Deposed King?', pp. 37–8.

himself ordered the death of an archbishop, and it may not be fanciful to imagine him haunted by guilt and seeking the powerful intercession of another murdered primate.

Whatever his motives, Henry may also have intended, as Wilson and Burden have suggested, 'to inaugurate a new royal mausoleum' at Canterbury.[73] If so, it was a short-lived project, for his son Henry of Monmouth resembled Richard II in his devotion to Westminster if in little else. Henry IV had abandoned Richard's funding of the rebuilding of the nave, but Henry V – shocked by its condition at his coronation – provided 1,000 marks a year, and by 1422 the gallery level was complete and the clerestory started.[74] In 1413 Henry ceremonially reinterred Richard's body in the Abbey; on 24 July 1415, on the eve of his Agincourt campaign, he made a will requesting his own burial there; and in November 1415, on his victorious return, he went in procession both to St Paul's and to the Abbey, making an offering at the Confessor's shrine.[75] Furthermore, when his close friend and companion Richard Courtenay, bishop of Norwich, died at the siege of Harfleur, Henry ordered his burial in the Abbey.[76] And in 1431 Lord Bourchier, the standard-bearer at Agincourt, was also buried in the Abbey, with an altar-tomb and a screen incorporating the *Non nobis domine* sung after the battle.[77] Clearly, one result of Henry's campaigns was to revive the Ricardian tradition of curial burials in the Abbey.

Henry V in fact made two wills, that of 1415 (long known and printed by Rymer) and a second in 1421 only recently rediscovered, as well as deathbed codicils.[78] He made detailed provision for his burial at the east end of the Confessor's chapel, including a combined two-storey tomb and chantry chapel. Work on the tomb was under way by the time of his funeral on 7 November 1422, and it was apparently complete by 1431. The elaborate chapel, ingeniously constructed on a bridge over the ambulatory, was added from 1437 by Cardinal Beaufort, and has been called the masterpiece of John Thirsk, the Abbey's master mason.[79] Allmand is surely correct in stating that Henry V consciously continued what had become – despite his father's example – a tradition of Abbey burial. He had seen St Denis; he would want to be buried in a similar mausoleum, especially as the Confessor was one of his patron saints; and 'it seems likely that he saw his own burial there as part of the honour and respect due to the royal dignity'.[80] His tomb-chest has recesses, and it has even been suggested that he was another royal candidate for canonisation; but the recesses were more probably intended to house the relics which had to be moved

---

[73] Wilson, 'Medieval Monuments', pp. 498, 505–6, following a suggestion of Woodruff and Banks; Burden, 'How do You Bury a Deposed King?', p. 38.

[74] Wilson et al., *Westminster Abbey*, p. 34.

[75] Christopher Allmand, *Henry V* (London, 1992), pp. 99, 173, 180; Paul Strohm, *England's Empty Throne: Usurpation and the Language of Legitimation, 1399–1422* (London, 1998), p. 115.

[76] L. E. Tanner, *Recollections of a Westminster Antiquary* (London, 1969), pp. 179–81.

[77] RCHM, *Westminster Abbey*, p. 37.

[78] *Foedera*, 3rd edn (10 vols, The Hague, 1739–45), IV, pt ii, pp. 138–9; P. Strong and F. Strong, 'The Last Will and Codicils of Henry V', *EHR* xcvi (1981), pp. 79–102. The document of 1417 in *Royal Wills*, pp. 236–42, is not strictly one of the wills: Allmand, *Henry V*, pp. 178–9; Strong and Strong, 'Last Will and Codicils', p. 80.

[79] W. St J. Hope, 'The Funeral, Monument and Chantry Chapel of King Henry the Fifth', *Archaeologia* lxv (1913–14), pp. 129–86; Brown, Colvin and Taylor, *King's Works*, I, pp. 488–9; Wilson et al., *Westminster Abbey*, pp. 125–8; Allmand, *Henry V*, pp. 180–1.

[80] Allmand, *Henry V*, p. 173.

from the east end of the chapel to make way for the tomb. (Both wills specified a location 'among the tombs of the kings in the place where the relics of saints are now housed'.)[81] It should be added that Henry's widow Catherine (d.1437) was originally buried in the Lady Chapel, but when that was demolished by Henry VII she was moved to Henry's tomb.

Space prevents a survey of all royal burials, but it is worth noting that in the century after 1350, as before, there was no common pattern even for close relatives. Richard II's uncle Thomas earl of Gloucester (d.1397) and his widow Eleanor (d.1399) were buried together beneath the floor of St Edward's Chapel, though not until after Richard's deposition.[82] Richard's other uncles, however, like the Black Prince, all chose burial elsewhere: Lionel duke of Clarence at Clare in Suffolk; John of Gaunt in St Paul's; and Edmund duke of York at King's Langley. Similarly, Henry V's brother Humphrey, duke of Gloucester, chose burial in St Albans Abbey, with which he had long had close ties, and immediately adjoining the shrine of St Alban.[83]

This survey can most appropriately conclude with the burial – or rather the burial intentions – of Henry VI, for the usual view is that that unhappy monarch decided in the 1450s, almost exactly two centuries after Henry III, on burial close to the Confessor's shrine. The evidence is posthumous and curiously circumstantial, for his only surviving will, dated 12 March 1448, is almost wholly concerned with his twin foundations at Eton and Cambridge, and stipulates no burial place for himself. In the event, when he was murdered in 1471, his supplanter clearly thought that burial in the Abbey could have made a focus for an opposition cult, and Henry was therefore buried at Chertsey Abbey in Surrey, only to be reburied by Richard III in 1484 – ironically not at Westminster, but in Edward IV's new chapel of St George at Windsor, and just opposite the tomb of Edward himself.[84]

Where, however, had Henry VI really intended to be buried? The evidence usually cited is that of an inquiry in 1498, when Henry VII was actively promoting the cult of his murdered predecessor and namesake. Henry Tudor had begun a new Lady Chapel at Windsor in 1496 to house his own tomb and a shrine to Henry VI, but the abbots at Chertsey and Westminster both intervened to claim the late king's body. Twelve elderly eyewitnesses then gave testimony, in circumstantial detail, that Henry VI had, some forty years before, selected a spot in St Edward's Chapel, where relics were then housed between the shrine and the tomb of Henry III. According to John Bothe, for instance, Henry had declared it fitting that he should be buried 'nyghe to Seint Edward where my fader and all my auncetours beth buryed'.[85] Their testimony was sufficient to persuade Henry VII to cease building at Windsor, to obtain papal permission to move Henry VI's remains to Westminster, and to begin a new Lady Chapel there in 1503 to house the tombs of both kings. If,

81 Stanley, *Historial Memorials*, 3rd edn, p. 155; Wilson et al., *Westminster Abbey*, p. 126; Strong and Strong, 'Last Will and Codicils', p. 89; *Foedera*, 3rd edn, IV, pt. ii, p. 138.

82 *Age of Chivalry*, ed. Alexander and Binski, pp. 510–11; Binski, *Westminster Abbey*, p. 200. The implication of Eleanor's will, 9 August 1399, is that this was their wish, but that it could not be fulfilled while Richard was king: *Royal Wills*, pp. 177–8, 185.

83 Nicola Smith, *The Royal Image and the English People* (Aldershot, 2001), pp. 18–28.

84 Bertram Wolffe, *Henry VI* (London, 1981), p. 352.

85 WAM, 6389**, printed in full in Stanley, *Historical Memorials*, 1st edn, pp. 506–14; 2nd edn, pp. 570–9; 3rd edn, pp. 600–8.

therefore, his plan had been fully carried out, the magnificent structure now called Henry VII's Chapel 'might today bear the name of Henry VI'.[86] And although Henry VI's canonisation process stalled, and his remains were never translated, the new Abbey chapel was completed by 1512, becoming a second royal mausoleum in the Abbey, for every monarch except four from 1509 to 1760 was buried there.

And yet the whole revived Westminster tradition may conceivably be based on a misinterpretation of Henry VI's intentions. The depositions of 1498 are, as Wolffe has drily remarked, 'not entirely above suspicion'. They were confessedly made some forty years after Henry VI's alleged remarks, and the one firm date cited by any witness (1458) is inconsistent with the other evidence he gave. Worse, some witnesses had the Abbey's master mason, John Thirsk, assisting the king; Thirsk left the Abbey for Windsor in 1449 and was dead by 1452.[87] It may even be, as Wolffe also argues, that Henry's determined care for Eton, as long as he was in control, speaks a different intention. 'One cannot doubt that if his own wishes had been fulfilled . . . he would surely have been buried by choice in his most glorious and most privileged minster of the Assumption of Our Lady at Eton.'[88]

---

[86] Wolffe, *Henry VI*, p. 357; Wilson et al., *Westminster Abbey*, pp. 70–1 (quotation from p. 70). A design for a monument to Henry VI, presumably for Westminster, is discussed in W. R. Lethaby, *Westminster Abbey Re-examined* (London, 1925), pp. 61–2, and reproduced in Sydney Anglo, *Images of Tudor Kingship* (London, 1992), p. 69.

[87] Wolffe, *Henry VI*, p. 357; John Harvey, *Gothic England*, 2nd edn (London, 1948), p. 98; John Harvey, *English Medieval Architects: A Biographical Dictionary down to 1550*, 2nd edn (Gloucester, 1984), pp. 295–6. Margaret Aston accepts the depositions as genuine, and dates the king's discussions to before 1452, but cites no evidence: 'Death', *Fifteenth-Century Attitudes*, ed. Rosemary Horrox (Cambridge, 1994), p. 219.

[88] Wolffe, *Henry VI*, p. 145. Intriguingly, statues of St George and St Edmund survive at Eton which are the only known figure-work outside Westminster by the master sculptor of Henry VII's chapel. Lindley, who points this out, dates them to c.1505–12, but had earlier given reasons in favour of an alternative dating of c.1479–82, when Bishop Waynflete (one of Henry VI's executors) had been completing the chapel: Lindley, *Gothic to Renaissance*, pp. 156–69.

LEGAL CULTURE:
MEDIEVAL LAWYERS' ASPIRATIONS AND PRETENSIONS

Anthony Musson

He 'was yn those quarters a great officer, as steward, surveier or receyver of Richemont landes, whereby he waxid riche and able to build and purchace'. So wrote John Leland, who travelled throughout England in the early sixteenth century recording details about manors and landed estates, concerning Thomas Metcalfe (d.1504), who was in the service of Richard, duke of Gloucester (the future Richard III) and was appointed chancellor of the duchy of Lancaster in 1483.[1] Metcalfe's building project was Nappa Hall in Yorkshire, which still stands today and whose external features remain remarkably untouched. We are fortunate to have a description of the 'before and after' in the true manner of a television make-over programme. Leland informs us that before Metcalfe got to work on Nappa Hall, there was 'but a cotage or litle better house, ontille this Thomas began ther to build in the which building 2 toures be very fair, beside other logginges'. The two towers are indeed an unusual feature of the hall. Comprising three storeys at the lower end rising to four at the upper, the towers flank the single storey hall, giving it a distinctive character.[2]

The comments made about Metcalfe might be taken as a model for many 'men of law' of the time, who were essentially self-made men, rising through the ranks of their profession (perhaps retained in royal and/or noble service) and seeking to invest their newly acquired money in landed estates. Land and property offered the obvious choice for investment. Chaucer describes his 'serjeant of the lawe' thus: 'So greet a purchasour was nowher noon/ Al was fee simple to hym in effect.'[3] In one reading at least this could mean that the serjeant was almost obsessively concerned with accumulating land: 'fee simple' could apply to land title, or more satirically to a lawyer's grasping desire for money. But this was not necessarily a universal characteristic of the profession: not every lawyer rose through the ranks, nor did those that did necessarily rise that highly. Undoubtedly some lawyers were simply unsuccessful and remained poor and insignificant. However, many men of law can be found to have desired to use their professional expertise to their advantage and to extend their landed base as a consequence. There may have been a variety of motivational factors, but it can be assumed on the basis of evidence presented here that they wanted to back up their pretensions to gentility and landed status with a visible sign of their wealth: the manor house.

---

1   *The Itinerary of John Leland*, ed. L. Toulmin Smith (5 vols, London, 1906–10), IV, p. 86.
2   A. Emery, *Greater Medieval Houses of England and Wales, 1300–1500* (2 vols, Cambridge, 1996–2000), I, pp. 382–3; M. Salter, *The Castles and Tower Houses of Yorkshire* (Malvern, 2001), p. 66. At one point in his writings, Leland refers to it as Knappa Castle: *Itinerary of John Leland*, IV, p. 33.
3   *The Riverside Chaucer*, ed. L. D. Benson, new edn (Oxford, 1987), p. 28.

This study, then, examines the interconnection between social relations and spatial structures and the media in which (and through which) social relations were formed and recreated.[4] It argues, in line with Matthew Johnson's 'study of old houses', that 'the structure and layout of domestic architecture relates not only to functional and economic considerations but also to the cultural and mental life of its users'.[5] Here this can be seen in a general desire for enhanced status that accompanied professional advancement in the law and its social manifestation in terms of the building (or acquisition and rebuilding) of manor houses. In examining these factors, the paper not only highlights the careers of individual lawyers and the fortunes of their families, but also assesses the style of the house, the choice of architectural design and the features of interest deployed within their living accommodation. From an analysis of these it is possible to gauge not only a family's relative status and standard of living, but also the extent to which lawyers were plugged into (and accepted by) the networks of both local and national society.

Drawing on a mixture of surviving architecture, the fruits of archaeological excavation, and contemporary (or near contemporary) documents and descriptions, the two main questions I shall be pursuing touch on the following areas: how did lawyers use architecture as a status-enhancing factor and to what extent were their concerns similar to or identifiable with those of the social group commonly referred to as 'the gentry'? In many ways the answers to these questions depend not simply upon the surviving evidence, but also upon whether the data concerning surviving examples of medieval lawyers' houses indicate that they were typical or atypical for the period. Were they following the latest fashions, or were they themselves determining to a certain extent the direction of those fashions? Were families' building projects financed solely on the back of the profits of a career in the law or afforded through other developments? An authoritative study of the influences on lawyers' aesthetics and the complexities of their family fortunes would require a more detailed survey than I have hitherto been able to accomplish. I shall nevertheless present some preliminary views, looking first at examples of status enhancement through use of architectural design and then at the acquisition of gentry status itself.

One of the most obvious methods of status promotion (one visible today physically and in the records) was to crenellate, that is fortify with battlements or *crenelles*, one's dwelling. The patent rolls often record licences granted by the crown (or, for the palatinate of Durham, the bishop) for this purpose.[6] Licences were in many ways a mere formality (for which it seems there were no specific criteria) and were routinely given upon payment of the necessary fee, which itself was fairly modest (enough to cover the cost of the parchment, seal and chancery overheads). While some crenellation was undoubtedly undertaken for military reasons, by and large it was an aesthetic statement, a sign of status-aspiration rather than, as some historians have suggested, a reflection of a genuine fear of violence.[7] Although the articles of the escheator included inquiry into 'castles and embattled houses . . .

---

[4] *Social Relations and Spatial Structures*, ed. D. Gregory and J. Urry (Basingstoke, 1985), pp. 1–3.
[5] M. Johnson, *Housing Culture* (London, 1993), p. 1.
[6] For a list of licences, see J. Parker, *Some Account of Domestic Architecture in England, from Richard II to Henry VIII* (2 vols, Oxford, 1859), II, pp. 400–22.
[7] C. L. H. Coulson, 'Freedom to Crenellate by Licence', *Nottingham Medieval Studies* xxxviii (1994), pp. 91–2, 97.

erected without the king's licence',[8] the acquisition of a licence to crenellate may not have been systematically enforced. The comparatively large numbers enrolled in the fourteenth century nevertheless indicate that people were willing to go through the bureaucratic process. It is likely that the bureaucracy was accepted because possession of a licence had advantages in social terms as it signified (and recorded) royal approval. As an aspect of aristocratic culture, it may have been thought of as a form of privilege that enabled the owner to display to the public the outward distinguishing marks of noble standing.[9] A commons' petition of 1371, which requested 'that every man throughout England might make fort or fortress, walls and crenellations on towers and battlements at his own free will',[10] may indicate that this privilege was indeed considered highly desirable. The petition may equally be taken to imply that the requirement for licensing was regarded as onerous; people thought that it should be enjoyed as of right by everyone.

Several lawyers, mainly judges, sought licences to crenellate in Edward II's reign, among them John Benstead for a dwelling near Westminster; Henry Scrope for his house at Kirkby Fleetham, Yorkshire; Henry's brother, Geoffrey Scrope, for his at Clifton on Ure; and Edmund Pashley for his property of La Mote in Sussex.[11] In Edward III's reign a licence was sought by Roger Hillary in 1346 for Bescote House in Staffordshire (now partly covered by the M6), and William Thorpe for his manor at Makeseye in Northamptonshire in 1374.[12]

The recorded licences indicate that permission was sought (and obtained) for building and outline something of the intended project. Any disparity between aspirations and resources, however, would obviously have placed a restraint on what was actually built.[13] We cannot be sure, therefore, that these crenellations were actually carried out, especially as all that remains of Henry Scrope's house at Kirkby Fleetham is the moated platform. In the absence of archaeological remains, Leland's description of Clifton as it stood in the sixteenth century (that it looked 'like a pele or castelet') offers the only direct link to the execution of the plan behind Geoffrey Scrope's licence to crenellate.[14]

Extensions to an existing property or 'make-overs' would imply that there was money to spare: refurbishment of or an addition to the house was a suitable way of announcing your prosperity or conversely, and more subtly, concealing economic difficulties in order to 'keep up with the Joneses'. Sir Geoffrey Scrope's addition of a new chamber to his manor house at Kingsbury in Middlesex, a dwelling that (unusually) already possessed one private room, suggests that he had money to spare, especially as this was not his main or sole residence.[15] Sir John Stonor, judge

---

8 *SR*, I, p. 240. For the escheator's duties in relation to these articles, see S. L. Waugh, 'The Origins and Early Development of the Articles of the Escheator', *Thirteenth Century England V*, ed. P. R. Coss and S. D. Lloyd (Woodbridge, 1995), pp. 89–113.

9 Coulson, 'Freedom to Crenellate', pp. 92–4, 97. 'His emblematic architecture (perhaps the more so if licensed) proclaimed his standing and his power to avenge and deter insult at law rather than by force, regardless of the shallowness of his moat or the fragility of his doors and window-shutters' (ibid., p. 118).

10 *RP*, II, p. 307.

11 Emery, *Greater Medieval Houses*, I, p. 421; Salter, *Castles and Tower Houses*, pp. 29, 52.

12 Emery, *Greater Medieval Houses*, II, p. 431.

13 Coulson, 'Freedom to Crenellate', pp. 94, 97.

14 *Itinerary of John Leland*, II, p. 2. The foundations may be in the cellar of Clifton Castle, Thornton Watlass: Emery, *Greater Medieval Houses*, I, p. 421.

15 D. J. M. Higgins, 'Judges in Government and Society in the Reign of Edward II' (unpublished DPhil thesis, University of Oxford, 1986), p. 194.

of common pleas in Edward III's reign, is recorded as considerably enlarging his house at Stonor Park between 1330 and 1350, rebuilding the hall and chapel and adding a solar wing.[16] This was equally a feature illustrative of the success of several fifteenth-century judges. Sir Roger Townshend, for example, who became a serjeant at law in 1478, and sat as a puisne judge in the court of common pleas from 1485 until his death in 1493, enhanced the family property of East Raynham Old Hall by adding a brick tower to the house and expanding various outbuildings during the period covering his legal career.[17]

Expansion of the physical space was one thing that could be calculated to impress; but what were the specific architectural features that signified (or can be perceived as indicating) that the owner wanted to enhance their status, or more particularly that they possessed gentry or noble status? Looking at the design of the house itself, the hall-based house is the most familiar model. Having an aisled hall carried considerably more cachet than an aisleless one. Recent archaeological work has revealed that Annesley Hall in Nottinghamshire, for instance, home of the active local man of law, John de Annesley, possessed the former.[18]

The hall itself was not simply a living space.[19] As the most obvious public area, its spatial measurements and setting mattered for providing initial perceptions of the status of the owner. A hall with a large floor area such as Horbury Hall (built around 1480 on an earlier site by Ralph Amyas, deputy steward of Wakefield)[20] offered an air of grandness and openness. There is also evidence of the use of a canopy beam over the dais end of the room. Curved ribs rose to a head beam ornamented on its two visible faces with carved panels on which are traces of the Amyas family arms. A spere truss separating the bay from the body of the hall was usually confined to the houses of nobility or the wealthiest gentry and is a distinguishing feature of Horbury.[21]

The structure of the house and its fabric were also important. T-shaped houses common in the fourteenth century were, by the fifteenth, supplanted by an H-plan structure. In the fourteenth century, timber-framed walls were replaced by stone walls. Interestingly, the frontage to the ground floor at Horbury Hall was of stone but was only half the normal height, and the rear wall was made of timber.[22] Fine masonry was highly prized until the mid-fifteenth century, during which period the use of bricks for the walls became fashionable. Such general stylistic markers can help to identify the trendsetters and trend-followers. The fifteenth-century lawyer, William Skipwith, who was also MP for Norwich in 1462, added (during the 1460s)

---

[16] Ibid. Leland described Stonor Parks when he visited it in the sixteenth century as having 'two courtes buyldyd with tymbar, brike and flynte': *Itinerary of John Leland*, V, p. 72.

[17] Emery, *Greater Medieval Houses*, II, pp. 84–6.

[18] M.W. Bailey, 'An Aisled Hall at Annesley Hall, Nottinghamshire', *Transactions of the Thoroton Society* lxxxvii (1983), pp. 85–6.

[19] The poet Langland complained 'Now hath ech rich a rule – to eten by hymselve/ In a pryvee parlour . . . / Or in a chambre with a chymenee, and leve the chief halle/ That was maad for meles, men to eten inne': William Langland, *The Vision of Piers Plowman*, ed. A. V. C. Schmidt (London, 1978), p. 103 (B-text, Passus X, 11. 98–101).

[20] Emery, *Greater Medieval Houses*, I, pp. 350–1. The present floor area of Horbury's great hall – 32 feet by 22 feet – is a reduction of the larger medieval space.

[21] *Rural Houses of West Yorkshire, 1400–1830* (Royal Commission on the Historical Monuments of England supplementary ser. viii, London, 1986), pp. 11–13, 15–16, 202.

[22] Ibid., p. 22.

to the early fourteenth-century, timber-framed, T-shaped block that comprised Sowre Hall in Norfolk a new block built of bricks at the upper end of the hall.[23]

An alternative to the T-shaped house was to have a tower house or an additional gatehouse (primarily for fashionable rather than defensive purposes). A surviving agreement for the building of a gatehouse in 1313 for John Bishopsden of Lapworth in Warwickshire (a keeper of the peace and local justice in the county) contains the details and dimensions that Bishopsden intended for the project. The room above the gatehouse, for instance, was to be 11 feet by 33 feet 9 inches, with two fireplaces and two privies.[24] Sir Robert Sillington's manor at Kirkby Bellars was described in late fourteenth- and early fifteenth-century extents of the manor as an imposing defensible residence (comprising a hall and fourteen chambers) surrounded by a moat with a gatehouse.[25] Drayton House in Northamptonshire, developed predominantly by Sir Simon Drayton in the early fourteenth century, comprised an open hall and cross wing within a large walled and a moated enclosure more than twice the size of that of nearby Barnwell Castle.[26] Baconsthorpe Castle, constructed by the Norfolk lawyer John Heydon in the 1440s, had an imposing gatehouse and a substantial courtyard house surrounded by a moat.[27] Moats were status symbols as well as having defensive capabilities. The status associated with a tower house is demonstrated by the way the fourteenth-century Lancashire administrator Richard Radcliffe was described in a document as coming from Radcliffe Tower, even though there is no evidence that his property, Radcliffe Hall, was ever a tower house in structure or design.[28]

Other architectural features, both external and internal, were valued. Chapels were never commonplace and their inclusion within the plan is indicative of social status (as well as religious devotion). The Stonor residence included a chapel, which is one of the surviving medieval parts of the house. Outward display, in the form of elaborate roof decoration, was highly fashionable; but before the fifteenth century, crown-posts were exclusively employed by those with (or wishing to exhibit) high status. Great Cobham Hall in Wethersfield, the principal family home of the Coggleshalls of Essex (who played an important role in the judicial administration of the county) comprises an early fourteenth-century hall with a contemporary crown-post roof.[29] Oriel windows were also symbols of prestige. Windows had the advantage of twin opportunities for enhancing status: the tracery of the windows, observable from the outside; and their light-enhancing properties (and colours), which could be appreciated from the inside. With some exceptions, surviving examples of glazed domestic windows tend to be from the fifteenth century. In this respect some lawyers appear to have been leading the way. The Norfolk judge, Sir Roger Townshend, whose family came to prominence through the fruits of his legal

[23] Emery, *Greater Medieval Houses*, II, p. 151.

[24] B. K. Roberts, 'Moated Sites in Midland England', *Transactions of the Birmingham Archeological Society* lxxx (1962), p. 34.

[25] D. Williams, 'Fortified Manor Houses', *Leicester Archaeological and Historical Society Transactions* 1 (1974–5), p. 7.

[26] J. Heward and R. Talory, *The Country Houses of Northamptonshire* (Swindon, 1996), p. 177; Emery, *Greater Medieval Houses*, II, p. 184.

[27] Emery, *Greater Medieval Houses*, II, pp. 49–50.

[28] Ibid., I, p. 243.

[29] Ibid., II, pp. 14–15; J. C. Ward, 'Sir John Coggeshale', *Transactions of the Essex Archeological Society* xxii (1991), pp. 61–6.

career, was particularly taken with windows as a feature. Roger put in a bay window (the ground-floor equivalent of an oriel) in the hall at East Raynham and in 1475–6 ensured that many of its windows were glazed.[30] Thomas Tropenell, steward to Robert, lord Hungerford, had an oriel chamber constructed at Great Chalfield in Wiltshire in about 1480.[31]

A particularly good example of a house reflecting the career of a successful lawyer can be found in the case of Sir John Knyvet, who inherited Southwick Hall on the death of his father, Richard, in 1352. The alterations made to the house reflect the outstanding success of John's legal career as he rose from serjeant at law (1354) to king's serjeant (1356–61) before being promoted to the court of common pleas as a puisne judge in 1361. He served on the bench of that court for four years before his appointment as chief justice of king's bench, a post he held for seven years. Knyvet then took over as head of the chancery in 1372, remaining there until 1375. Although Southwick Hall was already a substantial size, Knyvet built a three-storey extension in the 1360s on the west side of the existing two-storey tower that adjoined the cross wing. The building occurred in the very period he reached the apex of the profession. His rank and wealth clearly afforded him considerable luxury as well as comfort and aesthetic enjoyment. He enjoyed considerable private space, he contributed a private suite to an upper cross wing, and his rooms were airy (the solar was 18 feet by 16 feet) and highly decorated (including moulded corbels with carved heads). The first floor of the tower has traceried windows (with stone window seats). The house also boasts one of the earliest known oriel windows in England, suggesting that lawyers could indeed be the forerunners of architectural stylistic features.[32]

Status (and a concern for self-image) can be inferred from other features of the domestic arrangements, such as the covering of the walls, either by tapestries or wall paintings. Tapestries seemed largely the preserve of the monarch in the early fourteenth century, but by the turn of the fifteenth century had become a prominent feature in the halls and chambers of men slightly lower down the social scale who wanted to enhance their standing. Richard Scrope, son of the early fourteenth-century judge, Henry Scrope, had at Bolton Castle 'for the hall there my green tapestry woven with griffins with my arms worked in metal', and in his will left a 'bed of embroidered velvet with four sides or arras work and four tapestries of the same colour as the bed'.[33] Although painted walls were probably a normal feature in certain fourteenth-century houses, the painted chamber at Longthorpe Tower is a splendid and rare example of wall decoration. The owner of Longthorpe in the early fourteenth century was Robert Thorpe, steward of the abbot of Peterborough, and may have been a royal judge, or at least related to the royal judges and sometime chief justices Robert (d. 1372) and William Thorpe (d. 1375).[34]

This survey has cherry-picked architectural examples coinciding with owners who were legal professionals (in a wide sense). It should be pointed out, however, that there were often regional differences in the types of houses built or extended:

[30] Emery, *Greater Medieval Houses*, II, pp. 84–6.
[31] M. Wood, *The English Medieval House*, rev. edn (London, 1994), p. 105.
[32] Heward and Talory, *Country Houses of Northamptonshire*, pp. 306–8; Emery, *Greater Medieval Houses*, II, pp. 300–2.
[33] Wood, *English Medieval House*, p. 403.
[34] Wood, *English Medieval House*, pp. 399–401; Emery, *Greater Medieval Houses*, II, pp. 272, 274.

stone tower houses, for instance, tended to be favoured in the north (for their military or fire-resistant properties) rather than the courtyard houses of the midlands and south. As for the architectural detail, though, much also depended upon the knowledge and experience of the builder engaged: the north, it is said, generally lagged behind the contemporary trends in the south. The picture is complicated of course by the adoption of these features by others lower down the social scale at a slightly later date, and the advent of new fashions among those of high status. The fashion for halls spread down the social scale after 1370. The main difference thereafter was whether the hall was aisled or not.[35] The building of battlements had initially been the preserve of the uppermost reaches of society, but the practice percolated down to the knightly classes, and by Edward III's reign was also adopted by merchants, townsmen and monasteries. Crenellation was most popular amongst the gentry in the fourteenth century, with 237 recorded examples in the first half of the century and 101 examples in the years 1350–99. By the fifteenth century, crenellation seems to have declined in popularity. This possibly owed something to changes in architectural fashion, but may simply be a reflection of changes in enrolment or the sources for enrolments, since only eight licences were granted during Henry IV's reign, one in Henry V's, five in Henry VI's and three in Edward IV's.[36] In spite of any apparent change in fashion, some people clearly enjoyed this antiquated design. Ideally a detailed analysis would be able to pinpoint all the influences on different houses, but the measuring of where and when is an inexact science given the evidence and mixture of styles occurring through building accretions. Many houses developed piecemeal, depending perhaps on the level of current income available to spend on building or on the extent of financial optimism pending a lucrative appointment.

From a cultural point of view, this study of the architecture can tell us something about lawyers' concern for external image; but it can also offer an insight into the dynamics of county society. Coincidences in design suggest that the plans for at least some lawyers' houses may have been influenced by the residences of their clients or patrons. The internal plan of lawyer John Heydon's Baconsthorpe Castle in Norfolk bears similarities to the earl of Suffolk's castle at Wingfield (built in around 1385).[37] The slender bell tower at Harlsey Castle (home of the judge Sir James Strangeways) may have been influenced by the design of a similar tower at Mount Grace Priory (built in the 1420s), as the Strangways family were supporters of the priory in the 1450s.[38] It may also be that lawyers were influenced by the architecture of their colleagues' houses. Was Knyvet consciously copying Thorpe when adding his suite at Southwick? It certainly bears a strong resemblance to the cross wing at Longthorpe, added earlier in the century.

The preponderance of houses in a given county or area is also significant in terms of alliances and local networks. In the North Riding of Yorkshire, for instance, the supporters successively of Richard Neville, earl of Warwick, and of Richard, duke of Gloucester, built their own seats in a cluster around Middleham Castle.

---

[35] M. Thompson, *The Medieval Hall: The Basis of Secular Domestic Life, 600–1600AD* (Aldershot, 1995), pp. 138–9. See also J. T. Smith, *English Houses 1200–1800: The Hertfordshire Evidence* (London, 1992).

[36] Coulson, 'Freedom to Crenellate', pp. 93–4.

[37] Emery, *Greater Medieval Houses*, II, p. 50.

[38] Ibid., I, p. 413.

Metcalfe's Nappa Hall was extremely close, as was Sir Robert Dancy's Thorpe Perrow and Sir James Strangways' East Harsley. A little to the south, Strangways' daughter was responsible for developing Ripley Castle, while Sir John Savile, also connected with Neville, was based further south still at Thornhill. This clustering could also come as a result of marriages. Sir Thomas Acton (d. 1480), a trusted servant of the earl of Shrewsbury, married one of the sisters and heiresses of John Stapleton. A judicial colleague, Thomas Horde, who lived two miles away at Stapelton Moat Farm, married the other sister.[39]

The accumulation of wealth and its investment in land was not considered to be the sole or the definitive marker of gentry status. The Scrope vs. Grosvenor case in 1385, a dispute about arms heard in the court of chivalry, highlighted the contemporary feeling among some in the upper stratum of society that breeding mattered and that by definition lawyers were socially inferior: Richard Scrope had been told that he could not possibly be a 'gentilhomme' because his father had been a lawyer.[40] This was a somewhat disingenuous stance since his father, Henry, like all judges from Edward II's reign onwards, had been knighted on reaching the bench (a practice intended to emphasise the honour and dignity of serving the king in the highest royal courts). He had also been fortunate to have received the honour of having his coat of arms augmented by Henry de Lacy, earl of Lincoln, in respect of his service to the earl. Henry had gone on to achieve the distinction of becoming chief justice of king's bench, enjoying an income of around £250 to £350 that placed him midway between the income levels of a banneret and a lesser baron. Richard Scrope's father was undoubtedly not just any old lawyer.[41]

However, there was clearly a sense that, even though a lawyer might have the trappings of status, 'dignity' was still a prerequisite. This held true even for the elite advocates called to the order of serjeants at law. The use of the phrase *status et gradus servientis ad legem* (in the writ of call) may have been equatable with an estate, but in spite of Fortescue's contention ('nedum gradus sed et status') it did not confer *dignitas*.[42] Unlike the civilian tradition which (following Bartolus) held that doctors of law were knights for legal purposes, there was no equivalent of *seigneurie* or *chevalerie ès lois* for common law practitionerrs. Even though 'serjeant' was used as an addition when required under the Statute of Additions of 1413 and the elaborate call ceremony emulated that of a knight's *abdoument*, it was not until the sixteenth century that a shift occurred in the concept of dignity and the degree of serjeant at law was regarded as comparable to knighthood.[43]

By Edward III's reign, it had been established that promotion to the bench, to the chief law courts (of king's bench and common pleas), automatically brought with it

---

[39] Emery, *Greater Medieval Houses*, II, pp. 557–8.

[40] *The Controversy between Sir Richard Scrope and Sir Robert Grosvenor in the Court of Chivalry*, ed. N. H. Nicolas (2 vols, London, 1832), I, p. 181.

[41] B. Vale, 'The Profits of Law and the "Rise" of the Scropes: Henry Scrope (d. 1336) and Geoffrey Scrope (d. 1340), Chief Justices to Edward II and Edward III', *Profit, Piety and the Professions*, ed. M. Hicks (Stroud, 1990), pp. 92–8, 100–1.

[42] Sir John Fortescue, *De laudibus legum Anglie*, ed. S. B. Chrimes (Cambridge, 1949), p. 120.

[43] J. H. Baker, *The Order of Serjeants at Law* (Selden Society supplementary ser. v, London, 1984), pp. 34–5, 49–50. For the details of the knight's ceremony see M. Powicke, *Military Obligation in Medieval England* (Oxford, 1962), p. 68.

elevation to knightly rank (usually at the higher level of banneret).[44] This connection, once initiated, was maintained in order to emphasise and display the honour and importance of serving the king in high judicial office.[45] This association with the dignity of knighthood was then also externalised in other ways. Some lawyers endeavoured to project a knightly image either by participating in tournaments (as Geoffrey Scrope is reported to have done) or by being portrayed dressed in armour on their funerary monuments. A brass effigy in knightly attire of Sir Roger Hillary, justice of common pleas under Edward III, was made for the church at Walsall in Staffordshire; interestingly, given the debate outlined above, Henry Scrope was also depicted in armour on his tomb in St Agatha's, Easby in Richmond.[46]

Not all lawyers desired the social recognition associated with becoming *miles*. A number of royal judges and serjeants, among them Walter Friskeney, Robert Malberthorpe, Edmund Pashley, Gilbert Thoutheby and Geoffrey Scrope, were distrained for refusing knighthood in Edward II's reign.[47] Adam Bowes, a justice in the palatinate of Durham and briefly of the court of common pleas, was distrained to knighthood in 1327.[48] Interestingly, just as the crown at times had to resort to introducing monetary penalties in order to force those eligible to assume knighthood to do so (usually using the criterion of possession of £40 a year in lands and rents), so there are cases of lawyers exhibiting a reluctance to be called to the order of serjeant at law. In addition to their distinctive clothing, serjeants at law enjoyed exclusive rights of audience in the court of common pleas, and in the fourteenth and fifteenth centuries acted as assize justices in the provinces. It might be thought unlikely that these stereotypical seekers of status would refuse the opportunity to adopt this estate, especially as it guaranteed a certain amount of business and secured them prestige; but there is evidence that suitable candidates did indeed prefer to avoid the call. An obvious reflection of this is the fluctuating level in the penalty introduced by the king's council to deter those nominated as serjeants from refusing. Introduced at £5 in the 1370s, the penalty had increased to £100 a decade later. The level was then raised to 500 marks in 1412 before reaching an astronomical £1,000 three years later, suggesting that the king took the matter extremely seriously. In one case, evasion was accepted because the potential serjeant was too ill; but in the absence of explicit reasons in the records, it can only be surmised that there were various cogent factors affecting the take-up of the degree.[49] Some historians have suggested that it was on account of the extravagant expense involved in the call ceremony (which included the giving of gold rings and provision of a sumptuous feast) or the disincentive arising from the reduction in income that would result from restrictions placed on private practice, as well as the assumption of public duties which ensnared those who became serjeants and those later appointed

---

[44] *Select Cases in the Court of King's Bench VI*, ed. G. O. Sayles (Selden Society lxxxii, London, 1965), pp. xxiv–xxv.

[45] Higgins, 'Judges in Government and Society', p. 192.

[46] M. Stephenson, *A List of Monumental Brasses in the British Isles* (London, 1926), pp. 445–6; *Controversy between Sir Richard Scrope and Sir Robert Grosvenor*, I, p. 222; Baker, *Serjeants at Law*, pp. 70, 518, 536. For the significance of funerary monuments, see N. Saul, 'Parchment and Tombstone: Documents and the Study of Medieval Monumental Sculpture', *Archives* xxvii (2002), 97–109.

[47] PRO, C 47/1/8, mm. 14–15, 26, 30–31.

[48] PRO, E 198/3/19.

[49] Baker, *Serjeants at Law*, 28–30.

judges.[50] It may even have been the prospect of a commitment to a life based in London, which might have deterred those holding office or practising primarily in the provinces.

This last reason may be borne out in the case of John Heydon, who managed to secure an exemption in advance of call. Heydon was recorder of Norwich in the 1430s and early 1440s and secured his exemption in 1442 (a year before the next call).[51] His focus seems to have been resolutely on East Anglia, and his association with the administration of lands in the region belonging to the duchy of Lancaster may provide the motivation behind his desire to evade becoming a serjeant at law. In 1443 he became steward (jointly with Thomas Tuddenham) of the duchy's lands in East Anglia, was consistently a justice of the peace for the decade or so from 1441, and served as a member of numerous royal commissions in the region. He was also a member of the committee that drafted the act of attainder against the Yorkists. During this period it is noticeable that he expanded his landed interests (acquiring in 1442 the lease to the manor of Beeston in Norfolk, not far from his own home at Baconsthorpe, on the death of Sir Simon Felbrigg).[52] Heydon built Baconsthorpe Castle as a defensible residence consisting of a gatehouse and a substantial court-yard house (which envelops more than half the current site of the property). The earliest work on the house is datable to the 1440s, the period during which he achieved major prominence. John died in 1480. On inheriting, his son Henry (d. 1504), also a lawyer (in fact steward to Cecily Neville, the mother of Edward IV) enlarged Baconsthorpe further, having built earlier a house for himself in Kent at Wickham Court.[53]

The model of the successful lawyer becoming rich and building a house to reflect his status is a fairly simple one, and hardly an earth-shattering revelation. What is more interesting is the ability of the lawyer's family to perpetuate and extend the achievements of the founder. In this respect, the alterations made to houses, or their demise, can themselves chart or mirror changes to the fortunes of the family or families who owned or lived in them. Following the demise of Sir Simon Burley, former tutor to Richard II, who was executed by the Appellants in 1388, the family seat of Boncroft Castle was rescued in about 1399 by Simon's great-nephew, John Burley. John, who lived until 1415, was steward to the Fitzalan lordship of Oswestry; the construction work carried out on the property probably dates from the period of his ownership at the turn of the fifteenth century.[54] But not all families who enjoyed a meteoric rise were able to maintain their position. The well-respected chief justice of Edward III's reign, Sir William Shareshull, carefully accumulated estates in Staffordshire and Oxfordshire (including the manor of Shareshill in Oxfordshire), during his long career, but his son predeceased him and a failure of the male line in the early fifteenth century led to the extinction of the family and the scattering of the estates.[55] The residence at the place bearing his name was aban-

---

[50] Ibid., pp. 34–7.

[51] Ibid., p. 261.

[52] H. Castor, *The King, the Crown and the Duchy of Lancaster: Public Authority and Private Power, 1399–1461* (Oxford, 2000), pp. 95–8.

[53] Emery, *Greater Medieval Houses*, II, pp. 49–50.

[54] Emery, *Greater Medieval Houses*, II, pp. 52–3.

[55] There is archaeological evidence of building works carried out during the early fourteenth century. The manor of Shareshull boasted a moated site: Roberts, 'Moated Sites', p. 27.

doned in the later fourteenth century, at some point after Sir William's death in 1370.[56]

The model is more complex because lawyers might attain social prominence or build/obtain houses for reasons other than, or in addition to, their prowess in the law. Sir William Eure, who was active in the palatinate of Durham and has been described as 'an unscrupulous man of considerable legal talent' was, in addition, on active service in France at Agincourt and on the eastern marches in 1436–7. His father had acquired Bradley Hall from the family of that name, but William rebuilt or extended the house in the 1430s into what may have been an imposing courtyard residence with a two- or three-storey south range.[57] Fortunes could be made through military service (obtaining ransoms and booty), or through trade and investment. Eure was perhaps unusual in combining the two. In other cases, one member of the family provided a financial basis for a family's future success and another entered into a legal career that further increased the dynasty's wealth and prestige. As one twentieth-century commentator put it, a 'family which could afford to send the heir to be trained as a lawyer was placing its money where it could yield the most rapid and considerable social dividend'.[58]

The Bowes family of Streatlam Castle in County Durham built their initial fortunes on the legal activities of Adam Bowes. When Sir William Bowes married the heiress Matilda Dalton in the late fourteenth century, the family obtained Dalden Tower, a tower with a large hall to the side of it. Interestingly, it was the prowess of William's son, another William, in the French wars of the early fifteenth century that led directly to the building of one of the few major houses in the north-east of England during the century. William II is said to have sent home a plan and model of the castle that he hoped to build on his return from the continent, an undertaking he fulfilled in about 1430.[59]

Estates passing by marriage could provide a significant fillip to a family's fortunes and its ability to develop property holdings. Chief Justice Henry Green received Drayton House, which had been crenellated by Sir Simon Drayton, when he married Simon's sister and co-heiress in 1367. Sir William Shareshull's second marriage to Dionisia (widow of Sir Hugh Cokesey and daughter and heiress of William Botiller of Wemme) in 1357, at the ripe old ages of about sixty-seven, was an especial coup, as Dionisia was the inheritor of vast estates in Shropshire and Worcestershire. As Putnam remarked, 'that a "self made" man at the height of his career seemed an eligible husband for the lady Dionisia is a fact of considerable importance in social history'.[60] Judges' children or those of lawyers already possessing a foot in landed society tended to marry into county families, or alternatively they married the offspring of those who were similarly ascending through the ranks of society on the basis of their legal know-how. For some, therefore, there was an opportunity to perpetuate or increase the level of status within the county.[61]

The legacy afforded by successful lawyers offered an excellent platform for

---

[56] B. H. Putnam, *The Place in Legal History of Sir William Shareshull* (Cambridge, 1950), pp. 2–13.

[57] Emery, *Greater Medieval Houses*, I, pp. 55–6.

[58] E. W. Ives, *The Common Lawyers of Pre-Reformation England* (Cambridge, 1983), p. 32.

[59] Emery, *Greater Medieval Houses*, I, pp. 138–9.

[60] Putnam, *Shareshull*, p. 7.

[61] For some examples, see A. Musson, *Public Order and Law Enforcement: The Local Administration of Criminal Justice, 1294–1350* (Woodbridge, 1996), pp. 136–44.

further domestic expansion. Richard Scrope and Robert Bourchier, whose fathers had been royal judges in the early fourteenth century, reached the peerage following their own service in royal administration and sought to impress local society with their building programmes. Scrope's impressive Bolton Castle, for example, which was begun in about 1378 and finished by 1396 (four years before Richard's death), combines the uncompromising appearance of a traditional castle with complex domestic planning, including suites of chambers and lodgings of carefully graded size and status.[62]

Not all lawyers were from obscure backgrounds – some came from existing knightly families – but there were many who worked their own way up the social ladder. The building programmes undertaken by lawyers served to present them publicly as part of gentry society and disguise the fact that they owed their status to their professional expertise. What were the wider consequences of this innate desire to be part of gentry society? Although they were regarded by some as upstarts and not true 'gentlemen', most lawyers demonstrated great success in merging into local society – to such a degree, indeed, as to cause difficulties for their own profession. It was perceived that lawyers and landowners not only enjoyed mutual interests, but also conspired together to pervert the course of justice when one of their number was involved in court proceedings. The crown's practice of appointing judges and serjeants of the central courts to assize circuits and oyer and terminer commissions in areas where the lawyers had their own private interests, where they held lands or had family or other connections, proved to be a double-edged sword. On the one hand, royal government obviously deemed it appropriate that the justices should have some local knowledge of the area under their jurisdiction. An appreciation of the balance of power in the region, of the ascendancy or decline of particular families, of the topography and customs was probably a vital factor in trying to achieve a just outcome. On the other hand, their service in the locality highlighted the close professional relationship between lawyers/judges and the major landowners who retained them for their services.

These perceptions fed into contemporary popular literature, ballads and poems. In the *Gest of Robin Hood*, for example, the relationship between the justice and the abbot is stated explicity: 'I am holde with the abbot of cloth and fee.'[63] In Langland's *Piers Plowman* the connection between justice and wealth is apparent in the well-known character Lady Meed, a personification of the bribery that the poet felt riddled and demeaned the legal system.[64] Perceptions of the way that justice operated, while not necessarily reflecting reality, could not easily be altered. Equally, feelings in the upper social echelons often ran against lawyers: they were regarded as disturbing the traditional hierarchy of society because they had demonstrated that they were capable of making their own way up it.

The 'upwardly mobile' element, comprising not just lawyers but soldiers and merchants, may have caused social and political instability because their own titles to lands were new (and possibly insecure).[65] An example of the destructive nature of

---

[62] Emery, *Greater Medieval Houses*, I, pp. 303–11.

[63] R. B. Dobson and J. Taylor, *Rymes of Robin Hood: An Introduction to the English Outlaw*, rev. edn (Stroud, 1997), pp. 75, 86.

[64] A. P. Baldwin, *The Theme of Government in Piers Plowman* (Woodbridge, 1981), pp. 24–38.

[65] For the fifteenth century, see Castor, *Duchy of Lancaster*, pp. 145–6; C. Carpenter, *Locality and Polity: A Study of Warwickshire Landed Society, 1401–1499* (Cambridge, 1992), pp. 623–4.

disputes (in terms of damage both to relationships and, more literally, to living accommodation) comes from the Paston letters. William Paston, who was a successful lawyer and become a serjeant-at-law in 1417/18, bought Gresham Castle in Norfolk in order to enhance his family's landholdings; but there was sufficient doubt over the title for Robert Hungerford, Lord Moleyns, to register a claim. (Apparently Moleyns was encouraged in this enterprise by his neighbour, John Heyford, who is portrayed as a rival of Paston.) The dispute escalated when Moleyns entered the property and started claiming rents. Paston regained the house, but was then forced out again at a moment when Margaret Paston and some of the family's servants were occupying it. Allegedly Moleyns' men broke down the doors, 'myned down the walls of the chambre where-in [Margaret] was and bore here out at the yates'. Following this seizure, Moleyns' men escaped. Paston managed to reclaim the property a year later, but by then it was apparently unfit for habitation.[66]

The scale and manner of increasing landholding was a factor affecting social relations, and the replacing or eclipsing of established gentry families was then a potentially disturbing element in local society. Aggressive acquisition of neighbouring lands undoubtedly bred resentment, especially when carried out within a close-knit society and a well-defined area. The element of bad feeling probably deepened when the acquisition was a consequence of neighbours' financial difficulties. In the fourteenth century, for example, Geoffrey Scrope frequently loaned money to his neighbours in the North Riding of Yorkshire on the security of their lands. His brother Henry was equally active in advancing money and acting as a mortgage broker. At one time Henry was owed varying sums of money by at least three Yorkshire gentry; and when John de Wensley was unable to redeem his mortgages on the manor of Wensley, it was agreed that, on his death, title on the property would revert to Scrope.[67]

This study has examined the careers of various men of law of the fourteenth and fifteenth centuries. It has shown not simply that lawyers invested their money in land and property, but also that the law provided a conduit for clever men to progress in society, achieve positions of influence and (in some cases) enter the aristocracy. It has also indicated that the process was not necessarily straightforward and that there were a number of variations to the theme. We should certainly regard a study of lawyers' houses as an important corrective to a Westminster-oriented approach to law and the legal profession. Not only does such an approach neglect the provincial lawyers, who clearly operated in the counties with some financial success, so much so that they could afford to turn down the status-enhancing and potentially lucrative call to the order of serjeants at law; it also ignores the extent to which the fortunes (both personal and financial) of men practising in the central courts were intimately bound up in their families and the demands and politics of local society. It clearly mattered to them that they establish a family seat, accumulate lands and refurbish their manors; it mattered to them how they were thought about in the locality and they tried to promote an image of themselves and their status (actual or desired) through the design, architecture, furnishings and other accoutrements of their houses. Just as clothes and servants were important markers of status, so the impres-

---

[66] *Paston Letters and Papers of the Fifteenth Century*, ed. N. Davis (2 vols, Oxford, 1971–6), I, pp. 277–30.
[67] Vale, 'Profits of the Law', pp. 99–100.

sion gained from a country residence, both its external appearance and the various details within it (especially spatial measurements and interior allocations and ratios of public and private space) could go a long way to disguising true origins and determining the future by realising aspirations.

THOMAS OF LANCASTER'S FIRST QUARREL WITH EDWARD II

Andy King

See how often and abruptly great men change their sides. Those whom we regard as faithless in the north we find just the opposite in the south. The love of magnates is as a game of dice, and the desires of the rich like feathers.[1]

So wrote the anonymous author of the *Vita Edwardi Secundi*. He was decrying the fickleness of the earls of Lincoln and Warenne, who, having striven to procure the exile of Piers Gaveston in the spring of 1308, welcomed him back just a year later, when he was recalled from Ireland by Edward II in the summer of 1309. The relationship of Edward to his favourite was to dominate the politics of the first five years of his reign. His first act on becoming king had been to recall Gaveston, who was then in France, having been banished by Edward I.[2] Initially, this had not caused any great resentment; Lincoln and Warenne, and five of their fellow earls (including Lancaster) were the witnesses to the charter by which Gaveston was created earl of Cornwall, on 6 August 1307.[3] However, Gaveston's gross arrogance rapidly lost him their goodwill, though perhaps even more objectionable was the undue influence he exercised over royal patronage.[4]

Disaffection was already evident by the beginning of 1308, just seven months after Edward's accession. In mid-January, Edward and his court crossed to France for his marriage to Isabella, daughter of King Philip IV, leaving Gaveston behind as keeper of the realm. A group of magnates, who accompanied Edward, sealed letters patent at Boulogne on 31 January, pointing out that they were bound by their allegiance to uphold the king's honour and the rights of his crown, and promising to obtain redress and make amends for 'the oppressions that have been done and are still being done to his people day in, day out';[5] this juxtaposition was intended to imply a linkage between the redress of grievances and the upholding of the king's

---

[1]   *Vita Edwardi Secundi*, ed. Noel Denholm-Young (London, 1957), pp. 7–8. The possible identity of the *Vita*'s author is discussed by Noel Denholm-Young, *Collected Papers* (Cardiff, 1969), pp. 267–89. I would like to thank Michael Prestwich, Mark Ormrod, Len Scales and Beth Hartland for reading and commenting on various drafts of this piece, and Professor Prestwich for supplying several references.

[2]   'With the dead king not yet even buried', as Walter of Guisborough put it: *The Chronicle of Walter of Guisborough*, ed. H. Rothwell (Camden Society 3rd ser. lxxxix, London, 1957), p. 383.

[3]   The charter is discussed by Pierre Chaplais, *Piers Gaveston: Edward II's Adoptive Brother* (Oxford, 1994), pp. 27–34.

[4]   The most detailed accounts of the politics of the early years of Edward II's reign are provided by: J. S. Hamilton, *Piers Gaveston, Earl of Cornwall 1307–12* (London, 1988), pp. 37–51; J. R. Maddicott, *Thomas of Lancaster 1307–22: A Study in the Reign of Edward II* (Oxford, 1970), pp. 67–120; Chaplais, *Piers Gaveston*, pp. 23–43.

[5]   'les oppressiouns que ount estre feit et uncore se fount de jour en jour a soen people': J. R. S. Phillips, *Aymer de Valence, Earl of Pembroke 1307–1324* (Oxford, 1972), p. 316.

honour. The group – which included Anthony Bek, bishop of Durham, and the earls of Lincoln, Warenne, Pembroke and Hereford – was made up of courtiers and royal servants; these were therefore men who remained fundamentally loyal to the king, but who realised that reforms were necessary in the face of mounting opposition.[6] The strength of this opposition was starkly revealed when Edward returned to England; according to one chronicler, the *comites et barones* threatened to delay the king's coronation unless something was done about Piers Gaveston, who had acted with his customary haughtiness and lack of tact in Edward's absence.[7]

In the parliament that met at the beginning of March, Edward was presented with a demand for Gaveston's banishment; unable to accept this, he prorogued parliament, and both sides prepared for armed conflict. However, the king could muster only a handful of the earls and barons to his cause, whilst the opposition claimed the support of Edward's own father-in-law, Philip IV of France; when parliament reconvened at the end of April, Edward was eventually forced to back down. On 18 May, he agreed to send Gaveston abroad. He then contrived to put a face-saving gloss over this capitulation by appointing Piers as his lieutenant in Ireland – which did at least meet his opponent's demands for his removal from the country, if not perhaps in quite the manner they had envisaged.[8]

Evidently, the opposition to the king and his favourite encompassed most of the nobility of England. However, despite his later reputation as a steadfast and relentless opponent of Edward and his prominent role in the 'execution' of Gaveston, it would appear that this opposition did not, at this stage, encompass earl Thomas of Lancaster. The earl seems to have been close to Edward before his accession to the throne: after all, they were cousins. A surviving roll of letters written by Edward in 1304–5 contains five to Lancaster, couched in terms which suggest genuine affection; in one of them, Edward sends his sympathy as Thomas had been ill, and says that he hopes to able to come 'to see you and comfort you'.[9] The two men remained on good terms when Edward became king, and the earl remained steadfastly loyal to his royal cousin throughout the first year of his reign.[10] Thus, according to Guisborough, Lancaster was the only one of the earls who was unwilling to back Lincoln's demand, at the parliament of March 1308, for a written commission from the king for the reform of the realm;[11] this must have been particularly galling for Lincoln, for Lancaster was his son-in-law. Soon after this, Edward started to prepare for the possibility of civil war, changing the constables at some of the more strategically important of his castles and putting in men whom he believed to be trust-

---

6   Ibid., pp. 25–8.
7   'Annales Paulini', *Chronicles of the Reigns of Edward I and Edward II*, ed. W. Stubbs (2 vols, Rolls Series, London, 1882–3), I, p. 260.
8   Maddicott, *Thomas of Lancaster*, pp. 87–8; Hamilton, *Piers Gaveston*, pp. 51, 55–7.
9   *Letters of Edward Prince of Wales, 1304–5*, ed. Hilda Johnstone (Roxburghe Club, Cambridge, 1931), p. 122; Maddicott, *Thomas of Lancaster*, p. 6.
10   The *Flores historiarum* does describe Lancaster as being the focal point of opposition to Gaveston straight after Edward's coronation: *Flores historiarum*, ed. H. R. Luard (2 vols, Rolls Series, London, 1890), III, p. 142. But as Maddicott remarks (*Thomas of Lancaster*, p. 77), its author was 'rabidly pro-Lancastrian', and his account was undoubtedly distorted by hindsight; no other chronicle account mentions Lancaster as an opponent of the king this early in the reign.
11   *Guisborough*, ed. Rothwell, pp. 381–2; Maddicott, *Thomas of Lancaster*, p. 74. The *Annales Paulini* also recounts that, at this parliament, a single earl (*comes unus*) was reluctant to commit himself to reform; presumably, this too is a reference to Lancaster. 'Annales Paulini', pp. 262–3.

worthy; among these were Nicholas de Segrave and John de Segrave the elder, both prominent Lancastrian retainers. At the same time, Nicholas was appointed marshal of England. Clearly, Edward expected the earl to rally his retainers in his defence.[12] Lancaster's loyal support for the king throughout this period is demonstrated by the fact that he witnessed sixteen out of the forty royal charters issued during Edward's first regnal year, more than any other earl.[13]

Nor did this loyalty go unrewarded, for Lancaster received a steady stream of grants and favours. This culminated on 9 May 1308, when, at the height of the Gaveston crisis, he was formally granted the stewardship, to him and his heirs. This was a particular mark of his high standing in royal favour, for his father Edmund, the previous holder of the office, had specifically renounced any hereditary claim, and it had lapsed on his death; nor had Thomas tried to claim the title from Edward I.[14] Just six months after this grant, however, relations between the earl and the king suddenly broke down. On 22 November, the earl witnessed a royal charter at Chertsey, Surrey, and then withdrew from court.[15] There was probably nothing untoward in his departure, for after reaching Kenilworth on 23 November, he forwarded a petition to the king on behalf of the erstwhile abbot of Stoneleigh, Warwickshire; and on 1 December, Edward granted him the right to hold markets and annual fairs at two of his manors.[16] But after this, the king's patronage seems to have abruptly ceased; Lancaster was not to return to court for over a year, and witnessed no more royal charters until March 1310.[17]

By the summer of 1309, the earl had become a leading figure in the opposition to the king. Although his movements in the first half of that year are rather obscure, Lancaster may well have been prominent in the drafting of the hostile petition of eleven articles presented to the king at the parliament at Westminster at the end of April.[18] Certainly, despite having had no part whatsoever in procuring Gaveston's exile the year before, he now became implacably opposed to the recall of Piers. But most tellingly, Lancaster required letters of safe-conduct before he would agree to come to meet Edward at Kempston (Middlesex) at the end of May. Clearly, he no longer trusted him, and for all that the safe-conduct referred to him as 'nos cheres et foiaux monsire Thomas conte de Lancastre nostre chere cousin', their relationship was already on very poor terms.[19] It was to remain so for the rest of Lancaster's life;

---

[12] *CFR 1307–19*, p. 17; *CPR 1307–13*, p. 51; Hamilton, *Piers Gaveston*, p. 49. For the Segraves' Lancastrian connections, see Maddicott, *Thomas of Lancaster*, passim.

[13] J. S. Hamilton, 'Charter Witness Lists for the Reign of Edward II', *Fourteenth Century England I*, ed. N. Saul (Woodbridge, 2000), p. 6 and app. 1. Only the chancellor John Langton, Robert de Clifford, Hugh Despenser the elder and Miles de Stapleton witnessed more.

[14] Maddicott, *Thomas of Lancaster*, pp. 76–7, 87. As Maddicott points out, the grant of the stewardship was perhaps more a bribe to buy Lancaster's continued support at a critical juncture than a reward for past loyalty.

[15] This was to be the last of only four royal charters out of 54 witnessed by the earl during Edward's second regnal year: PRO, C 53/95, m. 13; Hamilton, 'Charter Witness Lists', p. 6 and app. 1.

[16] *CChR 1300–26*, p. 123; *CCW 1244–1326*, p. 281.

[17] Maddicott, *Thomas of Lancaster*, pp. 76, 92–3.

[18] See below, p. 40.

[19] *Foedera* (3 vols in 6 parts, London, 1816–30), II, i, p. 75; Maddicott, *Thomas of Lancaster*, pp. 95–106. The safe-conduct covered the earls of Pembroke, Hereford and Warwick, as well as Lancaster; it was guaranteed by the earls of Gloucester, Richmond, Arundel and Lincoln (the last being Lancaster's father-in-law).

and indeed, his prominent role in Gaveston's judicial murder served only to arouse Edward's 'mortal hatred'.[20]

How is this remarkable *volte face* to be explained? The only contemporary account to offer any sort of explanation is the *Vita Edwardi Secundi*, generally regarded as the most reliable of the chronicles of the reign, which relates that Lancaster was particularly offended, 'because one of his followers was removed from his office at the instigation of Piers [Gaveston]'.[21] Unfortunately, the author of the *Vita* was not considerate enough to name this familiar, and modern historians have so far failed to reach any consensus as to his identity.[22] The removal of crown officials and their replacement by Gaveston's adherents was certainly a controversial issue. According to the *Gesta Edwardi de Carnarvan*, it was this that first aroused hostility to Gaveston and led to his exile in 1308. The same charge featured in the lengthy indictment that constituted clause 20 of the Ordinances of 1311.[23] Nevertheless, it is unlikely that this was the root of Lancaster's dispute with the king, if only because of timing. This squabble evidently broke out in December 1308. At that time, Piers Gaveston had already been in exile for five months and would not return until seven months later. Certainly, Gaveston was able to exercise his influence over the king even from across the Irish Sea, for John de Charlton, his familiar, was granted the manor of Pontesbury, Shropshire, in March 1309, whilst he and Gaveston were still in Ireland.[24] Yet the *Vita* clearly indicates that the dismissal of Lancaster's follower (whoever he was) took place after Gaveston had returned to England, by which time Lancaster's enmity to the king was already established. The affair would undoubtedly have exacerbated this enmity, but it cannot have created it.

Lancaster's enmity to his royal cousin may, in fact, have its origins in a much more petty quarrel, involving a dispute with local officials of the crown, rather than Gaveston's undue influence over royal patronage. In September 1311, Edward II was forced to promulgate various Ordinances for the reform of the government of the realm, and prominent amongst the Ordainers who forced these reforms on the king was Thomas of Lancaster. Clause 13 of the Ordinances demanded the removal of all the evil counsellors who had badly advised the king; and in November, a 1311 petition was presented to Edward in which such men were named. A copy of this petition was preserved amongst the muniments of the London Guildhall, and it was copied *verbatim* into the *Annales Londonienses*; the relevant clause, from the Guildhall version, reads as follows:

---

[20] *Scalacronica, by Sir Thomas Gray of Heton, Knight*, ed. Joseph Stevenson (Edinburgh, 1836), p. 140.

[21] 'quia unus ex familiaribus suis procurante Petro eiectus erat ab officio suo': *Vita Edwardi Secundi*, p. 8 (my translation). For the highly contemporary nature of the *Vita*, see Chris Given-Wilson, '*Vita Edwardi Secundi*: Memoir or Journal?', *Thirteenth Century England VI*, ed. R. H. Britnell, R. Frame and M. Prestwich (Woodbridge, 1997), pp. 165–76.

[22] Suggestions include Nicholas de Segrave, the marshal, expelled from the court in August 1308 (Noel Denholm-Young, *History and Heraldry 1254–1310* [Oxford, 1965], pp. 133–4); Segrave's deputy, Jocelin de Branksecombe, replaced in 1311 by Arnald de Tilley, a probable associate of Gaveston's (Maddicott, *Thomas of Lancaster*, pp. 93, 117–18); and – taking a somewhat liberal definition of *officio* – the Lancastrian retainer Gruffydd de la Pole, caught up in a feud with the Gaveston adherent John de Charlton (Chaplais, *Piers Gaveston*, p. 70).

[23] *RP*, II, p. 283; 'Gesta Edwardi de Carnarvan', *Chronicles of Edward I and Edward II*, II, p. 34; Hamilton, *Piers Gaveston*, pp. 75–6.

[24] *CChR 1300–26*, p. 127 (contra Maddicott, *Thomas of Lancaster*, p. 93).

Item, Monsire Johan de Cherletone, Monsire Johan de la Beche, Monsire Johan le Sapy, Monsire William de Vaux, Sire Johan de Hothom, et Monsire Gerard de Sauvoie, soient oustez de office et de baillie, e hors du service le Roi; issint quil ne vignent pres du Roi.[25]

This same clause was also quoted in full (translated into Latin) in the *Gesta Edwardi*, although the rest of the petition was merely summarised briefly.[26] 'Monsire Gerard de Sauvoie' is identified as Gerard Salvayn by the *Annales* and the *Gesta* ('Gerard Salveyn' and 'Gerardus Salvayn' respectively). The *Annales* names 'sire Johan de Ockham' instead of 'Sire Johan de Hothom', but Hothum is confirmed by the *Gesta* ('Johannis de Hothome'). Similarly, the *Gesta* names 'Johannes de Bek' instead of 'Monsire Johan de la Beche', but the *Annales* confirms the latter.[27]

Of this group of six miscreants, four had close associations with Piers Gaveston, connections that had given them access to considerable royal patronage. John de Charlton, a man of obscure birth, had entered Edward II's household shortly before he became king, serving as Edward's chamberlain as well as Gaveston's *secretarius*. After his return from Ireland, Charlton was granted (in addition to Pontesbury) the hand of Hawys, heiress to part of the barony of Powys; consequently, he became involved in a protracted feud with Gruffydd de la Pole, who owned the rest of the barony, and did not scruple to use his influence with the king to gain the upper hand in this dispute.[28] John de Sapy, a yeoman of the king's household, was also a retainer of Gaveston, a connection that again proved profitable. In March 1310, he was granted the manor of Caldicot, Glamorgan, for life, a grant which was made hereditary twelve months later; in April 1311, he was granted the wardship of the lands of Urian de Seint Piere, during the minority of his heir; and in May, he was granted

[handwritten marginal note: 1311 custody of town of Hereford]

25 'Item, Sir John de Charlton, Sir John de Beche, Sir John de Sapy, Sir William de Vaux, Sir John de Hothom, and Sir Gerard de Salvayn, should be removed from office and from [their] bailiwick[s], and from the service of the king, so that they shall not come near the king': *Munimenta Gildhallæ Londoniensis*, ed. H. T. Riley (3 vols in 4 parts, Rolls Series, London, 1859–62), II, ii, pp. 682–90 (my translation); 'Annales Londonienses', pp. 198–202; Maddicott, *Thomas of Lancaster*, p. 117; cf. Ordinances, clause 13 (*RP*, I, p. 282).

26 'Gesta Edwardi', ed. Stubbs, II, pp. 40–1. Though compiled at the end of Edward III's reign, the *Gesta* was based on a contemporary set of annals kept at Bridlington Priory, Yorkshire, the writer of which had access to a copy of this petition preserved in a register of documents; therefore his information is likely to be reasonably accurate. John Taylor, *English Historical Literature in the Fourteenth Century* (Oxford, 1987), pp. 151–2; Antonia Gransden, *Historical Writing in England II: c.1307 to the Early Sixteenth Century* (London, 1982), pp. 9–10. The fact that the Bridlington chronicler choose to quote this clause in full, while only summarising the rest of the petition, may suggest that he considered this clause to be particularly significant (and may reflect the writer's knowledge of Yorkshire affairs); that a copy of the petition reached Bridlington suggests that it was deliberately circulated as propaganda, presumably by the Ordainers.

27 The substitution of 'Sauvoie' for 'Salvayn' was probably just a copyist's misreading (the names would have looked much more similar in a fourteenth-century hand than they do in modern Roman typeface). Bek was a retainer of Henry de Lacy, and subsequently of Thomas of Lancaster (Maddicott, *Thomas of Lancaster*, p. 61), so he is unlikely to have been objectionable to the Ordainers. As Bek is mentioned elsewhere in the Bridlington annals, the later compiler of the *Gesta* probably just assumed that 'Beche' was a variant of that name. The *Annales*' error may be explained by the fact that Ockham was the cofferer of the king's wardrobe (Maddicott, *Thomas of Lancaster*, p. 165), and therefore an obvious target for the Ordainers' ire.

28 Chaplais, *Piers Gaveston*, pp. 64–5; R. Morgan, 'The Barony of Powys 1275–1360', *Welsh History Review* x (1980–1), pp. 12–18 (and see n. 22 above).

custody of the town of Hereford.[29] William de Vaux was Gaveston's steward and was appointed as his attorney when Gaveston went into exile in 1311. He had previously been involved in the killing of a certain Thomas de Walkingham of Yorkshire and other felonies, for which he, Gaveston and five others received a royal pardon in September 1310. He was also able to obtain royal patronage through his association with Gaveston, notably, in January 1311, the custody of the lands of Robert de Roos (shared with Robert Darcy, another of Gaveston's retainers) and of Burstwick, Holderness. To add insult to injury, this latter grant was made on the same day as the pardon for the murder of Walkingham.[30] John de Hothum was one of the group of Yorkshire clerks who dominated the king's administration in the early fourteenth century. He made a career in the Dublin exchequer, gaining Gaveston's favour during the latter's sojourn in Ireland, and after coming back to England in his company, he succeeded Gerard Salvayn as escheator north of the Trent. His association with Gaveston was equally valuable; he was granted the wardship of the manor of Cottingham, Yorkshire, during the minority of the heir, and was presented to two Yorkshire livings while the archbishopric of York was vacant; he was promised further, and rapid, preferment until he held enough benefices to provide him with an income of £300.[31]

These men thus had close and profitable connections with Gaveston that made them objectionable to the Ordainers; these connections are well demonstrated by the fact that Hothum and Vaux were amongst those nominated as Gaveston's attorneys when he went into exile in 1311, and were appointed as keepers of, respectively, his London houses and Knaresborough castle in December 1311, just weeks after the Ordainers had demanded their removal from royal service. They should clearly be numbered amongst the 'complices et fautores Petri' mentioned in the *Vita Edwardi Secundi*'s account of these events, whose removal was demanded by clause 20 of the Ordinances.[32] John de la Beche seems not to have been a Gaveston adherent, though he was appointed keeper of Nottingham castle, which had been held by Gaveston until he went into exile. However, since 1308, he had been pardoned a total of over £195 on the farm of the manor of Henton, which he held by the king's gift. This was a prime example of what the Ordainers regarded as the wasting of the king's resources, condemned by clause 7 of the Ordinances.[33] All of these five also exerted their influence to obtain royal patronage for others, either their own followers or petitioners who doubtless paid for the privilege.[34]

The odd man out in this group is the Yorkshire knight Sir Gerard Salvayn. His only connection with Piers was that he had been sent to France in October 1311 to

[29] Hamilton, *Piers Gaveston*, p. 143 n. 50; *CPR 1307–13*, pp. 213, 335, 362; *CFR 1307–19*, p. 90.

[30] *CPR 1307–13*, pp. 277, 306, 397; *CFR 1307–19*, p. 71; Hamilton, *Piers Gaveston*, pp. 41, 76, 88, 91–2. The pardons for the killing of Walkingham may lie behind the Ordainers' complaint that Gaveston had been 'maintient robbeours, homicides, et les fait avoir le Chartre le Roi de pees, endenaunt hardement a mesfesours de pis faire': Ordinances, clause 20 (*RP*, I, p. 283).

[31] *CFR 1307–19*, pp. 52, 76; *CPR 1307–13*, pp. 212, 293, 337; Maddicott, *Thomas of Lancaster*, p. 165; J. L. Grassi, 'Royal Clerks from the Archdiocese of York in the Fourteenth Century', *Northern History* v (1970), pp. 21–2; J. R. S. Phillips, 'The Mission of John de Hothum to Ireland, 1315–16', *England and Ireland in the Later Middle Ages*, ed. J. Lydon (Dublin, 1981), pp. 64–5.

[32] *Vita Edwardi Secundi*, p. 21; *CPR 1307–13*, p. 397; *CFR 1307–19*, pp. 117–18; *RP*, I, p. 283.

[33] *CFR 1307–19*, p. 118; *CCR 1307–13*, pp. 85, 195; *RP*, I, p. 281.

[34] Instances include *CPR 1307–13*, pp. 57, 197, 199, 201, 270, 381; *CCW 1244–1326*, pp. 275 (a particularly revealing example), 366.

obtain a safe-conduct for him, and may have escorted him into exile (and possibly back again).[35] However, this need not suggest that Salvayn had any ties to Gaveston, for he had previously been employed on a mission to the French king by Edward I, in 1304;[36] it is probably this previous experience that explains his selection as an envoy in 1311. Neither does he appear to have enjoyed the royal bounty shared by the others named in this clause; apart from his fee as household knight, he received no recorded gifts from Edward II in this period (the only royal wardship he obtained was acquired by purchase from Hugh le Despenser) and his malpractices were on a purely local scale.[37] Thus, beyond the fact that, as a member of the royal household, he was an obvious partisan of the king, the only link between Salvayn and these others was that he was succeeded as escheator north of the Trent by Hothum. The Ordainers failed to demand the removal of any of the escheators for the south, so it would appear that somebody with influence over the Ordainers bore a grudge against northern escheators; and, of course, it was to the north of the Trent where the bulk of Thomas of Lancaster's estates lay, It is therefore unlikely to have been mere coincidence that Lancaster had come into conflict with Salvayn just at the time when he first fell out with Edward II.

In February 1309, Gerard Salvayn, then serving as escheator north of the Trent, had been ordered to appear at the next parliament to explain why he had taken into the king's hand the manor of Wilton, near Pickering in Yorkshire, held by John de Heslarton; and he was to return it in the meantime. A subsequent writ, in May, reveals that Salvayn had seized the manor as an estate held in chief that had been alienated without the king's licence. Wilton had been held by Roger Bigod, earl of Norfolk, who had granted it to John Lovel; Lovel in turn had granted it to Heslarton and his wife, occasioning Salvayn's intervention. Bigod had, of course, granted most of his lands away to Edward I in 1302, though retaining a life interest in them. It is therefore possible that, two years after Bigod's death in 1306, Salvayn believed that Lovel held Wilton in chief. Had this been the case, the seizure would have been perfectly legal, in accordance with a royal ordinance of 1256. However, a perusal of Domesday Book revealed that the soke of Wilton pertained to Pickering, an honor that Thomas of Lancaster held by inheritance from his father. Wilton was thus held of Lancaster, and not of the king, and Salvayn was duly ordered to desist from any further intervention. In fact, Wilton had been specifically excluded from Bigod's grant of his lands to Edward I, presumably for this reason.[38] It is rather more likely

---

[35] *CPR 1307–13*, pp. 228, 334, 404; *CCW 1244–1326*, p. 347; *Treaty Rolls 1234–1325* (London, 1955), nos. 490, 499; Hamilton, *Piers Gaveston*, pp. 89, 92; Chaplais, *Piers Gaveston*, pp. 75, 77; Maddicott, *Thomas of Lancaster*, p. 117.

[36] *CPR 1301–7*, p. 258; *CCR 1302–7*, pp. 169, 175, 219.

[37] *CPR 1307–13*, p. 114. In fact, Salvayn had done rather better under Edward I, who granted him markets, fairs and free warren on several of his manors and a licence to crenellate his house at Harswell: *CChR 1257–1300*, p. 435; *CChR 1300–26*, p. 37; *CPR 1301–7*, p. 160.

[38] *CCR 1307–13*, pp. 111, 139; *PW*, II, ii, p. 26; *Close Rolls 1254–56*, p. 429; *CCR 1296–1302*, p. 581; *CChR 1300–26*, p. 25. The circumstances of Bigod's grant to Edward I are discussed by K. B. McFarlane, *The Nobility of Later Medieval England* (Oxford, 1973), p. 262. The relevant entry in Domesday Book confirms that 'Wiltune' belonged to the jurisdiction of 'Pichering', which, in 1086, was held by the king: *Domesday Book*, ed. Abraham Farley (2 vols, London, 1783), I, p. 299b. This is, in itself, an interesting example of the use to which Domesday Book was put in the Middle Ages, and its status as an unimpeachable source of authority: cf. Anthony Musson, 'Appealing to the Past: Perceptions of Law in Later Medieval England', *Expectations of the Law in the Middle Ages*, ed. Anthony Musson (Woodbridge, 2001), pp. 168–9, 177–8.

that Salvayn knew precisely what he was doing, for he shared the lordship of two manors with Heslarton and would therefore have been reasonably familiar with Heslarton's affairs.[39] Certainly, one of his neighbours appears to have been well informed of – and very interested in – the precise terms of this grant, for somebody had copies drawn up of six deeds relating to the neighbouring manor of Thornton (which also pertained to Pickering), including a copy of a royal licence granted to Bigod when he surrendered his estates in 1302, permitting the latter to grant the manors of Wilton, Thornton and Levisham to whomever he wished. Another of these deeds was witnessed by Gerard Salvayn himself (along with John de Heslarton).[40]

Although the Salvayn family had long been established in Yorkshire, and had played a minor role in local affairs, Gerard was the first to make a significant career in the royal administration.[41] He took the opportunity to further his own local interests, buying several properties in the county; and it would appear that he had now turned to abusing his office to harass a neighbour by taking his lands into the king's hand. Such deliberate malpractice is suggested by the fact that, some time later, he seized some of Heslarton's livestock on the spurious grounds that Bigod had owed money to the king, and that as a tenant of lands formerly held of Bigod, Heslarton was liable to distraint for this alleged debt.[42] Nor was John de Heslarton the only person to suffer from Salvayn's malpractice; the mayor and citizens of York complained to the chancellor about an inquest *ad quod dampnum*, concerning a grant to St Leonard's hospital, which Salvayn had conducted improperly, without their knowledge.[43]

Gerard Salvayn may well have been acting on his own initiative in seizing Wilton, but Thomas of Lancaster had no reason to suppose that he was not acting in an official capacity. As far as the earl was concerned, his jurisdiction had been infringed by a royal official acting on royal business. The order for Salvayn to explain his actions is dated 2 February 1309; it is not unlikely that the seizure referred to had taken place in December, and was the immediate cause of the sudden cooling in relations between Lancaster and the king at the end of 1308. Certainly, the fact that the earl felt it necessary to obtain a confirmation of his franchisal charter at this time suggests that he considered his proprietary rights to be under threat.[44] An argument about the feudal status of a single Yorkshire manor may seem a very trivial matter to throw a previously loyal earl and cousin of the king into an opposition that was to last for the rest of his life, and which led ultimately to his execution at Pontefract. But if this was indeed the incident that first turned Lancaster against the king, its very triviality may explain why so few contemporary chronicles were able to offer

---

[39] *PW*, II, ii, p. 406. Salvayn and Heslarton had also served together as knights of the shire for Yorkshire in the parliament of 1305 (*CCR 1302–7*, p. 330).

[40] Durham Record Office, D/Gr 51, 54, 99, 104–6, calendared in *Greenwell Deeds*, ed. Joseph Walton, *Archaeologia Aeliana* 4th ser. iii (1927). The deeds were all copied neatly onto a single large sheet of parchment, in an early fourteenth-century hand.

[41] The careers of Salvayn and his relatives are conveniently summarised in C. Moor, *Knights of Edward I* (5 vols, Harleian Society, London, 1292–32), IV, pp. 203–5.

[42] *RP*, I, pp. 316–17; *Feet of Fines for the County of York 1300–14*, ed. M. Roper (Yorkshire Archaeological Society Record Series cxxvii, Leeds, 1965), nos. 115, 161, 191, 337, 349, 368, 422, 437.

[43] 'indebite . . . nobis nescientibus et omnino ignorantibus': PRO, SC 1/35/83.

[44] *CChR 1300–26*, p. 126, dated 4 March 1309; Maddicott, *Thomas of Lancaster*, p. 76.

any explanation of his move into opposition: they simply did not know about it.[45] Throughout his career, the earl was fiercely acquisitive and determined to protect his rights at all costs.[46] At the end of 1308, Edward was making every effort to win the opposition back to his side, in the hope that he could persuade them to allow him to recall Gaveston; these efforts included the liberal dispensation of his patronage.[47] Possibly, Lancaster resented this largesse to the king's recent opponents, feeling that his own loyalty had not been sufficiently valued. If so, the infringement of his rights over the manor of Wilton would have brought this resentment to a head; he could hardly have sat back and watched with equanimity as these rights were breached by a corrupt royal official on the make – an official, moreover, who was merely a jumped-up member of the local gentry in an area that the earl aspired to dominate.

Nor was Lancaster the sort of man to let mere matters of state obstruct his own personal feuds. He was quite capable of pursuing a petty personal vendetta even at the expense of his own best interests, as his treatment of Bartholomew Badlesmere was to demonstrate amply. Badlesmere was a royal favourite who turned against his benefactor after being supplanted in Edward's affections by the Despensers. In October 1321, the king besieged his castle at Leeds, Kent; but so great was Lancaster's contempt for this erstwhile courtier that he actually forbade his fellow rebels in the Welsh marches from relieving the castle, and subsequently refused to accept Badlesmere as an ally, despite the fact that, by this time, he clearly needed all the help he could get.[48]

Once Lancaster had withdrawn from the court, any quarrel with the king would have become self-perpetuating, for he would have not have received any favours while he was sulking on his own estates. Nor would he have been able to defend his retainers' interests, a situation that could easily have produced the dispute with Gaveston described by the *Vita*; and, of course, this would only have served to increase his resentment against the king. In all probability, Thomas was simply too proud to return to the court to beg for Edward's forgiveness, even after the Wilton dispute had been settled in his favour; and at this juncture, Edward had no great need of his support, for his political situation was steadily improving as he won the other earls back to his side. If neither Edward nor Thomas was prepared to back down (and both men seem to have particularly stubborn), a minor disagreement could easily have been blown up out of all proportion. And this appears to be just what happened.[49]

---

[45] Cf. Maddicott's comment: 'Tempers ran high, and some minor incident may have carried King and Earl forward to a breach which neither had foreseen' (*Thomas of Lancaster*, p. 93).

[46] For example, three years previously, the prior of Tutbury had complained that the actions of Lancaster's bailiffs had brought the convent nearly to destruction, in what appears to have been a dispute over jurisdiction: *RP*, I, p. 477; cf. *CPR 1301–7*, pp. 353–4, 405–6.

[47] Maddicott, *Thomas of Lancaster*, pp. 91–3; Hamilton, *Piers Gaveston*, pp. 67–9; *Vita Edwardi Secundi*, pp. 6–7. It was the success of Edward's efforts in this direction that provoked the author of the *Vita* to his famous comment on the inconstancy of magnates (see above, n. 1).

[48] *The Anonimalle Chronicle, 1307–1334*, ed. Wendy R. Childs and John Taylor (Yorkshire Archaeological Society Record Series cxlvii, Leeds, 1991), p. 102; Maddicott, *Thomas of Lancaster*, pp. 293–5.

[49] Maddicott comments of Lancaster's attitude to Badlesmere, 'his behaviour shows a surprising lack of a sense of proportion, an inability to distinguish between the main issues at stake and those which were trivial and personal' (*Thomas of Lancaster*, p. 295); it was just this sort of behaviour which would have led to a trivial dispute such as that over Wilton being blown up into a major quarrel.

That Lancaster's opposition to the king was shaped by his dispute with Salvayn is suggested by the fact that, as soon as Lancaster turned against the king, the activities of royal escheators became a matter of concern for the king's opponents. By virtue of his wealth and royal blood, Lancaster was the natural leader of any opposition faction and it would appear that he used the Dunstable tournament in the spring of 1309 to arrange a petition of grievances, presented at the parliament that met at Westminster on 27 April.[50] These grievances largely echoed those of the *Articuli super Cartas* of 1300, issues which had not prevented him from supporting the king until six months previously. Significantly, however, one of the few new matters raised by this petition was the subject of the last article:

> While various men of the realm hold their tenements in chief from the king, and they and their ancestors have held them from time beyond memory, the king's escheators come and seize their lands, and evict them by official inquests, without appeal to the king's court, by which the people feel much aggrieved.[51]

Although this does not correspond exactly with Lancaster's grievance over Wilton, the petition was supposed to reflect the grievances of the opposition as a whole, rather than those of any one individual magnate; certainly, the raising of the issue of unjust seizures by escheators at this time is unlikely to be coincidental. It is also possible that Lancaster's complaints were the cause of Salvayn's dismissal as escheator beyond Trent in December 1309. The latter had certainly not lost the king's favour for he was appointed sheriff of Yorkshire, for life, in the following March (an appointment which cannot have pleased Lancaster) and was admitted to the king's household on 8 June 1311.[52]

If Gerard Salvayn's activities as a royal escheator really were the initial cause of Lancaster's opposition to Edward, it is somewhat surprising to find that the same Gerard Salvayn was subsequently pardoned under the terms of the treaty of Leake as a retainer of Lancaster.[53] Even if Salvayn had had nothing to do with Lancaster's enmity with the king, it is still surprising to find the latter retaining a man whom the Ordainers had demanded should be removed from the king's presence. Nor was Lancaster usually the sort of man to let bygones be bygones, as his treatment of Bartholomew Badlesmere was to prove. How, then, is Lancaster's change of heart to be explained? In fact, by 1318 Gerard Salvayn had fallen from royal favour, so much so that he had had to grant his manor of Sandhall to Edward and make fine of £2,000 (subsequently remitted) to obtain a pardon for certain trespasses. Two of these offences in particular rankled with Edward, and were specified in his pardon: receiving a bribe of 40 marks from Robert de Lacy, and the seizure of the manor of

---

[50] *RP,* I, pp. 443–5; for the date and circumstances, see Maddicott, *Thomas of Lancaster,* pp. 97–8.

[51] 'Qe par la ou diverses gentz du Roialme tenent lour tenementz en chef du Roy, et unt tenuz eux et lour auncestres du temps dont memorie n'est, veignent les Eschetours le Roi, et seisent lour terres, et les oustent par enquestes q'il font de lour office, sanz appeller en la Court le Roy; dont le poeple se sente molt greve': *RP,* I, p. 445.

[52] *CFR 1307–19,* pp. 52, 86, 97 (Salvayn was replaced as escheator by John de Hothum); BL, Cotton MS Nero C.VIII, fol. 91. Salvayn was still in the royal household in 1314, when he is recorded as a banneret: PRO, E 101/378/6.

[53] *CPR 1317–21,* p. 228; *Select Cases in the Court of the King's Bench IV,* ed. G. O. Sayles (Selden Society lxxiv, London, 1957), pp. 86–8.

Metham.[54] The charge of bribery stemmed from a commission of oyer and terminer appointed in September 1314 to investigate the wrecking in a storm of a ship, said to be 'laden with silver in bar, gold florins, jewels and divers wares', much of which had been cast ashore near Scarborough; although wreck of the sea, and therefore legally belonging to the king, this treasure was seized by Lacy. This commission must have discovered evidence of corruption, for Salvayn was accused of accepting this bribe from Lacy's proceeds in return for neglecting to seize the goods for the king. Salvayn's dismissal from the shrievalty followed immediately after, and over the next year, various commissions were appointed to investigate his other mal-practices.[55] The seizure of Metham was one of these malpractices, committed at about the same time, though unlike his acceptance of Lacy's bribe, this seems to have been motivated by rather more than simple greed.

Metham had been held by John de Metham, who had been granted his inheri-tance jointly with his wife, Sibyl (an heiress in her own right), during his father's lifetime. Thus when John died in May 1312, leaving his twelve-year-old son Thomas as his heir, Sibyl was able to retain her husband's lands despite the fact that some were held in chief.[56] Obviously, this made her an attractive match, and by the begin-ning of June a certain Robert de Stiveton had already married her. Sibyl may well have been coerced, for Stiveton and several others were subsequently pardoned for her rape. This rapid wooing certainly aroused resentment locally, for Metham was plundered by a gang that included Laurence Hecks (from whom de Metham had rented land worth 15s) and Hugh Scot.[57] The latter was briefly imprisoned in 1313, along with Sibyl, as the result of a malicious indictment, and the feud ended with Hugh being killed by Stiveton at York in 1314, in the presence of the king. Not surprisingly, Stiveton then fled and his lands, and those of his wife, were taken into the king's hands. It was in the aftermath of this event, just before his dismissal as sheriff, that Salvayn seized Metham, along with Stiveton's other Yorkshire estates, assaulting the royal custodian in the process.[58]

Having initially denied any involvement in these events, Salvayn then claimed to have bought the marriage of John de Metham's son from the earl of Lancaster, though he stressed that 'the infant was peaceably seised of the manor a great time before Robert [de Stiveton] committed the felony [i.e. the killing of Hugh Scot]'. However, this cannot be taken as evidence that Salvayn was already moving into Lancaster's circle, for his account stretched the truth rather beyond breaking point. After John de Metham's death, Lancaster had claimed the wardship and marriage of

[handwritten marginal note: Bannockburn time]

---

[54] *CCR 1313–18*, p. 433; *CPR 1313–17*, p. 554. Salvayn's fall from grace is marked by the fact that he does not appear as a household knight in 1316–18 or in 1321–2 (cf. Society of Antiquaries MSS 120, 121; BL, MS Stowe 553). Salvayn had obtained Sandhall in 1307 (*Feet of Fines for the County of York*, no. 337; cf. above, n. 42).

[55] *CCR 1313–18*, pp. 232, 433; *CPR 1313–17*, pp. 249, 253, 312, 404, 425–6, 554; *CFR 1307–19*, p. 212. A month after the first investigation into Salvayn's conduct, commissions of oyer and terminer were appointed to investigate similar allegations against the sheriffs of the other counties of England (*CPR 1313–17*, pp. 143–4); though it is usually assumed that such enquiries were the result of pressure from the counties, this case demonstrates that the king himself had a direct financial interest in controlling corrup-tion amongst his officials.

[56] *CIPM*, V, no. 316 (writ issued 18 May) and cf. *Feet of Fines for the County of York*, no. 448; *CCR 1307–13*, p. 466; *CCR 1323–7*, p. 455.

[57] *CCR 1323–7*, p. 455; *CPR 1307–13*, pp. 476, 533–4, 535; *CPR 1313–17*, pp. 105–6.

[58] *CCR 1313–18*, pp. 6, 130; *CFR 1307–19*, p. 206; *CPR 1313–17*, p. 310.

his son, on the grounds that Metham and his wife held lands of him, at Pollington and Eggborough; however, he then sold the wardship to Nicholas de Metham (for £200, a sum which explains why Metham's estates were worth fighting over). It is quite possible that Salvayn had in turn bought the wardship from Nicholas, but while a later inquest recorded that Metham's son had entered these lands when of full age, the inquest *post mortem* on Metham himself found that his son and heir was only twelve years old, so he could not have been 'peaceably seised of the manor' at the time of his stepfather's felony just two years later. In any case, Lancaster had no right to sell the wardship and marriage of Metham's son to anybody, for the inquest *post mortem* had found that the marriage belonged to the king.[59]

Salvayn's involvement in what was essentially a family feud may be explained by the fact that he was personally acquainted with John de Metham; he had been appointed to a commission with him in 1311, and had acted as mainpernor for Sibyl in July 1312 when she was imprisoned for 'certain trespasses against the king'. Hugh Scot was evidently an associate of Salvayn's, being a party to an assault perpetrated by the latter in York in 1313.[60] On the other hand, Robert de Stiveton had played no part in royal administration, and was not a member of the circle in which Salvayn and de Metham moved;[61] it is not hard to imagine that his intrusion into this circle would have been resented. In a petition presented in parliament in 1315, John's son Thomas claimed that he had been granted the manor of Metham by Sibyl, his mother, following the death of his father, but before her marriage to Stiveton, and that it should not therefore have been subject to forfeiture after Stiveton's felony.[62] Thus, in seising Metham, Salvayn was not simply indulging in a piece of opportunistic banditry; rather, he was (ab)using his shrieval authority on behalf of Sibyl and Thomas, who were trying to get their lands back out of the king's hand. It is even possible that John de Metham had been his retainer, in which case Salvayn was simply exercising good lordship on behalf of his clients: indeed, inasmuch as he was coming to the aid of a widow in distress, Salvayn might even be said to have been acting from motives of chivalry.

Salvayn then faced a string of indictments for his various misdeeds as sheriff and escheator, indictments that hint at orchestration; it was undoubtedly this pressure that induced him to part with Sandhall, in exchange for a pardon, in October 1316, though he was still protesting his right in the matter. He obviously still felt aggrieved, for in July 1317 Stiveton was complaining that Sibyl had been abducted by a gang led by Salvayn, and including Thomas de Metham the elder, Nicholas de Metham, Thomas de Metham the younger and Jordan de Metham. (The younger Thomas was presumably John de Metham's son.) The fact that he was involved in the abduction of his own mother does suggest that Stiveton's marriage to Sibyl had

---

[59] *CCR 1313–18*, p. 130; *CCW 1244–1326*, pp. 408–9; *RP*, I, p. 304; *CIM 1307–49*, no. 565; *CIPM*, V, no. 316. It is interesting to note that John de Metham and Sibyl's joint tenancy seems to have effective in evading royal wardship, contra Scott L. Waugh, *The Lordship of England: Royal Wardships and Marriages in English Society and Politics 1217–1327* (Princeton, 1988), p. 102. Lancaster, however, does not appear to have been deterred by such legal niceties.

[60] *CPR 1307–13*, p. 308; *CCR 1307–13*, p. 542; *CPR 1313–17*, pp. 72, 73. Another of Sibyl's mainpernors was John de Hothum.

[61] Stiveton's career (or rather, lack of it) is summarised in Moor, *Knights of Edward I*, IV, p. 288.

[62] *RP*, I, p. 304. This claim may lie behind Salvayn's assertion that the young Thomas was 'peaceably seised of the manor' of Metham (cf. above, n. 56).

been against the wishes of her previous husband's family.[63] In these circumstances, it is hardly surprising that Salvayn should have turned against the king. As a supporter of the king during the crisis over Gaveston and the Ordinances, prominent enough to be singled out by the Ordainers, he must have assumed that his corruption would be overlooked by his royal master. This clearly demonstrates the difficulties that Edward faced with his own officials for much of his reign; any attempt to curtail their malpractices to any great extent might well lead to their defection to the baronial opposition. The king's attempts to discipline Salvayn simply had the effect of driving the latter into Lancaster's camp.[64] Nor is it surprising to find that Thomas de Metham, unable to obtain redress against an interloper who had taken over his father's lands, also became a follower of Lancaster, pardoned as such under the treaty of Leake. Similarly, John de Heslarton was prominent in the long list of those pardoned for Gaveston's death in October 1313.[65] Indeed, the relations of men such as these with Lancaster and with the king are a striking illustration of the enormous impact on the English shires of the factional squabbling that surrounded Edward's court.

The uncharacteristic willingness of the Thomas of Lancaster to forgive a former enemy such as Salvayn, and to retain him in his service, may be explained by the earl's changing priorities in Yorkshire. His already considerable landed interest in the county had been greatly enhanced by the death of his father-in-law, the earl of Lincoln, in February 1311, which had brought him the honor and castle of Pontefract.[66] This increasing dominance inevitably aroused wariness and resentment amongst his neighbouring magnates; this may have been a factor leading to the violent feud that broke out between him and John, earl Warenne, who held the nearby manor of Wakefield, with its impressive castle at Sandal, as well as Conisbrough in the south of the county.[67] However, the immediate – and rather more dramatic – cause of this feud was Warenne's abduction of Lancaster's wife, Alice, in April 1317. Warenne had marital problems of his own, and seems to have resented Lancaster's involvement in the Church's refusal to allow him an annulment; but many contemporaries (undoubtedly including Lancaster himself) suspected that

---

[63] *CPR 1313–17*, pp. 249, 253, 312, 352, 404, 425–6, 580; *CCW 1244–1326*, p. 450; *RP*, I, p. 306 (which reveals that Salvayn himself considered 'x mars ou xx mars' to be a suitable price for the king's renewed favour); *Select Cases in the Court of King's Bench IV*, pp. 86–8; *CPR 1317–21*, p. 81. Stiveton was detained for the murder of Hugh Scot in 1316, but had been acquitted by the following January (*CPR 1313–17*, p. 599; *CCR 1313–18*, pp. 390–1, 393); the fact that his complaint against Salvayn in 1317 was presented to the king by Roger Damory suggests that he had friends in high places.

[64] A comparison can be made with Robert le Ewer, another royal servant mentioned in the Ordainers' petition of 1311, who was pardoned for various 'trespasses, contempts, and disobediences'; le Ewer's prolific criminal career is outlined in Andy King, 'Bandits, Robbers and *Schavaldours*: War and Disorder in Northumberland in the Reign of Edward II', *Thirteenth Century England IX*, ed. R. Britnell, R. Frame and M. Prestwich (Woodbridge, 2003), pp. 123–5.

[65] *CPR 1317–21*, p. 228; *CPR 1313–17*, p. 21.

[66] Maddicott, *Thomas of Lancaster*, pp. 9–10.

[67] Note, however, that it is unlikely that 'fear of the earl of Lancaster' motivated Warenne's abstention from Edward II's Scottish campaign of 1314 (as suggested by Phillips, *Aymer de Valence*, pp. 73–4), for in November 1315 Lancaster wrote to the king requesting that Warenne (along with the earl of Arundel) be appointed to a commission to suppress the revolt of the erstwhile Lancastrian retainer, Adam Banaster (PRO, SC 1/21/190; Maddicott, *Thomas of Lancaster*, p. 176). This would suggest that, at this stage, Lancaster did not consider Warenne as an enemy, or even a rival.

Edward and his coterie had put Warenne up to it.[68] By the following autumn, Lancaster was conducting a full-scale private war against Warenne and would have been anxious to acquire as much local support as possible; thus present hatred of Warenne would have outweighed past resentment against Salvayn, particularly as the latter's own not insignificant lands lay in the area.[69]

Lancaster's changed priorities are clearly demonstrated by Salvayn's presence at a little gathering at Doncaster on 29 November 1318. Here, earl Warenne was forced to append his seal to two humiliating deeds, by which he surrendered all his Yorkshire lands and interests to Lancaster, and agreed to pay him the ruinous sum of £50,000 at Christmas. Salvayn was named third in the list of the twelve knights who witnessed these deeds: all of these men were prominent Lancastrian retainers, such as Robert Holland, John de Eure and Gruffydd de la Pole, and three of them were Salvayn's fellow-Yorkshiremen Adam de Swillington, Adam de Everingham and Warin de Scargill.[70] As a disgraced crown official, Salvayn would not have lacked for company in the Lancastrian affinity, for the earl recruited a significant part of it on the basis that any enemy of the king and his court was a potential friend to his own cause. He had retained Gruffydd de la Pole only after his dispute with John Charlton had already degenerated into private war. Later, in the aftermath of Gilbert de Middleton's robbery of the cardinals, he retained many of those who had been implicated in the affair, including John de Eure and Roger Mauduit. And John de Lilleburn, who seized the king's castle at Knaresborough in Thomas' name at this time, was another disaffected household knight.[71]

If a dispute over the manor of Wilton really did cause Lancaster's falling out with the king, then the earl's opposition was, at least initially, motivated entirely by personal concerns. The Ordinances of 1311, which were to form the basis of his political programme for the rest of his career, articulated complaints that largely dated back to the time of Edward I,[72] issues which had not prevented Lancaster from supporting Edward II for the first eighteen months of his reign. It has been supposed that his subsequent unbending commitment to these Ordinances indicates that he was largely responsible for them.[73] However, it might equally well suggest that he lacked the political imagination to come up with any programme of his own; or, more cynically, that they simply provided a convenient cloak of moral justification

---

68 The liveliest contemporary account is that of *Nicolai Triveti annalium continuatio*, ed. Anthony Hall (Oxford, 1722), pp. 20–2. For modern commentary, see F. R. Royston Fairbank, 'The Last Earl of Warenne and Surrey', *Yorkshire Archæological Journal* xix (1907), pp. 209–15; Maddicott, *Thomas of Lancaster*, pp. 197–8.

69 For Salvayn's lands, see *PW*, II, ii, pp. 404–7; *CIPM*, VI, no. 223.

70 PRO, DL 25/3575; E 42/101.

71 Maddicott, *Thomas of Lancaster*, pp. 38–43; Morgan, 'Barony of Powys', pp. 19–20; Andy King, 'Lordship, Castles and Locality: Thomas of Lancaster, Dunstanburgh Castle and the Lancastrian Affinity in Northumberland, 1296–1322', *Archaeologia Aeliana* 5th ser. xxix (2001), pp. 224–5; King, 'Bandits, Robbers and *Schavaldours*', pp. 127–8. The fluctuating loyalties of Edward II's household knights are discussed by Michael Prestwich, 'The Unreliability of Royal Household Knights in the Early Fourteenth Century', *Fourteenth Century England II*, ed. Chris Given-Wilson (Woodbridge, 2002), pp. 1–11.

72 Maddicott, *Thomas of Lancaster*, pp. 95–103; Michael Prestwich, 'The Ordinances of 1311 and the Politics of the Early Fourteenth Century', *Politics and Crisis in Fourteenth-Century England*, ed. J. Taylor and W. Childs (Gloucester, 1990), pp. 9–12.

73 Anthony Tuck, *Crown and Nobility 1272–1461* (London, 1985), pp. 64–5; on the other hand, the *Vita Edwardi Secundi* attributed the Ordinances to the earl of Warwick 'consilio ejus [et] ingenio ordinationes prodierunt' (p. 62).

for his continued antagonism to the king. Recent work on the disputes that led to the deposition of another ineffective English king, Henry VI, has tended to emphasise the importance of political concerns and principles in determining personal allegiances.[74] Similarly in Edward II's reign, the actions of such previously staunchly loyal magnates as Henry de Lacy and Aymer de Valence, both of whom put their names to the Boulogne declaration of 1308, cannot be explained purely in terms of personal concerns. Once he was in opposition to the king, even the earl of Lancaster presumably convinced himself that he was acting for the good of the realm; and certainly many others were convinced of his high-mindedness, enough to ensure his popular canonisation after his death. However, the initial cause of that opposition was nothing more abstract than personal grievance and local interests. Of course, it is possible that Thomas of Lancaster underwent a Damascene conversion in December 1308, experiencing a genuinely revelatory bout of concern for the public weal; but it is altogether more likely that his adoption of reforming ideals followed in the wake of his break with Edward, rather than causing it.

---

[74] John L. Watts, 'Ideas, Principles and Politics', *The Wars of the Roses*, ed. A. J. Pollard (London, 1995), pp. 110–33, for a convenient summary.

BRISTOL AND THE CROWN, 1326–31:
LOCAL AND NATIONAL POLITICS IN THE
EARLY YEARS OF EDWARD III'S REIGN

Christian D. Liddy

In October 1326 the town of Bristol was the scene of several dramatic episodes in the chain of events that would lead eventually to Edward II's deposition. Edward II fled from London upon Queen Isabella's arrival in England in September 1326 with a group of supporters including Roger Mortimer and Prince Edward; he made his way west, accompanied by the Despensers, his leading advisers. Unsure of London's loyalties at this critical juncture, he may have thought that he would find some support in south-west England and southern Wales, where the Despensers had constructed a major landed power base.[1] According to at least one chronicle, Edward made his way straight to Bristol on hearing of the queen's advance upon London.[2] The town itself was one of the Despenser possessions, having been awarded to Hugh Despenser the younger in October 1320 along with Bristol Castle and the neighbouring royal manor of Barton for a yearly rent of £210.[3] Before departing with the younger Despenser for the Bristol Channel, Edward made arrangements for the defence of Bristol, entrusting the elder Despenser with the custody of the castle and town.[4] Feeling abandoned by the Londoners, the king clearly did not want to lose another major town to his pursuers, particularly one which at this time was, in Froissart's words, 'large and prosperous and strongly fortified',[5] and a potential source, therefore, of both financial and military aid.

The queen and her forces continued to move west in pursuit, and were joined by a number of magnates at Gloucester, before arriving at Bristol towards the end of October to besiege the town and castle. Isabella had strong personal reasons for wanting to capture Bristol from the elder Despenser, since in March 1318 Edward II had granted her the profits of the town as part of the settlement of her dower before subsequently using the town's revenues as a form of patronage to reward the younger Despenser.[6] The queen expected the younger Despenser to render his account for the annual farm at the queen's exchequer, only keeping whatever profit he made in addition to the sum due, but this was not how he interpreted the king's grant. Even before September 1324, when her lands were formally seized by the king, she had lost financial control of some of her properties, including

1 For the location of the Despenser estates, see N. Fryde, *The Tyranny and Fall of Edward II* (Cambridge, 1979), appendix 1.
2 *Chronicon Henrici Knighton*, ed. J. R. Lumby (2 vols, Rolls Series, London, 1889–95), I, p. 432: 'Regina procedit Londonias, rex dirigit iter versus Bristolliam'.
3 *CFR 1319–27*, p. 33.
4 *Adae Murimuth Continuatio Chronicarum*, ed. E. M. Thompson (Rolls Series, London, 1889), p. 47.
5 Jean Froissart, *Chroniques*, ed. S. Luce et al. (14 vols, Paris, 1869–1975), II, p. 28.
6 For Isabella's dower, see *CPR 1317–21*, pp. 115–16.

Bristol.[7] When an investigation was undertaken between 1332 and 1336 into the debts outstanding to Queen Isabella, it was found that the younger Despenser had not paid a single penny of the £200 per annum accruing from Bristol, which was payable to the queen in accordance with the 1318 dower assignment.[8] This unpaid revenue included the income due from the period in which the queen's estates had been confiscated by the crown,[9] with the result that the total debt owing to Isabella from Bristol between 1320 and 1326 amounted to the large sum of £1,200. The retaking of the town from the Despensers, then, would have been especially significant to the queen.

The siege did not last long, however, thanks in no small measure to the Bristolians, who offered no resistance to the attacking army. According to Robert of Avesbury and Adam Murimuth, the elder Despenser, along with the town and castle of Bristol, quickly surrendered to the queen.[10] On 26 October 1326 the regime of Isabella and Mortimer and the process leading ultimately to Edward II's deposition began:[11] it was on this day at Bristol that new arrangements were made for the government of England on the grounds that the king had deserted the realm by fleeing into Wales, leaving the kingdom, in a very literal sense, 'without rule'. According to the official record of the event, an assembly comprising the most powerful magnates in England, including the bishops of Winchester, Ely, Lincoln, Hereford and Norwich and the earls of Norfolk, Kent and Lancaster, as well as 'other barons and knights then at Bristol', appeared before the queen and her son, Prince Edward, and, 'with the assent of the whole community of the realm there present', 'unanimously chose' the prince to act as keeper of the realm and to 'rule and govern the realm in the name and right of the king his father'. In William Stubbs's words, it was at Bristol that 'the ultimate purpose of the invasion was made known'.[12] The next day, Hugh Despenser the elder was brought before a group of magnates, including the king's brothers and Roger Mortimer, and sentenced to death for various treasonable offences,[13] after which, 'to the clamour of the people', according to Adam Murimuth, he was drawn through Bristol and hanged outside the town on the gallows used for common thieves.[14] At Bristol, on the following day, writs were issued by Prince Edward in his father's name, summoning a parliament to assemble in mid-December at Westminster.[15] Although parliament would be delayed until January 1327 when new writs were required after the capture of the king in

[7] For the confiscation, see *CFR 1319–27*, pp. 300–2, 308.

[8] PRO, E101/377/11, m. 1. I should like to thank Dr Jonathan Mackman for his help with this document.

[9] That the queen harboured claims to the revenue lost from 1324 is revealed in the Bridlington Chronicle, according to which one of the charges against the younger Despenser was that he had, through 'false conspiracy, ejected' Isabella from her dower lands, giving her daily wages instead, 'contrary to the estate and excellence of such a lady': 'Gesta Edwardi de Carnarvon Auctore Canonico Bridlingtoniensi', in *Chronicles of the Reigns of Edward I and Edward II*, ed. H. R. Luard and W. Stubbs (2 vols, Rolls Series, London, 1882–3), II, p. 89.

[10] *Robertus de Avesbury De Gestis Mirabilibus Regis Edwardi Tertii*, ed. E. M. Thompson (Rolls Series, London, 1889), pp. 282–3, and *Murimuth*, pp. 48–9.

[11] For what follows, see *CCR 1323–7*, p. 655.

[12] W. Stubbs, *The Constitutional History of England*, 5th edn (3 vols, Oxford, 1891–8), II, p. 377.

[13] For the judicial proceedings, see 'Annales Paulini', in *Chronicles of the Reigns of Edward I and Edward II*, I, pp. 317–18.

[14] *Murimuth*, pp. 48–9.

[15] For this and what follows, see *PW*, II, i, 350–2.

November, it was at this assembly that Edward II was formally deposed. Yet Bristol's role in the transfer of kingship was not complete. In October 1327 Edward II died in Berkeley Castle in somewhat dubious circumstances and, according to Adam Murimuth, the burgesses of Bristol were among those summoned (*fuissent vocati*) to view the former king's whole body (*ad videndum corpus suum integrum*) in order to provide the necessary proof of the king's natural death, though their actions did nothing, as the chronicler conceded, to dampen the rumours that he had been murdered.[16]

How should Bristol's participation in the events of autumn 1326 be viewed? The town had been thrust into the spotlight, through no choice of its own, primarily as a result of Edward II's flight westwards. Yet, though the evidence is thin, Bristol's burgesses cannot simply be reduced to the passive role of spectators. In 1329, for example, a Bristol mariner was granted a ten-year protection and safe-conduct for himself and his crew 'in consideration of service to Queen Isabella and the king at the time when they landed in England'.[17] Meanwhile, it would also be foolish to discount the sincerity of the popular applause that greeted the execution of the elder Despenser in Bristol in October 1326, for it can be assumed that the younger Despenser's position as a farmer of the profits of the town meant that the Bristolians would have experienced the rapacity of the Despensers at first hand. The commons' petition presented in the first parliament of Edward III's reign requesting that no bailiwick, whether city, borough or franchised town, 'be leased at farm except to those who have lands and tenements within the same bailiwick' perhaps betrays a Bristol influence, given the town's long-standing hostility towards outside farmers such as the younger Despenser.[18]

The question is how, if at all, Bristol benefited from its prominent position in the politics of 1326. May McKisack argued that the city of London played a critical role in disputed successions to the throne in the later middle ages, providing the element of popular acclamation necessary in such circumstances to quieten doubts about the legitimacy of the new regime, in return for which the city's rulers were able to strike deals with the crown.[19] In fact, as several commentators (including McKisack) have noted, London's participation in the events culminating in Edward II's deposition was much more extensive.[20] It was the London mob who, in mid-October 1326, rose up against the regime of Isabella and Mortimer and, in a famous episode described graphically in the *Annales Paulini*, attacked and robbed the London property of the king's treasurer, Bishop Stapledon, forcing him to flee to St Paul's, where he was hit on the head and then dragged into Cheapside to be beheaded. According to the author of the *Annales Paulini*, Stapledon's head was then sent to the queen who was residing at Bristol.[21] In January 1327 London's rulers were extremely active in pushing forward the deposition process, writing to parliament at Westminster to see

[16] *Murimuth*, pp. 53–4.

[17] *CPR 1327–30*, p. 442.

[18] *RP*, II, p. 8. For this animosity, see below, p. 54.

[19] M. McKisack, 'London and the Succession to the Crown during the Middle Ages', *Studies in Medieval History Presented to Frederick Maurice Powicke*, ed. R. W. Hunt, W. A. Pantin and R. W. Southern (Oxford, 1948), pp. 76–89.

[20] See ibid., pp. 81–3, and G. A. Williams, *Medieval London: From Commune to Capital* (London, 1963), pp. 295–8.

[21] 'Annales Paulini', p. 316.

if it would be 'willing to be in accord with the city' to crown the prince and to depose the king, and overseeing the oaths of allegiance to the new king sworn in the city's guildhall by a cross-section of the political community.[22] Yet it was the popular endorsement (*ad clamorem tocius populi*) of the decisions made by the main political actors in January 1327 that was acknowledged by both contemporary chroniclers and the new regime as absolutely vital in legitimising the transfer of royal authority, and it was the Londoners, swelling the ranks of the knights and burgesses assembling in parliament, who were central.[23] In the words of Gwyn Williams, 'Magnates and prelates had deposed a king in response to the "clamour of the whole people". That clamour had a distinct London accent.'[24] Most significantly, as in other uncertain successions, London's leaders were able to use their role as the *vox populi* to secure concessions from the crown. In this case, the city acquired a charter not only restoring corporate privileges lost during the visit of the eyre in 1321, but also granting the citizens 'the widest measure of administrative freedom London had yet attained'.[25]

On 26 October 1326, however, when the leading magnates in the kingdom met with the queen in Bristol to choose the prince as the keeper of the realm in what must surely be viewed as the first step in deposing Edward II, it was the Bristolians rather than the Londoners who acted as the *vox populi* to ratify the lords' decision. When the official record of the episode recounted that the decision had been made 'with the assent of the whole community of the realm there present', however stage-managed the scene, it is safe to assume that Bristolians were prominent among those giving their consent to the transfer of power.[26] Were Bristol's rulers able to exploit the town's central position in the political manoeuvring of October 1326 to their advantage in the same way that London's civic elite did? Did the new government acknowledge its indebtedness to the town by the grant of new constitutional privileges?

Measured by the evidence of royal charters, Bristol's experiences with the regime of Isabella and Mortimer were in sharp contrast to those of other English towns and cities in the period 1327 to 1330, despite the town's role in the deposition process. W. M. Ormrod has rightly drawn attention to the pattern of grants of urban charters under Isabella and Mortimer, demonstrating from the charter rolls the extent of the regime's generosity towards English urban communities. While it was by now customary for towns and cities to seek the confirmation of their chartered liberties at the accession of a new monarch, 'the sheer number of such grants made while

---

[22] Williams, *Medieval London*, p. 298, drawing upon *Calendar of Plea and Memoranda Rolls of the City of London, 1323-1482*, ed. A. H. Thomas and P. E. Jones (6 vols, Cambridge, 1926-61), I, pp. 11–19.
[23] The quotation is from the Lichfield Chronicle cited in M. Clarke, *Medieval Representation and Consent* (London, 1936), p. 184 n. 3. For comment, see C. Valente, 'The Deposition and Abdication of Edward II', *EHR* cxiii (1998), p. 865.
[24] Williams, *Medieval London*, p. 298.
[25] The quotation is from ibid., p. 299. For London's role in 1399 and 1461, see C. Barron, 'The Deposition of Richard II', *Politics and Crisis in Fourteenth-Century England*, ed. J. Taylor and W. Childs (Gloucester, 1990), p. 143; C. Barron, 'London and the Crown, 1451–61', *The Crown and Local Communities in England and France in the Fifteenth Century*, ed. J. R. L. Highfield and R. Jeffs (Gloucester, 1981), pp. 98–9.
[26] *CCR 1323–7*, p. 655. I should like to thank Professor Mark Ormrod for drawing this point to my attention and for sharing his thoughts on its possible implications.

Mortimer and Isabella were in power suggests something out of the ordinary.'[27] There was also something qualitatively different about these royal grants, in the sense that many were not recapitulations of existing charters, as was conventional at the beginning of a new reign,[28] but included additional privileges as well. Between 1327 and Edward III's assumption of power at the end of 1330, a significant proportion of the charters granted to towns and cities were not straightforward confirmations of already acquired liberties. Rather, urban communities including London, Southampton, Winchester, York, Lincoln and Gloucester received an inspection and confirmation of their charters with improvements.[29] Hence the concern expressed in the Northampton Parliament of 1328 about 'the many charters of royal franchises granted to the commonalties of great towns (*grantz villes*)' which had been issued since Isabella and Mortimer had assumed power and which were 'to the impoverishment of our crown'.[30] It was both the number and the type of charters which attracted contemporary criticism and which explain why the crown responded to the 1328 petition by ordering the scrutiny of the terms of the charters conferred upon urban communities since Edward III's coronation.

Bristol, however, is conspicuous by its absence from the charter rolls between 1327 and 1330. Indeed, the town did not even receive a simple confirmation of its existing liberties. Of the seventeen highest ranking towns and cities as measured by taxable wealth in 1334, Bristol was one of six urban communities not to secure chartered privileges in this period.[31] The omission of Bristol is most surprising given both its status as the wealthiest provincial town in this period and its involvement in the events of 1326. However, in 1331, after the collapse of the government under Isabella and Mortimer, the town acquired not one but two charters of confirmation, with additions.

What was the reason for this delay? There is no evidence that Bristol's rulers sought to obtain a charter through a petition, the normal means of securing valuable chartered privileges. It is this striking reluctance to approach the crown that needs specifically to be explored. First, the explanation of the reticence of Bristol's rulers lies essentially in the town's close, continuing (but hitherto obscure) association with the course of national politics after the succession crisis of 1326–7, in which the town was, in some ways, at the centre of the machinations of Isabella and Mortimer and one of their most prominent supporters, Thomas Berkeley, lord of Berkeley Castle in Gloucestershire. Second, Bristol's relationship with the crown during the early years of Edward III's reign was a formative one in the town's later history, helping to explain the town's celebrated charter of 1373, the first of its kind anywhere in England, which formally separated Bristol from the neighbouring shires of Gloucester and Somerset and transformed the town into a county in its own right.

---

27 W. M. Ormrod, *The Reign of Edward III: Crown and Political Society in England, 1327–1377* (London, 1990), p. 175.
28 L. Attreed, *The King's Towns: Identity and Survival in Late Medieval English Boroughs* (New York, 2001), pp. 35–6.
29 *CChR 1327–41*, pp. 7–9, 11–12, 47–8, 55–7, 97, 160.
30 *Select Cases in the Court of King's Bench V*, ed. G. O. Sayles (Selden Society lxxvi, London, 1957), pp. cxxxiii–iv.
31 A. Dyer, *Decline and Growth in English Towns, 1400-1640* (Cambridge, 1995), appendix 4 (London was in a league of its own), and *CChR 1327–41*, pp. 7–9, 11–13, 47–8, 52, 55–7, 82, 91–2, 97, 160, 176. The others were Newcastle upon Tyne, Boston, Norwich, Coventry and Canterbury.

There were two points of conflict between Bristol and the government under Isabella and Mortimer, both of which raised fundamental questions about the town's corporate identity and its right to self-government. The first arose from the disputed status of Redcliffe, a suburb of the town over which the Berkeleys, perhaps the most powerful landed family in the region in the early fourteenth century,[32] harboured claims of jurisdiction. The second issue related to the crown's use of the profits of Bristol to reward royal servants. Both problems had been major sources of tension between Bristol and the royal government from at least the later thirteenth century, but they were exacerbated in the period 1327 to 1330 and the town's rulers held the government of Isabella and Mortimer responsible. Certainly, the regime's intimate relationship with Thomas Berkeley would have serious repercussions locally.

Under Edward II the Berkeleys had suffered forfeiture of their lands and imprisonment as a consequence of their participation in the rebellion against the Despensers in 1321–2. Maurice Berkeley, the then head of the family, was imprisoned in Wallingford Castle, where he died in May 1326, while his son and heir, Thomas, was also incarcerated for his opposition.[33] Released from Pevensey Castle in Sussex upon Isabella's arrival in England in September 1326, Thomas joined the queen's forces as they headed west in pursuit of the king and, according to Adam Murimuth, passed from Gloucester through Berkeley, where the queen restored to Thomas the castle previously occupied by Hugh Despenser the younger, along with the honour of Berkeley in its entirety, before she headed for Bristol.[34] The restoration was given official endorsement in February 1327 when the order was issued to the escheator south of the Trent to deliver to Thomas his father's lands.[35] Yet this was only the beginning, for in the first few months of the new regime, Isabella and Mortimer looked on Berkeley as a key figure to keep the peace in the south-west counties.[36] Thomas also had personal connections to the government, since Roger Mortimer was his father-in-law,[37] and it was Berkeley Castle where Edward II ultimately found himself imprisoned after his removal from Kenilworth in the spring of 1327. Thomas Berkeley, moreover, was appointed to guard the former king, receiving a daily wage from the crown for his employment on 'special business of the king' while Edward was in his custody.[38]

In the reigns of Edward I and Edward II, Bristol and the Berkeleys had enjoyed a fractious relationship characterised by violence and open hostility. The subject which divided them was the status of Redcliffe, an extremely wealthy area of Bristol immediately south of Bristol Bridge on the Somerset side of the Avon within the town's walls, which was marked by a concentration of cloth workers and traders from whom most of the town's growing prosperity was derived. The Berkeleys maintained that Redcliffe was part of their manor of Bedminster, in which they

[32] N. Saul, *Knights and Esquires: The Gloucestershire Gentry in the Fourteenth Century* (Oxford, 1981), pp. 3–4.

[33] See the biographies of Maurice and Thomas in J. Smyth, *The Lives of the Berkeleys* (3 vols, Gloucester, 1883–5), I, pp. 223–361.

[34] *Murimuth*, p. 48.

[35] *CFR 1327–37*, p. 22.

[36] For his commissions, see *CPR 1327–30*, pp. 89, 130, 154. For comment, see T. F. Tout, 'The Captivity and Death of Edward of Carnarvon', *The Collected Papers of T. F. Tout* (3 vols, Manchester, 1932–4), III, p. 159.

[37] For this and what follows, see Tout, 'Captivity and Death', pp. 156–7.

[38] The quotation is from *CPR 1327–30*, p. 130.

claimed, in addition to the traditional obligation of suit of court owed by their tenants in Redcliffe to their court in Redcliffe St, extensive judicial rights including the assize of bread and ale, the attachment of thieves and possession of their own prison in Redcliffe St.[39] In sharp contrast, Bristol's rulers believed that the suburb was an integral part of the town under their single jurisdiction. The conflict between Bristol and the Berkeleys has been examined in some detail elsewhere.[40] Here it is simply worth noting that trouble flared in the first decade of the fourteenth century over the nature of the Berkeleys' manorial jurisdiction, as members of Bristol's civic elite, including the mayor, forcibly resisted the violent attempts by the Berkeleys and their officials to enforce suit of court and their right of arrest and imprisonment in Redcliffe St. In 1305 the king's justices found against the Berkeleys, seizing 'certain liberties' in the suburbs of Bristol pertaining to the manor of Bedminster into the king's hands. Although Maurice Berkeley had petitioned Edward II and his council in 1312 for their return, these privileges had not been restored to the family by the time of Isabella's invasion.[41]

There is little doubt that, at the beginning of 1327, Bristol's rulers would have been acutely aware of the potentially damaging implications of Thomas Berkeley's close associations with the new regime. In the first parliament of Edward III's reign, which met in February 1327 at Westminster, Thomas wasted no time in petitioning the crown for the restoration of the privileges pertaining to the manor of Bedminster and Redcliffe St, described provocatively as 'near to' (*iuste*) Bristol.[42] The manor, he argued, had belonged to his ancestors from time out of mind, with, among others, the rights of infangthief and view of frankpledge, as well as the enforcement of the assize of bread and ale, and he asked that he be allowed 'to regain his franchise' (*sa franchise reauoir*) which had been confiscated since 1305. Also notable was the inquisition held on 24 February 1327 to ascertain the lands held in Somerset by Maurice Berkeley, Thomas's father, in which it was found that he died seised of Redcliffe St, with the court which pertained to it.[43]

The extremely close links between Thomas Berkeley and the government of Isabella and Mortimer help to explain why the town's rulers chose not to approach the crown seeking either a confirmation or an extension of Bristol's corporate liberties. An exemplification of the town's existing liberties, especially the 1188 charter, which was the foundation of Bristol's corporate existence and which had determined the geographical limits of the town's liberty so as to incorporate the entire area south of Bristol Bridge including Redcliffe, was utterly pointless in a context in which real power lay elsewhere.[44] Moreover, there was little chance that

---

[39] For the late thirteenth-century royal inquests into the basis of the Berkeleys' liberties in Bristol, see *Rotuli Hundredorum* (2 vols, London, 1812–18), I, p. 177, and *The Great Red Book of Bristol*, ed. E. W. W. Veale (5 vols, Bristol Record Society ii, iv, viii, xvi, xviii, Bristol, 1931–53), II, pp. 104, 107.

[40] Most notably by S. Seyer, *Memoirs Historical and Topographical of Bristol and its Neighbourhood* (2 vols, Bristol, 1821), II, pp. 78ff. For a useful précis, see *Bristol Charters, 1378–1499*, ed. H. A. Cronne (Bristol Record Society xi, Bristol, 1945), pp. 39–41.

[41] *Rotuli Parliamentorum Anglie hactenus inediti*, ed. H. G. Richardson and G. Sayles (Camden Society 3rd ser. li, London, 1935), pp. 58–9.

[42] Ibid., p. 149.

[43] *CIPM*, VII, no. 97.

[44] Despite its theoretical incorporation of Redcliffe, the 1188 charter had, after all, been powerless in the past to prevent the assertion of the Berkeleys' rights in the southern suburb. Though the charter has been dated more recently to 1189x91 in *Accounts of the Constables of Bristol Castle in the Thirteenth*

the government under Isabella and Mortimer would look favourably upon any attempt by the town to secure, through chartered grants, the exclusion of the Berkeleys' claims to jurisdiction in the southern suburb.

Bristol's alienation from the regime was swift, for already by the second half of 1327 there were signs that the town's rulers had chosen a policy of deliberate disengagement from the wider affairs of the realm.[45] In the summer of 1327 'the mayor, bailiffs and more wealthy inhabitants' of the town exploited the opportunity provided by the crown's order to supply one hundred armed men for the military campaign against the Scots, in order to levy a tax which they used for their own purposes, while sending no-one to the north. Similarly, when instructed to return burgesses to a great council held at Lincoln in September 1327, they did not oblige. In both military and political matters, then, Bristol's civic elite had distanced itself from the government of Isabella and Mortimer.

The actions of Isabella and Mortimer only heightened Bristol's feeling of estrangement, loosening very quickly whatever residual attachments there were between the new government and the town. The crown's conduct towards the town's farm was the issue that would drive a further wedge between civic and royal government. In an urban context, the farm was a fixed annual sum rendered in lieu of individual payments owing to the crown from feudal revenues such as court profits, tolls, rents and escheats. Up until the late twelfth and early thirteenth centuries, the crown had leased the farm to towns and cities on a temporary basis, but the crown's financial needs meant that from this period leading towns acquired the privilege of farming the revenues due to the king on a permanent footing.[46] Bristol was a notable exception to this general pattern; since the reign of John the profits of the town were farmed during the king's pleasure by various individuals in addition to the burgesses in their corporate capacity. To the individuals who farmed the town, often the royally appointed constables of Bristol Castle, Bristol was a source of potential profit, for whatever they made over and above the fixed annual payment due to the crown was theirs to keep.[47] The town's rulers had complained without success to Edward I about the tendency of the royal government to lease Bristol at farm to profit-seeking outsiders in 1283.[48] The issue of the farm also played a prominent role in the serious disturbances that took place in Bristol between 1312 and 1316, involving opposition to the constable of the castle, Bartholomew Badlesmere, whom the burgesses accused of oppression, and for which the town's liberties were confiscated.[49] Edward II's grant of the castle and town of Bristol with the manor of Barton to the younger Despenser, first during royal pleasure and then, in June 1325, for life, was a continuation of the crown's policy towards Bristol's farm.[50]

and early Fourteenth Centuries, ed. M. Sharp (Bristol Record Society xxxiv, Bristol, 1982), p. 74, the customary reference is 1188, and I have followed this convention for the sake of convenience.

45 For what follows, see *CPR 1327–30*, p. 424.

46 D. M. Palliser, 'Towns and the English State, 1066–1500', *The Medieval State: Essays presented to James Campbell*, ed. J. R. Maddicott and D. M. Palliser (London, 2000), p. 130.

47 For the complex history of the town's farm, see the excellent discussion in *Bristol Charters, 1378–1499*, pp. 41–56.

48 *Rotuli Parliamentorum Anglie hactenus inediti*, p. 18, translated in *Bristol Charters, 1378–1499*, pp. 42–3.

49 E. A. Fuller, 'The Tallage of 6 Edward II (December 16, 1312) and the Bristol Rebellion', *Transactions of the Bristol and Gloucestershire Archaeological Society* xix (1894–5), pp. 171–278.

50 *CFR 1319–27*, pp. 33, 348.

On 1 February 1327, the day of Edward III's coronation, Queen Isabella's dower was restored with substantial additions, increasing the annual value of her landed estate from £4,500 to 20,000 marks. The town of Bristol, along with the castle and the manor of Barton, worth £210 per annum, was returned to the queen mother.[51] Initially she broke with tradition and granted the farm of the town to the burgesses of Bristol on a short-term lease payable at the queen's exchequer. As Bristol's rulers would tell the king and his council in the parliament of November 1330, the people of Bristol had been 'impoverished, destroyed and ruined by many great men (*grantz*) to whom the forbears of our lord the king had lately granted the farm of the said town', but that, 'in aid and profit of the said people', Queen Isabella had granted the farm to the burgesses of Bristol for a term of years.[52] Before long, certainly by December 1328, Sir Thomas Gurney, the infamous Somerset knight best remembered for his participation in the murder of Edward II in Berkeley Castle, now constable of Bristol Castle, was in receipt of the profits of the town.[53] Gurney had close ties not only to Thomas Berkeley, for he was a long-standing Berkeley retainer and Berkeley's deputy as keeper of Edward II, but also to Roger Mortimer, and it was through the latter's recommendation to Isabella, according to Bristol's 1330 petition, that Gurney had procured the farm.[54] The grant to Gurney, in which Mortimer was instrumental, raises the interesting possibility that the town's farm was a form of reward for the former's involvement in the murder of Edward II; certainly, the farm had long been a source of crown patronage. Indeed, on 16 August 1330, though clearly a piece of self-aggrandisement as he sought to establish a significant power base in the Welsh Marches, Roger Mortimer was rewarded with a lifetime grant of the keeping of the castle and town of Bristol explicitly for his 'good service'.[55] The key issue from Bristol's perspective, however, was that Thomas Gurney abused his position for illicit financial gain, committing extortion and many wrongs not only against the people of Bristol, but also against 'various other people of England, Ireland and Wales coming to the said town', who had responded by seizing the merchandise of Bristol burgesses trading in those parts. The language of the petition was highly coloured, providing a pointed contrast between the 'covetousness' of private farmers such as Gurney and the burgesses of Bristol, who represented themselves not as self-interested, but as concerned with the 'common profit', which would be upheld if the crown agreed to grant them the farm of the town. Yet the charges of embezzlement against Gurney are perhaps borne out by two writs of April and May 1331 relating to an investigation into the 'contents of a chest and certain casks which [Gurney], when he was constable of Bristol, had sent to the neighbouring abbey of Keynsham, there to be safely kept for him'.[56]

Meanwhile, the period 1327 to 1330 saw the eventual resolution of the Redcliffe dispute to the benefit of Thomas Berkeley. The issue took three years to settle in

---

[51] *CPR 1327–30*, pp. 66–9.

[52] PRO, C49/6/18 (i). Although undated, it has been possible to date the petition from both its contents and context.

[53] *CCR 1327–30*, p. 352, and PRO, C49/6/18 (i).

[54] Tout, 'Captivity and Death', p. 163. For Gurney's membership of the Berkeley affinity, see Saul, *Knights and Esquires*, pp. 69–71.

[55] *CFR 1327–37*, p. 187. For Mortimer's territorial ambitions, see D. A. Harding, 'The Regime of Isabella and Mortimer 1326–1330' (unpublished MPhil dissertation, University of Durham, 1985), ch. 3.

[56] J. Hunter, 'On the Measures taken for the Apprehension of Sir Thomas de Gournay', *Archaeologia* xxvii (1838), p. 278.

Thomas's favour. Significantly, it was Isabella, Bristol's potential patron, given her close financial interests in the town, who helped to bring the conflict to a satisfactory conclusion for the Berkeleys. Though the precise chronology is obscure, it would appear that a record and process of the Redcliffe dispute was brought before the king's council in response to Thomas's petition of 1327 seeking the restoration of his privileges in the southern suburb, after which the king ordered his chancellor to issue a writ to the royal justices to render judgment.[57] At the end of May 1330, Isabella wrote to the chancellor asking him to expedite the king's order 'graciously', regardless of the fact that the town was hers from the king's gift (*sans avoir regard a ce qe la ville de Brustuyt est en nostre mayn du doun le Roi nostre dit filz*).[58] At the very least, by intervening in this way, Isabella can only have been furthering the Berkeley cause, for it was Thomas who was seeking to force the issue. It is, therefore, perhaps no surprise that, just over a week later, Thomas received a royal inspeximus and confirmation of the Berkeley charters, including the one granting 'Bedminster with all its appurtenances and liberties and free customs pertaining to the aforesaid manor', of which Redcliffe was a part.[59] Bristol's ruling elite reacted with armed force to Thomas's victory, and in August 1330 the crown issued a commission of oyer and terminer to consider Thomas's complaint that, though he had been 'accustomed to have a court for his tenants . . . and others there' in Redcliffe, along with the assize of bread and ale, pillory and tumbrel, the mayor of Bristol, accompanied by the town's bailiffs and other prominent townsmen, had sought to undermine these and certain other unnamed 'liberties'. First they had rung the common bell to summon the commonalty of the town, before destroying the symbols of Thomas's legal authority in the suburb, namely the pillory and tumbrel, attacking his bailiffs, preventing the holding of Thomas's court, and abducting one of Thomas's bailiffs in Redcliffe, whereupon he was forced to swear an oath in the town's guildhall that 'he would not at any time make execution of the judgments of the court in that suburb'.[60]

Bristol could do little so long as 'the men whom common report associated with the crime [of Edward II's murder], Berkeley, Maltravers and Sir Thomas Gurney remained trusted agents of Mortimer and Isabella'.[61] With the arrest of Roger Mortimer at Nottingham Castle in October 1330,[62] Bristol's fortunes looked like they might change, particularly when, in the third week of October, Edward III instructed his sheriffs to ensure that all those who had complaints against the king's government during the period when it was in the hands of Isabella and Mortimer should appear at the parliament to be held at Westminster in the following month.[63] It was this assembly, moreover, which witnessed the trial of Mortimer and his accomplices for the death of Edward II, two of whom, Thomas Gurney and Thomas Berkeley, had been Bristol's oppressors.[64] Bristol's rulers did not need any official

---

57 *Rotuli Parliamentorum Anglie hactenus inediti*, p. 149.
58 PRO, SC1/38/193.
59 *CChR 1327–41*, pp. 178–9.
60 *CPR 1327–30*, p. 571.
61 Tout, 'Captivity and Death', p. 171.
62 The most recent study of this episode is C. Shenton, 'Edward III and the Coup of 1330', *The Age of Edward III*, ed. J. S. Bothwell (York, 2001), pp. 13–34.
63 *CCR 1330–3*, pp. 161–2.
64 *RP*, II, pp. 52–7.

encouragement and, in the course of the parliament, two petitions were presented to Edward III and his council. One was the specific complaint about Bristol's farm, the contents of which have already been discussed. The other petition comprised a lengthy series of requests, whose importance resonates far beyond the period 1327 to 1330.[65] Indeed, the petition set out an agenda some of which would only be addressed to the satisfaction of the town in the later fourteenth century.

The petition, from the 'mayor and community' of Bristol, asked first for a confirmation of Edward II's charter of 1322, which itself was a ratification of a 1300 confirmation exemplifying verbatim an 1188 charter and a 1252 charter.[66] It also requested a recapitulation of Henry III's 1247 charter, which, significantly given the recent troubles with the Berkeleys, had ruled that the 'burgesses of Redcliffe in the suburb of Bristol' should answer before the royal justices with the burgesses of Bristol.[67] There followed a series of fifteen requests seeking either a clarification or an explicit improvement of the town's existing chartered liberties. One asked that the burgesses be granted the town of Bristol with all the profits arising within its boundaries at fee farm (that is, in perpetuity),[68] a concession for which the townsmen promised to pay more than any of the constables or farmers had previously rendered to the king. Several clauses related to trade, including one that sought greater clarity than the 1322 charter provided on the types of customs duties from which the burgesses were quit throughout the king's realm, both within England and in Ireland, Wales and Gascony, specifying the miscellaneous customs by name.[69] Most of the others, however, concerned the town's legal privileges: one aimed to protect the burgesses from being impleaded, attached or distrained to appear outside the town in all cases except pleas of the crown; another sought to restrict the local powers of the court of the steward and marshal of the king's household to hear pleas of trespass and to limit the claims of the clerks of the market to enforce the assize of bread and ale and to examine weights and measures within the town and suburbs outside the verge, before the arrival of the king's household;[70] one called upon the king to provide chartered proof of the privilege of view of frankpledge; another wanted prisoners arrested and imprisoned within the liberty of the town to be delivered from the town's gaol and not elsewhere.

Many of these problems, such as the fee farm, were clearly long-standing. Indeed, the symbolic request that the burgesses of the town should elect their mayor continuously (that is, without the necessity of presenting him to the constable of the castle before whom he swore his oath, a requirement enshrined in the 1300 charter)[71] only makes sense in light of the fiscal subjection of the town by the

---

[65] For this and all further references to the document, see PRO, C49/6/18 (ii).

[66] For these earlier charters, see *Bristol Charters, 1155–1373*, ed. N. Dermott Harding (Bristol Record Society i, Bristol, 1930), pp. 8–13, 24–9, 44–7, 68–9.

[67] Ibid., pp. 22–3.

[68] To hold at fee farm meant 'to hold heritably, perpetually, at a rent; the fee, the inheritance, is let to farm': F. Pollock and F. W. Maitland, *The History of English Law* (2 vols, Cambridge, 1895), I, pp. 273–4.

[69] The concern arose from the imprecision of the clause in the 1188 charter of John, count of Mortain, establishing chartered immunity for the burgesses from 'all other customs throughout all my land and power': *Bristol Charters, 1155–1373*, pp. 10–11.

[70] The verge was an area covering a twelve-mile radius around the person of the king; for the operation of the marshalsea court, see W. R. Jones, 'The Court of the Verge: the Jurisdiction of the Steward and Marshal of the Household in the Later Middle Ages', *Journal of British Studies* x (1970), pp. 1–29.

[71] *Bristol Charters, 1155–1373*, pp. 44–7.

constable in the thirteenth and early fourteenth centuries. Yet there can be little doubt that these and other concerns were exacerbated by the town's experiences under the regime of Isabella and Mortimer. The recurrence of the issue of Redcliffe can only have persuaded the town's rulers of the need to tighten up the chartered basis of their claims to jurisdiction throughout Bristol. In 1327, for example, Thomas Berkeley had asserted his right to view of frankpledge in Redcliffe St, but, as Bristol's 1330 petition conceded, the burgesses' privilege of view of frankpledge had no documentary proof; their claim was based solely upon tradition, for they had held the right 'from time out of mind'.[72]

How was Bristol's petition received? The issue of the fee farm was resolved reasonably satisfactorily, though the town's rulers did not secure all that they wanted. On 14 December 1330, less than a week after the conclusion of parliament, the mayor, bailiffs and burgesses of Bristol were granted the annual farm of the town and the manor of Barton, but they were now expected to pay £240, a £30 increase from 1327. Also, this excluded the castle, which was to be kept at the king's cost, while the lease was not permanent, but was to last until Michaelmas next in the first instance and then for a further five years.[73] This pattern of short-term leases would continue until 1462, when Edward IV ended this practice in favour of a permanent grant of the farm to Bristol's burgesses.[74] Towards the end of December 1330, Edward III ordered a judicial commission to investigate whether the burgesses had, as they claimed, been accustomed to have view of frankpledge from time immemorial and whether it would be harmful to his interests if he did grant them this privilege by charter, but the inquiry did not take place until mid-August 1331.[75] In fact, when a royal charter was issued on 12 January 1331, the town simply received an inspeximus and confirmation of the charters of 1247 and 1322, with the extension of the mayor's powers of wardship over orphans and minors in the town so as to prevent embezzlement of their estates by their guardians, one of the numerous requests to have been made in the 1330 petition.[76]

One other issue, relating to the town's freedom from external pleas, was addressed in the January 1331 charter, but only in a highly irregular way. The key document was the 1188 charter of John, count of Mortain, issued to Bristol before he became king, in which he declared that no burgess of the town was to 'plead without the walls of the town concerning any plea except pleas of exterior tenements which do not pertain to the hundred of the town', a basic urban privilege and certainly common enough among English towns and cities by the second quarter of

---

[72] *Rotuli Parliamentorum Anglie hactenus inediti*, p. 149; the frankpledge system was indeed a very ancient institution of self-policing dating back to the Anglo-Saxon period: Pollock and Maitland, *History of English Law*, I, pp. 554–8. For its operation in an urban context, see S. Rees Jones, 'Household, Work and the Problem of Mobile Labour: The Regulation of Labour in Medieval English Towns', *The Problem of Labour in Fourteenth-Century England*, ed. J. S. Bothwell, P. J. P. Goldberg and W. M. Ormrod (York, 2000), pp. 140–5.

[73] *CFR 1327–37*, pp. 207–8.

[74] *Bristol Charters, 1378–1499*, pp. 51–5.

[75] *CPR 1330–4*, p. 61. Bristol had a copy of the crown's writ to the justices ordering an inquiry enrolled in its civic register, the Great Red Book, as well as a copy of the subsequent commission. See *Great Red Book*, II, pp. 108–10.

[76] *CChR 1327–41*, pp. 201–2. The mayor was empowered to seal recognisances with guardians so as to ensure that those in their care were not deprived of their inheritance. For further discussion, see *Great Red Book*, I, pp. 145–54.

the fourteenth century.[77] Bristol's ruling elite, however, wanted the crown's ratification of what it claimed was existing custom that a burgess should neither plead nor be impleaded (*quod nullus Burgensis placitet nec placitetur*) beyond the town's walls. It was this passive as well as active interpretation of the plea process, for which there was no documentary evidence in any of the town's existing charters, which concerned the mayor and bailiffs in 1330. Bristol's rulers were not alone in their sensitivity to this point, for in 1285 Edward I had granted a charter to Great Yarmouth, reciting the clause of a charter of King John to the East Anglian town in which it was declared that no burgess should plead outside the town for any plea except pleas relating to external property. Since then, Edward reminded the burgesses, the word ' "plea" has been interpreted actively and passively by our justices and by others of our counsel, on account both of the meaning of the word and the will of the grantor', and the king, 'willing to favour the said burgesses as to the wider declaration of the meaning of the said word', duly granted that from henceforth no burgess was to plead or be impleaded outside the town.[78] The desire of Bristol's civic elite for a similarly broad interpretation of the town's privilege of freedom from external pleas should be placed in the context of the jurisdictional conflict over the disputed status of Redcliffe, in which the townsmen had entirely justified misgivings that burgesses would be forced to appear in the Berkeley courts, not just in Redcliffe St, but elsewhere. Certainly, in the early fourteenth century there were several instances of townsmen being forcibly removed from Bristol's gaol and placed in Berkeley prisons outside the town.[79]

In the case of Bristol, unlike Great Yarmouth, the town did not receive a separate grant. Instead, an interpolation was made directly on the town's copy of the January 1331 inspeximus, altering the wording of the 1188 charter, so that the passive *vel placitetur* now appeared in the eleventh line of the text alongside the active form of the verb (Plates 1, 2).[80] It would be easy to view this interpolation as evidence that the town doctored the text for its own purposes, especially given that the additional words did not appear in the crown's version of the inspeximus preserved in chancery, while the document itself betrays obvious signs of tampering.[81] Yet the alteration and the document are in the same hand,[82] so it is possible that the truth was altogether less sinister, but equally interesting: namely, that the crown agreed to the town's request, instructing the chancery clerk to make the simple necessary amendment. The clerk, with the 1322 charter before him, must then have copied the correct form of the 1188 charter before realising somewhat belatedly, prompted perhaps by the townsmen, that an additional clause should have been included: hence the abrasion

---

[77] *Bristol Charters, 1155–1373*, pp. 8–9; *British Borough Charters, 1042–1216*, ed. A. Ballard (Cambridge, 1913), pp. 115–21; *British Borough Charters, 1216–1307*, ed. A. Ballard and J. Tait (Cambridge, 1923), pp. 148–55.

[78] *Bristol Borough Charters, 1216–1307*, p. 154.

[79] S. A. C. Penn, 'Social and Economic Aspects of Fourteenth-Century Bristol' (unpublished PhD dissertation, University of Birmingham, 1989), p. 251, using the evidence of royal assize rolls.

[80] BRO, Royal Charters and Letters Patent: 01249 (i).

[81] The nature of the change is explained by the editor of *Bristol Charters, 1155–1373*, p. 73: '*Bristollie placitet vel* is closely written over an erasure where *de Bristallo* must have stood and an abbreviation sign for *–ur* is added to the original, now the second, *placitet.*'

[82] My thanks to Dr Ian Doyle for his advice on this point.

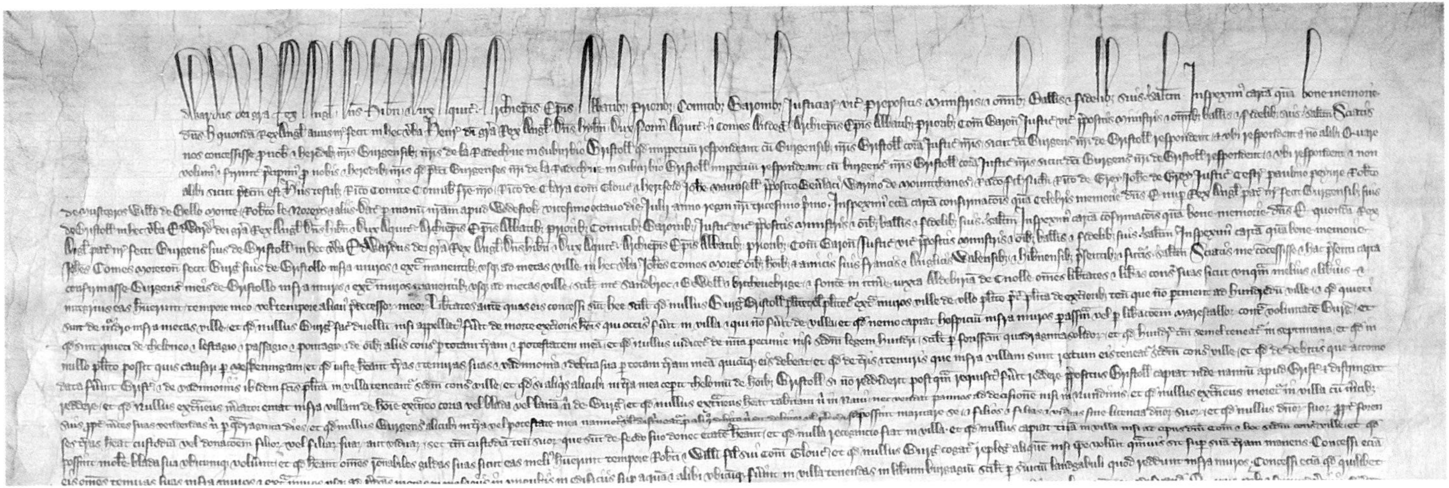

Plate 1 The opening section of Edward III's charter of January 1331 to Bristol. BRO, Royal Charters and Letters Patent: 01249 (i)

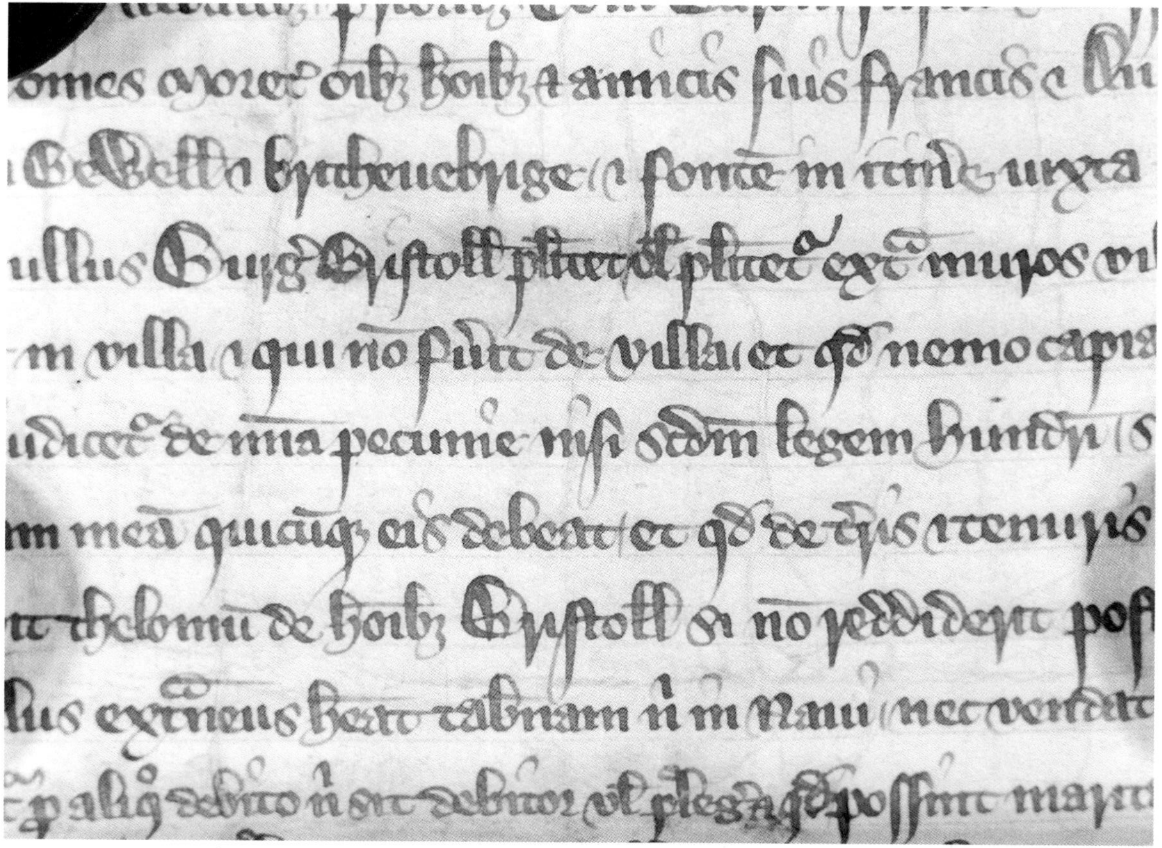

Plate 2 Edward III's charter of January 1331 to Bristol: detail showing erasure and interpolation in l. 11 of text. BRO, Royal Charters and Letters Patent: 01249 (i)

on the 1331 inspeximus.[83] Certainly, if this was an attempt at forgery, it was not very thorough, for the clause concerning freedom from external pleas first granted in the 1188 charter was also included in the 1252 charter, which was inspected and confirmed in January 1331, and here there was no similar interpolation.[84]

This striking inconsistency, coupled with the relatively lukewarm reception by the crown of the town's additional demands, explains why the town's rulers pressed for another inspeximus and confirmation of Bristol's chartered liberties in the same year. Though evidence is slim, it must have been as a consequence of the persistence of Bristol's leaders that, in August 1331 Thomas Berkeley released to the mayor and commonalty all his claims to various franchises within Redcliffe, including view of frankpledge, the assize of bread, infangthief and outfangthief, a prison, pillory and tumbrel, and surrendered his power to summon, distrain and hold pleas in the southern suburb.[85] At the parliament which assembled at Westminster at the end of September 1331, the mayor of Bristol reminded the king of the decision made in the town's favour by the justices appointed to examine the town's claim to view of frankpledge,[86] and on 16 October 1331 the burgesses of Bristol received an inspeximus and confirmation of the same charters that had been inspected and ratified at the beginning of the year. One difference was that both the town's copy of this confirmation and the crown's enrolment of the charter in the charter rolls incorporated the interpolation *seu placitetur* in the 1188 *and* 1252 charters.[87] Meanwhile, the burgesses were granted view of frankpledge 'in the town and suburb' of Bristol in perpetuity, as the town's rulers had first requested almost a year earlier.[88]

The petitioning process had been long and arduous, and there were still several issues on which the crown had not given Bristol's leaders the response they had been seeking. The crown's approach to the subject of Bristol's franchises in 1330–1 was extremely rigorous; the endorsement on the reverse of the 1330 petition indicated as much, stating that the town's existing charters should be confirmed, but that the king was awaiting advice on the additional requests. David Palliser has rightly pointed out, from the evidence of the way in which petition and charter often followed very closely, that towns knew what they were going to receive beforehand,[89] but this was definitely not the case for Bristol in 1330. Perhaps the experiences of the regime of Isabella and Mortimer had driven the town's leaders to ask for too much, particularly from a king who must have been aware of the liberality of the previous government in its distribution of royal favour, specifically its 'too many lavish concessions to towns'.[90] Yet more revealing is the way in which several of the requests rejected by the crown in 1331 were taken up again in the town's efforts to secure its 1373

---

[83] One can surmise that the chancery clerk who copied the inspeximus of January 1331 on to the charter rolls would have consulted the crown's own copy of the 1322 charter, which did not include the alteration.

[84] A 'curious discrepancy' also noted by the editor of *Bristol Charters, 1155–1373*, p. 73.

[85] *Great Red Book*, II, p. 111.

[86] Ibid., II, p. 110. The original petition is PRO, SC 8/97/4816.

[87] For the town's copy of the charter, see BRO, Royal Charters and Letters Patent: 01207, printed in *Bristol Charters, 1155–1373*, pp. 78–81. For further discussion of the textual issue, see *Bristol Charters, 1155–1373*, pp. 78–9.

[88] *CChR 1327–41*, pp. 231–2.

[89] Palliser, 'Towns and the English State', p. 129.

[90] Ormrod, *Reign of Edward III*, p. 175.

charter, but on this occasion they were granted, a consequence of the greater negotiating power enjoyed by Bristol in the third quarter of the fourteenth century.

A comparison between the 1330 petition and the petition that prompted the grant of the charter elevating Bristol to county status in 1373 is instructive, for in several cases the earlier requests were repeated practically verbatim.[91] For instance, the demand that, once elected, the mayor of Bristol should no longer have to swear his oath before the constable of the castle as was customary, but should make his oath before his mayoral predecessor in the presence of the commonalty of the town assembled in the guildhall, simply provided a more elaborate form of the principle of perpetual succession contained in the earlier petition.[92] The following two clauses in the 1373 petition sought to limit the intrusions of the steward, marshal and clerk of the market within the town and to ensure that prisoners detained in the town's gaol for offences committed within Bristol were delivered solely in the town, both of which had found earlier expression in 1330.[93] Meanwhile, the final demand in 1373 that the burgesses be allowed to assess by common consent taxes on their goods and rents for their own purposes, a right previously exercised by prescription, was a direct echo of a clause in the 1330 petition, even including the request that the money collected was to remain in the custody of two good men (*prodeshomies*) elected for the purpose.[94]

The duplication within the petitions of 1330 and 1373 reveals much about the highly organised nature of Bristol's civic archive in this period,[95] since the earlier document must have been preserved for future reference. But why was there a need for such repetition? The obvious answer is that the comprehensive agenda set out in 1330 had not yet been fully realised. In fact, some of those issues that had been resolved ostensibly in 1331 were still pertinent over forty years later. One of the first clauses in the 1373 petition articulated the town's wish that Edward III would confirm that 'no burgess of the said town shall plead or be impleaded outside the walls of the town'.[96] If the status of Redcliffe had been determined to the town's satisfaction in 1331, problems arising from Bristol's location on the border of Gloucestershire and Somerset remained. Since Bristol was not a county town, its burgesses could find themselves in Gloucester and Ilchester respectively for court sessions depending on whether they lived north or south of the Avon, and in 1354 and 1361 the town's bailiffs appealed successfully to the crown to stop cases of novel disseisin involving the urban property of Bristol burgesses being heard before the justices of the Gloucestershire assizes at Gloucester.[97] Their main defence was the clause that no burgess was to plead or be impleaded outside the walls of Bristol except in pleas concerning foreign tenures, and the royal justices were instructed to hear the cases in Bristol instead.

---

[91] The 1373 petition is in *The Little Red Book of Bristol*, ed. F. B. Bickley (2 vols, Bristol, 1900), I, pp. 115–26. The 1330 petition was in Latin, the later one in Anglo-Norman French.

[92] Ibid., I, pp. 121–2.

[93] Ibid., I, pp. 122–4.

[94] Ibid., I, pp. 125–6.

[95] The period also saw the emergence of a civic register, the Little Red Book, which was begun in 1344 as part of a wide-ranging reform of civic government.

[96] *Little Red Book*, I, pp. 116–17.

[97] Ibid., I, pp. 94–100.

Of those requests disregarded by the crown in 1330, the desire for royal approval of civic taxation was borne of a suspicion of external interference in the town's affairs, which had been heightened as a result of Bristol's misfortunes under Isabella and Mortimer. Though such royal authorisation was not forthcoming, Bristol's civic elite went ahead with its plans to compound for royal taxation and to organise its own fiscal contributions free from the interference of the Gloucestershire and Somerset tax collectors on either side of the Avon. Thus, in 1332 the mayor of Bristol, Hugh de Langebrigge, fined for £200 so that the 'goods within the town and suburbs' of Bristol 'shall not be taxed for this turn for the fifteenth and tenth granted to the king by the commonalty of the realm'. Two years later the then mayor, Roger Turtle, acquired the same exemption for the town in return for £220, and similar grants were made to Bristol in 1336 and 1337.[98] In the years following the renewal of the Hundred Years War in 1369, the need to raise civic taxes was greater than it had ever been in Bristol, for it was from this period that the town was approached regularly in its corporate capacity to raise loans for the war effort and to build barges and balingers at its own expense for royal naval service.[99] In this context, Bristol's leaders turned to the crown to legitimise their increasingly onerous financial demands upon their subjects.

Bristol's 1373 charter granted, with a few slight amendments, all of the requests contained in the town's petition, with the exception of the demand for exemption from the jurisdiction of the steward and marshal of the king's household and the clerk of the market, a privilege which was eventually bestowed upon Bristol in 1396.[100] Furthermore, in September 1373 Edward III ordered a perambulation of the boundaries of the new county so that they 'shall be set in certainty', a request for greater clarification of the extent of the town which had been rejected in 1330.[101]

What had changed between 1330 and 1373? The drain of the Hundred Years War after 1369 upon the crown's financial resources helps to explain the difference in the attitude of the royal government, and the payment of 600 marks into the king's chamber for the charter must have helped to oil the machinery of royal patronage.[102] Yet the main reason for the crown's changed response lay in Bristol's growing fiscal, military and political prominence within the realm in the second half of the fourteenth century, built largely upon its role as a source of shipping and loans in the war against the French. The events of 1326 demonstrated Bristol's importance in national affairs, but it had largely been the product of circumstance. From 1327 to 1330 the town's rulers stood apart from the magnate-dominated politics of the period, even if it was, in some senses, a self-conscious isolation, but they knew that their influence with the crown was limited, particularly as potential local patrons to whom they might have turned for assistance, such as Isabella and Thomas Berkeley, had interests inimical to those of the town. By 1373 Edward III's wife, Queen Philippa, to whom the king had granted the town of Bristol as part of her dower in January 1331,[103] had been dead for four years. Yet arguably Bristol's ruling elite did

---

[98]   *CPR 1330–4*, p. 337; *CFR 1327–37*, pp. 428, 486, 506.
[99]   For fuller details, see C. D. Liddy, *War, Politics and Finance in Late Medieval English Towns: Bristol, York and the Crown, 1350–1400* (forthcoming).
[100] *CChR 1341–1417*, p. 353.
[101] *Bristol Charters, 1155–1373*, pp. 142–5.
[102] Ibid., pp. 118–21.
[103] *CPR 1330–4*, pp. 55–6.

not need the patronage of such local lords. In the years around 1373 Bristol contained an extraordinary array of overseas merchants such as Walter de Derby, John de Stoke, Walter de Frompton, Richard le Spicer, Ellis Spelly and Thomas Knappe, who were not only dominant in local politics but extremely active in royal service with direct links to the crown, lending money and ships, acting as advisers to the royal government on maritime and commercial issues and even serving on royal diplomatic missions.[104] The war with France had transformed Bristol's leaders into significant players on the national stage, whose wishes the crown ignored to its detriment.

---

[104] See Liddy, *War, Politics and Finance*, for further discussion. Their exploits lived long in local memory and their achievements were remembered a century later: William Worcestre, *A Topography of Medieval Bristol*, ed. F. Neale (Bristol Record Society li, Bristol, 2000), passim.

MAPPING IDENTITY IN JOHN TREVISA'S ENGLISH *POLYCHRONICON*: CHESTER, CORNWALL AND THE TRANSLATION OF ENGLISH NATIONAL HISTORY

Jane Beal

John Trevisa finished translating the *Polychronicon*, a universal history of the world compiled from Latin sources by Ranulf Higden, into English on 18 April 1387.[1] The chronicle foregrounds geography in Book I, which Ranulf calls a *mappamundi* or a map of the world. The book begins at 'Inde' (a nice pun in Middle English) and concludes with England.[2] In the course of the geographical description of England, Ranulf devotes a disproportionate number of words to describing his native city of Chester, thus revealing his loyalty to that place. In a similar manner, Trevisa reveals his loyalty to Cornwall in a series of interpolated notes. These additions make clear that both compiler and translator associate personal identity with place of origin. Their references to Chester and Cornwall respectively reveal a relationship between identity and geography, but because Ranulf and Trevisa are loyal to *different* places, a new narrative tension arises between Ranulf's Chester and Trevisa's Cornwall in the English *Polychronicon*.

On one side, Ranulf's historical association with Chester, the acrostic he uses in the Latin *Polychronicon*, and his description of Chester from Book I of the *Polychronicon* give pride of place to Chester. Cornwall, though mentioned in passing by several authorities cited in Book I, receives no extended consideration from Ranulf. Trevisa responds to this silence by first acknowledging, then subverting, and finally criticising Ranulf's connection to Chester. Within the same narrative space, Trevisa tells his own side of the geographical story, interpolating several notes on his native Cornwall. In order to put Cornwall on the map of England and of the world (at least as that map is imagined in Book I of the *Polychronicon*), Trevisa insists on Cornwall's rightful place in the English nation, both as a shire and as a part of the see of Exeter, and on its contributions to English language instruction in grammar schools. Then in Book IV, following up on remarks

---

[1] The date is included in the colophon to Trevisa's English version: see *Polychronicon*, ed. Churchill Babington and J. A. Lumby (9 vols, Rolls Series, London, 1865–86). The English *Polychronicon* has also been edited from Huntington Library MS 28561 by Richard Seeger, 'The English *Polychronicon*: A Text of John Trevisa's Translation of Higden's *Polychronicon*, based on Huntington MS. 28561' (unpublished PhD thesis, University of Washington, 1975). For Trevisa's prefaces to the *Polychronicon*, see Ronald Waldron, 'Trevisa's Original Prefaces on Translation: A Critical Edition', *Medieval English Studies Presented to George Kane*, ed. Edward Donald Kennedy, Ronald A. Waldron and J. S. Wittig (Cambridge, 1988), pp. 285–99.

[2] For additional discussion of the graphic and prose *mappaemundi* in the *Polychronicon*, see David Woodard, 'Medieval *Mappaemundi*', *The History of Cartography, I: Prehistoric, Ancient, and Medieval Europe and the Mediterranean*, ed. J. B. Harley and David Woodard (Chicago, 1987), pp. 286–370; Evelyn Edson, *Mapping Time and Space: How Medieval Mapmakers Viewed Their World* (London, 1997); Jane Beal, 'John Trevisa', *British Writers Supplement IX*, ed. Jay Parini (forthcoming).

he makes in Book I, he makes comments which can be construed as emphasising the Cornish or Celtic contribution to English national identity as embodied by King Arthur. As a result, the geographical loyalties of the compiler and the translator of the *Polychronicon* pull against one another, creating a dynamic tension in the English chronicle that was not present in the Latin one.

To explore this tension, this study will first consider Ranulf's loyalty to Chester, secondly Trevisa's response to it, and thirdly Trevisa's loyalty to Cornwall. The fourth section will analyse Trevisa's translation of history in relation to matters of identity, loyalty and authority. As we shall see, Trevisa's fidelity to his place of origin motivates him to situate personal and regional identity within a context of English national identity. It also gives him the opportunity to make a clear argument for the validity of Geoffrey of Monmouth's *Historia regum Britanniae* and the historicity of King Arthur, a move with larger implications for the translation of history in vernacular culture.

Ranulf's loyalty to Chester

Ranulf Higden spent most of his adult life in the city of Chester. He joined the abbey of St Werburgh in 1299, as the colophons in at least two manuscripts of the Latin *Polychronicon* attest, and he died there in 1363.[3] While the exact location of his birth is unknown, Ranulf apparently remained in Cheshire throughout his life, with a single exception. On 21 August 1352, Edward III summoned him to Westminster to come 'with all your chronicles, and those which are in your charge to speak and take advice with our council on certain matters which will be explained to you on our behalf'.[4] It is unclear what these 'certain matters' might have been, though they may have been connected to affairs in France or Scotland. In any case, barring this trip to London, Ranulf, a Bendictine monk, seems to have stayed at home. As John Taylor notes, in the *Polychronicon*, Ranulf's 'observations from direct experience are almost all concerned with local affairs'.[5]

Ranulf clearly felt a sense of loyalty to Chester, and he linked his identity to his place of origin in an acrostic he added to the *Polychronicon*. The acrostic is made up of the letters that begin each chapter of Book I of the *Polychronicon*. Taken together, they read: 'Presentem cronicam compilavit Frater Ranulphus Cestrensis monachus' ('Brother Ranulf, monk of Chester, compiled the present chronicle'). This acrostic is fascinating because it inscribes three aspects of Ranulf's identity in the very fabric of the Latin *Polychronicon*: his roles as a Benedictine brother (*frater*), as the compiler of the universal history (*compilavit*), and as a monk, specifically of Chester (*monachus Cestrensis*). Clearly all three of these roles were vital to Ranulf or he need not have taken such care to make mention of them in his acrostic.

Interestingly, in the briefer acrostic which he incorporated into his preaching manual, the *Ars componendi sermones*, Ranulf included only his name and his place of origin: *Ars Ranulphi Cestrensis* ('The Art of Ranulf of Chester').[6] We might

---

3   The colophons appear in BL, MS Laud Misc. 619, and Oxford, New College MS 152.
4   John Taylor, *The Universal Chronicle of Ranulph Higden* (Oxford, 1966), p. 1.
5   Ibid.
6   Margaret Jennings draws attention to the uniqueness of a Benedictine monk composing an *ars praedicandi* in 'Monks and the *Ars praedicandi* in the Time of Ranulph Higden', *Revue Benedictine* lxxxvi (1976), pp. 119–28. She has also edited Ranulf's preaching manual in *The Ars Componendi*

deduce from this that Ranulf linked his personal identity first to his own name and then to his place of origin, the city of Chester. Ranulf's special interest in Chester is reflected in the *Polychronicon*.

In Book I, chapter 48, Ranulf depicts Chester in his own words. He begins the passage about Chester with a reference to his acrostic: 'There is another City of Legions of this name, where the present chronicle was finished, just as the head letters of this first book make clearly accessible.'[7] This reference stands as a marker in the text, drawing the medieval reader's attention to Ranulf's acrostic. Reading the capital letters at the beginning of the chapters of Book I leads to the discovery of Ranulf's name and identity. Ranulf deliberately placed this marker, this reference to his acrostic, at the beginning of his description of Chester. The effect is to link his name and identity to his place of origin once again.

In the description of his city, Ranulf locates Chester, formerly the Roman City of Legions, in the march of England toward Wales between two arms of the sea, Dee and Mersey. He describes the history of Chester, beginning with its role as a chief city of Venedotia or North Wales. According to Ranulf, the founder of the city is unknown, but some who see the great stone foundations of Chester suppose it was made by the Romans or giants rather than by the Britons. It is called Caerthleon in British speech, Legecestria and then Cestria in Latin, and Chester or the City of Legions in English, because Julius Caesar spent a winter there before attempting to win Ireland and the Orcades islands. Ranulf denies whatever William of Malmesbury dreamed (*somniaverit*) about Chester, explaining that the city has plenty of corn, flesh, fish, and prized salmon, as well as merchandise which it exports and imports. Close by are salt wells, metal and ore. Though the Northumbrians destroyed Chester, Elfleda, Lady of Mercia, rebuilt it. As Ranulf says, under the city are vaults and stonework engraved with ancient names (*antiquorum nomina*). Julius Caesar's name is among these. Ranulf reminds his readers that, at one time, Ethelfryd, king of Northumbria, killed nearly two thousand monks of Bangor monastery and that King Edgar once came to Chester with seven subject kings. Ranulf rounds off this geographical, etymological, and historical description of Chester with a poem that recapitulates several of the major points from his prose description.[8]

Trevisa's reaction to Ranulf's loyalty to Chester

In the English *Polychronicon*, Trevisa translates and responds to Ranulf's geographical loyalty to Chester in various ways. As we shall see, the translator's response somewhat undermines both Chester and Ranulf. This can be seen in Trevisa's *Dialogue between a Lord and a Clerk*, in his interpolated note on Ranulf's acrostic, and in yet another interpolated note on Ranulf's poem about Chester.

Trevisa begins the English *Polychronicon* with an original dialogue, the so-called *Dialogue between a Lord and a Clerk on Translation*. In the Lord's opening speech, Trevisa makes matter-of-fact reference to the *Polychronicon* and to Ranulf, specifically calling him 'monk of Chester':

Sermones of Ranulf Higden, O.S.B. (Leiden, 1991). For an English translation of this text, see Sally Wilson, *Concerning the Art of Preaching According to Ranulphum Cestrensis* (forthcoming).

[7]   *Polychronicon*, II, p. 76.

[8]   Ibid., II, 76–84.

> And so Ranulph, monk of Chester, wrot yn Latyn hys bookes of cronykes that discreueth the world aboute yn lengthe and brede and maketh mencyon and muynde of doyngs and of dedes, of meruayls and of wondres and rekneth the yeres to hys laste dayes fram the vurste makyng of heuene and of erthe.[9]

This initial reference to Ranulf is neither negative nor positive; it is simply descriptive. It acknowledges Ranulf's role as a monk and origin in Chester and moves on.

Trevisa's treatment of Ranulf's reference to his acrostic is similarly descriptive, but at the same time it is somewhat subversive. Remarking on Ranulf's reference, Trevisa interpolates:

> *Trevisa*: This is to vnderstondynge in the Latyn writynge and nougt in this Englische wrytyng, for it was not the same that made it in Laten and turned it into English. Nother it was yturned into English in the same place that it was made first in Laten. The hed letters of the chapiters of this first boke ywritte arewe as the chapiter standeth, a speleth this Laten reson: 'Presentem cronicam compilavit Frater Ranulphus Cestrensis monachus.' This Laten reson is to menyng in English, 'Brother Ranulph, monke of Chestre, compiled and made this present cronyk.'[10]

In some ways, Trevisa's interpolation is merely explanatory. However, in other ways, it draws attention to *difference*: the difference between Latin and English, between the compiler and the translator, between the place of compilation and the place of translation. The note does all this *before* re-inscribing Ranulf's acrostic and then translating it into English. It appears, then, that Trevisa's decision to draw attention to these differences translates the relevance and importance of Trevisa's role relative to the Latin *Polychronicon* and the new English audience. Without Trevisa, a reader of the English *Polychronicon* would be unable to understand Ranulf's cryptic reference to an acrostic because, in fact, the acrostic is lost in translation.

Trevisa's tendency to privilege his own role and the importance of his own explanation recurs in his interpolated note on Ranulf's poem. In Trevisa's English translation, the last four lines of the poem read as follows:

> Bacchus and Mercurius, Mars and Venus, also Lauerna,
> Proteus and Pluto reneth there in the towne.
> There Babilon lore,
> More mygt hath, truth the more.[11]

After the first two of these last four lines, Trevisa *interrupts* the poem with his own explanatory – but obviously outraged – interpolation. Following the allusions to the pantheon of Greek gods, Trevisa declares:

---

[9]   Waldron, 'Trevisa's Original Prefaces on Translation', p. 290. Note that Trevisa gives a three-part, generic definition of the *Polychronicon* as a chronicle consisting of a world map, a memorial of deeds and marvels and a reckoning of the years from the Creation to Ranulf's 'laste dayes'. The *Polychronicon* is thus a world history both spatially and temporally.

[10]   *Polychronicon*, II, p. 77.

[11]   *Polychronicon*, II, pp. 83, 85. Note that these lines, which translate Ranulf's Latin, make no reference to truth: 'Mars et Mercurius, Bacchus, Venus, atque Laverna, / Proteus et Pluto regna tenent inibi. / Ejus gens sequitur multum mores Babylonis, / Quae dum plus poterit, plus solet esse ferox.' As noted by the editors in ibid., II, p. 85n, 'the text seems corrupt; possibly *crouthe* (i.e. *croweth*) may be the true reading'.

Trevisa: God woot what this is to mene! But poetes in here manere of speche feyneth as they euerich kynde craft and leuynge hadde a dyuersite god, euerich from other; and so they feyneth a god of bataille and of figtynge, and clepeth hym Mars; also they feyneth a god of couetise of richesse and marchaundise, and clepeth hym Mercurius; and so Bacchus thei clepeth god of wyn; Venus, god of fairnesse and of loue; Lauerna, god of theft and of robberie; Proteus, god of falshede and of gyle; and Pluto, god of helle. And so hit semeth that this vers wolde mene that these feyned goddes regneth and beeth I-serued in Chestre: Mars with figting and cokkynge; Mercurius with couetise of richesse and of marchandyse; Bacchus with grete drinkynge; Venus with loue nought ful wys; Lauerna with theft and robberye; Proteus with falshede and gyle. Than is Pluto not vnserued, god of helle.[12]

Trevisa's explanation of Ranulf's 'feigning', his metaphors and their implications for life in Chester, makes Ranulf's city look like a regular den of debauchery, full of fighting, drinking, sex, stealing and lying. Ranulf's own emphasis, in both the prose and the poetic description of his city, was a little less lurid.

The point of Trevisa's explanation here seems twofold. On the one hand, he really is trying to explicate Ranulf's circumspect allusions to the Greek gods. Trevisa repeatedly insists that these gods are 'feigned', or made up, imagined by poets but totally unreal. One can almost discern Trevisa's pastoral concerns in this insistence. On the other hand, Trevisa makes Chester look like a very un-Christian sort of town, a characterisation that may taint Ranulf's association with the place. Trevisa might almost seem to say here, of the association between Ranulf and Chester, 'Bad company corrupts good morals.'

Taken together, Trevisa's responses to Ranulf's geographical loyalty to Chester are layered. In the *Dialogue between a Lord and a Clerk*, Trevisa accepts Ranulf's loyalty as a matter of course. In the note on Ranulf's acrostic, he explains the acrostic's reference to Chester, but in such a way that the explanation points to his own importance as a translator. In the note on Ranulf's poem about Chester, Trevisa changes the character of Ranulf's description of his home town, translating not only word for word, but also meaning for meaning – Ranulf's understated meaning for his own interpretation of Ranulf's metaphors. Trevisa's layered response creates a narrative tension between the translator and the compiler, a tension that builds in Trevisa's notes on his own place of origin.

Trevisa's loyalty to Cornwall

Trevisa's notes on Cornwall in the English *Polychronicon* appear to be motivated by several factors. First, of course, the translator has a natural interest in his own home county that he expresses as a matter of course in Book I. Secondly, Ranulf's tendency to favour Chester and ignore Cornwall may have inspired Trevisa to compensate in his English translation for what was, to his mind, lacking in the Latin version. This compensatory move on Trevisa's part also functions as a gesture of appropriation, rewriting the chronicle in English with a different geographical emphasis and inscribing identity through mapping-in-prose. Thus, thirdly, Trevisa

---

[12] Ibid., II, pp. 83, 85.

may have been motivated to discuss Cornwall as a means of claiming and asserting his own authority as the translator and creator of the vernacular English *Polychronicon*. His remarks in Book I on Cornwall's political, ecclesiastical, and linguistic situation all relate in some way to this third possibility.

Trevisa's first interpolation about Cornwall is essentially political. In it, Trevisa argues that Cornwall is a shire of England, an integral part of the greater nation. He makes this remark in reaction to Alfred of Beverly, who is cited in the *Polychronicon* and who had what Trevisa apparently regards as the unmitigated gall to count the shires of England without including Cornwall or the islands.

> *Trevisa*: Hit is wondre why Alfred summeth the schires of Engelond somdel as a man that mette; for Alfrede telleth the som of schires in this manere: 'There beeth in Engelond sixe and thritty schires withoute Conewayle and withoute the ylondes.' Why seith he nougt in this manere: 'There beeth in Engelond sixe schires with Cornwayle, and thritty other schires without the ilondes'? Eyther manere summynge is as vnredy as other. For to make a redy somme it schulde be i-writte in this manere: In Engelond beeth seuen and thritty schires, and so is Cornewayle acounted with the othere schires; and that is skilful. For Cornewayle is a schere of Engelond; for, as he seith, Cornwaile is in this Bretayne hym self, as it is aleide in the fourth chapitre of this firste book. Than hit is in oon of the chief parties of this Bretayne, that beeth Engelond, Wales, and Scotlond. But Cornewayle is nougt in Wales, for there is a grete see betwene, nother in Scotlonde, for there beeth many hondred myle bytwene. Than Cornwayle is in Engelond, and is departed in hundreds, and is i-ruled by the lawe of Engelond, and holdeth schire and schire dayes, as other schires dooth. Yif Alfrede seith nay in that, he wot nougt what he maffleth.[13]

In this interpolation, Trevisa insists that Cornwall is one of the 'chief parts' of Britain, which is made up of England, Wales and Scotland. Cornwall cannot belong to Wales, because a sea separates the two places, and it cannot belong to Scotland, because many hundreds of miles stand between. Cornwall belongs to England not only by reason of geography, but also because it is divided into hundreds, holds shire and shires days and is ruled by English law. In short, for Trevisa, Cornwall is a part of England because it is geographically, politically and juridically related to it. Alfred, in Trevisa's estimation, can be dismissed if he thinks otherwise.

Trevisa's second interpolation about Cornwall concerns its ecclesiastical situation. In it, Trevisa makes it a point to observe that West Saxon bishops' jurisdiction included, among other places, Cornwall: '*Trevisa*: Afterward me semeth by this lawe that Westsaxon conteyned Southeray, Southhampschire, Barrockschire, Wiltschire, Somersede, Dorsete, Deuenschire and Cornwayle.'[14] As with his insistence that Cornwall is a shire of England, so here Trevisa again is arguing for inclusion in England, this time based on ecclesiastical connections and historical precedent rather than on geographical, political or juridical affiliations.

Trevisa's third interpolation about Cornwall is perhaps his best-known note, and

---

[13] Ibid., II, p. 91. Trevisa believes that there is a reference to Cornwall in Book I, chapter 4, but there is no reference to Cornwall in the fourth preface to the *Polychronicon* or in chapter 8 (the fourth chapter from the last preface).

[14] Ibid., II, p. 121.

it concerns the linguistic contributions of Cornishmen to English language instruction in England.

> *Trevisa*: This manere was moche i-vsed to for firste deth and is sithe sumdel i-chaunged; for Iohn Conwaile, a maister of grammer, chaunged the lore in gramer scole and construccioun of Frensche in to Englische, and Richard Pencriche lerned the manere techynge of hym and of othere men of Pencrich, so that now, the yere of oure Lorde a thowsand thre hundred and foure score and fyue, and of the secounde kyng Richard after the conquest nyne, in alle the gramere scoles of Engelond, children leueth Frensche and construeth and lerneth an Englische, and haueth therby auauntage in oon side and disauauntage in another side; here auauntage is that they lerneth her gramer in lasse tyme than children were i-wonned to doo; disauauntage is that now children of gramer scole conneth na more Frensche than can hir lift heele, and that is harme for hem and they schulle passe the see and trauaille in straunge landes and in many other places. Also gentil men haueth now moche i-left for to teche here children Frensche.[15]

Here, Trevisa observes that, as of 1385, English children received instruction in English rather than French. The advantage of this, as Trevisa sees it, is that the children learn their grammar faster, but the disadvantage is that now English children know no more French 'than their left heel', and this is 'harm for them' when traveling overseas and in other foreign places. Interestingly, Trevisa attributes this monumental change in the educational system to two men, John Cornwall, 'a master of grammar', and his protégé, Richard Pencriche, observing that the latter went on to teach the English method to other men. This is not, of course, an implausible explanation, and it has been widely accepted because of the evidence showing that John of Cornwall taught grammar to boys preparing to attend Merton College at least from 1344 to 1349 and because of the evidence provided by the many extant manuscripts of his *Speculum gramaticale*.[16] However, Trevisa's loyalty to Cornwall ought to make us think twice about whether or not he is giving credit where credit is due. It is quite likely that several additional grammar teachers, not of Cornish origin, also helped implement the change from using French to using English as the language of instruction in grammar schools.[17]

Taken together, Trevisa's notes on Cornwall, though different in character from Ranulf's references to Chester, nevertheless indicate Trevisa's loyalty to Cornwall. Like Ranulf, part of his personal identity is clearly linked to his place of origin. In

---

[15] Ibid., II, p. 161.

[16] For further discussion of John of Cornwall and his contributions to English grammar school education, see Cynthia Renée Bland, *The Teaching of Grammar in Late Medieval England: An Edition, with Commentary, of Oxford, Lincoln College MS Lat. 130* (East Lansing, 1991).

[17] For discussions of the tradition of medieval grammatical instruction in England, see Sanford Brown Meech, 'Early Application of Latin Grammar to English', *Publications of the Modern Language Association* i (1935), pp. 1012–32; David Thomson, 'A Study of the Middle English Treatises on Grammar' (unpublished D.Phil. thesis, University of Oxford, 1977); David Thomson, *A Descriptive Catalogue of Middle English Grammatical Texts* (New York, 1979); David Thomson, 'The Oxford Grammar Masters Revisited', *Mediaeval Studies* xlv (1983), pp. 298–310; David Thomson, *An Edition of the Middle English Grammatical Texts* (New York, 1984); Jo Ann Hoeppner Moran, *The Growth of English Schooling, 1340–1548: Learning, Literacy, and Laicization in Pre-Reformation York Diocese* (Princeton, 1985).

the three notes summarised and analysed here, it is clear that Trevisa wants to emphasise Cornwall's inclusion in the larger realm of England, in geographical, juridical and political terms as well as ecclesiastical, historical and linguistic terms. The translator clearly emphasises Cornish contributions to England, which, Trevisa leads us to believe, include nothing less than giving the English language itself to English children.

Trevisa's notes on Cornwall do more than indicate his geographical loyalties, however. They also help to establish his authority for the vernacular English audience that he expects to read his translation of the *Polychronicon*. Perhaps anticipating unasked questions about his status as a Cornish translator of works from Latin into English, or perhaps desiring to please his patron Thomas, lord Berkeley, who had holdings in Gloucestershire and Cornwall, Trevisa stresses what he perceives to be the close and irrefutable connection between Cornwall and England. For Trevisa, the two are politically and ecclesiastically related; but beyond these organisational relationships, they also share linguistic interests. By pointing out Cornish grammar masters who teach using English, Trevisa highlights the contribution that Cornwall can make to the English language and English language instruction, even while he questions the abandonment of French to accomplish this. Like John of Cornwall, Trevisa himself is engaged in a project that disseminates information in the vernacular.[18] He could have translated the *Polychronicon* into French, but he did not do so; he translated it into English and, in the process, insisted that Cornwall was an important part of England and of English vernacular culture.

It comes as little surprise, then, that Trevisa had larger concerns with the translation of history and its implications for English national identity. These concerns are exemplified by Trevisa's insistence on the reliability of Geoffrey of Monmouth's *Historia regum Britanniae* and on the historicity of King Arthur. As we shall see, Trevisa's insistence is a reaction to Ranulf's ambivalent attitude toward Geoffrey, an ambivalence that the compiler repeatedly betrays in the Latin *Polychronicon*. Trevisa responds in detail to Ranulf's sceptical objection to Geoffrey in Book IV of the English *Polychronicon*, and his response demonstrates that Ranulf and Trevisa read history differently. It also demonstrates what the stakes are in the construction of vernacular history. In the case of the English *Polychronicon*, those stakes include a debate about whether the matter of England, and English national identity by extension, would verify the existence and accomplishments of King Arthur.

Trevisa's translation of history

The verity and reliability of English history, as written by Geoffrey of Monmouth in the twelfth-century *Historia regum Britanniae*, was the subject of much scholarly concern almost from the moment that it entered the English historical tradition. Ranulf, who had read widely in medieval chronicles (as the over two hundred sources he cites in the *Polychronicon* show), may have acquired from those same chronicles a suspicion that Geoffrey of Monmouth's version of English history was not to be trusted. He negotiates his distrust by treating Geoffrey as the mediator

---

[18] For further discussion of this aspect of Trevisa's work, see David Fowler, *The Life and Times of John Trevisa, Medieval Scholar* (Seattle, 1995); Ralph Hanna III, 'Sir Thomas Berkeley and his Patronage', *Speculum* lxiv (1989), pp. 878–916; Fiona Somerset, *Clerical Discourse and Lay Audience in Late-Medieval England* (Cambridge, 1998).

between himself and the named source of the *Historia*, the *liber vetustissimus* of Walter the Archdeacon. The first negotiation appears rather obliquely in the list of *auctoritates* which Ranulf gives in the second preface to his chronicle.

In that list, Ranulf names 'Walterus Oxonicum archdiaconus' as one of his sources; but unlike most of Ranulf's other sources, the title of the authority's work is not given. This is most probably because Ranulf did not know it. Instead, he knew *about* it from Geoffrey of Monmouth. According to the preface to the *Historia regum Britanniae*, Walter gave Geoffrey 'a certain very ancient book' which he then used as the source of his *Historia*:

> At a time when I was giving a great deal of attention to such matters, Walter, Archdeacon of Oxford, a man skilled in the art of public speaking and well informed about the history of foreign countries, presented me with a certain very ancient book written in the British language. The book, attractively composed to form a consecutive and orderly narrative, set out all the deeds of these men, from Brutus, the first king of the Britons, down to Cadwallader, the son of Cadwallo. At Walter's request, I have taken the trouble to translate the book into Latin.[19]

There has been considerable debate about the existence and authenticity of Geoffrey's source, beginning as early as 1198, when William of Newburgh condemned it in no uncertain terms.[20] However, Geoffrey of Monmouth's *liber vetutissimus* could very well have been a real book, not a metaphorical one standing for a collection of oral tradition passed on to him by the Archdeacon Walter. This can be true even if Geoffrey invents historical episodes out of whole cloth, uses unacknowledged sources, like Gildas, Nennius and William of Malmesbury, and implies that the 'British book' is his primary source when it is not.[21] Real or not, Geoffrey's motivation for claiming 'a certain very ancient book' as his source is obvious: the very 'ancientness' of his information would give it authority in the minds of his medieval audience and thus promote the version of English national history and identity which Geoffrey was seeking to create.

Ranulf Hidgen apparently shared Geoffrey's desire to appear authoritative through the use of the most ancient sources. This explains Ranulf's decision to list the book of Walter the Archdeacon as one of his forty *auctoritates*, even though it is unlikely that he had any access to it other than through the report of Geoffrey.[22] It

---

[19] *Geoffrey of Monmouth: History of the Kings of Britain*, trans. Lewis Thorpe (Harmondsworth, 1966), p. 51.

[20] See 'Geoffrey of Monmouth', *The Oxford Companion to English Literature*, ed. Margaret Drabble (Oxford, 1985), pp. 386–7. For an overview of the scholarly debate, see also Robert Huntington Fletcher, *The Arthurian Material in the Chronicles, especially those of Great Britain and France* (New York, 1906), pp. 49–57; D. R. Howlett, 'The Literary Context of Geoffrey of Monmouth: An Essay on the Fabrication of Sources', *Arthuriana* v (1995), pp. 25–69.

[21] Geoffrey Ashe provides good evidence for the existence of Geoffrey's source when he discusses the Camlann episode, the one episode in Geoffrey's *Historia* which the author specifically says came from the 'British book', which also appears in the *Chroniques de Saint Brieuc* independently of the *Historia*, suggesting that the *Historia* and the *Chroniques* shared a third common source, possibly the *liber vetutissimus*. See Geoffrey Ashe, ' "A Certain Very Ancient Book": Traces of an Arthurian Source in Geoffrey of Monmouth's History', *Speculum* lvi (1981), pp. 301–23.

[22] Ranulf's decision to list Walter the Archdeacon as a source when he only had Geoffrey of Monmouth may be paralleled by the twelfth-century French historian Gaimar, whose epilogue to the *Estoire des Engleis* refers to the book of Walter the Archdeacon, albeit without any reference to Geoffrey of

also foreshadows the series of moves that Ranulf makes in the *Polychronicon* proper to negotiate access to Walter's *liber* through Geoffrey's *Historia*. These negotiations can be grouped according to the names of three men: William of Malmesbury, Merlin and King Arthur.

In three remarks on William of Malmesbury, Ranulf refers to Geoffrey once to dismiss the reliability of the *Historia* and twice to affirm it. Then, in relating legends of Merlin in Book I, he apparently relies on Geoffrey but does not acknowledge him as a source. Finally, in an extended diatribe in Book IV, Ranulf rejects Geoffrey's *Historia* as a source of reliable historical information about King Arthur. This dismissive reaction to Geoffrey proves to be the proverbial last straw for John Trevisa, who translates Ranulf's objection only to refute it in the strongest possible terms. Trevisa asserts that Ranulf's points 'agens Gaufridus and Arthur' ought not to persuade any clerk that understands an argument, and he justifies this with recourse to the model of Christian readings of the four Gospels that harmonise or synthesize their differences. Beneath this justification, however, may be a motive related to Trevisa's loyalty to Cornwall. Geoffrey of Monmouth, unlike Ranulf Higden, gives tremendous pride of place to Cornwall in the *Historia regum Britanniae*, locating (among other significant events) the conception of King Arthur in Tintagel on the coast of Cornwall.[23] For Trevisa, then, affirming the value of Geoffrey's *Historia* means confirming the existence of an historical King Arthur and the contribution of Cornwall to English national history.

Before reaching the discussion of King Arthur in Book IV, the point where the narrative tension in the English *Polychronicon* breaks out into a full-blown disagreement, Trevisa has several opportunities to witness and translate Ranulf's reactions to Geoffrey of Monmouth, three of which occur in tandem with remarks on William of Malmesbury. For example, in Book I, chapter 47, Ranulf cites William's opinion that the hot baths of Bath were believed to have been established by Julius Ceasar. Ranulf then points out that Geoffrey of Monmouth believed that Bladud, a necromancer, had created them. By juxtaposing these two claims, Ranulf creates an opportunity to resolve the artificially constructed debate himself. He does so by asserting that the waters of Bath run over *venas sulphureas*, becoming hot thereby, and then spring up into the city.[24]

In the course of making these comments, Ranulf observes that William of Malmesbury had not seen Geoffrey's British book ('qui Britannicum librum non viderat'), and he adds that William wrote many things by relying on others or by his own conjecture. He finds it probable that Bladud did construct the city of Bath even if he did not build the hot baths for which it is famous. Thus, Ranulf relies on a portion of Geoffrey's information in order to dismiss William's and foreground his own explanation for the hot baths. In two later reactions to Geoffrey and William, Ranulf again relies on Geoffrey's historical information rather than William's, on these occasions completely rather than partially.

Monmouth. For an edition, translation, and commentary on Gaimar's epilogue, see Ian Short, 'Gaimar's Epilogue and Geoffrey of Monmouth's Liber Vetustissimus', *Speculum* lxix (1994), pp. 323–43.

[23] See E. M. R. Ditmas, 'A Reappraisal of Geoffrey of Monmouth's Allusions to Cornwall', *Speculum* xlviii (1973), pp. 510–24.

[24] *Polychronicon*, II, p. 58. As Galloway observes, Ranulf is indebted to Bede's *Ecclesiastical History* for this solution. Andrew Galloway, 'Latin England', *Imagining a Medieval English Nation*, ed. Kathy Lavezzo (forthcoming).

These remarks appear in Book I, chapter 48 and in Book IV, chapter 9, and in both cases they address the problem of attributing the inscription *Marii victoriae* (which appears in three-chambered place near Westmorland), to the correct Marius. William of Malmesbury believed that the inscription referred to an Italian consul while Ranulf, relying on information from Geoffrey's *Historia*, believed that the inscription referred to Marius, king of the Britons, who defeated Roderick, king of the Picts, in the same area where the inscription appeared. In both cases, Ranulf comments that William had not seen (*nusquam viderat*) or had not read (*non legisset*) Geoffrey's British book, and Ranulf does so presumably to lend support to his own reading of *Marii victoriae*.[25]

Thus far, then, it appears that Ranulf finds Geoffrey of Monmouth somewhat reliable and even appears to criticise William of Malsbury for his ignorance of the *Historia regum Britanniae*.[26] Of course, the matters up for dispute – the origin of hot water in Bath and the correct attribution of *Marii victoriae* – are not the most controversial matters of history. More specifically, they have nothing to do with King Arthur or with the construction of English national identity on a larger scale. When such matters do come up in the geographical description of Wales in Book I, chapter 38, Ranulf relies on Geoffrey of Monmouth but does not acknowledge him as a source.

The description of Wales is unique in the *Polychronicon*. It is the only chapter in verse, and it is the only chapter without named *auctoritates*. The 475 lines of rhymed couplets describe the Trojan origins of Wales, the etymology of its name, the produce of its lands, the customs of its people, and a selection of it marvels. For Ranulf, Wales is the daughter of Mother England and, among other things, the birth and burial place of Merlin. Ranulf mentions two Merlins in this chapter, points he derives from Gerald of Wales, but his ultimate and unacknowledged source for both of them is Geoffrey of Monmouth.[27]

Geoffrey of Monmouth invented the name Merlin or Merlinus by latinising the Welsh name Myrddin, and in Book VII of his *Historia* he introduced him as a young man prophesying before Vortigern in the 430s. When he realised that the original Myrddin, a seer, had lived much later, he created a poem called the *Vita Merlini* wherein he tried to reconcile the differences between the Merlin of the *Historia* and the new Merlin as he understood him when he wrote the *Vita*.[28] In the *Itinerarium*

---

25 Ibid., II, p. 70; IV, p. 416.

26 Of course, the 'British book' may be the *Historia regum Britanniae* or the source of the *Historia*, the *liber* which Walter the Archdeacon gave to Geoffrey of Monmouth. Ranulf's phrasing does not make the referent perfectly clear.

27 Given Ranulf's level of familiarity with both Gerald of Wales and Geoffrey of Monmouth, it is improbable that he would not recognise Geoffrey of Monmouth as the source of Gerald's information about Merlin. Indeed, Ranulf may have derived a part of his sceptical attitude toward Geoffrey from Gerald, as Gerald of Wales calls Geoffrey's *Historia* a 'fabulous history' that 'falsely maintains' even something as simple as the true etymology of 'Wales'. See *The Historical Works of Giraldus Cambrensis*, ed. Thomas Wright (London, 1863), p. 489. Additional evidence that Ranulf picked up his prejudice against Geoffrey of Monmouth from Gerald of Wales appears in Book V, chapter 20 of the *Polychronicon*. There, Ranulf cites Gerald's dismissing the Welsh belief that they will have kings agains when Cadwaladrus's bones are brought back from Rome: 'fabulosam reputo, sicut et historian Gaufridi in fine' (or, as Trevisa translates, 'but I holde that but a fable, as I doo the storie of Gaufidus in the ende') (*Polychronicon*, VI, pp. 160–1).

28 Geoffrey Ashe, Norris J. Lacy and Debra N. Mancoff, *The Arthurian Handbook*, 2nd edn (Garland Reference Library of the Humanities MCMXX, New York, 1997), p. 45.

Walliae, Gerald of Wales recognised that Geoffrey had created a composite figure, and he distinguished between the two in his eighth chapter:

> There were two Merlins; the one called Ambrosius, who prophesied in the time of king Vortigern, was begotten by a demon incubus, and found at Caermardin, from which circumstance that city derived its name of Caermardin, or the city of Merlin. The other Merlin, born in Scotland, was named Celidonius, from the Celidonian wood in which he prophesied, and Sylvester, because when engaged in a martial conflict, he discovered in the air a terrible monster, and from that time grew mad, and taking shelter in a wood, passed the remainder of his days in a savage state. This Merlin lived in the time of King Arthur and is said to have prophesied more fully and explicitly than the other.[29]

It is this passage that serves as the primary source for Ranulf's comments on two Merlins in Book I, chapter 38 of the *Polychronicon*. Ranulf acknowledges three works by Gerald of Wales as sources in his second preface, but does not do so anywhere in chapter 38 itself. This is notable because it is not Ranulf's usual practice. He generally favours the scholastic method of attributing passages to their sources even when he has abridged, paraphrased or expanded them considerably. The explanation for this may lie in the versified nature of chapter 38; perhaps Ranulf did not want to interrupt the poetic flow of his narrative at this point with citations. Whatever the reason, Ranulf does not mention either Gerald of Wales or his ultimate source, Geoffrey of Monmouth, in his three remarks on Merlin in his description of Wales.

The first reference, in line 202, refers to Merlin's prophecies (*Merlini vaticinium*) as a motivating factor in Welsh desires to fight against the Saxons. The second reference concerns the existence of two Merlins, and in the English *Polychronicon*, it appears in lines 308–73 as a kind of dialogue between Ranulf and Trevisa, who inserts his own opinion about the nature of Merlin's conception. Drawing on Gerald of Wales, Ranulf first identifies Merlin Ambrosius and says that he was fathered by an incubus. Trevisa interrupts here to say that fiends cannot engender their own children, but must first steal men and women's seed 'with craft', and by means of it make a woman pregnant. He adds that death does not slay fiends, but Merlin died, and so 'Merlyn was ergo no gobelyn.'[30] This interpolation is followed immediately by Ranulf's identification of the second Merlin as the man who had the two surnames Silvestris and Calidonius, who fled into the woods when he went mad, and who prophesied under King Arthur more openly than Merlin Ambrosius:

> Ad silvam tendens propere,
> Arthuri regis tempore;
> Prophetavit apertius
> Quam Merlinus Ambrosius.[31]

Earlier in this description, Trevisa adds his own note explaining the etymology of 'Sylvestris'.

---

[29] *Historical Works of Giraldus Cambrensis*, p. 452.
[30] *Polychronicon*, I, p. 421.
[31] Ibid., II, pp. 420, 422.

The discussion of the two Merlins in the chapter on Wales in the English *Polychronicon* reveals two important facts. First, it shows that Ranulf did not reject Arthurian legend *in toto*, as some readings of his later rejection of Geoffrey's *Historia* in Book IV imply.[32] Second, it shows Trevisa's interest in Merlin and, by extension, Arthurian lore, a point demonstrated again in Book I, chapter 48, when Gerald of Wales appears to question whether or not Roman messengers came to visit King Arthur in Caerleon:

> [Gerald of Wales] There the messangers of Rome come to the grete Arthurus court, yif it is leeful for to trowe. *Trevisa*: Yif Gerald was in doubt where it were leful for to trowe this other noo, it was nougt ful greet reedynesse to write hit in his bookes; as som men wolde wene. For it is a wonder sweuene i-mette for to write a long storie, to haue euermore in mynde, and euere haue doubte yit it be amys byleue![33]

Trevisa's frustration with Gerald of Wales' Latin qualifier, *si fas sit credere*, is obvious. It is notable because, although similar qualifiers appear elsewhere in the *Polychronicon*, Trevisa responds to it here when it is connected to King Arthur.

Given Ranulf's ambivalent treatment of Geoffrey of Monmouth, wherein he relies upon him partially but only to refute William of Malmesbury and wherein he uses his depiction of Merlin (via Gerald of Wales) but does not acknowledge him, it is perhaps somewhat surprising that he would decide to reject Geoffrey's *Historia* as a source of historical information about King Arthur in Book IV. Given Trevisa's previously demonstrated interest in Merlin, Arthur and Cornish contributions to English national history, on the other hand, his refutation of Ranulf's rejection is not really very surprising at all.

In Book IV, chapter 6, Ranulf once again comments on Geoffrey of Monmouth in reaction to the words of William of Malmesbury. William, speaking of Arthur, complains that he is the one about whom the Welsh tell deceitful fables (*fallaces fabulae*). Ranulf uses William's complaint as a pretext to criticise Geoffrey of Monmouth, who alone of all the historians praises King Arthur ('quem inter omnes chronographos solus Gaufridus sic extollit').[34] He goes on at length to identify those points in Geoffrey's *Historia* that he finds untenable: no Roman, French or Saxon sources record the successful exploits of Arthur in their countries; French historians make no mention of a King Frollo whom Arthur supposedly defeated; no Lucius, procurator of the Romans, was alive at the time Arthur is said to have killed him; and no Emperor Leo appeared to be ruling at the time Arthur did all his deeds. Ranulf does not accuse Geoffrey of falsifying history outright, but instead explains that each people likes to have its own hero and praise him excessively ('de suis laudibus attollere excessivis'): the Greeks have Alexander; the Romans, Octavian;

---

32 See, for example, John Housman, 'Higden, Trevisa, Caxton, and Arthurian Criticism', *Review of English Studies* xxiii (1947), pp. 209–17. For a response to Housman, see Ronald Waldron, 'Trevisa's "Celtic Complex" Revisited', *Notes and Queries* ccxxxiv (1989), pp. 303–7. Interestingly, Larkin has recently argued that Ranulf authored two Arthurian romances in Latin prose, which, if true, suggests that Ranulf participated in expanding the very tradition that he criticises. See Peter A. Larkin, 'A Suggested Author for *De ortu Waluuannii* and *Historia Meriadoci*', *Journal of English and Germanic Philology* (forthcoming).

33 *Polychronicon*, II, p. 77.

34 Ibid., V, pp. 332, 334.

the English, Richard; the French, Charles; and the Welsh, Arthur.[35] This is apparently enough to dismiss Geoffrey.

Trevisa, however, is unwilling to see Geoffrey's authority so disregarded, as he makes clear in one of his longest interpolations.

> *Trevisa*: Here William telleth a magel tale with oute evidence; and Ranulphus his resouns, that he meveth agenst Gaufridus and Arthur, schulde non clerke moove that can knowe an argument, for it foloweth it nougt. Seint Iohn in his gospel telleth meny thinges and doynges that Mark, Luc, and Matheu speketh nougt of in here gospelles, ergo, Iohn is nougt to trowynge in his gospel. He were of false byleve that trowede that that argument were worth a bene. For Iohn in his gospel telleth that oure Lordes moder and here suster stood by oure Lordes croys, and meny other thinges that non other gospeller maketh of mynde, and yit Iohn his gospel is as trewe as eny of hem al that they maketh. So they Gaufridus speke of Arthur his dedes, that other writers of stories speketh of derkliche, other maketh of non mynde, that dispreveth nougt Gaufrede his storie and his sawe, and specialliche of som writers of stories were Arthur his enemyes. It is wonder that he seith that no Frollo was kyng of Fraunce, nother Lucius procurator of the comynte, nother Leo emperour in Arthur his tyme, setthe that ofte an officer, kyng, other emperour hath many dyvers names, and is diverseliche i-nempned in meny dyvers londes; and in the thridde book, capitulo nono, he seith hymself that it is no wonder they William of Malmesbury were desceyved, for he hadde nougt i-rad the Brittische book; and yit they Gaufridus had nevere i-spoke of Arthur, meny noble naciouns speketh of Arthur and of his nobil dedes. But it may wel be that Arthur is ofte overpreysed, and so beeth meny othere. Soth sawes beeth nevere the wors they madde men telle magel tales, and som mad men will mene that Arthur schal come aye, and be eft kyng here of Britayne, but that is a ful magel tale, and so beeth meny othere that beeth i-tolde of hym and of othere.[36]

Trevisa is here at pains to address each one of Ranulf's arguments and offer another point of view, namely his own. He asserts that no clerk who knows how to recognise an argument should be moved by Ranulf's proofs and argues instead for a synthesising approach to reading chronicles, asserting in essence that the substance of Geoffrey's chronicle supplements the silence of other chronicles, filling in the gaps in the historical record.

Trevisa makes a persuasive rhetorical move when he takes the authoritative example of the Gospels as a model for harmonising chronicles. Trevisa notes that while the Synoptic Gospels generally agree with one another, the Gospel of John contains information that they omit, such as the reference to the presence of Mary and her sister at the foot of the Cross when Christ died.[37] If the differences between the Gospels had the same implications that the differences between the chronicles apparently do for William of Malmesbury and Ranulf, then the Gospel of John would be deemed false. According to Trevisa, 'He were of a wel fals byleve that

---

[35] Ibid., V, p. 336.
[36] Ibid., V, pp. 337, 339.
[37] See John 19:25.

trowede that that argument were worth a bene.' A failure to read correctly indicates a failure of faith; a man who reads contradictions in the chronicles like Ranulf does may well misread the Gospels, an action indicative of 'fals byleve' potentially bordering on heresy.

Having made a synthesising approach to chronicle reading a matter of Christian doctrine, Trevisa goes on to contradict each of Higden's four arguments against the authority of Geoffrey's chronicle as well as his explanations with precision and force. Trevisa observes first that chronicles which ignore Arthur's exploits might have been written by his enemies, and second that other sources may not mention a King Frollo, a procurator Lucius or an Emperor Leo because officers, kings and emperors often have many names and different ones in different countries. To dismiss Ranulf's explanations, Trevisa notes that Ranulf himself, in the ninth chapter of the third book,[38] observes that William of Malmesbury was deceived since he had not read 'the Bryttysch bok'.[39] Trevisa adds that Geoffrey is not the only source for Arthurian history, and finally, that although Arthur may be over-praised, so are many others, and 'Soth sawes beeth nevere the wors they madde men telle magel tales.' In other words, a truth inspiring a fabrication is not itself fabricated.

At issue here is more than the question of how to read history. Trevisa is clearly concerned with how to translate it for a vernacular English audience. If that audience accepts Ranulf's estimation of Geoffrey's *Historia*, it will lose a vital part of the tradition supporting the existence and accomplishments of an historical King Arthur. Trevisa is unwilling to allow that loss to go uncontested in the English *Polychronicon*.

Conclusions

As we have seen, Ranulf clearly associated his identity with Chester, as evidenced by his acrostics and descriptions, both prosaic and poetic, of his native city. Trevisa responded to this association by accepting it as a matter of fact but then by subverting it through interpolated notes. In one note, the one explaining Ranulf's absent acrostic, Trevisa shifted attention from the compiler to himself and his own importance as a translator. In another note, which explained references to Greek gods in Ranulf's poem, Trevisa changed Ranulf's emphasis on Chester as a relatively good city to an emphasis on the city as something like a den of debauchery. Trevisa's own geographical affiliation, his loyalty to Cornwall, emerges in additional notes that highlight Cornwall's inclusion in the larger realm of England as well as Cornwall's contribution to its nation. These conflicting geographical loyalties create a kind of narrative tension in the English *Polychronicon*, a tension that emerges as outright disagreement between compiler and translator in the estimation of Geoffrey of Monmouth's *Historia regum Britanniae* and the historicity of King Arthur. For Ranulf, Geoffrey's *Historia* is sometimes useful, but it is ultimately misleading in its claims about the scope of Arthur's conquests. For Trevisa, it supplies the information missing in other chronicles and a meaningful vision of

---

[38] Ranulf's remark actually appears in Book IV, chapter 9.
[39] 'The Bryttysch bok' here, as in Ranulf's earlier references, may refer either to Geoffrey's *Historia* or his source, Walter the Archdeacon's *Liber vetustissimus*.

England's past in which, as he well knew, Cornwall played a crucial part. Although Ranulf's interpretation enjoyed prominence in the many medieval Latin manuscripts of the *Polychronicon*, Caxton's 1482 printed edition of the English *Polychronicon* ensured that Trevisa's view would reach a much larger English audience and, together with the *Brut* chronicle, help to map the outlines of a unified English national identity.[40]

---

[40] For the relationship of printed editions of the *Polychronicon* and the *Brut*, see Lister Matheson, 'Printer and Scribe: Caxton, the *Polychronicon*, and the *Brut*', *Speculum* xl (1985), pp. 593–614. See also Edward Donald Kennedy, ed., *Chronicles and Other Historical Writing* (A Manual of the Writings in Middle English 1050–1500, viii, Hamden, 1989). For background information on William Caxton, see Seth Lerer, 'William Caxton', *The Cambridge History of Medieval English Literature*, ed. David Wallace (Cambridge, 1999), pp. 720–38. For Caxton's own ideas and ambitions for his edition of the *Polychronicon*, see his prohemye to the chronicle, which is reproduced in *The Prologues and Epilogues of William Caxton*, ed. W. J. B. Crotch (Early English Text Society, os, clxxvi, London, 1928).

EDWARD THE BLACK PRINCE AND EAST ANGLIA:
AN UNLIKELY ASSOCIATION

David Green

As his titles suggest, Edward the Black Prince, earl of Chester, duke of Cornwall, prince of Wales and Aquitaine, lord of Vizcaya and Castro Urdiales, did not have great landed estates in East Anglia. Yet it was from there, and particularly from Norfolk, that he drew a significant number of his affinity: well over fifty individuals, and among them some of the key members of his administration and military retinue.

Through the 'foreign manors' associated with the prince's demesne lands, particularly those of the duchy of Cornwall, estates were held throughout the country, including East Anglia. The most significant of these had previously been the honor of Eye, but this had passed to the Ufford earls of Suffolk with whom the prince was to establish close links. The prince's interests in the region were not extensive and his chief Norfolk estate did not come under his full control until 1358. It was then, with the death of his grandmother, Isabella, that the prince acquired Castle Rising and a share of the associated tollbooth at Lynn.[1] Neither the valor which was completed on the prince's death nor his inquisition post mortem indicate any other holdings in Norfolk,[2] although his marriage to Joan of Kent did provide their joint estate with property in Ormsby, two manors in Suffolk and various rights and holdings in Essex.[3] The limited nature of the prince's territorial interests is also indicated by the fact that the keepers of his fees in Norfolk and Suffolk always worked in a variety of counties and not always nearby.[4]

In the church of St Margaret in King's Lynn is a misericord on which is carved

---

[1]   John Berneye took control of Castle Rising, following Isabella's death, on 28 August 1358: *BPR*, IV, p. 261. Soon after this, Berneye was appointed steward of all the prince's lands in Norfolk at a wage of £5 a year, 1 October 1358: ibid., IV, p. 263.

[2]   PRO, C 47/9/57; *CIPM 1377–84*, pp. 67–77. The prince also had interests at East Carleton and briefly took control of Hunstanton manor after the death of Hamon le Strange in 1361 since it was held of Castle Rising and for which the family assumed certain garrison responsibilities at the castle: *CPR 1358–61*, 159; *BPR*, IV, pp. 408, 411–12, 422, 432; *Feudal Aids*, III, p. 640. The family, a cadet branch of Le Strange of Knockin, Shropshire, also held land at Ringstead and Holme-next-the-Sea in Norfolk. For further details see Hamon le Strange, *Le Strange Records, AD 1100–1310* (London, 1916); *Complete Peerage*, XII, i, pp. 343–5, 354–5.

[3]   *CIPM 1384–92*, pp. 110–11, 113–14. The bulk of her lands were in Lincolnshire. In addition, on the death of Thomas Sandwich, the purveyor of the prince's household, in 1360/1 the prince acquired further landed interests in Essex as Thomas had been in debt to the prince, 15 May 1361: *CCR 1360–4*, p. 188. For a description of these see *CIM 1348–77*, pp. 138–9.

[4]   Thomas Stanydelf also had responsibilities in Oxford and Berkshire and Richard Stratton worked in Oxfordshire and eight other counties. He was, in addition, a feodary of Wallingford and a bachelor of common law. See *BPR*, IV, pp. 258, 374, 414, etc.; A. B. Emden, *A Biographical Register of the University of Cambridge to 1500* (Cambridge, 1963), p. 562; Noel Denholm-Young, *The Country Gentry in the Fourteenth Century* (Oxford, 1969), pp. 126–7.

the arms of the prince of Wales and of the duke of Brittany (who received Castle Rising after the Black Prince's death), between which is the face of an unspecified royal figure, presumably Edward III. For the clergy and congregation of St Margaret's at least, the prince was or had been a significant presence. For the local aristocracy he was also an important figure, but by virtue of his status and not because of the property that he held in the region.[5]

It may be the case that the answer to the question of the presence of a large number of East Anglians in the Black Prince's retinue is self-evident, and based on two elements. First, the socio-economic climate: the region was prosperous[6] and yet comparatively free from dominating and domineering political and tenurial influence – although many men of some substance held land in the county.[7] Norfolk and Suffolk were both populous counties. Suffolk had 58,610 adults in 1377, including about 2,500 in Bury and some 1,500 in Ipswich. Only Yorkshire, Lincolnshire and Norfolk itself exceeded this number. There was also a weak manorial system, a high proportion of free men and, in some parts of Suffolk, a system of partible inheritance that meant more opportunities for possession of land. The growth of the cloth industry added to the economic and social dynamism of the area: some of the chief centres of cloth production, Hadleigh and Lavenham, were close to Joan of Kent's manors of Leyham and Kersey.[8] Secondly, there was the status of Edward of Woodstock himself: the Black Prince was the heir apparent and may have had a disproportionate influence over matters of political recruitment after Crécy and, particularly, after his own great victory at Poitiers.[9] However, if this latter point is accepted as a partial explanation of the prince's influence in the region, further consideration is needed both of the structure of the Black Prince's retinue (and its relationship to existing models of aristocratic retaining through bastard feudalism) and of the perennial questions of the nature and importance of the county community.

East Anglia in the fourteenth century, then, seems to have been as good a place as any to seek retainers, but not an area over which it was easy to exercise great political influence. In part, this was due to some aspects of what can be called a county/regional community. Certainly 'the structure of private authority in the

---

[5]   The area had been, and remained, a focus for the acquisition of ships and supplies for military expeditions. Edward II and Edward III relied on Norfolk to supply garrisons on the Scottish border and Yarmouth was particularly important for the arrest of ships in 1355: PRO, E 101/36/20; A. Saul, 'Great Yarmouth and the Hundred Years War in the Fourteenth Century', *BIHR* lii (1979), p. 109. The town again supplied vessels for the Rheims expedition of 1359–60 and for Robert Knolles' campaign in 1370.

[6]   For example, Great Yarmouth, in 1334 was only behind London, York, Bristol and Newcastle in terms of tax valuation, although it suffered disruption to its trade and fishing activities in the war and as a consequence of the plague: Saul, 'Great Yarmouth', pp. 105–6.

[7]   Simon Walker, *The Lancastrian Affinity, 1361–1399* (Oxford, 1990), p. 182; Roger Virgoe, 'The Crown and Local Government: East Anglia under Richard II', *The Reign of Richard II*, ed. F. R. H. Du Boulay and C. M. Barron (London, 1971), pp. 225–6.

[8]   Roger Virgoe, 'The Government and Society of Suffolk in the Later Middle Ages', *Lowestoft Archaeological and Local History Society* (1967–8), pp. 28–9.

[9]   Indentured retainers numbered only 21, but included the Norfolk men Baldwin Freville and Thomas Gissing as well as those with limited connections such as Nigel Loryng, Aubrey Vere and possibly Baldwin Bereford. Annuitants from Norfolk included John Bintree, Thomas Felton, Stephen Hales, James Audley, Baldwin Botetourt and Edmund Wauncy. See David S. Green, 'The Military Personnel of Edward the Black Prince', *Medieval Prosopography* xxi (2000), pp. 149–52, to which should be added Henry Eam and Richard Abberbury among the prince's life retainers.

region – the local sources of power and patronage – . . . is particularly difficult to define for East Anglia'.[10] The major landholders of the twelfth century, the Warennes, Bigods, Aubignys and Clares, had been swept aside and replaced by a fluid structure of landholding and authority at the highest level. The Bigod estates descended via the Seagraves to the Mowbrays. The estates of Thomas Brotherton were fragmented until 1382 when they came into the hands of Margaret Marshal. The honor of Clare passed via the Burghs to Lionel of Clarence and then to the Mortimers.[11] This lacuna was filled somewhat by the Uffords of Suffolk,[12] and the earls of March and Oxford, who all held sizeable estates in the region although without wielding great political influence. (Ecclesiastical lordship was particularly important in the region: the bishop of Norwich, the abbot of Ramsey, the bishop and prior of Ely and the abbot of Bury St Edmunds were also considerable landowners in the region.)[13] Robert, Thomas and William Ufford, Roger Mortimer, and John and Aubrey de Vere were all closely associated with the prince. Robert Ufford was titular head of the prince's council and a close military associate and Aubrey Vere received a sizeable annuity from the prince. The Bourchiers and Willoughbys also had large estates, and there were several influential gentry families such as the Carbonnels and Waldegraves who had links to the prince. Power and prestige were therefore 'more widely dispersed . . . than in many counties: there were many gentry families and large numbers of substantial freemen'.[14]

One of the key figures colouring the geopolitical complexion of Norfolk in the later fourteenth century was John of Gaunt, duke of Lancaster, who held extensive lands and liberties in the north of the county and, like his brother, drew on the area for many members of his affinity. As Helen Castor has demonstrated 'John of Gaunt . . . show[ed] little appetite for the challenge of establishing his rule in Norfolk, preferring instead to exploit his East Anglian revenues to support his political activities elsewhere. During the late fourteenth century therefore, the Lancastrian presence in the region . . . took the form of a disparate collection of retainers whose allegiance was not . . . exclusive, and whose local influence as a coherent and identi-

---

[10] Virgoe, 'Crown and Local Government', p. 225.

[11] In 1312 Edward II granted the Bigod estates to Thomas Brotherton (d.1338). These passed to his widow, Mary, and on her death in 1362 to her granddaughter, Joan Montague, wife of William Ufford, and on the latter's death in 1382 to Margaret, eldest daughter and heiress of Brotherton. Margaret died at Framlingham in 1399. *Medieval Framlingham: Select Documents, 1270–1524*, ed. John Rigard (Woodbridge, 1985), pp. 4–5. For further details see Rowena E. Archer, 'The Estates and Finances of Margaret of Brotherton, c. 1320–1399', *Historical Research* lx (1987), pp. 264–80. Margaret also held estates in Wales and the Marches. In 1353 she married Walter Manny, a military associate of the Black Prince and one of a large number of Hainaulters who were linked to him, mainly through to the influence of Queen Philippa. There was a strong Flemish/Hainaulter presence in Norfolk at this time, which may have developed after 1326 when a worsted manufactory was established in North Walsham. It contributed to the rebellion of Geoffrey Lister in 1381 in which Thomas Gissing, son of the prince's feofee, was involved and the rebels seized the lords Scales and Morley, and Stephen Hales in Norwich: *VCH: Norfolk*, II, pp. 481–3.

[12] Virgoe, 'Crown and Local Government', p. 225 n. 27.

[13] *CIPM 1391–99*, pp. 431–2, 439–43. John Fordham, the prince's secretary, clerk of his privy seal and executor of his will, had interests in Norfolk and was bishop of Ely, 1388–1426: PRO, E 101/398/5; David S. Green, 'The Household and Military Retinue of Edward the Black Prince' (unpublished PhD thesis, University of Nottingham, 1998), Appendix.

[14] Virgoe, 'Government and Society of Suffolk', pp. 29–30.

FIGURE 1. Norfolk members of the Black Prince's retinue and close associates

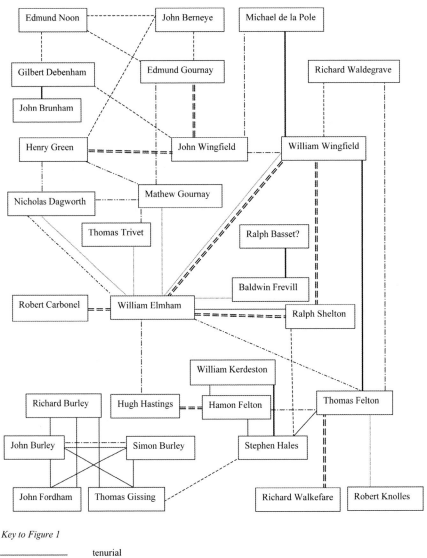

Key to Figure 1

———————	tenurial
··························	common military service
- - - - - - - - -	common administrative/governmental service
—··—··—··—··—	common diplomatic service
= = = = = =	legal associations
—·—·—·—·—·—	family ties
—··—··—··—··—	common service in affinity (before/after the Black Prince)
———————	other

fiable group was, at most, occasional.'[15] This bears considerable similarity with the apparent attitude of the Black Prince, except that he had a very small territorial base from which to start.

The prince's lands did not compare in size with those of his brother or indeed of many other lesser magnates in the region. The Lancastrian inheritance in Norfolk produced an annual income of just over £900. The lands of Richard Fitzalan (II), earl of Arundel, were valued at £200 in the 1390s. In the early fifteenth century, Michael de la Pole received around £500 from his East Anglian estates. The Mowbray family was the most significant landholder in Norfolk and Suffolk by the 1390s, and the dowager countess Margaret received £1,400 from these estates.[16] Castle Rising provided the Black Prince with just over £100 per year, but it appears that his rank and authority at court outweighed his limited tenurial influence.[17] As Nigel Saul has said: 'a magnate of national importance . . . could command the support of retainers in every county, many of them among the most substantial knights in the locality'.[18]

The case of the Black Prince, however, was somewhat special. Edward had benefited from his father's largesse in terms of land, but these estates were not areas heavily endowed with significant members of the nobility. Cheshire had a strong regional identity among the aristocracy but its members tended not to be individuals of high standing. This was also true of Cornwall. Although by no means deliberate, it did mean that the Black Prince had to recruit in parts of the country distant from where he held land since there were few members of the higher nobility who could be relied on to bring their own retainers within a greater affinity. With the benefit of hindsight, this can also be seen as rather beneficial. In those areas where the prince's lands did touch on those of important landholders, such as along the Welsh marches and in the principality of Aquitaine, there tended to be friction, which in the latter case led to open revolt and the reignition of the war with France in 1368–9.[19]

The representation of the prince's retinue in East Anglia was formed not only of vertical alliances but also of horizontal associations, and reflects the 'multi-directional currents of local society'.[20] Figure 1 is a crude means of showing some of these associations. It is based upon tenurial, military, financial and friendship links.[21] While it remains the case that '[e]xcept for certain members of the Paston circle and Margery Kempe very little is known about the private lives of even the

---

[15] Helen Castor, 'The Duchy of Lancaster and the Rule of East Anglia, 1399–1440: A Prologue to the Paston Letters', *Crown, Government and People in the Fifteenth Century*, ed. Rowena Archer (Stroud, 1995), p. 55; Walker, *Lancastrian Affinity*, pp. 182–209.

[16] *CIPM 1391–9*, p. 971; Walker, *Lancastrian Affinity*, pp. 183–4; K.B. McFarlane, *The Nobility of Later Medieval England* (Oxford, 1973), pp. 138–9.

[17] PRO, C 47/9/57 (1376 valor) (£90 [Rising], £26 13s 4d [Lynn tollbooth]); E. L. T. John, 'The Parliamentary Representation of Norfolk and Suffolk, 1377–1422' (unpublished MA thesis, University of Nottingham, 1959), pp. 22–3.

[18] Nigel Saul, *Knights and Esquires: The Gloucester Gentry in the Fourteenth Century* (Oxford, 1981), p. 258.

[19] See David Green, *The Black Prince* (Stroud, 2001), pp. 104–8 and references.

[20] Joel T. Rosenthal, 'Some Late Medieval and Mid-Tudor Norfolk MPs: Compare and Contrast', *Parliamentary History* xviii (1999), p. 295.

[21] 'Friendship in the fifteenth century, both in theory and practice involved a range of connections, material and spiritual, between tightly-knit groups of neighbours who might be chosen without regard to their social standing.' Philippa Maddern, ' "Best Trusted Friends": Concepts and Patterns of Friendship Among Fifteenth-Century Norfolk Gentry', *England in the Fifteenth Century*, ed. Nicholas Rogers (Stamford, 1994), p. 115.

most notable figures of late medieval Norfolk',[22] their public careers are more transparent. John Wingfield, William's cousin from Suffolk, was steward of the prince's lands and his business manager. John Brunham was chamberlain of Chester. Baldwin Freville was one of the prince's few life retainers. Thomas Felton, steward of the household, seneschal of Aquitaine and chamberlain of Chester, had manors at Litcham and elsewhere in Norfolk and his family was influential in the county.[23] Hales and Hamon Felton, Sir Thomas's elder brother, were returned to the first parliament of 1377, and Thomas was re-elected in the following October. In the retinue there was also a Duncan Felton who travelled to Aquitaine to join the prince in November 1367, although he may well have been from the Northumbrian branch of the family.[24] William Kerdeston the elder was a knight banneret of the household; his son was one of the Norfolk shire knights in 1378 and sat in the next eight parliaments.[25] Stephen Hales, Thomas Gissing, William Elmham and Edmund Noon were among the prince's retainers and annuitants.[26] Gissing sat for Norfolk in the Good Parliament. Elmham was witness to a quitclaim involving William Wingfield in 1377 and in 1380 both were part of a group who received a charter concerning a number of Norfolk manors. Wingfield acted as one of Elmham's attorneys when he went on crusade in 1383 and in 1386 both men witnessed a charter and served on a commission of array in Suffolk.[27] Edmund Noon, who fought in the rearguard action in Aquitaine and received an annuity from the prince in 1371, was sheriff of Norfolk and Suffolk in 1354–5.[28] Robert Carbonel, knight of the shire for Suffolk in the parliament of October 1385, was the half-brother of John Wingfield. On 30 August 1380, Carbonel made an enfeoffment of his lands and his feoffees included William Elmham and William Wingfield.[29] John Berneye, a yeoman of the prince, was steward of his lands in Norfolk as well as MP for Norfolk on four occasions between 1346 and 1368 and held land at Great Witchingham.[30] He acted on a number of royal commissions until December 1370.[31] In these cases he often acted in association with Edmund Gournay and Edmund Noon, as well as a case in 1359 with Gilbert Debenham, a lawyer on the prince's council, concerning the abbey of Bury St Edmunds that was witnessed by John Wingfield.[32]

---

[22] Roger Virgoe, 'The Divorce of Thomas Tuddenham', *Norfolk Archaeology* xxxiv (1969), p. 406.

[23] *CIPM 1377–84*, pp. 140–1.

[24] *CPR 1367–70*, p. 56.

[25] *BPR*, I, p. 80; *CIPM*, XI, pp. 72–8; John, 'Parliamentary Representation', p. 413; *Complete Peerage*, VII, p. 191.

[26] Elmham used his local knowledge and contacts while recruiting for Despenser's crusade, which also involved the prince's associates Thomas Trivet, Ralph Shelton and John Aleyn: James Magee, 'Sir William Elmham and the Recruitment for Henry Despenser's Crusade of 1383', *Medieval Prosopography* xx (1999), pp. 181–90.

[27] PRO, C 76/67/8; *CCR 1377–81*, p. 193; *CCR 1385–9*, p. 139; *CCR 1392–6*, p. 236; *CPR 1385–9*, p. 176.

[28] He became an esquire of the prince's chamber and later an esquire of the royal household under Richard II. PRO, E 199/29/25; *CPR 1377–81*, 199; John Roskell, Linda Clarke and C. Rawcliffe, *The House of Commons, 1381–1421* (4 vols, History of Parliament, Stroud, 1993), III, 841–3.

[29] John, 'Parliamentary Representatives', pp. 199–200. Carbonel was also a counsellor and annuitant of Margaret, duchess of Norfolk, and she was granted the wardship of his heir in 1397. Archer, 'Estates and Finances of Margaret of Brotherton', pp. 277 n. 92, 280.

[30] *BPR*, IV, pp. 261, 263; Roskell, Clark and Rawcliffe, *House of Commons*, II, p. 208; John, 'Parliamentary Representation', pp. 158–9.

[31] *CIM 1348–77*, 5–7, pp. 84, 123–5, 168, 285, 287.

[32] *CPR 1370–4*, pp. 106, 305; *CIM 1348–77*, p. 116. There were a succession of individuals named

A number of other associates had ties to East Anglia. Robert Knolles, the Cheshire-born *condotierre*, held Sculthorpe manor in Norfolk and was also the chief benefactor to Harpley church in the same county. The earl of Arundel was a close military and financial associate who lent considerable sums to the prince, as well as his wife and assorted members of his retinue.[33] Bartholomew Burghersh married the daughter of Richard Weyland of Fenhall and the Botetourts, Seagraves, Dagworths and Despensers, families with representatives in the prince's retinue, all had estates in Norfolk and Suffolk.[34] Ralph Shelton who fought in the Poitiers campaign also had interests in Norfolk, as did Nigel Loryng, the prince's chamberlain, since Henry of Grosmont, his former employer, had granted him an annuity there.[35]

As well as Thomas Felton, East Anglians were responsible for the administration of the prince's estates in Cheshire, Wales and Aquitaine. Mathew Gournay became seneschal of Landes. Robert Paris, the prince's chamberlain of North Wales and constable of Caernarfon castle, came from Cambridgeshire;[36] John Bintree, another Norfolk man, was constable of Chester and Rhuddlan.[37] Bintree had served Sir Walter Manny in a number of campaigns including the Brittany expedition of 1342–3.[38] Manny himself was sheriff and had near autonomy in Merioneth, adjacent to the principality of Wales; he married Countess Margaret, the widow of John, lord Seagrave, and daughter of Thomas Brotherton, earl of Norfolk.[39] Miles Stapleton married Joan, the widow of Roger le Strange of Knockin (d.1349) and daughter of Oliver Ingham, the former lieutenant of Gascony.

With the full acquisition of Castle Rising after Queen Isabella's death, the prince inherited a number of his grandmother's servants, some of who also had links to the late earl of Kent, the Fair Maid's former husband. He also acquired tenants of the estate and had responsibilities to those who received grants dependent upon it and the Lynn tollbooth.[40] For example, John Carleton, one of the prince's yeomen, was granted, with John Lancaster, all the lands in Chosley, Norfolk, which formerly had been held by Robert Holewell, later to be the sheriff of Caernarfon.[41] Carleton was

---

Gilbert Debenham in the fourteenth and early fifteenth centuries. Gilbert I (d.c.1369) also served Robert Ufford and John Wingfield. Roskell, Clark and Rawcliffe, *House of Commons*, II, pp. 760–1; Walter Debenham Sweeting, *A Record of the Family of Debenham of Suffolk* (London, 1909), p. 67.

[33] Fitzalan had land at Litcham, Dunham, Thetford, Bittering and Mileham. The last of these was significant since it controlled the road between Norwich and Lynn. Peter Wade-Martins, 'Norfolk Village Sites in Launditch Hundred', *East Anglian Archaeology* x (1980), pp. 42–3, 46. The west window of Mileham church, probably commissioned by Arundel in 1342, is one of the most important examples of fourteenth-century glass in the county.

[34] *VCH: Suffolk*, II, pp. 169–70, 172.

[35] *CCR 1354–60*, p. 334; Walker, *Lancastrian Affinity*, p. 185 and n. 18.

[36] He had been appointed by 4 September 1358: *BPR*, III, p. 307.

[37] Ibid., IV, p. 10; *CPR 1354–8*, p. 492.

[38] In this he lost one horse valued at 40 marks. Andrew Ayton, *Knights and Warhorses: Military Service and the English Aristocracy Under Edward III* (Woodbridge, 1994), pp. 240–1.

[39] *CPR 1343–5*, p. 113. He also held the manors of Stiffky and Holkham in Norfolk: *CPR 1340–3*, p. 333.

[40] *BPR*, IV, p. 81, 143, 375. On 18 February 1363, Reginald Hokere, yeoman of the chamber, was given a life grant of the water of Wiggenhall, Norfolk: *BPR*, IV, p. 486.

[41] 15 July 1358: *BPR*, IV, p. 259. Carleton had been resident in Norfolk for some time prior to this: *CPR 1354–8*, p. 391. He also purchased Iklingham manor, Suffolk, for £100, 1 August 1362: *BPR*, IV, pp. 461, 465, 469, 481–2, 550.

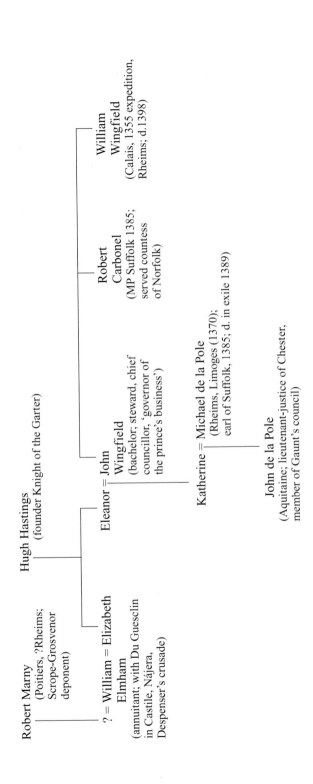

FIGURE 2. The Wingfield-de la Pole network and its service to the Black Prince

Robert Marny
(Poitiers, ?Rheims;
Scrope-Grosvenor
deponent)

Hugh Hastings
(founder Knight of the Garter)

? = William = Elizabeth
Elmham
(annuitant; with Du Guesclin
in Castile, Nájera,
Despenser's crusade)

Eleanor = John
Wingfield
(bachelor; steward, chief
councillor, 'governor of
the prince's business')

Robert
Carbonel
(MP Suffolk 1385;
served countess
of Norfolk)

William
Wingfield
(Calais, 1355 expedition,
Rheims; d.1398)

Katherine = Michael de la Pole
(Rheims, Limoges (1370);
earl of Suffolk, 1385; d. in exile 1389)

John de la Pole
(Aquitaine; lieutenant-justice of Chester,
member of Gaunt's council)

later granted a life annuity of £5, rising to £10, from the Lynn tollbooth, perhaps in connection with his responsibilities for auditing the Castle Rising accounts.[42] He may have been the same man who illuminated the charter granting Edward the principality of Aquitaine, and became clerk of the prince's privy seal and treasurer of Aquitaine.[43]

The estate also provided further patronage, ecclesiastical and secular, which in some cases changed hands regularly. John Rougham was presented to Rising church on 27 October 1361[44] and replaced by William Langham of Wighton soon after.[45] The prince maintained various officials in their positions, including the receiver of the lordship who was responsible for various repairs and the enclosure of the park at Rising.[46] The constable[47] and the surveyor of the chase were also retained. Both had links to the late earl of Kent and the latter was in receipt of an £8 annuity from him that was confirmed by Edward.[48] Baldwin Botetourt, master of the prince's horses and a member of his bodyguard at Poitiers, was later given a life commission to keep the chase,[49] and Richard Walkefare was granted the same office in 1362.[50] Walkefare was Thomas Felton's father-in-law, and it may have been this connection that ensured that he acquired the position as well as becoming a bachelor of the prince's household.[51]

In general, recruitment to the prince's retinue is something of a 'grey area', but it appears that in Norfolk one way by which this was undertaken was through kinship groups. In some instances mutual service to the prince can be observed within an extended family and over a number of generations. For example, the de la Pole and Wingfield families were closely associated and both contributed representatives to the prince's retinue (Figure 2). Similarly, the Le Strange family had some associations with the Black Prince, despite being more closely linked to John of Gaunt.[52] John, son of Hamon, married Eleanor, daughter of Richard Walkefare, and thus became Thomas Felton's brother-in-law (Figure 3).

---

[42] His wages for 24 April–15 August 1362 were £11 8s: *BPR*, IV, p. 474. He was given £10 to be deducted from the rent of Iklingham on 9 May 1364: *BPR*, IV, p. 527.

[43] *BPR*, IV, pp. 484, 502.

[44] Ibid., IV, p. 400. He was later presented to Henton Wallery church, the advowson of which the prince held through the minority of the heir of the earl of Northampton: ibid., IV, pp. 430–1.

[45] Ibid., IV, p. 443.

[46] Philip Pinchon was in office by 1 October 1358: ibid., IV, p. 264. He arranged the 'sure and safe keeping of the castle in consultation with Roger de Saham', the constable, on 14 February 1360. Repairs were made to the bridge, other areas and the castle on 26 March 1360 and 9 August 1362. £81 1s 2d was spent repairing a tower at Rising called 'Nightegale' on 8 July 1365. Ibid., IV, pp. 344, 346, 463, 471, 552, 559. The gate-keeper, Robert Carlel, probably also retained his office: ibid., IV, p. 344. Additionally, Thomas Stirston had been granted 4d a day by Isabella, which, at her request, the prince extended to a life grant: *CCR 1354–60*, p. 549.

[47] Robert Flemming was granted 6s 3d rent for good service to Isabella: *BPR*, IV, p. 304.

[48] John Herlyng was granted the office by Isabella on 6 November 1352 and it was ratified on 21 July 1353: ibid., IV, p. 98. He became usher of the king's chamber. The annuity was paid from Ormsby manor, Norfolk: ibid., IV, p. 460.

[49] Ibid., IV, p. 270. For details of Botetourt's career see Green, 'Household and Military Retinue', Appendix.

[50] *BPR*, IV, p. 470. He was replaced soon after by Simon del Hay, former forester of the estate, who in turn lost the office before being reinstated on 3 May 1365: ibid., IV, pp. 471, 492, 552.

[51] Felton named Walkefare as his attorney in the same year: *CPR 1361–4*, p. 232.

[52] John, 'Parliamentary Representation', pp. 588–99.

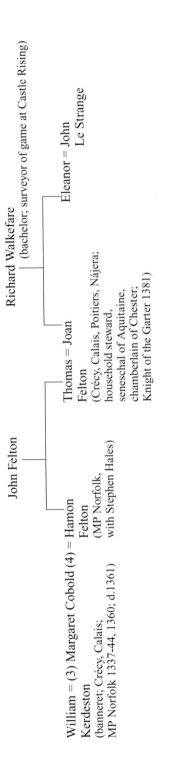

FIGURE 3. The Felton-Le Strange network and its service to the Black Prince

John Felton

Richard Walkefare
(bachelor; surveyor of game at Castle Rising)

William = (3) Margaret Cobold (4) = Hamon
Kerdeston   Felton
(banneret; Crécy, Calais;   (MP Norfolk,
MP Norfolk 1337-44, 1360; d.1361) with Stephen Hales)

Thomas = Joan
Felton
(Crécy, Calais, Poitiers, Nájera;
household steward,
seneschal of Aquitaine,
chamberlain of Chester;
Knight of the Garter 1381)

Eleanor = John
             Le Strange

Family ties underpinned the county community and such regional associations were also represented in other ways. A further Le Strange-Felton association can be seen in the grant of Tottingham manor by John to the prioress of Campsey Ash, Mary Felton. John was also closely acquainted with other members of the prince's retinue, including Ralph Shelton and Robert Ufford, the latter, among others, being appointed as his trustee in 1390.[53] One of Ufford's most significant areas of ecclesiastical interest and patronage was Campsey and he established close familial ties there.[54] In this manner, ecclesiastical and monastic patronage could also be indicative of county/regional sympathies. Thomas Felton and his wife, Joan Walkefare, were benefactors to Walsingham priory. Their feoffees, amongst who was Stephen Hales, granted two manors and an advowson in return for a chantry in which the priests were to celebrate masses for the prince, Joan, Thomas, and others. Hales himself also founded a chantry at Walsingham and Bartholomew Burghersh junior was buried there.[55] Common patronage of institutions is also evident in heraldry such as that above the west door at Salle church, Norfolk, which bears the Ufford, Morley and Kerdeston arms, although these commemorated later fourteenth- and fifteenth-century alliances. The glass in the east window also contains the quartered arms of Wingfield and de la Pole, and has been dated between 1415 and 1441. Particular chapels might be used to represent and reproduce bonds of friendship and mutual interest and this might also be demonstrated through gifts of vestments. If these were richly coloured and/or embroidered and used for the most important festivals, then at the focal point of such ceremonies would be the colours and heraldry of the donors. This was particularly significant in the context of the imposition of the sumptuary laws: such vestments would be all the more dazzling in comparison with the drab attire of the lower classes.[56]

It is clear that the prince took advantage of regional networks and the influence that they might exert from time to time. This is most clearly seen in commissions of various types that suggest a high level of self-interest being exercised by certain members of the local aristocracy. For example, in 1358 a commission of oyer and terminer demanded by the prince was given to John Wingfield, Robert Thorpe, Henry Green, Thomas St Omer, John Knyvet and John Berneye; all were directly or indirectly associated with the prince and could be assured to care for his interests.[57] Such commissions were not uncommon and were made all the more likely by the local knowledge and influence of the men who undertook them.

Such people were important since, despite the influence of certain magnates, local politics was dictated by local men. Roger Virgoe analysed this governing coterie in Norfolk during the reign of Richard II by examining the holders of the offices of sheriff, escheator, knight of the shire and other assorted commissions. This included a significant number of men who had links with the prince or who

---

[53] *CCR*, 1389–92, pp. 331–2.
[54] Roberta Gilchrist and Marilyn Oliva, *Religious Women in Medieval East Anglia* (Norwich, 1993), pp. 58–9, 62. Edmund Ufford made various grants to Campsey and was buried there as were many of the family: NRO, Norwich Consistory Court, Heydon register, fol. 93; *CPR 1358–61*, pp. 28, 295.
[55] Benjamin Thompson, 'The Church and Aristocracy: Lay and Ecclesiastical Landowning Society in Fourteenth Century Norfolk' (unpublished PhD thesis, University of Cambridge, 1989), pp. 147–8.
[56] C. Pamela-Graves, *The Form and Fabric of Belief: An Archaeology of the Lay Experience of Religion in Medieval Norfolk and Devon* (British Archaeological Reports cccxi, Oxford, 2000), pp. 85, 93, 100.
[57] *CPR 1358–61*, p. 159. See also *CPR 1361–4*, pp. 64, 205, 285, 529; *CPR 1374–7*, p. 138.

descended from men who had fought and served alongside him, such as the lords Morley, Scales and Willoughby and the knights William Elmham, Robert Knolles, Stephen Hales and Ralph Shelton. During the prince's lifetime, John Berneye, the steward of his lands in Norfolk and elsewhere, was regularly returned to the commissions of the peace, and other retinue members served as justices for short periods. Additionally some Norfolk retinue members served on commissions in nearby counties such as Thomas Gissing in Cambridgeshire and Thomas St Omer was justice of the peace and sheriff of both Norfolk and Suffolk.[58]

Parliamentary representation may also be used as a measure of the strength of a county community and also of the degree of magnate influence. Joel Rosenthal has, through an examination of MPs between 1386 and 1422, argued in favour both of the value of the concept of the county community as a tool of analysis and also of its influence over society in Norfolk. Among parliamentary representatives of the county there were, he states, 'innumerable . . . lines of networking'.[59] During the years of the prince's majority, members of the retinue represented the county on eight occasions, notably in the case of John Berneye from 1346 until the Good Parliament of 1376. In the prince's retinue, this pattern of domination of local elections was only surpassed by Shropshire, Herefordshire and the borough of Lostwithiel, all areas within or adjacent to the prince's demesne. (Wales and Chester, of course, did not return members to parliament.) The Suffolk knights of the shire were on five occasions associated with the prince in the same period, principally Edmund Wauncy, the prince's household steward, councillor and bachelor, and William Wingfield (although by the 1370s his loyalties lay with John of Gaunt).[60]

After the prince's death, Edmund Noon, Stephen Hales and Nicholas Dagworth also represented Norfolk, and Ralph Shelton and Edmund Thorpe can be added to Rosenthal's list of former Black Prince retainers, in addition perhaps to Hugh Fastolf.[61] However, there is no great evidence of royal pressure to influence parliamentary elections during Richard II's reign and these links were not unique or exclusive: for example the lords Morley were also associated with Noon, Hales and Fastolf.[62] Nonetheless, it is noteworthy that Richard II turned to Norfolk, as he was

---

[58] See, e.g., *CPR 1354–8*, pp. 227, 388, 554; *CPR 1361–4*, pp. 64, 285, 529. The St Omer family were from Mulbarton near Norwich.

[59] Rosenthal, 'Some Late Medieval and Mid-Tudor Norfolk MPs', p. 292 n. 5

[60] Borough of Bishop's Lynn: John Brunham, 1 May 1368. Norfolk: John Berneye, 11 September 1346, 14 January 1348, 17 April 1357, 1 May 1368; Thomas Gissing, 12 February 1376, 26 April 1376; Richard Walkefare, 5 February 1358. Suffolk: Edmund Wauncy, 6 October 1363, 20 January 1365, 4 May 1366; William Wingfield, 12 February 1376, 28 April 1376. David S. Green, 'Politics and Service with Edward the Black Prince', *The Age of Edward III*, ed. James Bothwell (York, 2001), pp. 62–5. Wingfield (seven times knight for Suffolk between 1378 and 1386) was also closely acquainted with William Ufford and Michael de la Pole: Virgoe, 'Crown and Local Government', p. 231.

[61] Fastolf is said to have been authorised to supply the prince's family, then living in Norfolk, with fish in 1356. This is rather peculiar since the prince was then in Gascony with much of his household to which the entry must refer since he was yet to marry. Fastolf was closely linked with other retainers and servants of the prince such as Lewis Clifford, Thomas Felton and Richard Stury. Roskell, Clark and Rawcliffe, *House of Commons*, III, pp. 55–9.

[62] Rosenthal, 'Some Late Medieval and Mid-Tudor Norfolk MPs', pp. 291–4 and nn. 5, 9. Robert Carbonel and William Berard (steward of the prince's lands in Norfolk and Suffolk and a manor in Essex from 3 June 1363) acted as JPs in 1383. Berard also became escheator of Norfolk and Suffolk. He was involved in an inquisition *ad quod damnum* concerning the younger William Kerdeston and a land grant

later to look to Cheshire, for support in the crisis of 1386 (a crisis which itself focused in part on a number of Norfolk and Suffolk men, including Dagworth, Elmham, Henry Green and Michael de la Pole). The call was largely ignored, and, apart from one or two well-known exceptions such as Simon Felbrigg, the king did not look to the region during his later campaigns of recruitment.[63]

It might be assumed, as has been observed in other parts of the country, that administrative, political and judicial duties in the county would be undertaken after a career of military service had provided individuals with the necessary status and perhaps the financial wherewithal. However, it should also be noted that this was a time of expanding opportunities for the lesser aristocracy, at least in terms of career options, and glory on the battlefield was not the only way to make a mark in society. Certainly in Norfolk between 1386 and 1421 'election to parliament came at no fixed time in a public career'.[64]

What was a 'Norfolk man'? How concentrated did property have to be in the county? Where else might an individual hold property, or from where might he receive rewards or annuities and still be considered a member of the local community? At what point did one's interests outside the area outweigh one's concerns within the county? Nicholas Dagworth, for example, came from a family with interests mainly in Suffolk and Essex. More particularly, John Chandos held the manor of Beccles but can hardly be considered to be a Norfolk man. This is a particular issue among those who served with the prince. If they fought alongside him, they fought in France or Castile. If they served in his administration or household or his chapels, unless they were at Castle Rising, they were in Chester, Wales, Aquitaine, Cornwall or in the prince's residences in and around London. They were not in East Anglia.

The wills of some of the protagonists are still extant, although they are not, in most cases, in good condition. What can be gleaned from this evidence is that, at least in testamentary terms, the East Anglian members of the Black Prince's retinue were not close. No other members of the retinue are mentioned in the wills of Thomas Gissing, Robert Carbonnel or John Berneye;[65] and while Ralph Shelton nominated William Wingfield as his executor in 1375, by this time Wingfield's association with the prince had ended.[66] Wingfield had been brought into the retinue through the influence of Baldwin Botetourt (d.1360) and John Wingfield (d.1361), and after their deaths he entered the service of the earl of Oxford and then John of

made to the prior and convent of Redlingfield. PRO, E 143/398/16; *BPR*, IV, pp. 496, 523. Morley, Hales and Ralph Shelton were active on various commissions but they were not so closely acquainted with the king that the Appellants saw it as necessary to remove them from the new commission of July 1388 (although Morley and Shelton were not reappointed subsequently): *CPR 1381–5*, p. 244. For the career of Nicholas Dagworth see Roskell, Clark and Rawcliffe, *House of Commons*, II, pp. 733–6; B. S. Capp, 'Sir Nicholas de Dagworth: The Career of a Royal Servant in the Fourteenth Century', *Norfolk Archaeology* xxxiv (1969), pp. 111–18.

63 Walker, *Lancastrian Affinity*, p. 205.

64 Rosenthal, 'Some Late Medieval and Mid-Tudor Norfolk MPs', p. 296.

65 NRO, Heydon register, fols 204–5 (Gissing); Joan Gissing, Thomas' wife, whilst giving £2 to the poor of her town and various other worthy causes, similarly made no mention of members of the late prince's retinue in her will of 1388. NRO, Harsyk register, fol. 101; Harsyk register, fol. 233 (Carbonel); Heydon register, fols 42–3 (Berneye). In Berneye's case this is not surprising since most of John's property and wealth passed to his sons, Thomas and Robert.

66 NRO, Harsyk register, fol 177. Shelton's son, also Ralph, was a feoffee of Joan, widow of Thomas Felton: Roskell, Clark and Rawcliffe, *House of Commons*, IV, 355–7.

Gaunt. There is no indication of retinue members among the beneficiaries or executors of his own will, dated 1398, but the document is badly damaged.[67]

William Elmham's will is also in a very poor condition. However, his wife left a detailed testament in 1419.[68] This notes bequests to individuals and institutions around her home in Westhorpe, Suffolk as well as to broader concerns such as the lepers of Norfolk, Suffolk and Essex and friars in Norfolk, Suffolk and Canterbury. There were also grants to Campsey Ash, and masses were requested for her own soul and William's. By this time, of course, there were few members of the prince's retinue left alive to be represented. Thomas Willoughby, one beneficiary, may have been from the Willoughby d'Ereseby family of Lincolnshire with which the prince was associated. The will does however, emphasise the family ties created either by co-membership of the retinue or independent regional associations or, as seems most likely, a combination of these influences. For example, grants were made to members of the Wingfield family, William and Robert, who were her nephew and cousin respectively. As Simon Walker has said of the Lancastrian affinity, 'Who a . . . retainer married; who witnessed his charters; who executed his testament – these were choices more usually determined by existing local contacts and loyalties than by membership of the . . . affinity.'[69] However, among the prince's retinue in Norfolk and Suffolk, membership of that retinue determined and was determined by local contacts and loyalties.

We may conclude with some pieces of material evidence: the Hastings memorial brass at Elsing in Norfolk, and the now lost Erpingham window in the Austin friary church of St Michael in King's Street, Norwich, both of which at once support and contradict the idea of a county community in Norfolk. The former is much the better known of the two examples and is one of the oldest and most interesting brasses in the country. Although much of it has been lost, rubbings and drawings from the eighteenth century reveal many of the side panels that have been removed in the intervening years.[70] Hastings himself was not directly associated with the prince. He died in 1347, not long after leading a diversionary expedition from Flanders to draw attention away from the *chevauchée* that would conclude at Crécy. He also had links to the Black Prince's retinue, and his daughter, Elizabeth, married William Elmham. His brass, which shows stylistic similarities with stained glass at Ely and the pre-plague East Anglian manuscript tradition, bears images of many of his comrades in arms, including Almaric St Amand, Ralph Stafford, Edward III, Lancaster, Warwick, Pembroke, Despenser and Grey.[71] Although these provide further links to the Black Prince, they are hardly indicative of a tightly knit county community. However, memorial brasses and funerary monuments remain a significant body of evidence, especially in Norfolk: only Kent and Essex have more surviving brass effigies. The memorial to Nicholas Dagworth at Blickling is part of a larger group

---

[67] NRO, Harsyk register, fols 249, 255; Roskell, Clark and Rawcliffe, *House of Commons*, IV, pp. 876–9; Green 'Household and Military Retinue', Appendix.

[68] NRO, Harsyk register, fols 288–9 (William Elmham); Hyrnyng register, fols 56–7 (Elizabeth Elmham).

[69] Walker, *Lancastrian Affinity*, p. 260.

[70] L. Dennison and N. Rogers, 'The Elsing Brass and its East Anglian Connections', *Fourteenth Century England I*, ed. N. Saul (Woodbridge, 2000), pp. 167–93.

[71] Hugh served in the household of Queen Philippa as her steward. It has also been suggested that he wore a wig. Barri Hooper, Stephanie Rickett, Andrew Rogerson and Susan Yaxley, 'The Grave of Sir Hugh de Hastyngs, Elsing', *Norfolk Archaeology* xxxix (1987), pp. 93–6, 98.

that includes armoured tributes to the Stapleton, Shelton and Felbrigg families. It has been suggested that these effigies were products of a set of motives concerned with demonstrating status and a shared cultural ethos, and that they show a cohesive and interrelated class that dominated county administration and provided military service to the crown.[72]

The Erpingham window is attested in Blomefield's *History of Norfolk* of 1805–10. The window was commissioned for the Austin friary church, an institution of some importance since it was chosen as the burial place of Thomas, lord Morley (d.1416).[73] The window is said to have consisted of eight lights, each with ten coats of arms, except the last, which had twelve. The names of the knights (but not their arms) were given, and an identification of both the knight and his blazon has been attempted although there may be difficulties with some of the attributions.[74] Sir Thomas Erpingham commissioned the window in 1419 'in remembrance of all the lords, barons, bannerets and knights, that have died without male issue in the counties of Norfolk and Suffolk, since the coronation of the noble King Edward III^d'.[75] The window included the arms of Robert Ufford, Richard Walkefare, Hamon Felton, Thomas Felton, William Elmham, Robert Knolles, Nicholas Dagworth, Thomas Gissing, Baldwin Botetourt and, more questionably, James Audley, Richard FitzSimon and John Verdon. That there were men with these names among those who fought with the prince (and, in case of Audley, was a close military associate and personal friend) is not in doubt; whether they were those same men is more questionable. Audley appears to have had few direct links to the region but his mother, Eva Clavering, was patron of Langley abbey.[76] This may have been enough in 1419 for him to have been considered a local man with a direct link to the county and perhaps therefore the community. Equally the cachet of including yet another member of the Garter and personal friend of the Black Prince may, with hindsight, have encouraged a tenuous link to be strengthened.

The Black Prince's retinue was, fundamentally, a military community formed by service overseas in a war. These were not the same sort of men that Nigel Saul described when he wrote that '[t]he fourteenth-century knight or rich esquire still lived a life which . . . was bounded by remarkably narrow horizons'.[77] Rather, such horizons could be remarkably expanded as a result of taking service with the Black Prince. Nor, clearly, were these the sorts of men who 'actively avoided magnates, seeking instead the support of close, reciprocal, functional relationships among their

---

[72] The brass to Ralph Shelton (d.1375), lost before the seventeenth century, is known to have carried a crested helm and French inscription: Jonathan Finch, *Church Monuments in Norfolk Before 1850: An Archaeology of Commemoration* (British Archaeological Reports cccxvii, Oxford, 2000), pp. 28, 37, 50–1.

[73] Colin Richmond, 'Thomas Lord Morley (d.1416) and the Morleys of Hingham', *Norfolk Archaeology* xxxix (1987), p. 2.

[74] Ken Mourin, *The Erpingham Window of St Michael at Conisford: The Austin Friary Church* (Norfolk Heraldry Society, Norwich, 2000).

[75] F. Blomefield, *An Essay Towards a Topographical History of the County of Norfolk IV* (London, 1808), pp. 86–8. The tradition continued and a number of knights who died with male children and had £100 per annum also had their arms put up, including members of the Felbrigg, Thorpe, Gerbrigge, Carbonnel and Bardolf families. See also Ken Mourin, 'Norwich, Norfolk and Sir Thomas Erpingham', *Agincourt, 1415*, ed. Anne Curry (Stroud, 2000), pp. 82–3.

[76] Audley petitioned the pope for an indulgence for the abbey: Thompson, 'Church and Aristocracy', p. 121.

[77] Saul, *Knights and Esquires*, p. 257.

neighbours, kin and marriages connections'.[78] However, they may show that such a distinction need not have been absolute. The Black Prince's retinue in East Anglia was a community within a community. It consisted of associations established through common regional landholding, local political interests or membership of the retinue of the Black Prince and reaffirmed by other links. But these associations were not necessarily independent or exclusive. This is a small survey, and associations will inevitably be more apparent between members of a group that worked and fought together. That there was a professional relationship between these men is not in doubt; it is more difficult to ascertain if this was a relationship that went beyond the professional or if it went beyond a shared association with the Black Prince. Perhaps in East Anglia we see two distinct but entwined communities, one linked to the shire and one associated with magnate affinities. In Norfolk, and more particularly in Suffolk, 'the community of the shire did exist but [these were] not simple or monolithic societies'.[79] Added to this, the character of the prince's demesne, the nature of his retinue and the political circumstances of the time created, in the context of his Norfolk retainers at least, an example of bastard feudalism *par excellence* through service in return for reward to a lord whose local territorial interests were little more than negligible.

---

[78] Maddern, 'Concepts and Practices of Friendship', p. 100.
[79] Virgoe, 'Government and Society of Suffolk', p. 30.

WILLIAM WYKEHAM AND THE MANAGEMENT OF
THE WINCHESTER ESTATE, 1366–1404

Mark Page

The bishops of Winchester were among the wealthiest and most powerful lords of medieval England, a position remarked upon by a number of contemporary writers. One fourteenth-century observer, noting the differences between the two cathedrals of Canterbury and Winchester and the wealth that supported them, declared that 'Canterbury hath the finer stable but Winchester the deeper manger'.[1] The bishopric of Winchester was indeed the richest in England throughout the later Middle Ages and on a par with the wealthiest in Europe as a whole. An income of about £4,000 a year in the late thirteenth century comfortably outstripped the £2,600 collected by the archbishop of Canterbury from his estate, or the £2,550 of the bishopric of Ely, or the £1,200 of the bishopric of Worcester.[2] Such great wealth sometimes gave rise to jealousy and suspicion. Matthew Paris worried that, as bishop of Winchester, Aymer de Valence (1250–60) would be 'second to none in England in wealth and power except possibly the king'.[3] Severe criticisms were expressed after the death of John of Pontoise (1282–1304), who was accused of misappropriating the revenues of the estate, at a personal profit of 40,000 marks. It was also said that 12,000 florins were found hidden in the ground next to his bed.[4] In the case of William Wykeham, suggestions of simony were made concerning his appointment, Edward III having made him guardian of the temporalities of the see 'for a certain large sum of money'.[5]

The wealth of the bishops of Winchester derived mainly from their possession of one of the largest and richest estates of medieval England, which extended far beyond the spiritual boundaries of the see. The diocese comprised the counties of Hampshire, including the Isle of Wight, and Surrey. The estate, on the other hand, included lands in a further five southern counties: Berkshire, Buckinghamshire, Oxfordshire, Somerset and Wiltshire (Map 1). Established in c.660, the see of Winchester benefited from its ancient associations with the rulers of Wessex, by whose pious gifts between the seventh and the tenth centuries the bishops acquired

---

[1] J. C. Dickinson, *An Ecclesiastical History of England: The Later Middle Ages* (London, 1979), p. 47. This paper is a revised and expanded version of a talk given at a conference on Wykeham held in Winchester in September 2002. I am grateful to the late Timothy Reuter for inviting me to speak and to the participants at the conference for their comments.

[2] J. Z. Titow, 'Land and Population on the Bishop of Winchester's Estates 1209–1350' (unpublished PhD thesis, University of Cambridge, 1962), p. 68a; F. R. H. Du Boulay, *The Lordship of Canterbury* (London, 1966), p. 243; C. Dyer, *Standards of Living in the Later Middle Ages*, 2nd edn (Cambridge, 1998), p. 36.

[3] *The Illustrated Chronicles of Matthew Paris*, ed. R. Vaughan (Stroud, 1993), p. 192.

[4] J. H. Denton, 'Complaints to the Apostolic See in an Early Fourteenth-Century Memorandum from England', *Archivum Historiae Pontificiae* xx (1982), p. 392.

[5] *DNB*, LXIII, p. 226.

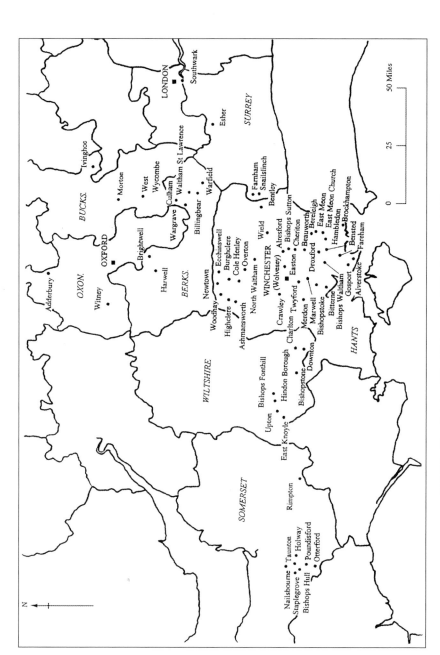

MAP 1. The Estate of the Bishopric of Winchester, c.1400

the bulk of their later medieval estate. Domesday Book reveals that, in the reign of Edward the Confessor, Bishop Stigand (1047–70) was possessed of most of the manors held by his thirteenth- and fourteenth-century successors. This paper examines Wykeham's stewardship of that estate during his long episcopate in the second half of the fourteenth century. Among the issues addressed are: the size of the estate and its changing composition under Wykeham's direction; the officials who managed the estate on the bishop's behalf; the chief sources of income from the estate and the uses to which the money generated was put; the productivity of the estate and the farming practices employed; and the problems which faced the bishop as a large landholder in the wake of the population collapse following the onset of plague. We begin, however, with a discussion of the main source of our evidence for the history of the estate: the Winchester pipe rolls.

The Winchester pipe rolls

The Winchester pipe rolls are enrolled accounts, a fair copy of the year's account, from Michaelmas (29 September) to Michaelmas, for the whole of the bishopric estate, which were drawn up from the individual manorial account rolls (or compotus rolls) after these had been corrected at audit. The pipe rolls were called *pipas* in Latin, their name reflecting the shape of the manuscripts when rolled, or perhaps the cylindrical case in which they may have been stored. In all, 191 rolls survive in broken series from 1208–9 until 1454–5. Thereafter, the accounts continue from 1456–7 until 1710–11 in the form of 137 parchment volumes. A total of 34 pipe rolls survive for the episcopate of William Wykeham, beginning at Michaelmas 1366, a little before Wykeham's election to the see in October of that year.[6] The series is complete with the exception of the accounts for just four years: 1380–1, 1391–2, 1397–8 and 1403–4.

The amount of information recorded in the Winchester pipe rolls is vast. Although the basic form of each manorial account changed very little over time, the details varied considerably. The accounts were divided into cash receipts, cash expenses, a grange account for the demesne's corn, and a livestock account. Under these four broad headings were entered many different types of information, relating to all aspects of medieval estate management. Cash receipts included: the rents paid by the bishop's tenants, minus any quittances (rebates given to tenants in return for serving as a manorial official) and defaults (rents uncollected because the land had been taken back into demesne); money received from the sale of demesne produce; and fines collected in the manorial court. By the time of Wykeham's episcopate, other sub-headings can also be found, such as those relating to the leasing of demesne assets, especially mills, and the sale of tenants' labour services, no longer required following the contraction of the demesne. Above all, tenements that remained unfilled as a result of the population collapse caused by successive waves of plague were leased out on a temporary basis to any willing to take them. Some of this cash was spent on the manor, to ensure that ploughs and carts were in working order, that manorial buildings were repaired, that tools and other equipment were available to use, and that the workers who brought in the harvest and threshed and winnowed the grain were fed and paid. Each type of grain was given its own

---

6   HRO, 11M59/B1/119–52.

account: how much was sown and reaped, how much was sold and how much consumed. The livestock of the manor was also recorded in the most minute of detail: how many were born, how many died, and how many were sent to market.

It is on an analysis of this information, recorded in the Winchester pipe rolls, that much of this paper depends. Yet it would be wrong to consider that the pipe rolls are the only source of evidence for a discussion of Wykeham's management of the Winchester estate. By the second half of the fourteenth century, compotus rolls begin to survive for a number of manors. These were the draft accounts which the reeves of individual manors brought at the end of the financial year to the audit and from which the pipe rolls were later engrossed. These rolls show that the reeves were habitually engaged in potentially heated debate with the auditors concerning the state of their accounts. The many crossings-out that are a characteristic of these rolls indicate the frequency with which the auditors disagreed with and disallowed the claims of the reeves. For example, it was often suspected that the reeve had sold grain or other produce for a higher price than that recorded in his account and that he had pocketed the difference himself. Thus, at Bishops Waltham in 1370–1 the five ox hides which the reeve claimed to have sold for 6s 8d were thought to be worth 10s by the auditors, and this was the price recorded in the pipe roll. The difference – 3s 4d – was charged to the reeve under the heading 'sales at the audit', which often amounted to a significant sum.[7]

Reeves were not only accused of undervaluing receipts. They were also suspected of recording expenses that were never in fact made. Thus, at Bishops Waltham in 1370–1, the auditors disallowed payments for a seed-basket and a basket for carrying corn supposedly purchased by the reeve for 1s 3d. Other payments, such as those made for the carting of wine to the bishop's residences, were also struck through.[8] Few of these details were transferred to the pipe rolls, our only clue to their existence appearing under the sub-heading 'allowances without writ'. By the time of Wykeham's episcopate, regular repayments were made to reeves, 'for various things charged above and disallowed by the auditors', in an attempt to keep arrears within reasonable limits. In the absence of the compotus rolls, therefore, potentially interesting information, relating to the supply of the bishop's household and other matters, is lost in the complex game of claim and counter-claim played out between the auditors and the reeves. They are thus not a source to be overlooked. Moreover, for those years in which the pipe roll is missing, the compotus rolls, in the event of their survival, are our only source of information.

Court rolls also begin to survive from the middle of the fourteenth century. These provide details about life on the manor that do not appear in the pipe rolls at all. Only the sums of money collected as fines were recorded there. Furthermore, inter-esting points about the bishop's management of his lands and tenants emerge from a reading of them. For example, at Bishops Waltham in 1390, attempts were made to force tenants to repair buildings which had become ruinous and to ensure that they did not demise land without paying the entry fine, two common complaints of lords throughout England at this time. Disputes between tenants are also reported. In 1390 John Newman complained that he was owed 2s 6d for a cartwheel sold by him

7   HRO, 11M59/B2/11/15; 11M59/B1/123, m. 35.
8   HRO, 11M59/B2/11/15.

to William Pigg.[9] Other documents relating to Wykeham's management of the epis-copal estate are some deeds concerned with the purchase of property, and the bishop's register.[10] This includes information about the appointment of manorial officials, the granting of land, the disciplining of tenants, and disputes with neigh-bouring lords. A single household account, for the period 1 April to 30 September 1393, also survives.[11]

The bishopric estate

At the beginning of his episcopate in 1366, Wykeham possessed a core of 28 manors and five boroughs in Hampshire, the heartland of the episcopal estate. A further 28 manors and five boroughs were held scattered across Berkshire, Buckinghamshire, Oxfordshire, Somerset, Surrey and Wiltshire.[12] Although most of these properties had been granted to the see before the Norman Conquest, the Winchester estate was not unchanging. Outlying manors, in Cambridgeshire and Hertfordshire, which were held by Bishop Stigand in 1066, were alienated or subinfeudated soon thereafter.[13] In 1284 the bishop lost possession of his properties on the Isle of Wight, which were appropriated to the crown by Edward I, and received in return four manors on Hampshire's southern coast that had formerly belonged to St Swithun's Priory.[14] More changes occurred under Wykeham, who was responsible for the recovery of a number of previously subinfeudated manors, including Benstead, Bereleigh, Cole Henley, Droxford Philip (all Hampshire), and Esher Matham (Surrey). The explana-tion for Wykeham's determination to bring back into demesne large areas of land that had been in the hands of tenants for centuries lies in part in his foundation and endowment of Winchester College and New College, Oxford.[15]

In 1381 the bishop alienated in mortmain the advowsons of Adderbury in Oxfordshire and Steeple Morden in Cambridgeshire to New College and in 1382 the advowson of Downton in Wiltshire to Winchester College. In order to ensure the permanency of these endowments, Wykeham took the precaution of compensating the bishopric for the resulting loss of income. Thus, in 1390 a quitclaim made by John de Bereleigh and Agatha his wife of a messuage and a mill, 205 acres of land, 10 acres of meadow, 60 acres of pasture, 50 acres of wood, and £2 0s 6d of rent in East Meon, Bereleigh and Drayton, was confirmed by Wykeham as being in compensation for the alienation of the advowsons. Similarly, the lands granted to the bishop by John de Blewbury in Droxford and Hamelin de Matham in Esher, as well as the manor of Bensted near Droxford granted by Philip St Clare, were all specifi-cally to make good the losses incurred through the endowment of the two colleges.

---

9   HRO, 11M59/C1/8/8.

10 HRO, 11M59/E2/159696; *Wykeham's Register*, ed. T. F. Kirby (2 vols., Hampshire Record Society, 1896–9).

11 *Household Accounts from Medieval England*, ed. C. M. Woolgar (2 vols., Records of Social and Economic History new ser. xvii–xviii, 1992–3), II, p. 721.

12 M. Page, *The Medieval Bishops of Winchester: Estate, Archive and Administration* (Hampshire Papers, xxiv, 2002), p. 6.

13 *VCH: Cambridgeshire*, VIII, pp. 35, 112–13, 120; *VCH: Hertfordshire*, III, p. 228.

14 *The Pipe Roll of the Bishopric of Winchester 1301–2*, ed. M. Page (Hampshire Record Series, xiv, 1996), p. ix.

15 For the following two paragraphs, see *The Pipe Roll of the Bishopric of Winchester 1409–10*, ed. M. Page (Hampshire Record Series, xvi, 1999), pp. xvi, xviii.

Wykeham also acquired land in Witney for the same purpose, although this was subsumed within the manor and was not accounted for separately in the pipe rolls.

The manor of Cole Henley near Whitchurch also seems to have been recovered from subtenants, appearing for the first time in the roll of 1379–80, but whether this too was related to Wykeham's endowment of the colleges is unclear. Accounts for a number of other manors also appeared for the first time during his episcopate, including Charlton (Wiltshire), Easton (Hampshire) and Snailslinch (Surrey). Charlton near Downton escheated to the bishop in 1375 on the death of Thomas Rivers without heirs, the see's tenure of the manor being confirmed in 1393. Easton near Winchester was a manor said to belong to St Swithun's Priory. Nevertheless, from 1383–4 onwards an annual account appeared in the pipe rolls. In fact, it would appear from later evidence that the priory was in possession of Lovington in the parish of Easton, while the manor itself belonged to the bishopric. Even so, the explanation for Wykeham's sudden possession of Easton in 1383–4 is by no means certain. Nor is the appearance in the rolls of the manor of Snailslinch near Farnham. It is possible that in some of these cases Wykeham was reacting to economic changes caused by the steep decline in population following successive outbreaks of plague. With land becoming increasingly available, certain manors held in fee may no longer have appeared attractive to their owners, allowing the bishop to resume possession and lease them instead for a term of years. If this was the case, it was certainly a development of which Wykeham took advantage, and which facilitated the endowment of his educational foundations.

The grant of tenancies in fee by the bishops of Winchester after the Norman Conquest has not been given close attention. Like other ecclesiastical tenants-in-chief, the bishop owed military service to the king. Indeed, it has been estimated that he was liable to supply some 70 knights to the royal army.[16] In order to discharge this obligation, the bishops subinfeudated parts of their estate, creating mesne tenants such as Walter de Tichborne, who held the Hampshire manor of Tichborne for two knights' fees of Henry of Blois in 1135.[17] These lands were resumed by the bishop on a temporary basis during minorities and an account of the manor was often included in the Winchester pipe rolls.[18] Thus, Wykeham collected the revenues of Tichborne in 1381–2, prior to John de Tichborne's coming of age in January 1385.[19] It has been observed that elsewhere in England the market in small lay estates became more active after the Black Death than it had been before.[20] The difficult economic circumstances in which some small landowners found themselves in the late fourteenth century may have encouraged the sale of outlying or unprofitable manors. For example, Bensted was a relatively minor possession of the St Clare family, whose main holdings were by this time in Kent.[21] The lack of heirs was another common reason for families to lose possession of an estate and, as at

---

[16] N. Vincent, *Peter des Roches: An Alien in English Politics 1205–1238* (Cambridge, 1996), pp. 62–4.
[17] *VCH: Hampshire*, III, p. 337.
[18] M. Page, 'A Note on the Manor of Limerstone, Isle of Wight', *Hampshire Field Club and Archaeological Society Newsletter* xxix (1998), p. 26.
[19] HRO, 11M59/B1/133, mm. 28d–29; *Wykeham's Register*, II, pp. 371–2.
[20] N. Saul, *Knights and Esquires: The Gloucestershire Gentry in the Fourteenth Century* (Oxford, 1981), pp. 229–30.
[21] C. L. Sinclair Williams, 'The Manor of Bensted St Clair', *Proceedings of the Hampshire Field Club and Archaeological Society* xlii (1986), p. 113.

Charlton, it was often a great magnate, such as the bishop of Winchester, who took advantage by securing title to the land.[22] Thus was Wykeham able to increase the size of the bishopric estate.

The administration of the estate

When Wykeham became bishop in 1366, most of the manors of the Winchester estate were still managed directly by the episcopal administration, as they had been since the beginning of the thirteenth century. The leasing of the demesne was a fifteenth-century rather than a fourteenth-century development on the bishopric estate, although the first steps towards it were taken during Wykeham's tenure of the see. Direct demesne farming demanded a different kind of administration from that employed to supervise an estate that was leased. A hierarchy of officials existed to keep a close check on every aspect of the management of the estate. In charge of the estate's finances was the treasurer or receiver, to whose office at Wolvesey Palace money sent from the manors was delivered. Under Wykeham each of his three treasurers remained in office for considerable lengths of time: William Renaud from the beginning of the episcopate until 1374; John de Ketene from 1374 until 1395; and Simon Membury from 1395 until Wykeham's death in 1404. All three were trusted advisers and served the bishop in other ways: for example, by acquiring property on behalf of Winchester College, or by inquiring into the state of the hospital of St Mary Magdalen in Winchester.[23]

Other payments from the manors were made directly to the treasurer or clerk of the household, to provide for the bishop on his itinerary. Thus, in 1381–2 seven salmon worth £1 4s 10d were delivered to Robert Perle, treasurer of the household, from the episcopal fishery at Bitterne. In addition, £53 5s was sent by the reeve of the manor to John de Ketene at Wolvesey Palace.[24] It is likely that both treasurers, of Wolvesey and the household, acted as auditors of the estate and served on the bishop's council, along with the steward and clerk of the bishopric.[25] The steward was a more peripatetic official than the treasurer and stood at the head of the bishop's manorial administration. He, or the clerk of the bishopric, visited each manor twice a year to preside at the tourns (or law-courts) of Martinmas (11 November) and Hockday (the second Tuesday after Easter), and to ensure that the demesnes were being managed effectively.[26] For instance, at East Meon in Hampshire in 1403, the steward, Thomas Chelrey, conducted an inquisition into the free status of a tenant at the Hockday tourn, to which the clerk of the bishopric, Richard Prewes, was a witness.[27] Another of Wykeham's stewards, William Ringbourne, was appointed in 1386, remaining in office until the end of the fourteenth century. He

[22] C. Given-Wilson, *The English Nobility in the Late Middle Ages* (London, 1987), p. 129.

[23] D. Keene, 'Town into Gown', *Winchester College: Sixth-Centenary Essays*, ed. R. Custance (Oxford, 1982), pp. 56–7; *VCH: Hampshire*, II, p. 198.

[24] HRO, 11M59/B1/133, m. 34.

[25] E. Swift, 'The Machinery of Manorial Administration with Special Reference to the Lands of the Bishopric of Winchester 1208–1454' (unpublished MA thesis, University of London, 1930), pp. 52–3.

[26] Swift, 'Machinery of Manorial Administration', pp. xxvi–xxvii.

[27] *The Register of the Common Seal of the Priory of St Swithun, Winchester, 1345–1497*, ed. J. Greatrex (Hampshire Record Series, ii, 1979), p. 27.

was a prominent figure in Hampshire, serving as sheriff and representing the county in parliament.[28]

Below the steward in the hierarchy of the estate's officials were the constables of the castles of Farnham and Taunton, and eight or nine bailiffs, each responsible for a small group of geographically related manors. Indeed, the creation of formal bailiwicks appears to have been accomplished during Wykeham's episcopate.[29] The bailiffs were charged with holding the manor court in between sessions of the steward's tourn and with overseeing the farming of the demesne, particularly the ploughing and the harvest.[30] Both constables and bailiffs received wages from the manors under their control. For example, Robert Chesenal, constable of Farnham Castle, received £10 a year in 1381–2, a figure which had not increased since 1278.[31] In the same year the bailiff of the bailiwick of Bishops Waltham, William Somerford, collected wages of £6 from the manor of Bishops Waltham, together with a further £2 from Droxford and £2 from Bitterne, a total of £10 in all.[32] Both steward and bailiff might supervise particular aspects of the management of the estate, such as the building works undertaken by Wykeham at his residence at Highclere. Accommodation for the bailiff and his horses was provided at Highclere, repairs to which were carried out in 1368–9.[33]

Finally, in charge of an individual manor was the reeve, who was usually an unfree tenant of the estate. The reeve was responsible for everything produced and consumed on the manor. His duties were manifold: organising the cultivation of the bishop's demesne and the care of the livestock, with the help of hired workers and of whatever labour services were due from the tenants; buying and selling corn to best advantage; seeing that the grain was effectively threshed and properly stored; and looking to the good order of the farm buildings and implements. He also collected the rents due from the bishop's tenants and the fines imposed in the manorial court. He distributed wages both in cash and kind, and finally, at the end of the year, handed over the profits of the manor to the bishop's treasurer.[34] Although a contemporary treatise on estate management recommended that reeves should serve for no more than a year, this advice was frequently ignored. For example, William Dameme was reeve at Cheriton from 1343 until his death in 1387. Unlike the bailiffs, reeves did not receive a salary. Instead, they were granted a reduction in the rent for their holding and small gifts of grain and stock. That some, like Dameme, were willing to serve for such long periods of time suggests, perhaps, that opportunities for petty corruption and bribery existed and were exploited.[35]

---

[28] *Wykeham's Register*, II, p. 386; *Register of the Common Seal*, p. 201.

[29] Titow, 'Land and Population', p. 6; T. Mayberry, *Estate Records of the Bishops of Winchester in the Hampshire Record Office* (Hampshire County Council, 1988), pp. 17–18.

[30] *Pipe Roll of the Bishopric of Winchester 1301–2*, pp. xvii–xviii; Swift, 'Machinery of Manorial Administration', pp. xxiii–xxiv.

[31] HRO, 11M59/B1/133, m. 17d; E. Robo, *Medieval Farnham* (Farnham, 1935), pp. 26, 44.

[32] HRO, 11M59/B1/133, mm. 33d, 34–34d.

[33] G. D. Dunlop, *Pages from the History of Highclere, Hampshire* (Oxford, 1940), pp. 38–9, 44, 47–8.

[34] P. D. A. Harvey, *Manorial Records*, 2nd edn (British Records Association, Archives and the User, v, 1999), p. 5; E. Miller and J. Hatcher, *Medieval England: Rural Society and Economic Change 1086–1348* (London, 1978), p. 193; *The Pipe Roll of the Bishopric of Winchester 1210–11*, ed. N. R. Holt (Manchester, 1964), p. xliv.

[35] D. L. Farmer, 'The *Famuli* in the Later Middle Ages', *Progress and Problems in Medieval England*, ed. R. H. Britnell and J. Hatcher (Cambridge, 1996), p. 225.

Under the supervision of the reeve was often a substantial workforce, usually known to historians by the Latin term *famuli*. They included beadles, carters, cowherds, dairymaids, haywards, oxherds, park-keepers, ploughmen, shepherds, smiths, swineherds and so on. During the course of the fourteenth century, the way in which these workers were paid began to shift. In 1305–6 over 60 per cent of *famuli* on the Winchester estate were rewarded with a reduction or cancellation of their money rent and labour services, together with occasional payments of grain or stock. However, by 1381–2 this figure had fallen to 41 per cent and the bulk of the manorial staff now received regular stipends in cash and kind. This development resulted largely from an unwillingness by tenants to fill service holdings, following the collapse in the population after the Black Death, and their preference to be paid in cash. Although the bishop of Winchester had to accept this change, nevertheless he was sufficiently powerful to impose an almost uniform pay structure across the whole of his vast and scattered estate, and to prevent wages rising, at least until the end of the fourteenth century. Under Wykeham, most male *famuli* received about 4s a year in cash and a quarter of grain (usually barley) every 10 weeks.[36]

The administrative structure of the Winchester estate appears not to have changed much during Wykeham's tenure of the see. Eleanor Swift's analysis of the functions of the bishop's council, exchequer and wardrobe also suggests that no major innovations were introduced in the late fourteenth century.[37] There is, however, one indication of an administrative development. On all his manors the bishop had the right to collect the amercements imposed on his tenants in the royal courts, and in Hampshire this prerogative was extended to include several hundreds that were dominated by the lands of other lords. Until the 1370s the money raised from these fines was accounted for in the pipe rolls by the bishop's marshal. Thereafter, this role was assumed by the bailiff of the liberty. The change of title appears to have been of some significance, coinciding as it did with a marked tightening up of the bishop's income from jurisdiction and incidents.[38] Wykeham was evidently seeking to maximise this particular portion of his revenues.

The income and expenditure of the estate

The Winchester pipe rolls give no overall total for the annual revenue of the episcopal estate. Instead, such figures have to be compiled from the individual manorial accounts. Table 1 outlines the general dimension of Wykeham's income at intervals throughout his episcopate, following the practice adopted by Harriss in his study of Henry Beaufort (1404–47).[39]

The amount of money delivered to Wykeham's treasurers from the estate appears to have been remarkably stable throughout his episcopate, ranging from about £3,500 to £3,800 a year. To this sum must be added the proceeds from the sale of the estate's wool, most of which was transported to Wolvesey and its sale organised from there. No accounts for this trade in wool survive but it is likely to have been worth between about £200 and £300, sufficient to bring the annual income from the

36 Farmer, 'The *Famuli* in the Later Middle Ages', pp. 211, 219–20, 227, 231.
37 Swift, 'Machinery of Manorial Administration', pp. 1–94.
38 Ibid., p. 102; *Pipe Roll of the Bishopric of Winchester 1409–10*, p. xix; D. Keene, *Survey of Medieval Winchester* (2 vols., Oxford, 1985), I, p. 72.
39 G. L. Harriss, *Cardinal Beaufort* (Oxford, 1988), pp. 411–12.

TABLE 1. Annual income of the Winchester estate under Bishop Wykeham

Year	(1) Arrer.	(2) Rec. c. Arr.	(3) (Receipts)	(4) Et debet	(5) Lib. den.
1370–1	£1,182 9s 2d	£7,982 10s 8¼d	£6,800 1s 6¼d	£5,726 4s 10½d	£3,712 11s 10½d
1381–2	£1,514 3s 7½d	£6,742 9s 8¾d	£5,228 6s 1¼d	£5,218 18s 0d	£3,567 11s 10½d
1392–3	£1,584 3s 0d	£6,558 9s 6¾d	£4,974 6s 6¾d	£5,281 4s 0½d	£3,551 3s 3¼d
1402–3	£330 15s 6¼d	£5,575 3s 5¾d	£5,244 7s 11½d	£4,385 18s 10d	£3,783 8s 3¾d

Source: HRO, 11M59/B1/123, 133, 143, 152.

Key:
(1) Arrears: these were written off at least once during Wykeham's episcopate.
(2) Total receipts, from rents, fines and the sale of produce, plus arrears.
(3) Total receipts minus arrears: this figure is not in the accounts.
(4) Total receipts less administrative costs and capital investment.
(5) Payments to the treasurer of Wolvesey after local expenditure under warrant (including payment to the household on itinerary). (Payments to the household totalled £340 18s 5d in 1370–1, £416 11s 0d in 1381–2, £447 2s 1¼d in 1392–3, and £442 16s 2½d in 1402–3.)

estate close to £4,000.[40] Few other lords of Wykeham's generation could command an income as large as this, and certainly no other bishop. Only major secular lords, such as the dukes of Lancaster, received more from their estates.[41] The money raised from the Winchester estate in the late fourteenth century was closely comparable to that collected by the bishops a hundred years before.[42] The Black Death and the resulting changes to the manorial economy appear not to have made much difference to the financial well-being of the bishopric. Yet changes had taken place over the course of the fourteenth century.

After 1350 rents generally constituted the largest single component of the bishop's annual income, rising from around £1,600 in the middle of the fourteenth century to some £1,800 at the beginning of the fifteenth century.[43] Since rents were fixed by custom and were neither raised nor lowered to reflect prevailing economic conditions, any increase in the amount of rent owed must represent an enlargement in the area of land held by the tenants. After the Black Death this usually meant land leased from the demesne, which the bishop no longer wished to farm himself. Yet, although rents rose under Wykeham, they seem to have become more difficult to collect. Arrears mounted sharply during his episcopate, almost certainly as a result of tenants defaulting on their payments in an era of declining land values. So severe was the problem that in 1402 Wykeham largely wrote off the massive debts owed by his reeves.[44] The importance of the bishop's rental income to the money delivered every year to his treasurers, therefore, should not be overstated.

The income from the bishop's own farming of the demesne remained substantial under Wykeham. Sales of grain were particularly important and fluctuations in this source were mirrored by changes in the overall revenues of the estate. Thus, the higher receipts of 1370–1 compared with those of later years recorded in Table 1 were largely the result of the exceptionally high prices received for grain in that year.[45] Wykeham's income from grain declined over the course of his episcopate, from an average of around £1,330 a year in the period 1370–9 to about £939 in 1380–9 and £849 in 1390–9 (Figure 1).[46] This reflected a wider trend, as the population of England fell under the onslaught of plague. As Farmer has shown, following a few years with prices exceeding 8s for a quarter of wheat, there began in 1376–7 a remarkable period of low prices. In all but four of the next 24 years, wheat cost less than 6s a quarter. The price in 1392–3 was the lowest for over a century, and it was never as low again.[47] Thus, in this year the estate's receipts fell below £5,000. A similar correpondence between grain prices and total income occurred on the Winchester estate before the Black Death.[48]

Whatever the annual income of the estate, however, the cash delivered to the bishop's treasurers appears to have remained roughly the same. This was apparently

[40] *Pipe Roll of the Bishopric of Winchester 1409–10*, p. xxiv.

[41] Dyer, *Standards of Living*, p. 36.

[42] *Pipe Roll of the Bishopric of Winchester 1301–2*, pp. xx-xxi; Titow, 'Land and Population', p. 68a.

[43] Titow, 'Land and Population', pp. 57–8; *Pipe Roll of the Bishopric of Winchester 1409–10*, p. xxv.

[44] *Pipe Roll of the Bishopric of Winchester 1409–10*, p. xxviii.

[45] D. L. Farmer, 'Prices and Wages', *The Agrarian History of England and Wales III, 1348–1500*, ed. E. Miller (Cambridge, 1991), pp. 502–3.

[46] Figure 1 is based upon the net grain income of the estate (grain sold less grain bought) calculated by J. Z. Titow in his unpublished notes: HRO, 97M97/B1.

[47] Farmer, 'Prices and Wages', pp. 434–5.

[48] Titow, 'Land and Population', p. 67.

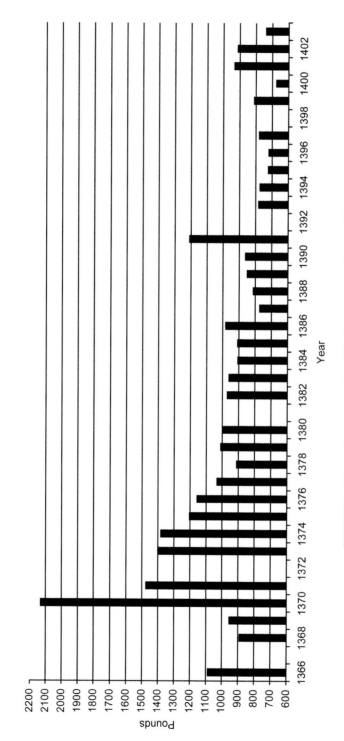

FIGURE 1. Net grain income of the Winchester estate, 1366–1404

achieved by reducing manorial expenditure, which fell steadily over the course of Wykeham's episcopate. Levels of investment undoubtedly declined as a result of the contraction of demesne farming in the later fourteenth century. Fewer ploughs were required to cultivate a diminishing demesne, there were fewer carts, fewer horses and oxen were kept, and fewer labourers were needed to plough, harrow, sow, weed, and harvest the grain. Indeed, such trends can be discerned even before the Black Death.[49] Nevertheless, it remains unclear whether deliberate steps were taken to reduce manorial expenditure in order to maintain payments to the bishop's exchequer at a familiar level. Moreover, in one area of expenditure, on the bishop's palaces and other residences, Wykeham was not inclined to economise. Construction work on the palaces at Bishops Waltham, Highclere and Southwark, on the castle at Farnham, and on the court-house at East Meon was extensive during Wykeham's episcopate and was largely funded out of manorial revenues.[50] However, the more grandiose building projects, at Winchester Cathedral, Winchester College, and New College, Oxford, for which Wykeham is most remembered, were paid for out of the bishop's household income, for which accounts do not survive.

Farming practices and agricultural productivity

Most of the manors of the Winchester estate practised mixed arable and livestock farming.[51] Under Wykeham, the importance of the pastoral sector was enhanced. The sown acreage of the demesne had begun to contract from as early as the 1270s and continued to decline throughout the fourteenth century. At the beginning of Wykeham's episcopate, the number of acres sown regularly exceeded 7,000. By its close in the early fifteenth century, fewer than 6,000 acres were under the plough (Figure 2).[52] This decline was not particularly pronounced and followed a well-established pattern both on the Winchester estate and on other demesnes. Some of the arable discarded by the bishop was leased to the estate's tenants. The remainder was turned over to pasture. As a result, Wykeham was able to increase the size of the bishopric's sheep flock.

The number of sheep on the estate rose sharply in the years immediately following the Black Death. This was probably in response to changed economic conditions, which favoured less labour-intensive farming in an era when workers were in short supply. The highest annual total was reached in 1369, soon after Wykeham became bishop, when there were nearly 35,000 sheep. Thereafter, numbers fell back slightly but, in spite of some fluctuations, there remained around 33,000 sheep on the Winchester estate until the end of the fourteenth century. The

---

49 *Pipe Roll of the Bishopric of Winchester 1409–10*, p. xxvii; Titow, 'Land and Population', pp. 41–2.

50 J. N. Hare, 'Bishop's Waltham Palace, Hampshire: William of Wykeham, Henry Beaufort and the Transformation of a Medieval Palace', *Archaeological Journal* cxlv (1988), pp. 222–54; C. Phillpotts, 'Plague and Reconstruction: Bishops Edington and Wykeham at Highclere, 1346–1404', *Fourteenth Century England I*, ed. N. Saul (Woodbridge, 2000), pp. 115–32; M. Carlin, 'The Reconstruction of Winchester House, Southwark', *London Topographical Record* xxv (1985), pp. 33–57; Robo, *Medieval Farnham*, p. 152; E. Roberts, 'William of Wykeham's House at East Meon, Hants', *Archaeological Journal* cl (1993), pp. 456–81.

51 B. M. S. Campbell, K. C. Bartley and J. P. Power, 'The Demesne-Farming Systems of Post-Black Death England: A Classification', *Agricultural History Review* xliv (1996), pp. 131–79.

52 Figure 2 is based upon the adjusted total area under seed calculated by J. Z. Titow in his unpublished notes: HRO, 97M97/B1.

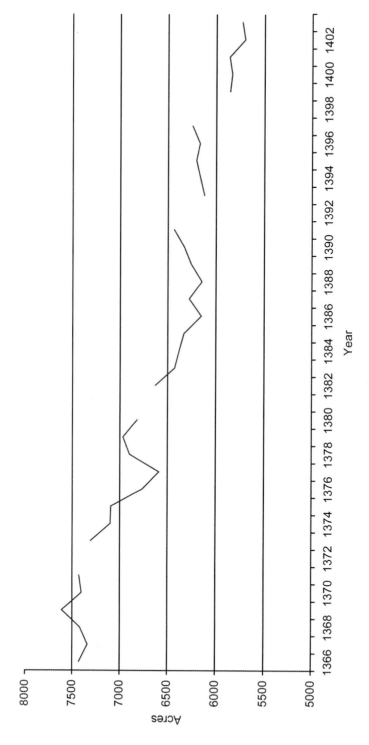

FIGURE 2. Number of acres sown on the Winchester estate, 1366–1404

rapid expansion of the flock coincided with a period of declining yields of wool. Fleece weights fell rapidly in the 1370s and did not recover for the remainder of the Middle Ages. However, no clear relationship between productivity and population size has been established.[53] Instead, other factors may have been at work. The quality of the wool produced depended to some extent on the skill of the shepherds who tended the flock.[54] Good shepherds may have been harder to find in an era of general labour shortage, leading to a decline in productivity. In addition, wool prices were low in the late fourteenth century, providing little incentive to maximise yields.[55] On the other hand, the increased purchasing power of the population, benefiting from rising wage rates, led to a growth in the consumption of meat, including mutton.[56] Wykeham may have sought to capitalise on the improved standards of living of the peasantry and townspeople by removing large numbers of sheep (often called kebbs) for sale in the market.[57] Although the scale of this trade has yet to be determined, the likelihood is that it was not inconsiderable. At Rimpton in Somerset, for example, specialised fattening grounds for sheep were in use from the 1340s.[58] Wool undoubtedly remained the principal cash crop of sheep-farming in the later Middle Ages, but other sources of income, from the sale of stock, skins, milk, cheese and butter, were also important.[59]

The rise in the number of sheep kept on the Winchester estate may have contributed to the improvement in grain yields achieved in the late fourteenth century.[60] On most manors the yields of wheat, barley and oats were higher during Wykeham's episcopate (especially in the 1380s) than they were during those of Bishops Edington (1345–66) and Beaufort (1404–47).[61] An increase in the availability of manure, however, would only benefit grain yields if the compost was adequately spread. At Rimpton, changed grazing practices and the high cost of labour limited the amount of dung which reached the arable.[62] If similar circumstances applied across the estate, alternative explanations need to be sought for the improvement of yield figures in the late fourteenth century. One possibility is that, by sowing the seed more thinly, higher yield ratios could be achieved. This seems to have occurred on some of the bishopric's manors, although the evidence is problematic and far from conclusive.[63] Another explanation is that Wykeham's episcopate coincided

---

[53] M. J. Stephenson, 'Wool Yields in the Medieval Economy', *Economic History Review* 2nd ser. xli (1988), pp. 378, 385–7.

[54] C. Thornton, 'Efficiency in Medieval Livestock Farming: The Fertility and Mortality of Herds and Flocks at Rimpton, Somerset, 1208–1349', *Thirteenth Century England IV*, ed. P. R. Coss and S. D. Lloyd (Woodbridge, 1992), pp. 40–1, 43.

[55] T. H. Lloyd, 'The Movement of Wool Prices in Medieval England', *Economic History Review Supplement* vi (1973), pp. 19–20; Farmer, 'Prices and Wages', pp. 462, 513.

[56] Dyer, *Standards of Living*, pp. 158–9, 202.

[57] E.g. *Pipe Roll of the Bishopric of Winchester 1409–10*, pp. 265, 284.

[58] Campbell, Bartley and Power, 'Demesne-Farming Systems', pp. 178–9; C. Thornton, 'The Determinants of Land Productivity on the Bishop of Winchester's Demesne of Rimpton, 1208 to 1403', *Land, Labour and Livestock: Historical Studies in European Agricultural Productivity*, ed. B. M. S. Campbell and M. Overton (Manchester, 1991), p. 209.

[59] E. Miller, 'Farming Practice and Techniques: The Southern Counties', *Agrarian History of England and Wales III*, pp. 295–6.

[60] D. L. Farmer, 'Grain Yields on the Winchester Manors in the Later Middle Ages', *Economic History Review* 2nd ser. xxx (1977), pp. 563–4; Miller, 'Farming Practice and Techniques', pp. 289–90.

[61] Farmer, 'Grain Yields', pp. 557–60.

[62] Thornton, 'Determinants of Land Productivity', p. 200.

[63] Farmer, 'Grain Yields', pp. 564–6.

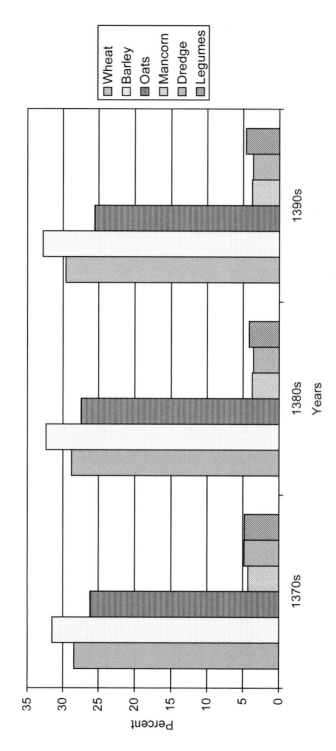

FIGURE 3. Percentage of crops sown on the Winchester estate, 1370–99

with a period of good weather that was kind to arable farmers, or that by altering crop rotations the harvest could be improved.[64] On the other hand, the contraction of the demesne and the cultivation of legumes appear not to have affected yields of grain to any significant degree.[65] Undoubtedly the factors involved varied according to the particular circumstances of individual manors. For most, however, the folding of sheep on the arable remains the most likely explanation for an increase in yields.[66]

Wheat, barley and oats were the principal crops grown on the estate in the late fourteenth century, together with very much smaller quantities of mancorn, dredge and legumes (Figure 3). However, there was considerable regional variation between manors (Figure 4).[67] On the northern manors of the estate (Brightwell, Harwell and Wargrave in Berkshire; Ivinghoe, Morton and West Wycombe in Buckinghamshire; and Adderbury and Witney in Oxfordshire), significant quantities of dredge (mixed oats and spring barley) were cultivated. Much of this crop, together with large amounts of barley, was used to make malt for brewing.[68] Dredge was commonly sown on demesnes in Berkshire, Buckinghamshire and Oxfordshire in the late fourteenth century, a specialism that had its antecedents in the years around 1300.[69] Likewise, rye and rye mixtures (including mancorn, a mixture of rye and winter barley) tended to be grown only in particular areas, notably central and north-eastern Oxfordshire and northern Buckinghamshire, where it was particularly favoured by the peasantry.[70]

On the western manors of the estate (Bishops Fonthill, Bishopstone, Downton and East Knoyle in Wiltshire; and Rimpton and Taunton in Somerset), the pattern of crop production corresponded much more closely to that of the estate as a whole, with barley, wheat and oats as the dominant grains. This was characteristic too of other demesnes in the area.[71] Similarly, on the bailiwicks of East Meon (East Meon, East Meon Church, Fareham and Hambledon) and Bishops Sutton (Alresford, Beauworth, Bishops Sutton, Cheriton and Wield) in Hampshire, barley, wheat and oats were the crops most widely sown, albeit with considerable manorial variation. This pattern had changed little since the period before the Black Death, during which time it also characterised the Hampshire manors of St Swithun's Priory.[72] To a large extent, therefore, crop production on the Winchester estate was determined by local ecological and commercial factors that influenced the lords of other manors to a similar degree. In other words, there was little out of the ordinary in the farming practices pursued by Wykeham.

---

64 Miller, 'Farming Practice and Techniques', pp. 289–90; P. D. A. Harvey, 'Farming Practice and Techniques: The Home Counties', *Agrarian History of England and Wales III*, p. 262.

65 Farmer, 'Grain Yields', pp. 561–4.

66 E. Newman, 'Medieval Sheep-Corn Farming: How Much Grain Yield Could Each Sheep Support?', *Agricultural History Review* 1 (2002), p. 179.

67 Figures 3 and 4 are based upon the decennial average as a percentage of total crop production for each manor of the estate calculated by J. Z. Titow in his unpublished notes: HRO, 97M97/B1.

68 E.g. *Pipe Roll of the Bishopric of Winchester 1409–10*, pp. 119, 137–8.

69 Harvey, 'Farming Practice and Techniques', p. 260; B. M. S. Campbell, J. A. Galloway, D. Keene and M. Murphy, *A Medieval Capital and its Grain Supply: Agrarian Production and Distribution in the London Region c.1300* (Historical Geography Research Series, xxx, 1993), pp. 114, 120.

70 Harvey, 'Farming Practice and Techniques', p. 259.

71 Miller, 'Farming Practice and Techniques', p. 287.

72 HRO, 97M97/C1 (J. Z. Titow, 'Field Crops and their Cultivation in Hampshire, 1200–1350, in the Light of Documentary Evidence'), pp. 9–11.

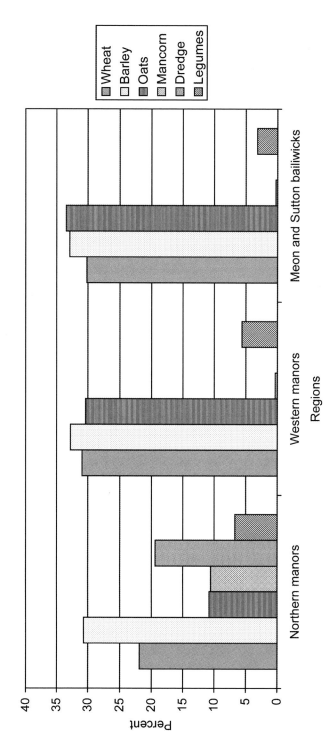

FIGURE 4. Percentage of crops sown on the Winchester estate in selected regions, 1370–99

Leasing and the end of direct management

Regular outbreaks of plague in the second half of the fourteenth century precipitated a sustained reduction in the population of England, which in turn shifted the economic balance of power away from landlords in favour of their tenants. One of the ways in which this change of fortunes manifested itself on the Winchester estate was in the inability of bishops to attract sufficient tenants to fill all the customary tenements that had been held before 1349. The problem was at its most severe in 1350–1, immediately after the initial catastrophe of the Black Death. But the effects of the first outbreak of plague were relatively short-lived. By 1355–6 many vacant tenements had been filled, particularly on populous manors such as Bishops Sutton and Taunton. Under Wykeham, however, a stagnant population combined with a more trenchant opposition among the peasantry to the obligations of serfdom led to a renewed rise in the number of customary tenements lying vacant. The bishop was able to lease some of this land to tenants on an *ad hoc* basis, for rent only, for which they were not obliged to pay an entry fine, render labour services, or owe other servile dues. By this means Wykeham recovered most of, and sometimes more than, the rent originally due to him, but his dissatisfaction with the policy was occasionally made clear with the note that the land was leased only 'until someone should come to fine for the same'.[73]

One reason why tenants may have been reluctant to enter customary tenements on the old terms was that, in spite of the contraction of the demesne, labour services remained a significant feature of life on the Winchester estate. In 1376–7 between 14 and 98 per cent of the labour services owed by tenants on 35 manors continued to be exacted by the bishop, many of them at harvest-time (Table 2).[74] Most of the remainder were commuted in return for cash payments, as they were wholesale on manors such as Farnham and Bishops Waltham.[75] The availability to the bishop of labour services appears to have been one factor in the decision to transfer from direct management to leasing during Wykeham's episcopate. A more important consideration, however, was probably the size of the demesne.

Towards the end of Wykeham's episcopate, in 1402–3, only about a dozen manors were leased, and these were among the smallest of the bishop's possessions.[76] They included places such as Bensted, Bereleigh, Cole Henley, Droxford Philip, Easton and Snailslinch, which Wykeham had brought into demesne following the foundation of Winchester College and New College, Oxford. Other manors leased by Wykeham were Ashmansworth, Culham, Morton, Otterford, Wield and Witney. Some of these too (for example, Ashmansworth) were demesnes on which the sown acreage was relatively small. As a result, the profits of direct farming were limited, providing little incentive for the bishop to retain control following the collapse of grain prices in the later fourteenth century. Other manors were larger but lacked an adequate supply of labour services, an important consideration in an era of rising wage demands. Wield, for example, possessed a small tenant

---

[73] J. Z. Titow, 'Lost Rents, Vacant Holdings and the Contraction of Peasant Cultivation after the Black Death', *Agricultural History Review* xlii (1994), pp. 97–114.
[74] Table 2 is based upon an analysis of the *opera* accounts recorded in the pipe roll of 1376–7 (HRO, 11M59/B1/129) by J. Z. Titow in his unpublished notes: HRO, 97M97/B5.
[75] Titow, 'Land and Population', pp. 39, 41a.
[76] *Pipe Roll of the Bishopric of Winchester 1409–10*, pp. xxii–xxiii.

TABLE 2. Percentage of labour services worked on the Winchester estate, 1376–7

Percentage	*Manors*
10–19.9	Fareham, Hambledon, Taunton
20–29.9	Alresford, Wargrave, Highclere, Overton
30–39.9	Rimpton
40–49.9	Bishops Fonthill, East Knoyle, North Waltham, Bishopstoke, Wield, Brightwell
50–59.9	Twyford/Marwell, Bitterne, Bishopstone, Bishops Sutton
60–69.9	Ashmansworth, East Meon
70–79.9	Cheriton, Downton, Burghclere, Crawley
80–89.9	Harwell, West Wycombe, Ivinghoe, Woodhay, Adderbury, Ecchinswell
90–100	Morton, East Meon Church, Merdon, Bentley, Beauworth

Source: HRO, 97M97/B5; 11M59/B1/129.

population in relation to the size of the demesne and had relied on hired labour even before the Black Death.[77] At Witney, on the other hand, the lack of labour services resulted from the unwillingness of tenants to accept holdings on the old terms, with the result that the bishop was obliged to commute works on a large scale.[78] Finally, three of the manors leased by Wykeham (Morton, Otterford and Wield) had also been at farm for varying lengths of time before the Black Death.[79]

The scale of leasing under Wykeham was thus relatively limited. The number of manors leased was small and they were among the least valuable of the bishop's possessions. They included manors with no tradition of direct management within the estate, as well as some that had been leased even during the more propitious economic circumstances of the thirteenth century. Moreover, Wykeham retained in his own possession one of the most lucrative aspects of late fourteenth-century farming: sheep. Thus, at Ashmansworth, Culham, Witney and elsewhere, the bishop maintained his responsibility for the sheep flock and continued to collect the fleeces and skins.[80] As a result, the farms Wykeham was able to command were relatively small, ranging from less than £2 to no more than £17 a year. By contrast, Wykeham's successor, Henry Beaufort, who leased larger and more valuable manors, including the sheep, was able to attract lessees willing to pay up to £80 a year in the first decade of his episcopate.[81]

The end of direct management on the Winchester estate was not finally achieved until 1473. Under Wykeham, a wide variety of manorial resources were let at farm, from dovecotes and fisheries to pasture and piglets. Standardised returns were placed upon such livestock as capons, chickens and geese; in effect, their offspring were being leased to the reeve, so that the same numbers were recorded in the pipe

---

[77] Titow, 'Land and Population', p. 38.
[78] A. Ballard, 'The Manors of Witney, Brightwell, and Downton', *Oxford Studies in Social and Legal History V,* ed. P. Vinogradoff (Oxford, 1916), pp. 199–200.
[79] Titow, 'Land and Population', p. 7.
[80] E.g. *Pipe Roll of the Bishopric of Winchester 1409–10*, pp. 94–6, 145–6, 254–6.
[81] Ibid., pp. xxii–xxiii.

rolls year after year.[82] However, Wykeham cannot be considered to have withdrawn very markedly from the most profitable sectors of direct demesne farming, especially the production of grain and wool. This was left instead to his successors, Beaufort and Waynflete, in the even more challenging conditions of the fifteenth century. In his attitude to leasing, therefore, Wykeham adopted a more cautious approach than many of his contemporaries, including the archbishops of Canterbury, who leased 18 of their 30 demesnes between 1381 and 1396.[83]

Conclusions

The episcopate of William Wykeham coincided with a turbulent period for the landlords of medieval England. The lower levels of population prevailing after the Black Death gave rise to a multitude of potential problems: the scarcity of tenants and labourers, rising wage rates, falling food prices, and deteriorating social relations, which culminated in the Peasants' Revolt of 1381. The records of Wykeham's management of the Winchester estate reflect these developments and reveal his officials' attempts to cope with the changing circumstances of the times. In general terms, the administration may be said to have succeeded in weathering the new conditions. The income generated by the estate remained at a level closely comparable to that achieved in the late thirteenth and early fourteenth centuries. Farming practices were adapted, where necessary, to take advantage of particular market forces, and few manors became so unprofitable or difficult to manage that the bishop decided to lease them.

The evidence presented in this paper affords a largely generalised view of Wykeham's management of the bishopric estate. Relatively little account has been taken of the fact that the economic and social changes occurring in England in the late fourteenth century were often intensely local in their effect. The 34 Winchester pipe rolls surviving between 1366 and 1404 contain more than 2,000 separate manorial accounts. Only a detailed examination of these will reveal precisely the different policies pursued and outcomes achieved on each of the 60 or so manors of the bishop's vast and scattered estate. To date, only Rimpton in Somerset has received the close attention necessary for an integrated analysis of the whole demesne economy. However, this small and relatively isolated manor can hardly be regarded as typical of the estate as a whole.[84] Research is also under way into the response of the bishop's tenants to changes in landholding in the post-Black Death era.[85] Nevertheless, until further studies are forthcoming our understanding of the agrarian economy and society of the Winchester estate will remain incomplete and our explanations of the developments occurring under Wykeham must remain couched in general terms.

---

[82] Thornton, 'Efficiency in Medieval Livestock Farming', p. 43; e.g. *Pipe Roll of the Bishopric of Winchester 1409–10*, pp. 100, 225, 239, 363.

[83] C. Dyer, *Making a Living in the Middle Ages: The People of Britain 850–1520* (London, 2002), p. 332.

[84] Thornton, 'Determinants of Land Productivity', pp. 184–8; B. M. S. Campbell, *English Seigniorial Agriculture, 1250–1450* (Cambridge, 2000), pp. 382–5.

[85] Reseach funded by the Leverhulme Trust, undertaken by J. Mullan, supervised by R. H. Britnell and P. D. A. Harvey, entitled 'The Transfer of Customary Land on the Estate of the Bishopric of Winchester, 1350–1415'.

A LANCASTRIAN POLITY?
JOHN OF GAUNT, JOHN NEVILLE AND
THE WAR WITH FRANCE, 1368–88

Mark Arvanigian

It has become almost axiomatic to point out that the political life and aspirations of John of Gaunt were, in an English context, quite singular. His life and career have, over the past decade, been the subject of much interest by students of later medieval English politics.[1] First as earl of Richmond, then as duke of Lancaster, Gaunt's relentless political machinations were the genesis of a distinct, Lancastrian 'party'. This in turn provided him with a power base of great regional authority, which was capable of serving not only his own changing interests, but also of providing his son the one great treasure that the duke never allowed himself: the throne of England. The origins of Gaunt's political circle, and of Lancastrian polity generally, begin with the French campaigns of his youth, and with the assembly in his retinue of a close-knit group of soldier-politicians. This group of knights, barons and magnates – many his tenants or neighbours in the north – was initially assembled for war in France but became, for him and his son, an important basis for domestic political power.

John of Gaunt thus made a formative contribution to Lancastrian government through the creation of a large, durable, flexible and effective political organisation, which we might term his affinity. Its most prominent early members – quite apart from those involved in routine estate management and functions of local governance within his English dominions – were those originally assembled for military service abroad. Over time, however, his pattern of retaining shifted, reflecting his new-found interest in domestic political affairs following the death of his father. He quickly became the leader of the north's political community, cemented by his appointment as royal lieutenant of the Scottish Marches, a position which was probably modelled on those held by his brothers, Lionel and Edward, in Ireland, Wales and Aquitaine. As John's interests shifted from the Continent back to England, so too did many leading northerners not already in his service gravitate toward him. These men, who were valuable in part because they wielded influence of their own, in turn received patronage and offices from both the crown and the duchy of Lancaster. It is these men who would later prove to be instrumental in Henry Bolingbroke's *coup*, and who would assume important positions in his government.[2]

[1] Simon Walker, *The Lancastrian Affinity, 1361–1399* (Oxford, 1990), p. 36; Helen Castor, *The King, the Crown and the Duchy of Lancaster: Public Authority and Private Power, 1399–1461* (Oxford, 2000), pp. 23–4.
[2] A. L. Brown, 'The Reign of Henry IV', *Fifteenth Century England, 1399–1509*, ed. S. B. Chrimes, C. D. Ross and R. A. Griffiths (Manchester, 1972), pp. 1–24; D. L. Biggs, 'The Reign of Henry IV: The Revolution of 1399 and the Establishment of the Lancastrian Regime', *Fourteenth Century England I*, ed. Nigel Saul (2000), pp. 195–210.

The great wealth of the duchy of Lancaster made Gaunt exceptional in England, his financial means exceeding even that of the wealthy earl of Arundel. In this capacity, he was probably matched only by his elder brother, the Black Prince – though he derived much of his wealth from (and spent most of his time in) Aquitaine; in any case, the two princes stood head and shoulders above their English contemporaries. Gaunt's aspirations also dwarfed those of his potential rivals; as Professor Goodman has shown, his political horizons lay in a wider, European theatre, rather than merely in the English countryside. Those aspirations were consistent with his father's plans for establishing all of his children abroad. It seems that, in trying to extend his own power in the 1350s and 60s, Edward III employed a strategy of projected power, through familial advancement.[3] In adopting the 'family firm' approach, as conceived of earlier by Henry II, Edward's goal was to extend Plantagenet influence throughout Western Europe through the deeds and advantageous marriages of his vigorous children.

At length, John of Gaunt also adopted this approach, but with himself in the role of political godfather, to the mutual benefit of himself and his offspring.[4] Over time, he expanded that approach to include not only Henry Bolingbroke's siblings, but also his half-siblings and their spouses. Thus, through the application of this strategy, Gaunt came to define his conception of 'family' more liberally: by the 1390s, it included the Beaufort clan, children by his long-time mistress (then duchess), Catherine Swinford. They would make significant contributions to Lancastrian governance from the very start of in the reigns of Henry IV and Henry V – contributions based initially upon royal and ducal preferment in Gaunt's own lifetime. Specifically, the duke and Henry assisted John Beaufort, later marquis of Dorset and earl of Somerset, and Henry Beaufort, later cardinal and bishop of Winchester, in the establishment of their own retinues in the 1390s.[5] In 1397, the marriage of Ralph, lord Neville of Raby, to Joan Beaufort solidified an important relationship for both families, and cemented for Ralph not only the earldom of Westmorland, but also a central position in Lancastrian circles. His own (numerous) offspring from this marriage became important supporters of the house of Lancaster in the fifteenth century. Clearly, the rise to prominence of this family, in common with many northern families in the period, began years earlier, in the reign of Edward III. Ralph's father, John, was an important figure in Gaunt's retinue, a soldier and diplomat in France and Scotland. This essay will examine his career and influence, and his role in the genesis of a distinct Lancastrian polity in the late-fourteenth century.

Coinciding with his tenure as earl of Richmond, Gaunt's affinity included such northern barons as the lords Roos, Scrope, Neville and Percy.[6] John Neville was the son and heir of Ralph, lord Neville of Raby, from whom he inherited a large patrimony in the north. Ralph had been keeper of the forests north of the Trent, keeper of the royal fortress of Bamburgh, and had once served as the steward of Edward III's

---

3   W. M. Ormrod, 'Edward III and his Family', *Journal of British Studies* xxvi (1987), p. 400.

4   John Gillingham, *The Angevin Empire*, 2nd edn (London, 2001), pp. 116–25.

5   Walker, *Lancastrian Affinity*, pp. 35–7.

6   Walker, *Lancastrian Affinity*, pp. 262–84. Henry Bolingbroke would build on all of these connections, and add more northern barons to this list.

household in France.[7] In 1346, several weeks after Crecy, Ralph and his son served together against the Scots at the battle of Neville's Cross.[8] Because of his role in the capture of David Bruce, John de Coupland is perhaps the best remembered of those who fought in the battle. However, 'Sir Ralph Neville' also features prominently in a number of contemporary chronicles, which cite his capture of numerous Scottish prisoners and his willingness to absorb the cost of a monument commemorating the battle, fought on a hill above the River Wear, very near the city of Durham. The monumental cross was to be placed on a road running directly between his castle at Brancepeth and Durham.[9] Thus, as a result of lord Neville's gesture, what contemporaries generally referred to as the battle of Durham has come down to us as the battle of Neville's Cross.[10]

Although the Nevilles could boast of estates throughout the north-east, in Swaledale, Wensleydale, the Vale of York, and scattered around the North Riding, their principal residence in the fourteenth century seems to have been the palatinate of Durham. While often absent from the region for long stretches, like his father, John Neville remained essentially a Durham man, and Raby Castle, near the Tees in South Durham, was his principal residence. The manor and castle of Brancepeth, near Durham City, also served for use as a frequent base for conducting both his own business and that of the bishop; as early as 1380, John held a seat on the bishop of Durham's temporal council.[11] Eventually to become a march warden, John followed his father as keeper of the royal forests north of the Trent, an additional source of influence. That influence would swell with the statutory powers of a march warden and a closer connection with John of Gaunt, the king's lieutenant in the region, in the 1380s.[12]

Neville's connection to Lancaster came first from the latter's need for experienced soldiers.[13] John Neville had been captain of a company of men in France in 1359, and entered into Gaunt's formal employment with the receipt of his first annuity at Brancepeth in 1366.[14] The following year he served as an executor of his late father's will, and with the exception of a single abbreviated journey to France in 1369, spent the next three years on royal commissions in the north, where he participated in the property market and established his own affinity.[15] He became

---

[7] Charles R. Young, *The Making of the Neville Family in England, 1166–1400* (Woodbridge, 1996), p. 104.

[8] *The Anonimalle Chronicle*, ed. V. H. Galbraith (Manchester, 1927), p. 27.

[9] Michael Prestwich, 'The English at the Battle of Neville's Cross', *The Battle of Neville's Cross, 1346*, ed. David Rollason and Michael Prestwich (Stamford, 1998), pp. 4–5. This was also the opinion of Thomas Sampson in a letter to his friend. For a translation of that letter, originally quoted by Froissart, see Mark Arvanigian and Antony Leopold, 'Illustrative Documents', *Battle of Neville's Cross*, p. 136. For Ralph Neville's role in constructing the monument itself, see J. Linda Drury, 'The Monument at Neville's Cross', *Battle of Neville's Cross*, pp. 85–6.

[10] For a short discussion, see Drury, 'The Monument at Neville's Cross', p. 85.

[11] PRO, DURH 20/114/8.

[12] R. L. Storey, 'The Wardens of the Marches of England towards Scotland, 1377–1489', *EHR* lxxii (1957), pp. 593–615.

[13] Gaunt retained Neville initially for service abroad in 1366–7. *Foedera* (20 vols, The Hague, 1704–35), III, ii, p. 812; Walker, *Lancastrian Affinity*, p. 276.

[14] Anthony Goodman, *John of Gaunt: The Exercise of Princely Power in Fourteenth-Century Europe* (Harlow, 1992), p. 298.

[15] For the formal accounting of Neville's part in the French campaign of 1369, see PRO, E 101/315/28. Prominent members of his own affinity included Roger Fulthorp, Thomas Surtees, John Conyers (his

co-warden of the East March in 1368 with Henry, lord Percy, and the old bishop of Durham, Thomas Hatfield.[16] This was followed by the acquisition of estates through his attorneys in Northumberland (from the widow of Geoffrey Scrope) and then around the manor of Raskelf, near the city of York.[17] At length, Neville acquired the manor of Raskelf in its entirety and granted it as a conveyance to use to his retainer, Sir Thomas Surtees of Durham.[18] He then completed the business of his inheritance, when he and his co-executor (and retainer), John Birtley, rendered their account of the forests north of the Trent, as his late father's executors, at the exchequer.[19]

The late-1360s also saw the dismantling of Edward III's plans for creating a web of influence through his children. W. M. Ormrod has convincingly argued that Edward conceived of the application of Henry II's family dynasty, to be achieved through the promotion of his children's interests abroad. He has further argued that while these aspirations were formulated before the making of the treaty of Brétigny, they were already in the process of unravelling by the late-1360s.[20] October 1368 brought the death of Edward's second son, Lionel of Antwerp, duke of Clarence, who had recently married Violante, daughter of the powerful Galeazzo Visconti, duke of Milan. Moreover, from Edward's standpoint, June 1369 brought the saga of the marriage of Louis de Mâle's daughter and sole heir, Margaret, to an unsatisfactory conclusion. Edward III had desperately hoped for a marriage between Margaret and his younger son, Edmund of Langley, and spent much of the 1360s pursuing this.[21] However, after some years of prevaricating, Margaret married instead Charles V's brother, Philip of Burgundy, effectively ceding Flanders to Burgundy and completing an important shift of the diplomatic landscape of north-west Europe, very much to Edward III's disadvantage.

All of this coincided with the disintegration of English diplomatic gains enshrined in the Bretigny agreement. By the late-1360s, a number of Gascon nobles, led by the count of Armagnac, were challenging the seigniorial rights of the Black Prince as lord of Aquitaine, bringing suits against him before Charles V in Paris rather than Edward III, their nominal overlord.[22] Armagnac arranged for the marriage of his nephew, the sire d'Albret, to Charles' sister-in-law, Marguerite de Bourbon, and Albret in turn soon renounced his allegiance to the Black Prince and the English crown. Richard Barber has identified this as a diplomatic turning point for the French king, who took the opportunity to challenge English control of the whole province. Whether Charles sensed a weakness in the English position in Aquitaine, or in the personages of Edward III and his eldest son, is uncertain.[23]

---

receiver-general by 1383), William Blakeden, and Sir Ralph Hastings. For some of their associations, see *CPR 1367–70*, pp. 201 (commission of oyer et terminer), 428 (inquisition).

16   *RS*, II, p. 2.

17   Chris Given-Wilson, *The English Nobility in the Late Middle Ages* (1987), pp. xii–xiii.

18   PRO, E 212/34. For the grant of Raskelf manor to Surtees, see PRO, E 40/416.

19   PRO, E 210/1222. John would later be granted these forests, and pass them on, at length, to his son, Ralph, confirming the office's informal, but real, inherited status.

20   Ormrod, 'Edward III and his Family', p. 417.

21   Ibid., pp. 412–13.

22   The French king certainly had undermined the prince's authority for much of the 1360s, though a fundamental change came at the session of the estates in January 1368, when a number of Gascon nobles objected to paying their share of a proposed *fouage*. Richard Barber, *Edward, Prince of Wales and Aquitaine* (London, 1978), pp. 209–15.

23   Ibid., p. 215.

Certainly, the Black Prince would soon be incapacitated (permanently, as it turned out) by an illness that saw his departure from Aquitaine and the French war almost altogether.[24] Whether this can be extrapolated into a diplomatic advantage, it is nonetheless the case that by 1369, the English aspirations expressed in the Brétigny treaty were in serious abeyance; Edward III's wish that his influence be expressed through his children was therefore becoming elusive.

The events in France in the late-1360s, and particularly the English response in 1369, were significant for Gaunt and his affinity.[25] The 1369 campaign would mark his first French command, and thus was significant in terms of retinue formation, as he strengthened ties with a number of experienced commanders. Simon Walker has shown that important members of the Lancastrian affinity first came into service around 1369, though many had existing ties to Gaunt, either as tenants in Richmondshire or through another prior tenurial or service connection.[26] Many had been granted protections in 1366, in anticipation of the Spanish campaign that ended with the English victory at Najera.[27] For those already in his service, connections with Gaunt and the crown were strengthened in 1369. In recognition of the role he would now play in Gaunt's war retinue, John Neville was in that year made a knight of the Garter.[28] The 1369 campaign proved also to be something of a turning point for Edward III's personal rule, as it began one of the most intensive periods of fighting in the French war, and witnessed the final collapse of his aspirations for the royal children. While the campaign itself was less than fully successful, some historians have argued that the duke and his retinue were essentially blameless in its outcome.[29] Anthony Goodman has shown that the contemporary accounts of the stalemate between Gaunt and the duke of Burgundy seem to differ along national lines; nonetheless, they generally agree that a sort of paralysis overtook both commanders, probably stemming from their unwillingness to risk a major defeat in the field.[30]

In any event, familial loss soon overshadowed the failure of Gaunt's first important command. How and how much this affected the character of English government and the activities of the duke and his retainers merits some consideration. Duchess Blanche, heiress of Henry of Lancaster and she who, through marriage, had raised Gaunt's prospects immeasurably, died in September of 1368. Following this, in 1369, Queen Philippa herself fell mortally ill.[31] Both were enormously

---

[24] The Black Prince's final campaign finished with the successful but ultimately damaging sack of Limoges in 1370, after which he returned to England, never to fight again. David Green, *The Black Prince* (Stroud, 2001), chapter 7. Edward had meant to lead the 1369 campaign himself, but was prevented by the queen's death. W. M. Ormrod, *The Reign of Edward III: Crown and Political Society in England, 1327–1377* (London, 1990), p. 33.

[25] For the full picture of English retinues in the campaigns of these years, see J. W. Sherborne, 'Indentured Retainers and English Expeditions to France, 1369–80', *EHR* lxxix (1964), pp. 718–46.

[26] Walker, *Lancastrian Affinity*, p. 27.

[27] *Foedera*, III, ii, p. 812.

[28] George Holmes, *The Good Parliament* (Oxford, 1975), p. 68. This probably marks the adoption of the bull's head as his personal heraldic symbol.

[29] James Sherborne, 'John of Gaunt, Edward III's Retinue and the French Campaign of 1369', *Kings and Nobles in the Later Middle Ages: A Tribute to Charles Ross*, ed. Ralph A. Griffiths and James Sherborne (Gloucester, 1986), pp. 56–7; Sydney Armitage-Smith, *John of Gaunt* (London, 1904), pp. 72–4.

[30] Goodman, *John of Gaunt*, pp. 230–32.

[31] Blanche died on or around 12 September 1368: Goodman, *John of Gaunt*, pp. 46–7.

popular, and the queen especially was the beloved matron of the kingdom, as well as being an important figure in the royal court.[32] If some disarray in Edward's court followed her demise, it would certainly explain why Gaunt saw fit to cut short his stay in France, and return to England having served only half of his contracted time.[33] As it happened, 1369 proved also to be a milestone in the government's French policy, in that it marked the beginning of a five-year period that saw the government move the prosecution of the French war to the top of its agenda. Politically, that year also saw the rise to prominence in royal government of William, lord Latimer, who became steward of the household in 1369. Latimer was a wealthy former soldier and a confidant of John of Gaunt and John Neville, who would add his voice to those most influential with the king in the coming years.[34]

For his part, in May 1370, lord Neville became admiral of the king's fleet north of the Thames and the *de facto* keeper of the Newcastle customs house.[35] By July, he had been made co-warden of the East March, sharing that responsibility with several others.[36] The English crown mounted another French campaign behind the royal princes in 1370, and John played the role of ferryman, most notably organising transport to Normandy for an army led by Sir Robert Knolles, in advance of his *chevauchée*. This had originally been planned as just one component of a much larger expedition, destined ultimately for Gascony, along with other armies under the command of Gaunt and the Black Prince.[37] Yet as the latter failed to materialise, the campaign overall amounted to very little. Lord Neville spent much of his time in 1370–1 dealing with other admiralty business, in particular overseeing a complex set of negotiations involving the English seizure of two Genoese trading vessels, each holding cargo of significant value. As the case dragged on through the autumn, he and the king's other admiral, Guy de Brienne, were eventually granted leave to negotiate directly with the doge of Genoa on the king's behalf, with the hope of bringing the matter to a swift conclusion.[38]

Important changes had also taken place in the management of English territories in France. By 1371, Gaunt had replaced the ailing Black Prince as the king's lieutenant in Aquitaine, and he would later marry Constance, daughter and heir of the ousted Catalan king Enrique of Trastamara. In taking these steps, he seems to have fully assumed his brother Edward's interests and aspirations in France and Spain, becoming in some ways the embodiment of English foreign policy in these regions. As Gaunt's servant, the focus of lord Neville's career also shifted away from the Scottish border, toward the royal court and its chief interest: the war with France. In February 1371, his earlier indenture with Lancaster was confirmed.[39] In it, Neville was bound by the familiar terms of life service, receiving an annuity of 50 marks in peacetime and 500 marks in times of war. In the latter, he and his men – five knights, twenty men-at-arms and twenty mounted archers, which he was bound to

---

[32] Ormrod, *Reign of Edward III*, p. 34; Barber, *Edward, Prince of Wales*, p. 227.

[33] Sherborne, 'John of Gaunt', p. 56.

[34] Michael Prestwich, *The Three Edwards: War and State in England, 1272–1377* (New York, 1980), p. 286.

[35] *Foedera*, III, ii, p. 892. John's father, Ralph, seems to have first purchased for the family the farm of the customs of Newcastle on 20 May 1360, for a sum of £85.

[36] *Foedera*, III, ii, p. 895.

[37] Young, *Neville Family*, p. 120; Barber, *Edward, Prince of Wales*, p. 223; *Foedera*, III, ii, p. 896.

[38] PRO, E 101/30/22; *CCR 1369–74*, pp. 216–17, 224, 234–5.

[39] For this and what follows, see *CPR 1370–4*, p. 46.

provide for wartime service – also received their share of whatever wages Gaunt might negotiate from the crown, and a share in any attendant spoils. In that same year, his friend, Latimer, became Edward III's chamberlain, and as a result of his influence (and Gaunt's), lord Neville took his place as steward of the royal household. Moreover, he and members of his immediate household (his chamberlain, his grooms and several attendants) were explicitly welcome as resident guests at Gaunt's palace of the Savoy. However, this had become insufficient to his needs: though busy much of the year gathering his inheritance and gaining full rights to the Neville patrimony, by late 1368 John had purchased a significant residence of his own in London, presumably anticipating greater residential requirements in the capital.[40] The details of the indenture, the appointment to the stewardship, and the purchase of a London residence all demonstrate his improved prospects as a courtesan and politician, as he took charge of the king's household.

Formally, as Chris Given-Wilson has shown, the offices of chamberlain and steward were roughly equal in status.[41] In practice, however, the stewardship was recognised as a stepping stone to the chamber; the latter offered access to the king's person, and with it the prospect of tremendous influence. Contemporaries understood the power of this office, evidenced by the frequent animosity reserved for its most prominent holders, such as the exquisite unpopularity of the younger Despenser with the political community during the reign of Edward II. The power of the chamberlain was also a primary issue in the two most confrontational parliaments of the fourteenth century. In the Good Parliament of 1376, Latimer was expelled (albeit temporarily) from the household and public life under a cloud, while in the Merciless Parliament of 1387 the Commons and their allies took more severe measures against Richard II's chamberlain and long-time tutor, Sir Simon Burley. Access to the king's person, by way of the chamber, was coveted as a route to power, and its potential for delivering that power often made it the focus of intense political scrutiny.

By comparison, the stewardship was less controversial. Certainly, the office could be linked with (occasionally excessive) royal influence – as was amply expressed by the Commons and their backers in 1376. Yet the steward was also an officer of state, and as such was occasionally called upon to preside over public matters – appearing at the head of inquests or trials, for example – and thus avoided becoming a lightning rod for such intense opposition. If as steward Neville's access to the king's person was inferior to that of the chamberlain, his duties may also have been more onerous, including, with the above, the general coordination of the household. Moreover, while the new chamberlain was unlikely to leave the company of the king for long periods, the steward might be forced to do so. Lord Neville often served as an ambassador and commissioner during his years as household steward (see below), and his absences from court have caused some historians to suppose that he was less involved with the mismanagement of government and other improprieties alleged by the Commons in 1376.[42] Perhaps this was so: he certainly did not amass the riches allegedly misappropriated by Latimer, Lyons and their co-conspirators in the early 1370s.

---

40 *CCR 1364–8*, p. 350, 355, 416.
41 For what follows, see Chris Given-Wilson, *The Royal Household and the King's Affinity: Service, Politics and Finance in England, 1360–1413* (London, 1986), pp. 72–5.
42 Prestwich, *Three Edwards*, p. 103.

Nonetheless, lord Neville's influence over affairs was significant, and his reward commensurately great. The chief interest of the government remained the prosecution of the war in France, and as an experienced military commander, his attentions were turned in that direction. By early 1372, he had sworn out an indenture to act as chief negotiator of a treaty with Duke John de Montfort of Brittany, Edward III's new son-in-law.[43] Neville appointed his friend and neighbour in the north, Thomas, lord Roos of Helmsley, as his attorney in England, empowering him to act on his behalf in all matters of consequence during this absence.[44] Roos was a significant Yorkshire landowner, soldier and long-time member of Gaunt's military retinue. His father, William, fought as a commander in the earl of Arundel's division (some 2,000 strong) at Crécy, along with his friend and Yorkshire neighbour, lord Willoughby.[45] After witnessing the elevation of his patron, Henry of Grosmont, to the duchy of Lancaster in 1350, William Roos served as a naval commander against the Spanish off Winchelsea.[46] He died campaigning in Prussia with Henry of Grosmont in 1351, when he left his estates to his son, Thomas.[47] Thomas, lord Roos of Helmsley, campaigned with Grosmont's eventual heir, John of Gaunt, in 1369, 1370, 1372 and 1373, and like Neville had been in receipt of a Lancastrian annuity since 1366.[48] Long-standing colleagues and associates in private matters, Neville and his neighbour remained close over the years. In December 1371, lord Roos sold him the estates of the late William Everingham for £200 during the minority of his heiress.[49] As a direct result of Neville's lobbying, Roos was excused a forfeiture in 1371, and by August, 1372, he was paying John an annuity of £40.[50] Over the years, John would purchase numerous estates from him in Yorkshire, including Baildon and Thornton, near Craven, with many outlying rents and appurtenances.[51] Neville also acted as his executor in 1373, when Roos accompanied Gaunt on his famous *chevauchée* through northern France; he received a Lancastrian annuity until 1380, when he retired from military life altogether.[52]

As the new patriarch of a large and ambitious family, John Neville was already the focus of the aspirations of others by 1370, when the stewardship and his first important command in France created further opportunities for patronage. For example, at least one family member (a cousin, William) accompanied him to Brittany as a fee'd retainer.[53] A brother, Sir Robert Neville, was also a Lancastrian retainer and frequently served under John's command.[54] He had experience in Brittany, and was often utilised there by the crown. In 1371, Robert was commissioned by the king to negotiate with the duke of Brittany over the return of Becherel and other provinces, and over a possible long-term alliance between Edward and

43 PRO, E 30/280.
44 PRO, E/101/32/24.
45 Jean Froissart, *Chronicles*, trans. G. Brereton (Harmondsworth, 1968), p. 84.
46 Ibid., p. 114.
47 *Knighton's Chronicle, 1337 to 1396*, ed. G. H. Martin (Oxford, 1995), p. 112.
48 *JGR 1379–83*, II, no. 945; Walker, *Lancastrian Affinity*, p. 280. John Neville also was retained perhaps for the first time by the duke, for service abroad, in 1366–7. *Foedera*, III, ii, p. 812.
49 *CPR 1370–4*, p. 158.
50 Ibid., pp. 27, 194.
51 PRO, E 210/4426. The estates were ordered delivered to Lord Neville on 8 July: PRO, E 326/221.
52 He died in 1384. Goodman, *John of Gaunt*, pp. 288–9.
53 Young, *Neville Family*, p. 120.
54 Walker, *Lancastrian Affinity*, p. 276.

John de Montfort.[55] Sir Robert became a significant figure in Lancastrian circles over the next several years, and would ultimately be returned to twelve Parliaments by the Yorkshire electors.[56] Another younger brother, William – an experienced soldier who had already campaigned with John at least once – replaced his brother as admiral of the north.[57] In 1372, he swore out his own indenture for service in France with the crown, and was one of the sea captains charged with ferrying lord Neville's army to Brittany.[58] He continued as admiral of the north for several years, rendering annual accounts for his activities with the exchequer and serving as a leading figure in the defence of the coast.[59] Charles Young has argued that William was sufficiently well thought of by the crown for the government to entrust him on more than one occasion with the collection of large sums of money.[60] This was probably so, and Sir William in turn became a source of patronage for other family members as well as tenants and northern associates, as his retinue roll aptly demonstrates.[61] In this way, just as the Neville brothers had each received their entrée into high political circles at the behest of family members and friends, so too did they provide similar patronage for others.

It seems that the French campaign of 1372 had the full backing of the king and his advisors, yet it was to be an unwieldy undertaking. Planned as a four-pronged affair, it began with an expedition in August, led by the king and the Black Prince, to relieve the siege of La Rochelle following the earl of Pembroke's disastrous defeat at the hands of a Spanish fleet. However, this enterprise experienced notoriously poor luck in getting under way, and by October it had finished without incident, the weather ultimately causing its abandonment.[62] Having sworn out protections in June, lord Neville was to lead a much smaller second force, on the order of 1,000 men-at-arms and archers, to Brest in support of the besieged duke of Brittany.[63] He was to be reinforced there by Sir William Neville and his sailors, along with their human cargo: a land army under the command of William Montague, earl of Salisbury. Securing an alliance with the duke of Brittany had lately been the focus of much English diplomatic effort, and as the former marshal of Brittany (1365), Sir Robert Neville accompanied John on this expedition.[64] Having first cut his military teeth in the Crécy campaign in the company of the Black Prince, Robert had since shown himself an able commander over the years.[65] A fee'd Lancastrian retainer, he campaigned with Gaunt in 1367 and 1369 and, naturally enough, served as one of the envoys to Brittany with lord Neville in 1371.[66] Indeed, members of the royal household had much experience in Brittany: lord Latimer himself had served as an

[55] *Foedera*, III, ii, pp. 927–8.
[56] Walker, *Lancastrian Affinity*, p. 240n.
[57] PRO, E 320/280; E 101/68/5/111; E 101/68/5/116.
[58] PRO, E/101/68/5/105.
[59] PRO, E 101/68/5/112.
[60] Young, *Neville Family*, p. 121.
[61] PRO, E 101/32/24; E 101/33/13.
[62] Richard Barber, *Life and Campaigns of the Black Prince* (Woodbridge, 1979), p. 138. The king and his army were perhaps seven weeks at sea without favourable wind. This comes from a translation of the chronicle of Chandos Herald, whose master was a famous member of the Prince's retinue and who may well have had good information on this undertaking.
[63] *Anonimalle Chronicle*, p. 71; *Foedera*, III, ii, p. 948.
[64] Michael Jones, *Ducal Brittany, 1364–1399* (Oxford, 1970), p. 42.
[65] Froissart, *Chronicles*, p. 84; Young, *Neville Family*, p. 116.
[66] Walker, *Lancastrian Affinity*, p. 276; Jones, *Ducal Brittany*, p. 67.

English officer there, from which assignment he was later accused of making a size-able and untoward profit by the Good Parliament.[67]

The final prong of the 1372 campaign was to be led by Lancaster himself, who at Calais would assemble his largest command to date and one of the largest English armies yet put into the field in France, over 6,000 men in all.[68] In the meantime, in April of 1371, his brother-in-law, the earl of Pembroke, had been made the king's lieutenant in Aquitaine.[69] Brought about for the purpose of strengthening the defences in Aquitaine in anticipation of renewed hostilities, the earl instead succumbed at La Rochelle, and was taken prisoner.[70] The personal commands of Gaunt, Pembroke and the household officers certainly support the contention that all were committed to a belligerent war policy by 1371, perhaps wishing to reassert the advantage and momentum gained by Gaunt and the Black Prince at Najera to re-establish the gains of Bretigny. Indeed, as part of this overall strategy, Edward III had himself invested much, through his renewed alliance with the duke of Brittany. As part of Duke John IV's marriage settlement, and just days before a treaty between the two was announced, he was granted the valuable and strategic English earldom of Richmond.[71] This had been confiscated by Edward III on the death of John III, who died childless; it was first granted to Queen Philippa, and then to John of Gaunt in 1351.[72]

The return of Richmond to the duke marked an important transaction, enrolled at Westminster before a gathering of the court. Edward required Richmond, and Gaunt did his part by granting it to the crown, for the purpose of completing the alliance with Brittany. Yet Lancaster did not personally bear the cost of his father's diplomatic gesture; he was richly compensated by the crown with other English lands, including the lordships of Knaresborough and Tickhill. While Richmond had been strategically important to Gaunt as the lynch pin of his northern estates (and his greatest single holding in North Yorkshire), his compensation proved more than generous.[73] Moreover, the duke of Brittany rarely enjoyed the fruits of his English earldom, as shown in his repeated petitions of Richard II's council for the payment of vast sums owed to him.[74] The honor was anyway confiscated in 1381 by the English government, which in turn farmed its components to various members of the northern baronage, including, respectively, Henry Percy, John Neville, Henry Fitzhugh, Ralph Lumley and, finally, John Neville's son, Ralph.[75] Few of these ever showed much of a compunction to remit the sums owed to de Montfort's receiver, and their arrangements with the royal exchequer indicate that the sums were anyway

---

[67] Holmes, *Good Parliament*, pp. 126–30, is the most complete exposition of the charges of extortion against Latimer by the 1376 parliament. Jones, *Ducal Brittany*, pp. 52–3, 167, further explains the Breton context.

[68] Holmes, *Good Parliament*, p. 23.

[69] *Foedera*, III, ii, p. 941.

[70] Anthony Tuck, *Crown and Nobility, 1272–1461: Political Conflict in Late Medieval England* (1985), p. 142.

[71] *Foedera*, III, ii, p. 953.

[72] PRO, DL 10/309; Goodman, *John of Gaunt*, pp. 29–30.

[73] *JGR 1379–83*, I, no. 11. Prestwich, *Three Edwards*, pp. 286–7, termed this a 'diplomatic necessity'. PRO, DL 10/309; SC 6/1092/13; DL 10/339.

[74] *Proceedings and Ordinances of the Privy Council of England*, ed. N. H. Nicolas (7 vols, London, 1834–7), I, p. 47; Jones, *Ducal Brittany*, p. 193; *CPR 1381–5*, p. 540; *CPR 1396–9*, p. 13.

[75] Jones, *Ducal Brittany*, pp. 189–95.

highly negotiable.[76] The matter of Richmond was not finally dealt with until Henry IV granted the earldom to Ralph Neville in 1399, for the term of his life.[77] Thus, although Gaunt had surrendered the lordship in 1372, his political interests were nonetheless hardly suborned in Richmondshire, as his retainers generally retained control of it for the remainder of his life. Although willing to use it to help buy success in the French campaign, through his affinity the duke had also engineered a broad continuation of his own hegemony in Richmondshire, and gained healthy compensation, to boot.

The 1372 campaign itself was in fact carried out with significant difficulty. Lord Neville's army faced a considerable delay at Southampton, during which the crown made a number of urgent appeals to local tradesmen warning of the impropriety and potential hazards of overcharging the king's soldiers for supplies during its stay there. Only in mid-October, after a delay of several months, did the force finally depart from English shores.[78] It landed in Brittany on or around 16 October, with a force totalling about 1,000 men, divided more or less equally between men-at-arms and archers.[79] The delay had proved costly: in the interim, the duke of Brittany had decided (or had always planned) not to pay liege homage to Edward in the event of the latter becoming king of France.[80] The commitment of the English to a high-profile and expensive campaign, and their delay in putting it in motion, seems to have provided him sufficient opportunity to alter the terms of his agreement with King Edward, *ex post facto*. Ironically, as Michael Jones points out, this new condition was simply the duke echoing Edward III's own thinking on provincial relations with the French crown, in his own role as duke of Aquitaine.[81]

Lord Neville's force initially had success in Brittany, relieving John IV's position at Brest, which had lately been in English hands as part-payment for the Richmond honor – an exchange that would later be repeated by Richard II. The two men quickly came to a formal agreement on the crown's behalf, and Neville assumed the prestigious, if rather expensive, office of captain of Brest, where he remained until 1374, when he surrendered the post to Sir Robert Knolles.[82] Over that time, de Montfort borrowed significant sums from lord Neville, for which he was not reimbursed anytime soon by the English government; indeed, this was consistent with the financial difficulties faced by a number of captains of Brest.[83] At any rate, it was Neville's aim in 1372 to move inland from Brest, hopefully with French attention diverted away by the arrival of the English host. Unfortunately, renewed English in-

---

[76] Jones, *Ducal Brittany*, pp. 189–91.

[77] Ralph, Lord Neville of Raby (1388) and first earl of Westmorland (1397), died in 1425.

[78] The length of his stay at Southampton is uncertain, though it has been suggested that he remained there for fifteen months, during which time the crown tried to commission ships to carry his party across the Channel. The account of one William Beaufrey shows that the small army was finally ferried across by local ships, though Neville's brother may also have been involved in arranging their transport. PRO, E 101/32/22.

[79] Young, *Neville Family*, p. 120.

[80] Jones, *Ducal Brittany*, p. 70.

[81] Ibid.

[82] *RP*, II, p. 328; *Foedera*, III, ii, p. 953; *Anonimalle Chronicle*, p. 71; Sherborne, 'Indentured Retinues', pp. 726–7.

[83] Sherborne has shown that Lord Neville was remunerated just over £4,073 by the crown for the mustering of the retinues themselves and their transport from England, though he reckons this to have been around £750 below the agreed amount. Sherborne, 'Indentured Retinues', p. 726; Jones, *Ducal Brittany*, Appendix E.

volvement in Brittany proved immediately unpopular with the Breton nobility, and in spite of an avowed loyalty to their duke, they invited Charles V's able constable, Bertrand du Guesclin, to intervene on their behalf. This he promptly did, besieging Neville at Brest and rendering impotent the thrust of the proposed invasion.[84] At length, the siege was lifted by forces led by Sir William Neville, the earl of Salisbury, as well as John of Gaunt at the head of his great force, though by that time de Montfort had fled to England, and the opportunity to press on had been lost.[85] Indeed, in spite of the considerable sums spent on the campaigns of the early 1370s, very little had actually been achieved. The truce at Perigueux, made in the spring of 1374, ended the campaign, and it was widely felt in England that an opportunity had been missed.[86] In spite of chronic financial difficulties, Neville and his army continued to hold Brest until 1374, when the command was transferred to the capable hands of Robert Knolles and John Devereaux before Neville's return to England.[87] Gaunt seems to have funnelled money to Neville during his captaincy at Brest, and even before his return began the process of gaining remunerating for him for his losses, as evidenced by his activities at the Savoy in June of 1373.[88]

Neville's role in the widely derided Breton campaign proved politically damaging to him in the short term. Charles Young has shown that he was charged by the Good Parliament with failing to meet certain financial obligations at Brest.[89] Whether the charge was made in good faith is not known; it is likely, however, that the undoubted cash shortfall had in fact emanated from the general direction of the royal treasury. By way of response, Neville complained loudly in parliament and elsewhere of the government's failure to adequately underwrite his nearly two-year defence of Brest.[90] Moreover, he was actually remunerated by the exchequer after his departure from government in 1376, part of which was earmarked as repayment of an outstanding debt, still owed him from his stint in Brittany. Neville himself was probably one of the crown's many occasional creditors in its French endeavours; as the 1376 parliament made clear, Latimer was very much in the business of arranging loans to the king, investments that often boasted very favourable rates of return.

However, there may also have been some merit in the commons' assertion that Neville was paid for a larger and more effective army than he actually brought to Brittany in 1372. As James Sherborne points out, an experienced and ambitious soldier was unlikely to sabotage his own military fortunes for the sake of short-term financial gain.[91] As no record of a response to this from the commons exists, his version of events may well have been accepted. Nonetheless, Professor Holmes has certainly shown that Neville, like Latimer, made significant financial gains in this period.[92] However, the parliamentary charge of financial malfeasance may also

84 Tuck, *Crown and Nobility*, p. 143.
85 Goodman, *John of Gaunt*, p. 234.
86 Armitage-Smith describes the endeavour as a 'fiasco'. Armitage-Smith, *John of Gaunt*, pp. 116–17, 122.
87 Despite his lack of resources, Neville seems to have withstood a rather large French siege, by offering hostages and managing resources. Jones, *Ducal Brittany*, p. 147.
88 *JGR, 1379–83*, II, no. 1332.
89 Young, *Neville Family*, p. 120.
90 Jones, *Ducal Brittany*, p. 147; Holmes, *Good Parliament*, p. 130.
91 Sherborne, 'Indentured Retinues', p. 727.
92 Holmes, *Good Parliament*, pp. 108–34, outlines the financial charges made by the 1376 parliament against Latimer, Neville and Lyons in particular. The charge against Neville which dealt with his stint in

demonstrate the degree to which the two men symbolised wayward royal policy, in Neville's case its exponent abroad. Clearly, some saw him not as a servant of an active and independent royal will, but rather as something like an architect of royal policy himself, and therefore personally culpable for that policy's failure. But how much influence did he wield? We can be certain that at certain junctures in the early 1370s, Neville, Latimer and others had a naked, direct influence on royal policy; the 1376 parliament knew it, and cited egregious examples where it could.[93]

John Neville's influence with the king seems to have lacked any specific roots, though its development may yet be pieced together. Tradition points to the death of Queen Philippa in 1369 (along with that of Lionel of Antwerp a year earlier) as coinciding with the decay of Edward's familial and diplomatic settlements of the 1360s.[94] Whether or not the queen's death was itself a catalyst for Edward's decline in vigour, it certainly seems to have opened up of the royal court to mischief. Anthony Tuck and others agree that, from about 1371 onward, Neville and his father-in-law, Latimer, were the dominant figures in the household and the court. Their influence over the king was thought to have exceeded even that of the royal princes, and Michael Prestwich has argued that Latimer and other courtiers effectively directed royal patronage.[95] This point should not be overstated: Edward's real decline into ineffectualness still lay some years hence. However, we might ask whether, as a political reality, the king's dotage should be seen as a progressive decline, perhaps taking place over a few years rather than assuming the form of an abrupt collapse. Ormrod has pointed out that strong royal will was still evident in the early 1370s, and that it was only around 1375 that we can discern its diminution.[96] Yet Edward's increasing willingness to listen to and respond positively to the opinions and applications of his steward and chamberlain offered both men significant opportunities to expand their influence. As early as 1371, both Neville and Latimer were able to secure pardons for a number of their own servants and allies, often for murders and other serious felonies.[97]

Yet influencing policy was not directing it. After all, the king was sufficiently vigorous to campaign personally in 1369 and 1372, being denied the opportunity only by personal tragedy and poor weather, respectively. Moreover, the rise of certain other important courtiers, like Alice Perrers, posed challenges to and placed limitations on any ambitions Latimer and Neville may have harboured, collectively or individually.[98] Rosemary Horrox has rightly described the court as anything but monolithic; it was instead a heterodox organism, a political arena where a variety of interests competed simultaneously for the king's interest, favour and patronage.[99]

Brittany is discussed ibid., p. 130, which hints that he may also have tried to profit by taking fewer men than he had contracted for with the king to Brest on the campaign.

[93] The startling degree to which Latimer especially was organising patronage, against what the nobility especially thought was its 'natural grain', is discussed in Ormrod, *Reign of Edward III*, pp. 115–20.

[94] Ormrod, 'Edward III and his Family', pp. 416–17.

[95] Tuck, *Crown and Nobility*, p. 141; Prestwich, *Three Edwards*, p. 286.

[96] Ormrod, *Reign of Edward III*, p. 118.

[97] For Neville, see the cases of William Johnson of Tynemouth (Northumberland) and John Hoton of Yorkshire; for Latimer, see, in October 1371, pardon granted to one Zenobe Martin, a Lombard. *CPR 1374–7*, pp. 136, 195–7.

[98] Holmes, *Good Parliament*, pp. 68–69.

[99] Rosemary Horrox, 'Caterpillars of the Commonwealth? Courtiers in Late Medieval England', *Rulers*

Access to the king undoubtedly gave the household officers unique influence over royal policy (as contemporaries understood well), and this King Edward was far from the vigorous young king that had led victorious armies at Crécy and Poitiers. Nonetheless, evidence for unusual influence over policy by Neville or Latimer is quite limited in these years, and such influence seems to have been confined to relatively short periods, perhaps during moments of royal infirmity. Edward III, though certainly showing the effects of age, nonetheless remained the master of his court and government in the early 1370s. It seems therefore straightforward: Latimer and Neville were looked upon favourably, and this led to their promotion.

Edward's continued direction also probably precluded any great competition between members of the household on the one hand, and Gaunt and the earl of Pembroke on the other, over control of wartime policy and the direction of patronage.[100] There is in fact very little evidence of discord between Gaunt and the household officers. Latimer was a wealthy former soldier, and with his son-in-law lord Neville's assistance, he parlayed that wealth into significant political influence and still further wealth. No parliament was held between 1373 (when the Commons still believed the French campaign to be proceeding acceptably) and the Good Parliament of 1376, and it was here that the greatest abuses were alleged against members of the household. Neville had been steward and a councillor from 1371 to 1376. He became steward of the temporalities of the see of York during its vacancy, and was clearly a defining factor in the elevation of his brother, Alexander, to the archbishopric. In 1374, he witnessed his brother's consecration at the head of a large contingent of barons, perhaps a demonstration of his growing power.[101] With his return from Brittany, it is clear that the crown still owed him significant sums from his time at Brest, and he set about the business of replenishing his stock of ready money.[102] A number of enrolments made in chancery bare this out. In 1375, he exchanged his annuity of £100 from the exchequer for a similar annuity from Penrith, in Cumberland, presumably to expand his influence there.[103] He sold land to Sir Robert Knolles, and took a single loan of 2,000 marks from the executors of the earl of Pembroke in late 1374, which must have required at least the tacit approval of the crown.[104]

However, some have viewed these as anomalies. Prestwich has argued that Neville actually received few tangible rewards from his time at the centre of royal governance, and that they paled in comparison to Latimer's.[105] Holmes has concluded that his prominence in the financial and military charges brought by the commons in 1376 surely were the result of the opposite being true.[106] Clues seem to lie in John Neville's origins. In spite of his experience as a soldier and a courtier, Neville remained essentially a north-country baron, and his stint as steward produced a significant expansion of his landed interests in that region. He held the

and Ruled in Late Medieval England, ed. Rowena E. Archer and Simon Walker (London, 1995), pp. 14–15.

[100] Ormrod, 'Edward III and his Family', p. 417.
[101] *CPR 1370–4*, pp. 432, 449.
[102] *JGR, 1379–83*, I, nos. 163, 170.
[103] *CPR 1374–7*, p. 182.
[104] Ibid., p. 105, 194–5.
[105] Prestwich, *Three Edwards*, p. 287.
[106] Holmes, *Good Parliament*, p. 68 and passim.

temporalities of the archdiocese of York remanding them to his brother in June 1374.[107] By May 1375, he had received *seisin* of his late mother's dower lands and reunited (to its fullest extent) the Neville patrimony in the north-east, combining it with his newly acquired estates. He also gained an annuity from the lordship of Penrith, formerly of the Richmond lordship and now in the hands of the crown.[108] This marks the beginning of the Nevilles' landed interests in the north-west, which had traditionally been the province of families such as the Dacres, Cliffords and Umfravilles.[109] Moreover, this interest became essentially permanent, and over the succeeding decades the Nevilles would eclipse all other families in the region.[110]

Also in 1375, Neville assumed control of the considerable dower lands of Elizabeth, widow of John Mowbray, in the North Riding (which served as a complement to his own lordship of Sheriff Hutton) and he gained a portion of the Yorkshire estates of Walter Fauconberg.[111] As with Penrith, his interest in the Fauconberg lands presaged a more determined one for his offspring in later years. Additionally, in keeping with his *modus operandi* during the final months of Edward's reign, he manipulated the distribution of the balance of the Mowbray lands, naming his associates as the eventual trustees.[112] Indeed, subtle intimations of his influence can be found in numerous royal grants and commissions, in which he had an explicit voice in royal governance. Here, on numerous occasions, decisions are made by the king explicitly crediting Neville's recommendation as the decisive factor in the king's judgement.[113] We can therefore cautiously, but firmly, accept that John Neville's influence in government in the first half of the 1370s was significant, and that his rewards, though perhaps less obvious than those of Latimer or Lyons, were strategically important to his own political and financial circumstances. This is reflected in the strategy of the Good Parliament: though not its primary target, Neville's association with Latimer and his alleged fraud over payments taken for the 1372 Brittany campaign became the focus for enmity (although the campaign's perceived failure was certainly another factor).[114] At least one observer felt that a purging of the household was a necessary step in ridding the king of bad counsel, and returning the nation to sound fiscal governance.[115]

Yet to some degree, all of this misses the point. The most important result of Neville's prominence at court was in cementing his relationship with Gaunt. In 1370, Lancaster had retained him under the now-familiar terms: service for life, in

---

[107] *CPR 1370–4*, p. 449.
[108] *CCR 1374–7*, p. 138. It was confirmed in that same July and again in October (ibid., pp. 144, 177).
[109] For a map showing the extent of Clifford holdings in Westmorland, see Given-Wilson, *English Nobility*, p. xx.
[110] *CPR 1374–7*, p. 182; *CCR 1374–7*, p. 159. Storey has chronicled the rise of Neville hegemony in the West March in the fifteenth century, and includes a map showing the spread of baronial holdings in the Northwest. See R. L. Storey, *The End of the House of Lancaster* (London, 1966), pp. 105–23; there is a useful map of the family's estates on p. 107.
[111] *CPR 1374–7*, pp. 74, 232.
[112] Ibid., p. 253.
[113] See, for example, ibid., pp. 250, 253, 254, 255, 256–7.
[114] The latter seems a slightly narrow view: the resumption of hostilities in France in 1369 had led to virtually nothing in the way of tangible English successes by this time. Neville's 'failure' in Brittany should perhaps be viewed within the broader context of general military ineffectiveness on the part of the English.
[115] Thomas Walsingham, *Historia Anglicana*, ed. H. T. Riley, (2 vols, Rolls Series, London, 1863–4), I, p. 320.

peace and war.[116] Goodman, in his analysis of Gaunt's personal associations, judged that the two men had also become friends. Neville served as a banneret in the duke's army, and in various other capacities until his own death in 1388.[117] This certainly contradicts the notion that Gaunt (with Pembroke) was in a kind of competition with the leading householders; instead, it seems that Lancaster was quietly at work bolstering his own influence through others. Ever the pragmatist, Gaunt strengthened existing connections with leading figures of the court and household, including Neville and Latimer.[118]

Yet his Lancastrian connections and their various requirements had a unique influence on Neville's approach to national policy, as he increasingly found his interests intertwined with the duke's.[119] Gaunt's relationship with Latimer, while cordial, was more remote.[120] Not a 'Lancastrian' *per se*, Latimer was neither a fee'd retainer nor a member of Gaunt's affinity. His own personal wealth and position in government probably precluded such a patron–client relationship, something that cannot be said of a number of other Lancastrian barons, all of whom were rooted in the north in a way that Latimer was not.[121] After a distinguished military career, William Latimer spent his 'retirement' amassing influence in high political circles: he was truly a courtier. Conversely, Neville was at root a Durham and Yorkshire magnate, with most of his landed interests and holdings located north of York, just one of many recruited by Gaunt.[122]

As a courtier and household officer, John Neville was acting at least in part as Gaunt's partisan between 1371 and 1376, even as the latter continued his frequent absences from court.[123] Goodman is surely correct in noting that the Good Parliament made no objection to any influence Gaunt might have wielded through his numerous fee'd retainers in the household, most notably Scrope of Bolton, John Ypres, and Neville.[124] Yet the fact that the commons did not complain about Gaunt's influence does not disprove its existence; the Commons may not yet have seen anything especially untoward or malign in Gaunt's influence in royal government. By 1376, the king's decline was palpable indeed, and with the death of the Black Prince occurring during the parliament's proceedings, Lancaster was almost certainly regarded by some as a vigorous symbol of stability and legitimacy. He was, after all, a unique figure in England: a prince of the royal blood with eyes fixed on a wider European stage – and an attractive potential, natural leader for an otherwise rudderless government.

Though he never secured a return to court, John Neville certainly demonstrated that he believed himself that Gaunt was the backbone of royal government, and he

---

[116] He was retained at a cost of 100 marks a year. *CCR 1364–8*, p. 350. See also *JGR 1379–83*, I, no. 7; Given-Wilson, *Royal Household*, p. 148. For a full list of Gaunt's retainers, see Walker, *Lancastrian Affinity*, pp. 262–84.

[117] Goodman, *John of Gaunt*, p. 106.

[118] Historians have recognised the possibility of a patronage relationship developing from this. See, for example, Young, *Neville Family*, p. 128.

[119] *CPR 1370–4*, p. 46.

[120] Armitage-Smith, *John of Gaunt*, p. 128.

[121] Walker, *Lancastrian Affinity*, Appendix I.

[122] These included the lords Fitzhugh, Roos, Scrope, Percy and Greystoke, as well as other, junior members of these same families. Walker, *Lancastrian Affinity*, pp. 31, 73, 280–1.

[123] Ibid., pp. 68, 69n.

[124] Goodman, *John of Gaunt*, p. 55.

continued to serve him in numerous capacities.[125] Holmes has shown just how ephemeral the measures taken by the Good Parliament proved to be.[126] The continual council, created by the Good Parliament and with whom the commons' hopes for so-called 'good government' rested, lasted just a few months.[127] The Hilary Parliament itself, though not, as was once thought, packed with Lancastrian retainers, was nonetheless of a different temperament than its predecessor.[128] Reasons for this remain somewhat unclear, though perhaps some evidence can be found in the composition of the intercommuning committee, the body charged with mediating between the commons and the lords. Missing from the slate of four magnates during the Hilary Parliament (though present in 1376) was, for example, the earl of March, a principal architect of the Good Parliament's belligerence toward the household. Present instead were four barons with connections broadly favourable to Gaunt. Henry Percy and Thomas Roos were Lancastrian retainers, and would likely have acted as partisans. Walter Fitzwalter of Essex had originally been belligerent to Gaunt, but his attitude changed sometime before 1382 and he died campaigning with Lancaster in Spain in 1386.[129] The Hilary Parliament may have occasioned that change. The final member was Ralph, lord Basset, an old soldier and prominent commander in Gaunt's army during the 1373 campaign.[130] Basset became disillusioned with its slow progress and with his retinue's lack of pay; unusually, he abandoned the duke as a result, and hastened an early return to England.[131] However, lord Basset was back acting as a charter witness at the Savoy by 1374, the two clearly having mended any rift.[132] The following August, Basset sold the custody of a French prisoner taken during that campaign to the crown for the handsome sum of 12,000 francs – a transaction incidentally witnessed by both Latimer and Neville.[133] It is difficult not to see the quiet hand of the duke of Lancaster at work in these matters.

Moreover, Ralph Basset's attachment to Gaunt strengthened further when he entered into a marriage alliance with another prominent Lancastrian family from their region, the Greys of Codnor. There, he secured the marriage of his daughter and co-heiress, Elizabeth, to Richard, later fourth lord Grey of Codnor, an important Lancastrian servant. Simon Payling has shown that this marriage and control of the Basset estates were critical in elevating the Greys out of the minor baronage and into the English first rank.[134] In fact, it was the making of their political fortunes. To that point, the Greys' Derbyshire estates were relatively minor, and they were anyway just one of a small group of barons utterly overshadowed in the region by Gaunt; the Basset marriage elevated them to the top of that group, and made them attractive

[125] Given-Wilson, *Royal Household*, pp. 73, 158–9.

[126] Holmes, *Good Parliament*, p. 160.

[127] T. F. Tout, *Chapters in the Administrative History of Medieval England*, 6 vols (Manchester, 1920–33), III, pp. 306–9.

[128] Walker, *Lancastrian Affinity*, p. 239.

[129] Goodman, *John of Gaunt*, p. 292.

[130] Sherborne, 'Indentured Retinues', p. 728.

[131] Jones, *Ducal Brittany*, p. 91.

[132] *JGR 1379–83*, I, no. 159.

[133] *CPR 1374–7*, p. 134.

[134] Simon Payling, *Political Society in Lancastrian England: The Greater Gentry of Nottinghamshire* (Oxford, 1991), pp. 90–1.

duchy retainers.[135] Thus, while not himself a fee'd Lancastrian retainer, Basset certainly fits into that group of minor barons aligned with, and patronised by, Gaunt on an ad hoc basis, often on foreign campaigns. He was a peripheral member of the Lancastrian affinity, and would certainly have seen sense in supporting the duke's interests in the Hilary Parliament, particularly in the absence of royal opposition.

Intriguingly, David Green has argued recently, against tradition, that there is little credible evidence for enmity between John of Gaunt and his brother, Edward. The chief evidence for the alleged stand by the Black Prince against Lancaster's ambitions comes from Walsingham, whose credibility on this subject must be questionable.[136] Moreover, Gaunt's phenomenal unpopularity in 1381 was probably presaged by the genuine mistrust of and enmity against him displayed by Peter de la Mare and the commons in 1376 – without the support of Edward of Woodstock, who willingly allowed Gaunt to supplant him in Aquitaine and Spain. But if the Black Prince was silent on the subject of Gaunt's ambition, his father was not. Both Walsingham and Froissart tell us that it was the king that undid the work of the Good Parliament, when, as a result of his own infirmity, he handed the reins of government over to Lancaster.[137] Edward's death in 1377 brought with it the onset of conciliar government, one that was heavily influenced by Gaunt. Although he had formally retired, Walsingham, at least, believed strongly that the duke remained the guiding hand behind royal government, and that the makeup of the council owed much to his influence.[138] All of this points to the 1376 parliament as an anomaly, a genuine protest against those close to the king – Gaunt in particular – who were judged too powerful and influential, particularly in light of the naked profiteering of Latimer, Lyons and others. Through it all, however, Edward's loyalty to his sons, and theirs to him and to each other, seem never to have been in much doubt; all remained mutually supportive.

Perhaps the power of the duke of Lancaster alone is sufficient to explain the political resurrection of John Neville. Following the deaths of the earl of Pembroke in 1375 and the Black Prince in 1376, new leadership was required in Gascony, and Neville was duly made the king's lieutenant in Aquitaine on 10 June 1377, with all the attendant 'pro-consular' powers once enjoyed there by the prince of Wales.[139] The *Anonimalle Chronicle* tells of John's delay in reaching Aquitaine, first spending a few months at Plymouth during which he could not secure carriage for his army. He arrived in Bordeaux on 8 September with a force of a thousand men-at-arms and 2,000 archers, charged with the task of assisting the king of Navarre in accordance with a treaty recently made between him and the English.[140] Neville's tenure in Aquitaine, which lasted from 1378 to 1381, was generally thought to be a success, and he has been credited by some historians with halting, albeit temporarily, the thrust of French incursions into Gascony.[141]

---

[135] Walker, *Lancastrian Affinity*, p. 211.
[136] Green, *Black Prince*, p. 117.
[137] Froissart, *Chronicles*, p. 195; *Chronicon Angliae*, ed. E. M. Thompson (Rolls Series, London, 1874), p. 103; Goodman, *John of Gaunt*, p. 57; N. Saul, *Richard II* (London, 1997), pp. 20–1.
[138] *Historia Anglicana*, I, p. 339.
[139] PRO, E 30/284; *Foedera*, IV, i, p. 43. These powers included the coinage of money, the making of war and the pardoning of rebels.
[140] *Anonimalle Chronicle*, pp. 119–20.
[141] Young, *Neville Family*, p. 121.

Thereafter, the failing diplomatic situation with Scotland drew his attention back to England, and to new challenges in the north. Alistair Macdonald has recently shown that with the accession of Richard II, there came a sharp increase in northern border warfare between England and the Scots.[142] To combat this, Gaunt was called upon to oversee the northern march, and stabilise border defences. Through his retinue, Gaunt was already patron to a sufficient stable of northern barons that, with even the Percies loyal to him, we may style him 'lord of the north', as Professor Hicks once styled Richard, duke of Gloucester.[143] Yet when Gaunt failed to quell border hostilities, he turned to his most experienced captain for assistance. In 1381, lord Neville provided soldiers for the duke's retinue for service in England, and was rewarded handsomely for it.[144] That year, Gaunt made him warden of the East March and governor of Berwick, then of the West March and governor of Carlisle in 1383,[145] where his retinue comprised 120 men-at-arms and 240 archers, a more substantial force than had previously been stationed there.[146] These developments should also be seen in the light of the new dispute between Lancaster and Percy: Neville's return to the north was looked upon with considerable disfavour by the new earl of Northumberland, Henry Percy. As the diplomatic situation worsened in late 1383, Percy was once more appointed warden of the northern marches, though it was now an appointment specifically to be held in jointure with lord Neville.[147] With a number of barons and magnates – many from his own retinue – to choose from, it is difficult to avoid the conclusion lord Neville was patronised by Gaunt in this period as a deliberate counterweight to Percy authority. There was certainly nothing unusual in naming multiple march wardens in times of hostility. Yet the elevation of a Neville to parity in office holding with the earl of Northumberland must have seemed significant to contemporaries. The Percies had for years been instrumental in the defence of the north; Neville had not, though his family had been similar in stature to their Percy rivals before the latest outbreak of hostilities. Hostile to evolving Percy power in the region, Lancaster may have seen Neville as its perfect counterweight.

In 1383, the duke of Brittany's English lordships of Boston and Richmond were confiscated by the crown, and many of their constituent estates, particularly in the north of Yorkshire, were granted to lord Neville as partial repayment for a still-outstanding debt from his service in France.[148] In addition, Gaunt arranged for the formal repayment to him of a sum in excess of £7,000 from the exchequer, at the rate of £1,000 a year.[149] Moreover, Neville continued to receive his lifetime annuity of 100 marks from the lordship of Richmond.[150] With the shift in English diplomatic policy away from alliance with Brittany, and with the crown's subsequent recovery

[142] Alastair J. MacDonald, *Border Bloodshed: Scotland and England at War, 1369–1403* (East Lothian, 2000), p. 45.

[143] Michael Hicks, *Bastard Feudalism* (Harlow, 1995), p. 60.

[144] *Foedera*, IV, i, p. 128.

[145] PRO, E 404/13/88, no. 43. Comprehensive discussion of the march wardens can be found in Storey, 'Wardens of the Marches', pp. 593–615.

[146] Henry Summerson, *Medieval Carlisle: The City and its Borders from the Late Eleventh to the Mid-Sixteenth Century*, 2 vols (Kendal, 1993), I, p. 320.

[147] MacDonald, *Border Bloodshed*, p. 75.

[148] Jones, *Ducal Brittany*, p. 191.

[149] *CPR 1381–5*, p. 273.

[150] Jones, *Ducal Brittany*, p. 184.

of Richmondshire from John de Montfort, the king gained substantial political capital in the north of England. With the agency of John of Gaunt and a history of service (now in the Scottish borders) to his credit, a large portion of this was directed toward lord Neville.

He persisted in the West March until 1384, when the king again named warden of the East March and governor of Berwick-upon-Tweed. The renewal of hostilities along the border, and the ongoing hostilities between Gaunt and the Percies, seemingly made him an important alternative in this capacity. Control of the East March also allowed Neville to draw more efficiently on the resources of his estates in Durham and north Yorkshire, and on the growing influence and maturity of his retinue in the north-east.[151] It also confirmed that the crown viewed him as a viable march warden in times of open hostility, and his status as a rival to the Percies, previously thought indispensable in wartime. In 1383, Neville expanded his family's coal mining operation on south Tyneside when he purchased lands at Winlaton, near Gateshead, and two years later was building additions to the royal castle at Bamburgh, his family's old charge.[152] Later that year, with an army of his own, he accompanied Richard II to on his campaign to Scotland, a very grand affair that included many of the great magnates of the kingdom.[153] We know that Neville was still in command of Carlisle at the time, as a new governor had to be found to replace him; in the interim, he left behind a portion of his army to man the city's battlements.[154] As border uncertainty continued to plague Richard II's government, and the aura of the Percies as peacekeepers grew, Neville presented a unique alternative, their only potential counterweight in the north. He thus spent the remainder of his career in the service of the crown and the duchy of Lancaster in the Scottish borders; following his death in 1388, his eldest son, Ralph, largely replaced him in this capacity.

But John Neville's career also speaks to broader issues. Edward III's attempt to expand his own influence through his children, with the energies and aspirations of his progeny delicately woven into those of their father, was a partial, if short-lived, success. Ormrod is surely correct to point out that Edward's longevity was his essential undoing, in that he outlived both his cohort and the reasonable life span of his plans.[155] Edward's military fortunes suffered both from the loss of the commanders that had achieved so much for him prior to Brétigny, and from the infirmity of his finest commander, the Black Prince.[156] Yet King Edward's strategy was founded upon the twin principles of family loyalty and his own personal belief that his sons would faithfully adhere to it. The willingness of Edmund of Langley and Lionel of Antwerp to be utilised in this way, so often with disappointing results, is testimony to this. So is the mutual support generally displayed between Gaunt and Edward of Woodstock, especially over the Black Prince's aspirations in France and Spain, and

---

[151] PRO, E 101/68/10/239; E 101/73/2/28.

[152] PRO, E 101/458/31; E 210/4096; E 210/4425.

[153] MacDonald, *Border Bloodshed*, p. 89.

[154] Summerson, *Medieval Carlisle*, I, p. 320; MacDonald, *Border Bloodshed*, p. 89.

[155] Ormrod, 'Edward III and his Family', p. 415.

[156] *The Wars of Edward III: Sources and Interpretations*, ed. Clifford J. Rogers (Woodbridge, 1999), pp. 201–2; and Green, *Black Prince*, pp. 117–30, who very ably captures the general mood of the political community as Edward and the prince became inactive and their chivalric deeds faded further from the collective memory.

Gaunt's assumption of these during his infirmity. Tellingly, Lancaster retained the good faith of both the king and his elder brother in the years leading up to their deaths – faith that proved well founded, as Gaunt remained an important pillar of royal government for many years, in spite of incessant popular fear of his personal ambitions.

It is from these antecedents that Gaunt became legitimate heir to his father's approach to dynastic politics. In spite of the fact that little provision had been made for the royal accession of the young (and vulnerable) Richard II – and despite the fact that many expected Gaunt to usurp the throne for himself at the earliest opportunity – the duke showed himself to be loyal to his nephew. It certainly may be that he replaced English royal aspirations with similar ones in Castile: Gaunt was for many years styled 'king of Castile' in the records after his marriage to Constance, and for years he sought to press those claims, politically and militarily. However, this ought not overshadow his essential loyalty to his king, and his rejection of his own usurpation of the crown of England, which must have been far preferable to him than a Castilian version. The very fact of Richard's reign is surely evidence for the success of Edward III's attempt to engender family solidarity in his children.

Secondly, however, Gaunt adapted Edward's 'family firm' approach and techniques to his own circumstances. In the process, he created an extended family and affinity that stretched the length and breadth of the English political community; it reached its apex in the north of England, where the Nevilles of Raby formed its central core. As early as his expulsion from the household in 1376, John Neville's primary loyalty already lay firmly with the duke of Lancaster, and he in turn became a focus for the duke's private livery.[157] Neville became a Lancastrian banneret, and led a group of six important retainers who each named fellow Lancastrian retainers as executors.[158] While service and financial relationships could found these loyalties, it was through marriages and the co-mingling of interests that they were cemented. The Neville entry into the Lancastrian *milieu* began with John Neville's service to Gaunt in France, deepened over time as his career was promoted, and was finally cemented when his eldest son, Ralph, married Gaunt's daughter, Joan Beaufort, in 1397. For the political culture of the nation, these developments would carry great significance. Ralph Neville, also earl of Westmorland by 1397, became perhaps the strongest single supporter of Henry IV among the country's great magnates.[159] In engendering these affinities, Gaunt acted with purpose: in his last years, many of his retainers and associates transferred their services (and loyalties) to Henry Bolingbroke and to his Beaufort children.[160] Henry's ability to translate this kind of political support into the tools of effective government was an important component of his own success as king.

Chris Given-Wilson has described John of Gaunt's territorial extension of power

---

157 Details of his turbulent stint in the royal household can be found in Given-Wilson, *Royal Household*, pp. 133, 148–53.

158 This from a total of 58 surviving Lancastrian wills. Interestingly, one of the other five, William Balderston, named as executor of his will Thomas Langley, a former colleague in the duke's service, one of John of Gaunt's and later Henry IV's clerks, and bishop of Durham 1406–37. See Walker, *Lancastrian Affinity*, p. 111.

159 His brother, Thomas Neville, Lord Furnival, became Henry IV's long-serving treasurer, and a fixture in his council.

160 Walker, *Lancastrian Affinity*, pp. 36–7.

into the north as a process of co-operating with local grandees and patronising them well, eventually absorbing them into his own retinue. Dacre, Roos, Willoughby, FitzHugh, de la Pole, Scrope and most importantly, Neville – even Percy – all entered the Lancastrian orbit in this way.[161] Yet in some cases, Gaunt did more than this: some, like the Nevilles, achieved his inner circle, and he promoted their interests as members of his family. They and their offspring became important Lancastrian partisans – evidenced most spectacularly in 1399. Gaunt displays the all the hallmarks of having understood Edward's 'family firm' concept; his creation of a lasting dynastic party was the backbone of a distinct, Lancastrian polity.

---

[161] Given-Wilson, *English Nobility*, pp. 173–4.

'HEARTS WARPED BY PASSION':
THE PERCY–GAUNT DISPUTE OF 1381

Kris Towson

The title of this paper comes from a passage in the Westminster Chronicle describing a meeting of Richard II's council at Berkhamsted on 9 October 1381. This meeting was convened 'to recall hearts warped by passion to the proper courses of harmony and peace, lest intensified ill-feeling between the estranged nobles should cause the sparks of sedition, still smouldering, to be fanned into a blaze which would destroy the whole of England'.[1] The passage concerns a dispute in the summer and autumn of 1381 between two of the most powerful magnates in England, Henry Percy, earl of Northumberland, and John of Gaunt, duke of Lancaster. At one point the two men brought armed retinues to the streets of London and the dispute threatened the very stability of the realm.[2] The situation was all the more shocking in that it appeared to represent the sudden and complete collapse of a long-standing, friendly and cooperative relationship.

From childhood, Percy had been very close to his Lancastrian cousins: according to the Alnwick chronicle, he was raised partly in the household of his uncle, Henry of Grosmont, first duke of Lancaster.[3] His close ties to the house of Lancaster continued after the death of Duke Henry and the accession of John of Gaunt to the duchy. Throughout the 1370s, Percy and Gaunt continued to work closely together. Percy accompanied Gaunt on the latter's ill-fated campaign across France in 1373. In 1377, Percy and Gaunt worked together in an attempt both to extend the jurisdiction of the marshal over the city of London and to support Wyclif against Bishop Courtenay in a raucous confrontation at St Paul's. Walsingham delights in telling us that on the day following the uproar at St Paul's, Percy and Gaunt were interrupted in the middle of an oyster luncheon and forced to flee together across the Thames to escape a mob. Later in the same year, as marshal and steward of England respectively, the two lords battled crowds and over-eager champions in an attempt to keep the coronation of Richard II running as smoothly as possible.[4] Four years later,

---

1   *The Westminster Chronicle 1381–1394*, ed. L. C. Hector and B. F. Harvey (Oxford, 1982), p. 21. A version of this paper was read at the 2001 Fifteenth Century England conference at Bristol. I am indebted to the participants there for their comments and suggestions, and would also like to thank Chris Given-Wilson, David Green and April Harper for their generous assistance.

2   *Westminster Chronicle*, p. 21; *RP*, III, p. 98.

3   'He in his youth was brought up sometimes in the king's court; sometimes with his uncle, the illustrious and first duke of Lancaster, and he was greatly beloved and familiar to him.' 'Cronica Monasterii de Alnewyk', ed. W. Dickson, *Archaeologia Aeliana* 1st ser. lii (1844), p. 42.

4   *The Chronicle of Adam Usk, 1377–1421*, ed. Chris Given-Wilson (Oxford, 1997), pp. 7, 8n., 9; Anthony Goodman, *John of Gaunt: The Exercise of Princely Power in Fourteenth-Century Europe* (Harlow, 1992), p. 61; *Chronicon Angliae*, ed. E. M. Thompson (Rolls Series, London, 1874), pp. 123–4; Thomas Walsingham, *Historia Anglicana*, ed. H. T. Riley (2 vols, Rolls Series, London, 1863–4), II, p. 337.

however, their relationship was to take a dramatic turn for the worse as a result of a series of events, misunderstandings and over-reactions during and after the Peasants' Revolt of 1381.

From the outset of the 1381 rising, Gaunt was one of the principal targets of the rebels. His name was first on the list of 'traitors' presented to the king by the rebels, and his magnificent London manor of the Savoy was utterly demolished by the rebels. It was at the sacking of the Savoy that the rebels made the most dramatic demonstration of their utter contempt for the duke by destroying rather than looting the contents of what was then considered to be the finest private residence in all England.[5]

The sheer violence and intensity of the hatred of the rebels for the duke led even those closest to him to be wary of offering assistance. For example, Abbot Kereby of Leicester (a house of which Gaunt was an important patron) refused to allow Gaunt's goods to be placed within the abbey's precinct for safe keeping, for fear of reprisals by the rebels.[6] Even more dramatically, Gaunt's own wife, the Duchess Constance, was turned away from the gates of the duke's own castle at Pontefract.[7] Like Abbot Kereby, the keeper of Pontefract was fearful of the wrath of the rebels, and the duchess was forced to travel by night to the rather run-down and leaky Knaresborough castle, where she was at least more honourably, if less comfortably, received.[8]

At the time of the outbreak of the Peasants' Revolt, John of Gaunt was on the Scottish marches negotiating an extension of the truce between England and Scotland. He had first been appointed the king's lieutenant in the marches in February 1379, a commission renewed and elaborated in September 1380 and again in May 1381. As lieutenant, Gaunt had been given the authority to negotiate, enforce or even suspend truces as he saw fit, as well as to supervise English defences.[9] For those – particularly Percy – who had previously held powers as wardens of the marches, Gaunt's appointment must have been seen as a significant intrusion into their accustomed sphere of influence. For all his wealth, power and status, Gaunt was a relative outsider to the border political community.[10] Suddenly, the northern magnates found themselves subordinate to one who, with the notable exception of the castle of Dunstanburgh in his barony of Embleton, lacked any significant landed basis for his new position on the marches. The new position may have seemed

---

[5] *The Anonimalle Chronicle*, ed. V. H. Galbraith (Manchester, 1927), pp. 139, 141–2; *Knighton's Chronicle, 1337–1396*, ed. G. H. Martin (Oxford, 1995), pp. 215–17.

[6] *Knighton's Chronicle*, pp. 228–30.

[7] Goodman, *John of Gaunt*, p. 308.

[8] In the summer of 1381, Knaresborough was evidently in need of significant repair: 'le graunt toure et les autres tourres et maisons deinz nostre dit chastel de Knaresburgh enbusoignent grandement de plumbe et des autres reparillementz deinz brief temps pur eschivere greindre costages', John of Gaunt to Robert de Morton, receiver of Knaresborough, 2 June 1381. *JGR 1379–83*, II, no. 542; Goodman, *John of Gaunt*, p. 309; *Knighton's Chronicle*, p. 230. The *Anonimalle* chronicler suggests that the duchess stayed briefly at Pontefract before leaving for Knaresborough because of doubts she had for her safety: *Anonimalle Chronicle*, p. 153; Simon Walker, *The Lancastrian Affinity, 1361–1399* (Oxford, 1990), p. 236.

[9] Goodman, *John of Gaunt*, p. 76; *RS*, II, pp. 27–9, 36; C. J. Neville, *Violence, Custom and Law: The Anglo-Scottish Border Lands in the Later Middle Ages* (Edinburgh, 1998), p. 67; R. L. Storey, 'The Wardens of the Marches of England towards Scotland, 1377–1489', *EHR* lxxii (1957), pp. 595–6.

[10] For a discussion of the English Lancastrian estates, see S. Armitage-Smith, *John of Gaunt* (London, 1904), pp. 214–29, also map facing p. 218.

particularly ominous to Henry Percy. In November 1380, Gaunt appointed his deputies to hold a march day to obtain 'due and reasonable' compensation for infringements of a truce that had previously been agreed between Percy and Archibald Douglas.[11] Percy therefore found himself having to pursue compensation through Gaunt and to place his claims in the hands of Gaunt's adherents.

The role played by John of Gaunt's appointment as lieutenant of the march in provoking the quarrel between the duke and Percy has recently been played down.[12] The present interpretation focuses more on the confrontation between Percy and Gaunt at the council of Berkhamsted in August 1381 than on any tensions that may have been building between the two men in the period before the Peasants' Revolt. Percy's violent eruption at Berkhamsted was a reaction to the charges of disobedience, betrayal and ingratitude that Gaunt laid before the king there, rather than the result of any simmering resentment that he may have felt towards Gaunt.[13] It is certainly tempting to suggest that such an intrusion into his sphere of influence might have alienated Percy in the months prior to the Peasants' Revolt. The earl was a proud man who jealously guarded what he had come to assume was his rightful position as the leading border magnate, and it presumably irritated him to be so suddenly relegated to a secondary (or indeed, in the case of the infringements of the Percy–Douglas truce noted above, a tertiary) position. Recent work has questioned the extent to which Percy dominated the marches in terms of the retaining of Northumberland gentry.[14] However, while Hardyng's oft-quoted comment that the Percys 'had the hearts of the people [of the] north'[15] was an exaggeration, it does not necessarily follow that Percy himself did not, by 1381, consider the north to be his rightful sphere of influence.

For all this, however, there is no real indication that Gaunt's new position on the marches was itself sufficient to threaten the destruction of the long-standing friendship and working partnership which had for so long existed between earl and duke. Gaunt's appointment did not mean the exclusion of Percy from marcher offices. Except for one brief period during the winter of 1379–80, when the magnates were removed from the offices of wardens of the marches and replaced by members of the gentry, Percy was the senior warden on the east march from July 1377 to December 1381.[16] Percy's possible concern at the advent of Gaunt into the politics of the far north was not, in itself, sufficient to provoke him into an attack on the duke. It may, however, have made him less inclined to place himself in harm's way in order to protect Gaunt. And this was exactly what Gaunt was seeking in the summer of 1381.

According to Thomas Walsingham, news of the Peasants' Revolt first reached Gaunt prior to the conclusion of his negotiations with the Scots on 18 June 1381. Henry Knighton concurs with this. Although the *Anonimalle* chronicler states that the duke first received the news only while travelling back to England after

---

11 *JGR 1379–83*, II, no. 1206. Archibald 'the Grim' Douglas would become the third earl Douglas in 1389. Michael Brown, *The Black Douglases* (East Lothian, 1998), p. 88.

12 Simon Walker, 'Letters to the Dukes of Lancaster in 1381 and 1399', *EHR* cvi (1991), p. 73.

13 Walsingham, *Historia Anglicana*, II, p. 44.

14 Andy King, ' "They have the Hertes of the People by North": Northumberland, the Percies and Henry IV, 1399–1408', *Henry IV: The Establishment of the Regime, 1399–1406*, ed. Gwilym Dodd and Douglas Biggs (Woodbridge, 2003), pp. 139–59.

15 *The Chronicle of John Hardyng*, ed. H. Ellis (London, 1812), p. 378.

16 Storey, 'Wardens', pp. 609–10.

concluding the negotiations, Walsingham's and Knighton's versions seem more plausible. Not only was Walsingham well informed, but Knighton had direct access to information provided by his Lancastrian patrons. There are also certain entries in John of Gaunt's Register that support this version of events. On 17 June, Gaunt sent several orders that indicate that he was shifting his household north from Leicester to Pontefract, presumably in order to distance it from the rising in the south.[17]

Another reason to prefer the chronology suggested by Walsingham and Knighton is the timing of the arrival from London of a royal sergeant at arms bearing news of the uprising. The sergeant at arms left London for the north on 11 June, and returned to the city on 22 June.[18] Given the distance involved, he must have arrived in Berwick on or about 17 June: any sooner or later would require one leg of the journey to have been completed in less than five days, a seemingly impossible task. By 17 June, therefore, the duke was informed that something was happening in the south that posed a threat to the stability of the realm in general and to his own interests in particular. In terms of the true magnitude of that threat, however, he would as yet have known nothing. On 11 June, the day the sergeant at arms left London for the north, the rebels were still two days removed from their domination of London and the destruction of the Savoy, and three removed from the executions of the archbishop of Canterbury and his fellow victims. Gaunt therefore saw no reason to react to the new information with panic measures. He ordered the victualling and garrisoning of several of his castles both in Wales and in the north of England, but was careful not to betray his anxiety to the Scots while negotiations were still underway.[19] Prudent precautions were called for, but there was as yet no cause for real alarm.

Gaunt appears to have remained ignorant of the full gravity of the situation in the south until at least 20 or 21 June. Following the conclusion of the negotiations with the Scots on 18 June, he moved his household from Berwick, which had served as his base during his stay on the March, to Bamburgh, whence he continued to conduct routine duchy business.[20] Sometime on 20 or 21 June, however, sufficient substantive news of the rebellion must have filtered up to Bamburgh to cause genuine concern. By 22 June, Gaunt had obtained a safe conduct from the earl of Carrick,[21] and had received the less than welcome news that Percy was unwilling to open his doors to him.[22]

Percy's message was delivered by two of his associates, Sir John Hothum and Thomas Motherby. Hothum's ancestors were long-time tenants of the Percy manor

---

[17] The earls and dukes of Lancaster were patrons of Knighton's abbey at Leicester. Antonia Gransden, *Historical Writing in England II: c.1307 to the Early Sixteenth Century* (London, 1982), pp. 178–81; *Anonimalle Chronicle*, p. 152; *JGR 1379–83*, II, nos. 541, 551; Walsingham, *Historia Anglicana*, II, pp. 41–2; *Knighton's Chronicle*, p. 233. Walter Bower also delights in telling of the duke receiving the news of the revolt on his way back to England, then 'humbly' asking for asylum from the Scots in something of a state of panic. Again, there is no reason to prefer this version to those of Knighton and Walsingham. Walter Bower, *Scotichronicon VII*, ed. A. B. Scott and D. E. R. Watt (Aberdeen, 1996), p. 391.

[18] PRO, E 364/16, m.10; E 403/484 (11 June); Walker, 'Letters', p. 70n.

[19] *JGR 1379–83*, II, nos. 530–6; Walsingham, *Historia Anglicana*, II, pp. 41–2; *Knighton's Chronicle*, p. 233.

[20] *JGR 1379–83*, II, nos. 537–9, 1097, 1176–7.

[21] The son of Robert II of Scotland and the future Robert III of Scotland. *JGR 1379–83*, II, no. 1186.

[22] Percy had previously invited the duke to dine with him at Alnwick: *Anonimalle Chronicle*, p. 152; *Knighton's Chronicle*, p. 233.

of Topcliffe in the North Riding of Yorkshire, and the family appears to have maintained quite close ties to their Percy lords well into the fifteenth century.[23] Apart from his serving as a witness to a charter of enfeoffment dating from 1383, however, there is nothing else to indicate that Sir John served Percy in an official capacity following the delivery of this message to Gaunt.[24] Motherby, by contrast, is frequently recorded as a member of Percy's circle, appearing mainly in the roles of attorney and mainpernor.[25] Such connections no doubt proved useful to him in advancing his public career: he served as knight of the shire for Northumberland in the Salisbury parliament of 1384,[26] sat on a number of royal commissions (in one case serving with Percy's son Hotspur) [27] and in 1390 was made controller of customs at Newcastle upon Tyne.[28]

Percy's messengers were therefore well known and loyal to him. Particularly in the case of Motherby, it is somewhat surprising to find that these two men were later accused of having blatantly exceeded their brief in delivering their message to Gaunt: in doing so, they would have risked the wrath not only of the duke but also of their own patron. It is also unclear as to where and when Gaunt was told by Percy's messengers that the earlier offer of hospitality had been withdrawn. While Knighton asserts that the meeting took place almost before the gates of Alnwick, where Gaunt had expected to be welcomed and entertained by the earl, other chroniclers are less specific.[29] Whether the meeting took place at Alnwick, at Bamburgh or at some point in between, and whether it was on 20 or 21 June is, perhaps, less important than what actually transpired at the meeting, and the repercussions thereof.

Any attempt to determine just what was said to Gaunt by Hothum and Motherby must begin with the credence given to the messengers by Percy with the agreement of John Gilbert, bishop of Hereford and the earl of Stafford.[30] In this document, Percy, Gilbert and Stafford simply advised Gaunt that, in view of information received both in privy seal letters and from a spy who had been present among the

---

[23] As early as January 1303, a John Hothum was witness to a grant by which Henry Percy, great-grandfather to the first earl, gave the manor of Pocklington, the advowson of the church of Nafferton and some land to the abbot of Meaux: *The Percy Chartulary*, ed. M. T. Martin (Surtees Society cxviii, Durham, 1911), pp. 43–4, 116, 213–14, 228, 230, 233; Walker, 'Letters', p. 72n. A later Sir John Hothum (d. 1460) was still receiving 'fees' from the Percies as late as 1453–4: J. M. W. Bean, *The Estates of the Percy Family 1416–1537* (Oxford, 1958), pp. 92 n.1, 97.

[24] *CCR 1381–5*, p. 403.

[25] *CFR 1369–77*, p. 306; *CFR 1377–83*, pp. 126, 137, 195.

[26] Charles Henry Hunter Blair, 'Members of Parliament for Northumberland (September 1327–September 1399)', *Archaeologia Aeliana* 4th ser. xi (1934), pp. 71–2.

[27] *CPR 1388–92*, pp. 30, 356.

[28] Ibid., p. 356.

[29] Walker, 'Letters', p. 70. Walsingham ignores altogether the confrontation between the messengers and Gaunt: Walsingham, *Historia Anglicana*, II, pp. 42–3.

[30] PRO, C 49/12/11:

> Ceste cedule fust mise en parlement par Moderby esquier en disant qe ce fu sa credence et celle credence il dist et nul autre.
>
> La credence countee al duk de Lancastre par Mons' John de Hotham et Motherby est tiel.
>
> Monseignur, les sires de Hereford, Stafford et Northumbr' se recomaundent a vous et vous envoient que, eiant regarde sibien as lettres du privee seal directez au count de Northumbr' come as novelx as luy countez par un de ses varletz esteant entre les comunes a Londres le iour de corpore Christi et lendemain prochein ensuiant tanqe a heure de None, lour counsaille est sanz meillour avys de vos chivaliers et esquiers que vous vous reteignez en le chastell de Bamburgh et y demurer pur du temps tanqe vous soiez bien appris del estate du roy et del affaire des comunes.

commons in London, their advice was that Gaunt should maintain himself in Bamburgh castle for the time being. This is hardly the curt, rude message one would expect to be necessary to shatter such an apparently strong and long-standing association and to trigger such a remarkable dispute. Percy, Gilbert and Stafford appear simply to have been counselling caution on the part of Gaunt, saying that, unless he had better advice from his own people, they would urge him to stay at Bamburgh until he was more fully informed as to the situation in the south.[31] There is no mention in this credence of a refusal to show hospitality, nor of a refusal to allow Gaunt entry into any castle in Percy's keeping. This, however, is precisely what Knighton claims to have been the content of the message delivered by Hothum and Motherby.[32]

The advice given by Percy, Gilbert and Stafford in the credence is remarkably level-headed considering that Percy's spy had been present in London at the time of the sacking of the Savoy and the executions of the archbishop of Canterbury and the treasurer of England.[33] As well as news of actual events in London, the valet would surely have acquainted Percy with the many rumours then circulating about Gaunt. It was said that Gaunt's southern castles lay in ruins, and that two bands of armed rebels, each 10,000–strong, were scouring the country for him. It had also been put about in the south that Gaunt was leading an army of 20,000 Scots against the king. Although the Scots had in fact offered Gaunt an army to lead against the rebels, the duke had rejected the offer with the boast that, if such an army entered England, 'they would find fighting enough before ever they reached York'.[34]

There is also the question of the privy seal letters mentioned in the credence as having been sent by Richard II's government to the earl of Northumberland. Although their exact contents remain unknown, it is possible that they were letters sent by the king at the insistence of the rebels, and as such would no doubt have spelled bad news for Gaunt.[35] As Percy would later produce these letters in parliament in an attempt to explain his actions,[36] it seems likely that they contained some information or instructions that he used to justify his hesitation in offering support to Gaunt. However well or poorly informed Gaunt may have been at this time, Percy, Stafford and the bishop of Hereford were becoming all too aware of the growing extent of the emergency in the south.

The available evidence suggests that Percy's envoys had seriously overstepped their bounds when delivering their message to the duke. First, although no threat of exclusion from Percy-controlled castles was contained in the credence itself, Knighton makes it very clear that such a threat had been made. Indeed, Gaunt ultimately decided that it was necessary for him to seek shelter with his adversaries in Scotland. However, even if Percy had refused to admit Gaunt into any castle that he controlled, the Lancastrian stronghold of Dunstanburgh was close at hand, on the coast between Alnwick and Bamburgh. Although the castle may have been in need

---

[31] Hereford and Stafford had been John of Gaunt's fellow commissioners at the recent march day: *RS*, II, pp. 35–6; PRO, E 403/484; E 364/15, m. 5; E 364/16 m. 2; Walker, 'Letters', p. 68.

[32] *Knighton's Chronicle*, pp. 234–5.

[33] *Anonimalle Chronicle*, p. 145; *Westminster Chronicle*, pp. 5–7 and 7n.

[34] Goodman, *John of Gaunt*, p. 81; Walsingham, *Historia Anglicana*, II, pp. 42–3; Walker, 'Letters', p. 71.

[35] Goodman, *John of Gaunt*, p. 82.

[36] See below, p. 151.

of renovation at that time,[37] it was nonetheless an imposing structure and must have been a tempting option for the duke. For Gaunt to decide to flee to Scotland, it is evident that Hothum and Motherby made some sort of suggestion or threat regarding the duke's safety in England that was not explicit in the credence itself. This view gains support from the fact that, when the Percy–Gaunt dispute finally came before parliament in November 1381, Gaunt was particularly incensed at the two messengers, seeking and securing their imprisonment in the Tower for having said more to him than had been authorised.[38]

An alternative and intriguing possibility raised by Knighton's chronology of events is that Gaunt expected to be turned away by Percy and made preparations to turn this possibility to his advantage. Knighton wrote that, as soon as the extension to the truce had been agreed, Gaunt sought permission to come to Scotland with his retinue.[39] From this, it is clear that Knighton believed Gaunt to have applied for his safe conduct well before the confrontation with Percy's messengers. In the credence given by Percy to his messengers, it is stated that Percy's actions were based in part on the information received from a spy present among the rebels in London on 13 and 14 June. Allowing at least five, and most likely six, days for the trip from London to Alnwick, the earliest that Percy could have received the news from his spy would have been 19 or 20 June. As the negotiations for the extension of the truce were concluded on 18 June, Knighton's sequence of events clearly has Gaunt requesting his safe conduct one or two days before any possible encounter with Percy or his agents. If his account is to be believed, Gaunt either had a convenient and coincidental desire to visit Scotland or foresaw some eventuality that would require his hasty removal from the country.

Walsingham's account of Gaunt's movements and motives at this time is rather less specific than Knighton's. Walsingham agrees with Knighton that Gaunt accelerated the negotiations upon hearing of the uprising in the south, and that (with what he viewed as extraordinary concessions) the truce was extended before the Scots received news of the troubles.[40] He does not, however, say that Gaunt requested his safe conduct prior to the Scots learning of the revolt. Rather, he states that Gaunt doubted the loyalty of those around him – not only Percy, but also his own knights and those who held castles in the north.[41] Walsingham may therefore suggest that Gaunt doubted the certainty of Percy's loyalty. What remains unclear is just why this was so, and exactly when Gaunt came to this conclusion. Did he, as Knighton's account suggests, simply suspect that Percy would not support him? Or had he already met Hothum and Motherby and come to the realisation that it would be both unsafe and unwise for him to remain in England?

---

[37] During the years 1380–1, Gaunt was experiencing some difficulties with John Lewyn, the mason he had hired on to improve the castle's defences in 1380. Goodman, *John of Gaunt*, pp. 309–10.

[38] 'En quel temps monsire Johan de Hothum, chivaler, et Thomas de Motherby esquier, furont mys en le toure de Loundres en prisone pur mesme la cause al suyt del duc et en eese de son coer, qare ils furont messagiers al duc depar le count par lettres de credence; et come fuit mys sour eux ils dissoient al duc plus qils ne furont charges.' *Anonimalle Chronicle*, p. 155.

[39] *Knighton's Chronicle*, p. 233.

[40] Walsingham both justified these concessions and took a shot at Gaunt by writing: 'But the extraordinary circumstances of the aforesaid uprising accounts for the extraordinary nature of this concession, for it would justifiably have caused anybody, even the most worthy of people, to have been confused and terrified.' Walsingham, *Historia Anglicana*, II, pp. 41–2.

[41] Ibid., II, p. 42.

Assuming that, as Knighton claims, Gaunt asked for the safe conduct immediately following the conclusion of negotiations on 18 June, there remains an unexplained four-day delay between the making of the request and the earl of Carrick's issuing of the safe conduct on 22 June in Melrose.[42] Carrick and Gaunt were both present when the truce was concluded,[43] so there should have been no time lost in locating and petitioning the earl. Although it would have been understandable for Carrick to check his own intelligence before issuing a safe conduct, four days does seem a rather long delay. Because of the unexplained gap between the conclusion of the truce and Carrick's issuing of the safe conduct, Knighton's chronology must be suspect. It is more likely that, rather than anticipating Percy's decision to withdraw his offer of hospitality and requesting the safe conduct prior to the conclusion of the negotiations, Gaunt made his request after having already met Hothum and Motherby. It is possible that the duke and the envoys could have met late on 20 June, but it is more likely that they did so on the following day. This would have allowed six days for the messenger from London to reach Alnwick, and one for Percy, Stafford and Hereford to consider the news and to prepare the credence and for Hothum and Motherby to locate Gaunt.

The encounter between Gaunt and Percy's messengers marked only the beginning of their dispute. Relations between the two lords took a further turn for the worse at a series of council meetings held by the king between August and October 1381. At the first of these, held at Reading on 4 August, Gaunt accused Percy of having been 'not only disobedient, but unfaithful and ungrateful as well'[44] towards him during the summer crisis.[45] The language used by Gaunt in making these accusations illustrates that this was very much a personal, and not simply a political, dispute. Gaunt had clearly been deeply hurt by what he saw as his cousin's betrayal of their friendship. Emotions continued to run high following the Reading council, leading to a violent confrontation between Gaunt and Percy during a feast held at Westminster on 15 August.

In the wake of the duke's accusations against Percy, their failure subsequently to settle the dispute, and what was evidently a rapidly deteriorating situation, the king summoned the earl and duke to a council to be held at Berkhamsted on 9 October, which was intended

> to reconcile the duke of Lancaster and the earl of Northumberland, who, from having been close friends, had for particular reasons become deadly enemies. The king therefore sought by interposing the efforts of his magnates to recall hearts warped by passion to the proper courses of harmony and peace, lest intensified ill-feeling between the estranged nobles should cause the sparks of sedition, still smouldering, to be fanned into a blaze which would destroy the whole of England. But when the assiduity of the councillors had been exhausted in vain endeavour, the two disputants departed in undiminished, or even increased, hostility.[46]

---

42 *JGR 1379–83*, II, no. 1186.
43 Stephen Boardman, *The Early Stewart Kings: Robert II and Robert III* (East Lothian, 1996), p. 117.
44 Walsingham, *Historia Anglicana*, II, p. 44
45 Armitage-Smith, *John of Gaunt*, p. 255; Goodman, *John of Gaunt*, p. 89; Walsingham, *Historia Anglicana*, II, p. 44.
46 *Westminster Chronicle*, p. 21.

At Westminster, the king had intervened on Percy's behalf, making excuses for him and asking that his uncle Gaunt contain his anger. At Berkhamsted, however, Percy would allow no one to speak for him. In reply to Gaunt's accusations, he loosed a volley of verbal abuse that nearly led to the estranged friends engaging in a judicial duel.[47] Still more importantly, his outburst and his refusal to obey the king's order to remain silent so enraged Richard II that Percy found himself 'arrested as being guilty of lèse-majesté'.[48] He was in fact only released after the earls of Warwick and Suffolk stood surety for him and guaranteed that he would come to the next parliament to answer the charges against him.[49]

Even with this charge of lèse-majesté having been made against him, Percy seems to have sought out opportunities for further confrontation with the duke. In the days leading up to the parliament, the gamesmanship continued. Although accompanied by a large number of armed men, Gaunt did not consider it safe to enter the city of London. Percy, however, not only brought his own body of armed supporters but also made the most of the Londoners' hatred of the duke. He and his supporters confidently entered the city and received the hospitality of the citizens, Percy even going so far as to become a citizen himself.[50] With both Percy and Gaunt coming to parliament with sizeable bodies of armed retainers, the king found it necessary to issue an injunction that none from either side should come armed to parliament, further illustrating the extraordinary extent to which this dispute had escalated.[51] This injunction having been given, the parliament then proceeded to consider the dispute in a somewhat more secure, if no less tense, atmosphere.

Gaunt began by reciting his grievances against Percy, who was obliged by the king to remain silent and to prepare his answers for the following day.[52] When he was given an opportunity to speak, Percy first repeated the charges made against him by Gaunt, then produced the four privy seal letters which had been sent to him in June at the time of the Peasants' Revolt. Although we do not know the contents of these letters, it is certain that they contained information or instructions which, according to Percy, justified his actions of 21–22 June.[53] The following day, Gaunt brought a new series of charges against Percy, against which the *Anonimalle* chronicler felt Percy defended himself well. Gaunt also had his revenge against the messengers Hothum and Motherby, securing their imprisonment in the Tower for having overstepped the bounds of their credence.[54] Parliament having 'been uselessly extended for a long time on account of the aforesaid dispute',[55] and both sides having had, over five days, an opportunity to air their grievances and make their defences, the king finally took their complaints into his hands. On 9 November,

---

[47] Percy even went so far as to throw down his gage before Gaunt in the presence of the king. Ibid.; Goodman, *John of Gaunt*, p. 89.

[48] Walsingham, *Historia Anglicana*, II, p. 44.

[49] Ibid.

[50] Ibid., II, pp. 44–5; *Westminster Chronicle*, p. 21.

[51] *Anonimalle Chronicle*, p. 155; Walsingham, *Historia Anglicana*, II, p. 44; *Westminster Chronicle*, pp. 21–3.

[52] *Anonimalle Chronicle*, pp. 154–5.

[53] Ibid., p. 155.

[54] Ibid. Interestingly, being committed to the Tower does not seem to have greatly harmed the careers of Hothum and Motherby, nor did it end their associations with Percy.

[55] Walsingham, *Historia Anglicana*, II, p. 45.

Percy brought proceedings to a close, and his dispute with Gaunt to a formal end, by kneeling before the king and offering an abject apology.[56]

The most interesting aspect of this apology is that it deals almost entirely with the events at Berkhamsted, and not the original cause of the dispute, Percy's refusal of hospitality during the Peasants' Revolt. In fact, it is only the last paragraph that refers to the events of June – the so-called 'other matter'. The previous four paragraphs of the apology are all concerned with offence given to both the king and the duke by Percy's actions at Berkhamsted. Clearly, it was Percy's public outburst against Gaunt at Berkhamsted that most offended the duke. By acting in such a manner before the king, and ignoring royal commands to remain silent, Percy had drawn Richard's ire as well, and it was this that necessitated such a meek apology.

An interesting point raised by the dispute is the role played by the king in the resolution of disputes between the great men of the realm. This was one of the most important responsibilities of a medieval monarch, and Richard II's later failure to fulfil the obligation in a satisfactory and equitable manner during the Hereford–Norfolk dispute of 1398 was to be a primary factor in his downfall. The Percy–Gaunt dispute also bears similarity to another, earlier, example. In 1332, John Grey and William Zouche had similarly been called before Edward III and his council to settle a dispute. That meeting was not only the scene of 'hot words' between the two disputants, but also very nearly ended in disaster for Grey after he placed his hand on his dagger and withdrew it partly from its scabbard. Drawing a weapon – even partly – in the presence of the king was a serious offence, and Grey was only released from prison after several magnates petitioned the king on his behalf.[57] Although Percy did not go as far as Grey in that he did not actually draw a weapon, he did throw down his gage in the presence of the king. Fortunately Gaunt did not respond in kind, and the dispute did not end in bloodshed.[58]

---

56 *JGR 1379–83*, II, no. 1243. The document may be translated thus:
  My most honourable liege lord [Richard], whereas in your high and honourable presence at Berkhamsted, without leave or licence from you, my liege lord, I offended you by my ignorance, in answering my lord of Spain, here present, otherwise than I should in reason have done and in throwing down my gage before him, I submit myself to your grace and ordinance, and pray that you pardon my offence.
  And my lord of Spain [Gaunt], whereas at Berkhamsted in the presence of my most redoubtable lord the king, I, by my ignorance, gave answer otherwise than I should have done to you, my lord, who are son to my redoubtable lord the king, whom God absolve, and uncle to my redoubtable liege lord the king, here present, and so high person and of such very noble and royal blood as you are, my lord. And also to you, my lord, who are the greatest lord and the highest person of the realm after my liege lord the king, here present, and I of your blood and alliance, having thrown down my gage before you in the presence of my liege lord the king, here present, I beg your pardon and your honourable lordship.
  My liege lord, as to the disobedience towards you, God knows that it was never my wish or my intention to disobey in any way your royal majesty. And if there was any [disobedience] through ignorance, I submit myself to your gracious ordinance. My lord of Spain, if any disobedience was done to you through ignorance or otherwise, that was not my intent and I pray that you will pardon me your anger.
  And as to the other matter concerning the disloyalty charged against me, I was not always so wise or well advised always to do what is best, and in so much as I have not carried out my duty to your lordship as naturally and fully as I could have done and as I was bound to do, it weighs heavily on me and I beg your good lordship, which I desire with all my heart.
57 *RP*, II, pp. 65–6.
58 Another example of a magnate being forced to make an abject apology to Gaunt before parliament arose in 1394, when the earl of Arundel made a series of accusations against both the king and Gaunt. His

Considering the heated atmosphere in which Percy and Gaunt confronted each other in parliament, Richard II did well to bring the dispute of 1381 to a formal end. Unfortunately it is unclear whether Richard himself or his advisors were responsible for the settlement of the dispute. We are told that he took the dispute 'into his own hands', but this may well have only been a conventional phrase. However, in spite of the fact that Richard was only fourteen years old, one has only to consider his actions in calming the rebels at Smithfield to see that he was capable of asserting an authority beyond his years. Whether it was the king or his advisors who finally settled this dispute, it is obvious that they were much more effective than Richard himself would prove to be seventeen years later.

Who was to blame for the Percy–Gaunt dispute? In considering Percy's actions of 21–22 June, we have to remember that he was both ill informed of events in the south and unsure of the king's attitude towards John of Gaunt.[59] At that time, the only definite information he had concerning the Peasants' Revolt was that the rebels had taken control of London, burnt the Savoy and executed, among others, the archbishop of Canterbury and the treasurer. If the terms spelled out in the credence are to be taken as Percy's intended message to Gaunt, it is difficult to fault his judgement. Ignorant of the true extent of the danger to the south, but aware that something very serious and potentially disastrous was taking place, Percy's advice to lie low was certainly prudent. This advice had also been given with the agreement of the earl of Stafford and the bishop of Hereford. Exactly what Hothum and Motherby said to Gaunt, we shall never know, but it is apparent that their message was sufficient both to drive Gaunt to seek refuge in Scotland and to draw his ire in parliament.

For his part, Gaunt must be excused for being offended at his former ally's refusal to honour an earlier offer of hospitality. Percy's failure to stand by their friendship and offer his support came not only as a political disappointment, but also as a personal shock and affront to his honour. However, his stubborn refusal to listen to Percy's explanations was itself responsible for Percy's remarkable outburst at Berkhamsted and the subsequent parliamentary drama.

Both men had been placed in extremely difficult and uncertain positions. Neither could be sure about the course of events in London; nor could either be certain of the other's motives or status, let alone the attitude of the king. In such a situation, Gaunt's usurpation of what Percy had considered to be rightfully his own position of authority on the marches may have proved the proverbial last straw. Unsure as he was of the king's disposition towards Gaunt, Percy would have had little inclination to risk both his own standing with Richard and his own personal safety for the sake of someone he felt was intruding into his rightful sphere of influence. Had Percy been better informed of events in the south, and particularly of the king's disposition towards Gaunt, he might well have reacted more hospitably to Gaunt. As it was, jealousy combined with uncertainty to prevent such a course of action and, instead, to generate this remarkable dispute.

main accusations were that the king and his retainers were improperly wearing the livery of the duke; that Gaunt was so overbearing in council and parliament that the earl and others found it impossible to express themselves as they wished; that the king's support of Gaunt's continental ambitions was excessive; and that the grant of the duchy of Aquitaine to Gaunt had been against the interests of both the king and the realm. Arundel's accusations were quickly and robustly refuted by the king, and the earl was, like Percy in 1381, forced to beg forgiveness before parliament. *RP,* III, pp. 313–14.

59 Walker, 'Letters', p. 72.

THE REASONS FOR THE BISHOP OF NORWICH'S ATTACK OF FLANDERS IN 1383

Kelly DeVries

Henry Despenser, bishop of Norwich, is generally thought of as one of the most celebrated losers of the Hundred Years War. Ostensibly launching a crusade in 1383 against the heretical followers of the 'anti-pope', Clement VII (pope in Avignon), on behalf of the 'true' pope, Urban VI (pope in Rome), he is vilified for leading his forces instead against the supporters of Urban in the southern Low Countries, along the coast of Flanders and at Ypres. There he met a quick defeat, first at the hands of the besieged Yprois and then by running away from the opportunity of fighting the Franco–Burgundian armies led by Philip the Bold, duke of Burgundy. Norman Housley calls his military actions 'humiliating';[1] to May McKisack the crusade was 'deplorable', 'a total failure';[2] while to George M. Wrong, 'the crusade settled nothing; no burdens were lightened by it and many were heavier'.[3] This is not to mention the fact that the bishop himself, in defending his actions on the crusade before a tribunal judging his impeachment was unwilling to accept any of the blame for the defeat, dismissing his failure simply with the notion that the Ghentenaars had made him do it: that he bore no responsibility in the matter.[4]

The purpose of this article is not to revise Despenser's reputation. He was not a good military leader, nor was he tried unjustly. He had not converted a single heretic; he had not punished the French; he had not succeeded in opening the recently closed markets of Flanders to English wool; and, more importantly, he had abused indulgences, had misused funds, and had profited from his willingness to retreat back across the Channel from France without doing battle with Philip the Good, all of the things for which he was put on trial for impeachment. On the other hand, Bishop Henry Despenser has been misjudged by those historians who have dismissed his 'Ghentenaars made me do it' trial rationalisation. The following words, the preliminary ideas of a thesis to be worked out in a more lengthy work on the bishop of Norwich's crusade, take the position that the Ghentenaars really did make Despenser do it, that his actions in Flanders were not at his direction, but at the command of the rebel leadership in Ghent, those seeking sovereignty from the French and Burgundians. Without looking at Bishop Henry Despenser's crusade from the Flemish perspective, its actions and failure cannot be completely understood.

---

[1] Norman Housley, 'The Bishop of Norwich's Crusade, May 1383', *History Today* xxxiii (1983), pp. 15–20.
[2] May McKisack, *The Fourteenth Century* (Oxford, 1959), p. 431.
[3] George M. Wrong, *The Crusade of 1383 Known as That of the Bishop of Norwich* (London, 1892), p. 90.
[4] The best work on the case made against the bishop of Norwich is Margaret Aston, 'The Impeachment of Bishop Despenser', *BIHR* xxxviii (1965), pp. 127–48.

The bishop of Norwich's 1383 crusade came at a time when there was a confluence of three historical events important to the history of the Hundred Years War. First, it was a time of incredible downturn in English military achievements. The death of Edward the Black Prince in 1376, followed the next year by the death of his father, King Edward III, left a military leadership vacuum of significant proportion. Richard II's lack of interest in pursuing the fighting in France has been perhaps overstated, but the young king was certainly not the general that his father had been, nor was his uncle, John of Gaunt, and victory over the peasants at home in England only went so far to boost the morale of a defeated populace.[5] Secondly, at the same time, the French had replaced their defeated military leadership of the middle of the fourteenth century with King Charles V, Bertrand du Guesclin and numerous others. These generals whittled away at the English military acquisitions and holdings until only Aquitaine, Ponthieu and Calais remained effectively in English hands on the continent.[6] Thirdly, as important was the Flemish situation. The county of Flanders had held an extremely important position throughout the early part of the Hundred Years War. The Flemings had stood by Edward III through his early victories and, despite recent English problems, ties remained strong, especially in Ghent.[7] This was not lessened by the 'Ghent War', begun in 1379 by the townspeople of Ghent as a Flemish rebellion against their count, his son-in-law and heir, Duke Philip the Bold of Burgundy, and the French king, Charles V.[8]

It is difficult in knowing exactly why this revolt occurred. Almost every different historian writing on the origins of the 'Ghent War' has a different interpretation as to its origins. These range from political to economic, to social, to sociological, to religious and to the choosing between an English or a French alliance.[9] What is clearer is that, initially at least, the Ghentenaars had success in pursuing this war. Their first military strike of the conflict,[10] on 7 October 1379, against the French and French-

---

5   The notion that Richard II was not interested in pursuing war is certainly a theme of Anthony Steel, *Richard II* (Cambridge, 1941). Recent efforts to disprove this include: J. J. N. Palmer, *England, France and Christendom, 1377–99* (London, 1972); Nigel Saul, *Richard II* (London, 1997); and, most recently, Anne Curry, 'Richard II and the War with France', *The Reign of Richard*, ed. Gwilym Dodd (Stroud, 2000), pp. 33–50.
6   On this period in the Hundred Years War, see Edouard Perroy, *The Hundred Years War*, trans. W. B. Wells (New York, 1951), pp. 146–86; and Jean Favier, *La guerre de cent ans* (Paris, 1980), pp. 327–66. On the reign of Charles V and his role in the Hundred Years War, see Françoise Autrand, *Charles V: Le sage* (Paris, 1994); and on Bertrand du Guesclin see Yves Jacob, *Bertrand du Guesclin, connétable de France* (Paris, 1999), and M. S. Coryn, *Bertrand du Guesclin, 1320–1380* (Paris, 1980).
7   Marc Haegeman, *De anglofilie in het graafschap Vlaanderen tussen 1379 en 1435: Politieke en economische aspecten* (Anciens Pays et Assemblees d'Etats/Standen en Landen xc, Kortrijke-Heule, 1988), remains the best work on the relationship of England and Flanders after the death of Edward III.
8   The 'Ghent War' is in need of a monograph-length study, but for the moment the article by Maurice Vandermaesen and Marc Ryckaert, 'De Gentse opstand (1379–1385)', *De Witte Kaproenen: De Gentse opstand (1379–1385) en de geschiedenis van de Brugse Leie*, ed. M. Vandermaesen, M. Ryckaerts and M. Coornaert (Ghent, 1979), pp. 7–31, will have to suffice as the best overall look at the conflict.
9   I have looked into these in my dissertation, 'Perceptions of Victory and Defeat in the Southern Low Countries during the Fourteenth Century: A Historiographical Comparison' (unpublished PhD thesis, University of Toronto, 1987), and will attend to them at greater length in a longer work on the Ghent War.
10   The initial blow of the Ghentenaars against the count of Flanders came on 5 September 1379, when they murdered his bailiff to the town, Rogier van Outrive. Following this, a popular government was immediately installed in the town, and legates were sent to the other regions of the county announcing the rebellion of Ghent and asking others to join the independence movement. See Vandermaesen and Ryckaert, 'De Gentse opstand', pp. 12–14; and David Nicholas, *Medieval Flanders* (London, 1992), p. 228.

allied garrison in the Flemish town of Oudenaarde, was a siege using gunpowder weapons in what may have been one of the earliest sustained gunpowder artillery bombardments of any location. Froissart claims that the Ghentenaars 'fired and fired their cannons against those in the town'. So intense was this bombardment, with many of the projectiles seeming to pass over the walls and fall into the town, that the inhabitants of Oudenaarde were forced to cover their houses with dirt to protect their roofs from fire.[11] The Flemish count, Louis of Male, was not in Oudenaarde at the time, but instead had sought refuge in the nearby town of Dendermonde. It, too, underwent attack. Both of these engagements forced Louis to seek respite and some succour. He sued Philip van Artevelde for peace, asking his son-in-law, Philip the Bold, duke of Burgundy, to be the mediator in this dispute with his subjects.[12]

A peace treaty extremely favourable to the Ghentenaars was signed on 1 December 1379, but Louis clearly never meant to abide by its provisions (although it did buy him some time to regroup and build his forces), as the following summer the count went to war against the rebels, recapturing Ypres and occupying Courtrai, both important rebel towns. Furthermore, the important, but until then non-aligned town of Bruges, decided to side with the count against its economic and often political adversary, Ghent. This allowed Louis, in the autumn of 1380, even to besiege Ghent itself. Ultimately, however, Louis of Male did not prove to have sufficient forces to effectively besiege this large town, the second largest in northern Europe, and with his supplies dwindling and winter approaching, he was forced to raise his siege and again agree to peace.[13]

Of course, this peace did not hold for very long either. Throughout 1381 and into 1382, the two sides fought each other in several fruitless engagements, with the rebels directing their military activity from Ghent against Bruges, and the comital forces responding from Bruges against Ghent.[14] It was not until 3 May 1382 that a more significant contest was fought, at Bevershoutsveld, outside the town of Bruges.[15] It was a hard-fought battle, one that the Ghentenaars fought with a urgency that seemed not to be with the Brugeois. The Ghentenaars were desperate, as the Flemish harvests had been destroyed from the constant warfare of the preceding three years and what little food was available in 1382 had gone to Bruges, which had the support of Count Louis of Male.[16] In the battle, the Brugeois, who

---

[11] Jean Froissart, *Chroniques*, ed. S. Luce et al. (14 vols, Paris, 1869–1975), IX, pp. 196–201. See also Vandermaesen and Ryckaert, 'De Gentse opstand', pp. 14–15; Richard Vaughan, *Philip the Bold: The Formation of the Burgundian State* (London, 1962), p. 21; David Nicholas, *The Van Arteveldes of Ghent: The Varieties of Vendetta and the Hero in History* (Ithaca, 1988), p. 141.

[12] Vaughan, *Philip the Bold*, pp. 21–2; Vandermaesen and Ryckaert, 'De Gentse opstand', p. 15; Nicholas, *Medieval Flanders*, p. 228; Perroy, *Hundred Years War*, pp. 188–9; Henri Pirenne, *Histoire de Belgique II: Du commencement du XIVe siècle à la mort de Charles le Téméraire* (Brussels, 1903), pp. 191–2.

[13] Froissart, *Chroniques*, X, pp. 60–3; Vaughan, *Philip the Bold*, pp. 22–3; Vandermaesen and Ryckaert, 'De Gentse opstand', p. 15; Pirenne, *Histoire de Belgique II*, pp. 192–3.

[14] Vaughan, *Philip the Bold*, p. 23. Froissart, *Chroniques*, X, pp. 63–218, concerns himself much with the travels made and skirmishes fought by the two sides. But in the final reckoning of the greater Ghent War these engagements meant very little.

[15] See Kelly DeVries, 'The Forgotten Battle of Bevershoutsveld, May 3, 1382: Technological Innovation and Military Significance', *Armies, Chivalry and Warfare in Medieval Britain*, ed. Matthew Strickland (Stamford, 1998), pp. 280–94.

[16] Froissart, *Chroniques*, X, pp. 5–8.

were also celebrating their annual Holy Blood procession and may have been more inebriated than sensible, rushed out of the protective walls of their town and into the gunpowder weapons of the Ghentenaars.[17] These weapons had been prepared to fire on the walls of Bruges, but instead discharged their projectiles into its militia. Jean Froissart describes this action:

> The Ghentenaars placed themselves on a hill and they gathered themselves all together. Then they fired more than three hundred cannons all at the same time. And then they turned around on a hub and ordered themselves, placing the Brugeois with the sun in their eyes, which distressed them greatly. Then they attacked them crying 'Ghent!' At the moment that the Brugeois heard the voices of the Ghentenaars and the firing of the cannons and saw that they were about to be brutally attacked, they, like cowards and villains, opened their lines and allowed the Ghentenaars to enter among them without putting up any defence. And they flung down their weapons and fled.[18]

The *Chronique de Flandre* confirms what Froissart writes:

> The Ghentenaars moved themselves and their artillery forward. Which artillery fired a blast with such a furor that it seemed to bring the [Brugeois] line directly to a halt.[19]

The Brugeois fled in a hurried rout, rushing for the safety of their town. The Ghentenaars pursued them, showing little mercy.[20] The Ghentenaars even were able to enter the town, where their slaughter of the count's adherents continued.[21] However, the chief prize of the rebels, Louis of Male, was not to be found among the dead or captured, for the count had successfully escaped from his enemies.[22]

Without the Flemish count's capture, there was to be no end to the rebellion

---

[17] 'Chronicon comitum Flandriae', *Corpus chronicorum Flandriae I*, ed. J. J. de Smet (Brussels, 1837), p. 248; Oliver van Dixmude, *Merkwaerdige gebeurtenissen vooral in Vlaenderen en Brabant van 1377 tot 1443*, ed. J. J. Lambin (Ypres, 1835), p. 11. See also 'Chronicon comitum Flandriae', p. 240; 'Chronique de Flandre', in *Istore et croniques de Flandres*, ed. Kervyn de Lettenhove (2 vols, Brussels, 1879–80), II, p. 247.

[18] Froissart, *Chroniques*, X, pp. 31–2: 'Adont ceulx de Gand se missent en ung mont et se recueillirent tous ensamble et fisent tout à une fois desclicquer plus de IIIc canons, et tournèrent autour de ce plasquiet, et misent ceulx de Bruges le souleil en l'ueil, qui mout les greva, et entrèrent dans eulx, en escriant: "Gand!" Sitost que ceulx de Bruges oyrent la voix de ceulx de Gand et les canons desclicquer, et que il les veirent venir de front sur eulx et assailir asprement comme lasches gens et pleins de mauvais convenant, il se ouvrirent tous et laissièrent les Gantois entrer dans eulx sans d'effence nulle et jettèrent leurs bastons jus et tournèrent le dos.'

[19] 'Chronique de Flandre', II, p. 247: 'Ils se reboutèrent tous en leur artillerie que ils firent à coup tirer par telle fureur que ce sembloit ung droit fourdre venant d'en hault.'

[20] Froissart, *Chroniques*, X, pp. 31–2; Jean Juvénal des Ursins, 'Histoire de Charles VI, roy de France, et des choses mémorables advenues durant quarante-deux années de son règne depuis 1380 jusques à 1422', *Nouvelle collection des mémoires pour servir à l'histoire de France*, ed. J. F. Michaud (Lyons, 1851), II, p. 351; *Chronique du religieux de Saint-Denis contenant le règne de Charles VI, de 1380 à 1422*, ed. Louis Bellaguet (6 vols., Paris, 1839–52; repr. Paris, 1994), I, p. 168.

[21] Froissart, *Chroniques*, X, pp. 33–4; 'Chronique de Flandre', II, p. 247; 'Chronicon comitum Flandriae', p. 240; 'Rijmkroniek van Vlaenderen', *Corpus chronicorum Flandriae IV*, ed. J. J. de Smet (Brussels, 1865), pp. 870–1.

[22] There are several versions of Louis' escape from Bruges. For a recounting of these see DeVries, 'Forgotten Battle of Bevershoutsveld'.

favourable to the Ghentenaars, even though they had captured Bruges and soon would have Ypres and Courtrai back in their control. Again they began a siege of Oudenaarde using large numbers of gunpowder weapons.[23] Still, despite such artillery, the garrison and townspeople of Oudenaarde refused to surrender, hoping that they would be rescued.

Louis of Male quickly travelled to Paris, where he petitioned his son-in-law, Philip the Bold, and Philip's nephew, the recently crowned Charles VI, for aid against the rebellion. The French king could hardly refuse such a petition, especially after Philip the Bold convinced his nephew that to allow Flanders to rebel without punishment would fuel the already hot fires of independence in his own towns.[24]

Charles VI and Philip the Bold gathered their armies and moved north towards the southern Low Countries. The Flemings put up some relatively small and futile resistance at Commines,[25] but Ypres surrendered without a fight.[26] Before the Franco-Burgundians could move on to Bruges, however, scouts reported that a Flemish force had amassed between Ypres and Bruges near West Rosebeke. Philip van Artevelde, perhaps cocky because of his recent, relatively simple victory over the Brugeois at Bevershoutsveld, believed it was to his advantage to meet his enemy in open battle. He had selected an advantageous terrain and awaited the arrival of the Franco–Burgundian forces.[27] The battle of Rosebeke was fought on 26 November 1382.

At Rosebeke Philip van Artevelde was not able to repeat his previously successful gunpowder weaponry-determined tactics. Although he had chosen the battlefield and had ordered his lines 'very subtly and in good order', according to the *Chronique de Flandre*, with one line interspersed with *canons et engiens*,[28] it seems that he was unable to discharge these in the face of the enemy's attack, as he had at Bevershoutsveld. Instead, the far more numerous Franco–Burgundian soldiers were able to rush the Flemings and quickly defeat them.

The battle of Rosebeke was a resounding defeat for the Ghentenaars and other Flemish rebels, and among the dead left on the battlefield lay Philip van Artevelde. The remnants of van Artevelde's force fled to the safety of Ghent and nearby towns. The rebel siege of Oudenaarde was raised, and Bruges submitted again quickly to the authority of the count.[29] Yet Ghent refused to surrender, even after being offered

---

[23] Froissart, *Chroniques*, X, pp. 247–9.

[24] On the petitions of Louis to Philip the Bold and Charles VI, see Vaughan, *Philip the Bold*, p. 16; Pirenne, *Histoire de Belgique II*, p. 197; Palmer, *England, France and Christendom*, p. 20; Françoise Autrand, *Charles VI: La folie du roi* (Paris, 1986), p. 124.

[25] The quotation comes from Froissart, *Chroniques*, XI, pp. 13–14. See also *Chronique du religieux de Saint-Denis*, I, pp. 192–6; Jean Juvénal des Ursins, 'Histoire de Charles VI', pp. 353–4; *Chronographia regum Francorum*, ed. H. Moranville (Paris, 1891–7), III, pp. 41–2; *Chronique des quatre premiers Valois (1327–1393)*, ed. S. Luce (Paris, 1862), pp. 305–6; *Chronique du bon duc Loys de Bourbon*, ed. A.-M. Chazaud (Paris, 1876), pp. 167–9; *Chronique des règnes de Jean II et de Charles V*, ed. R. Delachenal (Paris, 1910–20), IV, pp. 24–6; Autrand, *Charles VI*, pp. 126–28.

[26] *Chronique des règnes de Jean II et de Charles V*, IV, pp. 27–30; Jean Juvénal des Ursins, 'Histoire de Charles VI', p. 354; *Chronique du religieux de Saint-Denis*, I, pp. 200–2; *Chronique du bon duc Loys*, pp. 169–70; *Chronographia regum Francorum*, III, pp. 41–2; 'Chronique de Flandre', II, p. 214; Autrand, *Charles VI*, pp. 129–30.

[27] Autrand, *Charles VI*, p. 131.

[28] Chronique de Flandre', II, pp. 214, 251.

[29] 'Chronique de Flandre', II, pp. 216–17, 266–7; van Dixmude, *Merkwaerdige gebeurtenissen vooral in Vlaenderen en Brabant*, p. 16; 'Chronicon comitum Flandriae', p. 242; *Chronique des règnes de Jean II et Charles V*, p. 31; Autrand, *Charles VI*, 134–5.

amnesty (at a high cost in reparations). And the Franco–Burgundians were unable to proceed against the still rebellious city as winter was approaching. As a parting gesture, however, they marched on Courtrai, which had sided with Ghent in this rebellion, burned the town, and returned to France with the armour and golden spurs which had hung in the town's church of Notre Dame since being captured at the battle of Courtrai eighty years previously.[30]

His victory at Rosebeke established Charles VI's military legacy early, something that his contemporary biographers would later remember during the king's bouts of mental instability.[31] It also confirmed the growing military reputation of Philip the Bold, which ultimately would give him a military as well as political legitimacy when he took over the rule of the Flemish county two years later. But it did not end the rebellion. The Ghentenaars still held out.

Although Flemish relations with the English during the time of Edward III had always been strong, by the end of this king's reign this strength had begun to decline. After his death, English activity, militarily or diplomatically, in Flanders had almost entirely ceased. With Richard II on the throne and the English wool staple established in Calais,[32] there was little interaction between the once very close allies; and what little there was, was Ghent-initiated and Ghent-directed. Throughout the 'Ghent War' especially, representatives from this rebellious Flemish town had tried to reinvigorate the English–Flemish friendship, undoubtedly hoping to pull them into the conflict. Ghentenaar ambassadors even offered Richard II title to the county of Flanders and promised to recognise his right as king of France.[33] But the English king, who obviously had his own rebellious subjects to deal with,[34] refused to accept Flemish allegiance or to enter into the 'Ghent War'. Nor did his subjects, at least until after the battle of Rosebeke.

Undoubtedly this Flemish defeat was one of the provocations for Henry Despenser, bishop of Norwich, to preach a crusade in England. It is not the purpose of this study to discuss the bishop's speeches, his parliamentary fight, his recruitment of men and gathering of funds, or his ability to interest the participation of more experienced military leaders, Hugh Calveley or William Elmham.[35] Instead, this article will investigate the military history of Despenser's crusade and the role played in it by Ghent.

On 17 May 1383, the bishop of Norwich's force disembarked at Calais. Almost immediately they turned away from French-held territory, lands whose inhabitants

---

[30] Froissart, *Chroniques*, XI, pp. 69–70; *Chronique du religieux de Saint-Denis*, I, pp. 228–9; Jean Juvénal des Ursins, 'Histoire de Charles VI', p. 356; van Dixmude, *Merkwaerdige gebeurtenissen vooral in Vlaenderen en Brabant*, p. 16; 'Chronique de Flandre', II, pp. 217–18.

[31] See especially Jean Juvenal des Ursins, 'Histoire de Charles VI', p. 353; *Chronique du religieux de Saint-Denis*, I, pp. 188, 218, 230; Christine de Pizan, *Le livre des fais et bonnes meurs du sage roy Charles V*, ed. S. Solente (2 vols, Paris, 1936–40), II, pp. 25–6.

[32] This staple had been moved from Bruges to Calais in 1362. See McKisack, *Fourteenth Century*, pp. 353–4; David Nicholas, 'Economic Reorientation and Social Change in Fourteenth-Century Flanders', *Past and Present* lxx (1976), p. 9.

[33] According to Thomas Walsingham, *Historia Anglicana*, ed. H. T. Riley (2 vols, Rolls Series, London, 1863–4), II, p. 71.

[34] So evident during the Peasants' Revolt of 1381.

[35] These points will be addressed more completely and at length in a future book on the Ghent War and the bishop of Norwich's crusade. In the meantime, see the comments of Wrong, *Crusade of 1383*; James Magee, 'Sir William Elmham and the Recruitment for Henry Despenser's Crusade of 1383', *Medieval Prosopography* xx (1999), pp. 181–90.

favoured Pope Clement VII, and marched towards Flanders, a county whose inhabitants favoured Pope Urban VI, the same pope in whose support Norwich crusaded. On 19 May the English captured Gravelines without conflict and began a siege of Bourbourg.[36] Leaving a few troops behind to continue that siege, which ended successfully a few days later, the bishop of Norwich captured Dunkirk, again without any conflict, and on 25 May had his first real engagement with enemy troops a few kilometers up the coast, outside Dunkirk. This was a victory for the English, but it slowed their advance as well as losing them several soldiers.[37] At this point the bishop turned east, towards Ypres, and laid siege to the town on 9 June. Froissart claims the English believed that the townspeople 'would surrender completely when they saw the land surrender to them'.[38]

As the English were making this progress, Ghentenaar armies marched towards Damme, outside Bruges, and, again, towards Oudenaarde. Damme, without a protective garrison, fell quickly. So, surprisingly given to its previous history, did Oudenaarde. The Ghentenaars also moved to Ypres, arriving a short time after the English.[39] So far, it looked like a successful campaign, although certainly not the crusade against the Clementines anticipated by some of the English, including Sir Hugh Calveley.[40] But Ypres did not surrender as expected. For whatever reason, the Yprois decided to put up an active defence. So the English and Ghentenaars began the by now customary gunpowder artillery bombardment of the town's fortifications. Almost all the contemporary chronicles of this siege recount the heavy bombardment and its destructive results. 'Many were killed by [the English and Flemish] artillery,' writes Jean Froissart.[41] The *Chronique de Flandre* agrees, adding the story of 'one stone shot from a cannon at night [that] fell among three houses on the rue de Boesingues. And this stone fell onto the roof of a woman who was asleep on her bed. But because she was a woman of God, she was not hurt.' The anonymous chronicler concludes, 'Thus God saved the people of Ypres.'[42] (This sentiment is still somewhat held by the Yprois, who have continued to revere a statue of the Madonna, now mounted above the entrance to the post-World War I reconstructed Cloth Hall, as influential in saving the town from the English siege of 1383.)

Despite the intensive bombardment, the fortifications of Ypres held. This may be because of the large water-filled moats around the town, to which almost all of the

[36] Froissart, *Chroniques*, XI, pp. 95–7; 'Chronique de Flandre', II, pp. 285, 293, 307; Walsingham, *Historia Anglicana*, II, pp. 88–90; *The Westminster Chronicle 1381–1394*, ed. L. C. Hector and B. F. Harvey (Oxford, 1982), pp. 38–9. For the siege of Bourbourg, an interesting study is Gustave Monteuuis, 'Le siège de Bourbourg en 1383', *Annales du comité flamand de France* xxii (1895), pp. 259–313.

[37] Froissart, *Chroniques*, XI, pp. 97–9, 102–3; 'Chronique de Flandre', II, pp. 285–6, 293, 307; Walsingham, *Historia Anglicana*, II, pp. 90–3; *Westminister Chronicle*, pp. 38–41.

[38] Froissart, *Chroniques*, XI, p. 107: 'Il avoient imaginacion et intencion que la ville d'Ippre se renderoit tantos quant il veroient le païs rendu.' See also ibid., XI, pp. 107–8; 'Chronique de Flandre', II, pp. 281, 283, 286–91, 293–320; Walsingham, *Historia Anglicana*, II, pp. 95–6; *Westminister Chronicle*, pp. 44–7.

[39] Froissart, *Chroniques*, XI, pp. 111–12.

[40] Ibid., XI, pp. 93–4. According to Froissart, Calveley continued to have problems with the bishop of Norwich's divergence from his stated crusade: ibid., XI, pp. 99–100, 102–4.

[41] Ibid., XI, p. 121: 'et que mout perdoient de leur artillerie.' See also 'Chronique de Flandre', II, pp. 294, 298, 309, 311–12, 317.

[42] 'Chronique de Flandre', II, p. 298: 'Après avint que une pierre d'un canon fu trait par le ville parmi trois maisons en le rue de Boesingues, par nuit, et le pierre fu trouvée dalés une femme qui dormoit à son lit, dont le femme Dieux looit que elle n'en fu pas grevée. Ainsi sauvoit Dieux ciauls d'Ippre.'

same chroniclers also refer.[43] Many of the shots fired from the besieging weapons may have missed hitting the walls or gates of the town; many others, based on the story above, flew over them into Ypres itself. Evidence for this may also be found in the fact that, when most of artillery-related destruction is reported in the contemporary sources, it is almost entirely in the town and among the inhabitants and their domiciles and not against the fortifications. With this explanation, one may understand why, after two months and one final assault, on 10 August, the bishop of Norwich decided to abandon his participation in the siege (leaving his own gunpowder weapons and other military materiel, according to Henry Knighton).[44] The bishop and his army retreated to Calais; by the middle of September, he had also given up Bourbourg, Dunkirk and Gravelines;[45] and by the beginning of October he had returned to England, where he would be tried for abusing indulgences, misusing funds and personally profiting from his willingness to retreat across the Channel without doing battle with Charles VI or Philip the Bold.[46] (It seems that the bishop had negotiated his retreat with these two enemy leaders, benefiting financially from it.)[47]

The most frequently asked question about the bishop of Norwich's crusade, then and now, is why, after his stated purpose both in raising men and funds in England was so clearly to fight against the heretical Clementines, he changed his direction once he landed on the continent and led his forces against Urbanists. Henry Despenser certainly must have known that the Flemings followed Pope Urban VI. In fact, there is sufficient evidence to suggest that, once the bishop actually entered Flanders, the Flemish count, Louis of Male, even sent two ambassadors, Jean Vilain and Jean Moulin, to him to explain that Louis supported Pope Urban, as did his county's inhabitants.[48] However, this also did nothing to stop the bishop or to change his direction. Why not? Could Henry Despenser, bishop of Norwich, an ecclesiastic of some esteem prior to this crusade,[49] have been so stupid as not to realise the difference between the Urbanist Flemings and the Clementine French? In short, the answer is that the Ghentenaars made him do it, as Despenser would later claim. That can be the only explanation. Despenser's moves, combined with those of the Ghentenaars, give a military rationale to his campaign.

Let us return to the initial march of the two armies in this campaign. As Henry Despenser made his march up the coast and against Ypres, the Ghentenaar armies marched against Damme and Oudenaarde and captured them. This left three of the five most important Flemish towns in Ghent's hands: Ghent, Damme and

---

[43] Froissart, *Chroniques*, XI, p. 121; and 'Chronique de Flandre', II, pp. 288–9, 297, 312.

[44] *Knighton's Chronicle, 1337–1396*, ed. G. H. Martin (Oxford, 1995), pp. 326–29. See also Froissart, *Chroniques*, XI, pp. 120–1; Walsingham, *Historia Anglicana*, II, pp. 98–9.

[45] Froissart, *Chroniques*, XI, pp. 126–37; 'Chronique de Flandre', II, pp. 290–1, 320; Walsingham, *Historia Anglicana*, II, pp. 102–4.

[46] Froissart, *Chroniques*, XI, pp. 152–3; Walsingham, *Historia Anglicana*, II, p. 104; *Westminster Chronicle*, pp. 46–7; *Knighton's Chronicle*, pp. 328–9. Walsingham, *Historia Anglicana*, II, pp. 99–100, insists that the bishop of Norwich wished to continue the crusade after his failure at Ypres by invading Picardy, but that his military leaders opposed this plan. Despenser enters Picardy anyway, but returns to Gravelines and then to England once he realises the approach of the French army. No other contemporary source (English, French or Flemish) supports this interpretation.

[47] Aston, 'Impeachment of Bishop Despenser', pp. 127–48.

[48] Froissart, *Chroniques*, XI, pp. 100–1, 115–16.

[49] On the history of Henry Despenser see Wrong, *Crusade of 1383*, pp. 10–17.

Oudenaarde. Only Ypres and Bruges remained under comital control. It was a strategy that benefited the Ghentenaars in their rebellion. But it was not the English crusading cause, as no Clementines were ever attacked.

When was this plan formulated? It is possible that it occurred in England, before Despenser's departure for the continent. It is known that Frans Ackerman, the Ghent admiral and leader of the rebellion after the death of Philip van Artevelde, visited England after the battle of Rosebeke, undoubtedly to ask for English assistance.[50] It is probable that he met with and encouraged the bishop of Norwich at this time. Perhaps the two also planned this strategy then. Yet this would make Despenser much more duplicitous than even the most anti-Despenser critic has suggested. Besides, there is no evidence to support this idea.

More than likely, the plan to alter the bishop of Norwich's crusade was hatched at Calais once the bishop and his troops had arrived at the port on 17 May and before they left on 19 May. But what sources are there to substantiate this theory? No French or English sources mention the changing of Despenser's mind at Calais or a meeting between Ghentenaars and the bishop there. This should not be considered a significant problem, however, as none of the French chronicles and only Thomas Walsingham and the Westminister Chronicle among the English sources even mention Henry Despenser at Calais;[51] the others seem to have the bishop off to Gravelines or Dunkirk directly.[52] It is the less frequently used Low Countries' sources that clarify what happened at Calais, in particular the contemporary writings of the *Chronique de Flandre* (also known as the *Istore et croniques de Flandre*) and Jean Froissart.

We must turn first to the *Chronique de Flandre*. The anonymous author of one version of this chronicle,[53] whom the Baron Kervyn de Lettenhove, its editor, claims was a Ghentenaar, reports that, after landing at Calais, the bishop sent *une chevalier* to Ghent to announce the crusaders' arrival. 'And that being done,' he writes, 'the populace of Ghent put together around 20,000 men [exaggeration is, as always in chronicles, allowed] and marched towards Ypres to assist the English [and this is the important phrase] *who were then assembled at Calais*.'[54] Why include the Ghentenaars unless a concerted strategy had been formulated between the English and the Ghentenaars to regain recently lost Flemish territory?

---

[50] Froissart, *Chroniques*, XI, p. 83. See also François Quicke, *Les Pays-Bas à la veille de la periode Bourguignonne, 1356–1384: Contribution à l'histoire politique et diplomatique de l'Europe occidentale dans la seconde moitié du XIVe siècle* (Brussels, 1947), pp. 342–3.

[51] Walsingham, *Historia Anglicana*, II, p. 88; *Westminster Chronicle*, pp. 38–9.

[52] *Knighton's Chronicle*, pp. 326–7, and the continuation of the *Eulogium historiarum sive temporis*, ed. F.S. Haydon (3 vols, Rolls Series, London, 1858–63), III, pp. 356–7, pick up the story with the bishop's attack at Gravelines and Bourbourg.

[53] In the edition of the 'Chronique de Flandre' by Kervyn de Lettenhove, there are several different variations of each 'partie' of the text. These are identified, after the initial reading, as 'autre relation', and may be separate readings of the same original chronicle. (Large parts of one version seem even to have been translated as the *Chronographia regum Francorum*.) Kervyn de Lettenhove identifies the original chronicler as a Ghentenaar, which he takes from his reading of the text; certainly this seems justified by the amount of material on Ghent and especially on the Ghent War, although the chronicle finishes in 1383, before the completion of the war. It is badly in need of a new edition.

[54] 'Chronique de Flandre', II, p. 281: 'Et vint uns chevaliers d'Engleterre par-deviers ceuls de Gand, ausquels il dist que briefment seroient reconfortés des Englès. Et, ce fait, les gens de Gand se misent ensemble jusques à XXm hommes et alèrent viers Yppre pour là attendre les Englès *qui pour lors s'asamblèrent à Calais*.' (Emphasis mine.)

Of course, this still might mean that such a plan had been made in England and not in Calais. But this is where Jean Froissart illuminates matters. Froissart, who composed this final redaction of his chronicle fairly soon after the events which he relates, does not report the same movements or the same chronology of movements as does the *Chronique de Flandre*. However, he does include two conversations had by the bishop of Norwich at Calais, which suggest that this is when Despenser made the decision to change his purpose and the reasons that influenced this decision. The first conversation, with a group of his companions, has Despenser tell his fellow crusade leaders that they would not be attacking Boulogne or St Omer (the two nearby Clementine sites mentioned by Froissart):

> because Flanders is the land of attack, and it ought to be attacked because of the power of the king of France there. Also, we are not able to make a better exploit, all considered, nor a more honourable one than to reconquer that place'[55]

Sir Hugh Calveley was apparently not with this group and, after discovering this change of plans, rushed into the bishop's residence and exclaimed:

> We were supposed to destroy the Clementines, and you want us to go into Flanders and not against the lands of the duke of Burgundy and the king of France. You do not want us to go forward with this. But I would entreat you that the count of Flanders and all the Flemings are also good and loyal Urbanists as we are.[56]

To this Froissart has Despenser answer:

> Oy, Oy [Froissart's French is 'Oïl, oïl'], Sir Hugh, you would have us attack the kingdom of France and not elsewhere. But would it not be more profitable for us to enter Flanders along the rich frontier of the sea, against Bourbourg, Dunkirk, Nieuwport, and into the castellaneries of Bergues, Cassel, Ypres and Poperinghe? And the lands which I have named to you, as I have been informed by the burghers of Ghent, *who are in our company*, will not fight against us.[57]

Of course, Froissart is notorious for making up dialogue that he could not possibly have heard or recorded. But, even if the accuracy of the words cannot be guaran-

---

[55] Froissart, *Chroniques*, XI, p. 92: 'Nous ne poons partir ne issir des portes de Calais nullement, que nous n'entrons sus terre d'anemis, car c'est France de tous costés, otant bien vers Flandres comme vers Boulongne ou Saint Omer, car Flandres est terre de conquès, et l'a conquis par poissance li rois de France. Ossi nous ne porions faire milleur exploit, tout consideré, ne plus honnerable que dou reconquerir.' Despenser's entire speech here rationalises his decision to move into Urbanist-held territory. Most of this rationalisation revolves around the injustices of the count of Flanders towards his subjects and sounds suspiciously as if it was given to him by Ghentenaar propagandists.

[56] Ibid., XI, p. 93: 'se nous poons destruire les Clementins. Se nous alons en Flandres, quoi que li païs soit au duc de Bougongne et au roi de France, nous nos fourferons, car j'entench que li contes de Flandres et tout li Flamenc sont ossi boin et vrai Urbanistre que nous sommes.'

[57] Ibid., XI, p. 94: 'Oïl, oïl, messire Hue, vous avés tant apris ou roiaulme de France à chevauchier que vous ne savés chevauchier ailleurs. Où poons nous mieux faire nostre pourfit que de entrer en celle rice frontière de mer de Bourbourc, de Dunquerque, de Noefport et en la castelerie de Berghes, de Cassel, de Ippre et de Popringhe? En che païs là que je vous nomme, sicom je fui enfourmés des bourgois de Gand *qui sont chi en nostre compaignie*, il ne furent onques guerriiet.' (Emphasis mine.)

teed, it is safe to suggest that two things can be established in this dialogue. First, the decision to change attack plans was made at Calais and not previously; note Calveley's reaction to Despenser's resolution. Second, this strategic change was made at the behest of the Ghentenaars who were present at Calais, probably from the very arrival of the bishop and his crusaders and probably numbering among them Frans Ackerman, as it is written that he then led the English up the coast and to Ypres. The Flemish knight sent to Ghent, as recorded in the *Chronique de Flandre*, was sent there after the Ghentenaars had effectively changed the bishop of Norwich's mind, undoubtedly to report that their rebellion should once again become an offensive one.

This also gives the reason for Despenser's abandonment of the siege of Ypres on 10 August, barely two months into it. The reasons given for this by English chroniclers of the time, and echoed by modern historians – which include the lack of siege machines (despite Thomas Walsingham's descriptions of both gunpowder and non-gunpowder artillery pieces among the besiegers),[58] dysentery[59] and even the large approaching relief army of Philip the Bold – are not accurate.[60] Henry Despenser left Ypres because he had been lied to by the Ghentenaars, who had promised the bishop that the Yprois 'will not fight against us'. The Flemings aligned with the French and Louis of Male did fight back, and they fought well.

In fine, then, the Ghentenaars really did make Henry Despenser do it: which, unfortunately for most modern English commentators, means that the story of the bishop of Norwich's crusade in 1383 is more a Flemish than an English one.

---

[58] Walsingham, *Historia Anglicana*, II, pp. 98–9.
[59] *Eulogium historiarum*, III, p. 357.
[60] Froissart, *Chroniques*, XI, pp. 116–17; *Knighton's Chronicle*, pp. 326–7; *Chronique des règnes de Jean II et de Charles V*, III, pp. 55–7.

LOYALTY, HONOUR AND THE LANCASTRIAN REVOLUTION: SIR STEPHEN SCROPE OF CASTLE COMBE AND HIS KINSMEN, c.1389–c.1408

Alastair Dunn

On 2 August 1400 the court of the constable and marshal of England met at the Moot Hall in Newcastle upon Tyne to hear an appeal by John Kighley, esquire, against Sir Stephen Scrope.[1] Kighley's charge was the gravest that could have been brought – that Scrope 'and other great persons', gathered at the manor of Bingbery in Kent in December 1399, had plotted to murder King Henry IV. This hitherto ignored appeal of treason sheds new light on both the Epiphany Rising, and the broader discourse within the political community in the aftermath of the Lancastrian revolution.

In 1990 Simon Walker charted the dramatic downturn in the fortunes of the Abberburys, an Oxfordshire gentry dynasty who had been closely associated with the court of Richard II, but had failed to weather the storm of his deposition.[2] More recently he has analysed the career of Janico Dartasso, the Gascon squire who remained loyal to Richard II but, in marked contrast to the Abberburys, reinvented himself in Lancastrian service.[3] This article intends to apply the same examination to Sir Stephen Scrope, and to draw some conclusions as to why his experiences following the 1399 revolution resembled those of Dartasso more than those of the Abberburys and the other Ricardian 'recusants'.

Sir Stephen Scrope's alleged identification as a party to the 'Epiphany Rising' – the failed Ricardian re-adeption of January 1400 – put him in a highly precarious position. Several knights personally known to Scrope, including Benedict Cely, Thomas Blount and Bernard Brocas, had endured traitors' deaths at Oxford and London in January 1400, while the leading conspirators, the earls of Kent, Huntingdon and Salisbury and lord Despenser, had been lynched in an outburst of popular anti-Ricardian sentiment.[4]

The fall of Richard II in 1399 had created a flurry of personal challenges arising from the deep personal hatreds that had been festering within the kingdom's

---

[1]   BL, MS Additional 9021 (Anstis' transcriptions of proceedings before the Court of Chivalry), fols 238–45, 250, 266–74. I would like to thank Rees Davies, Chris Given-Wilson and Simon Walker for their help in the preparation of this article.
[2]   S. K. Walker, 'Sir Richard Abberbury (c.1330–1399) and his Kinsmen: The Rise and Fall of a Gentry Family', *Nottingham Medieval Studies* xxxiv (1990), pp. 113–40.
[3]   Simon Walker, 'Janico Dartasso: Chivalry, Nationality and the Man-at-Arms', *History* 84 (1999), pp. 31–51.
[4]   A. Rogers, 'Henry IV and the Revolt of the Earls, 1400', *History Today* xvi (1968), pp. 277–83; D. Crook, 'Central England and The Revolt of The Earls', *Historical Research* lxiv (1991), pp. 403–10; J. L. Leland, 'The Oxford Trial of 1400: Royal Politics and The County Gentry', *The Age of Richard II*, ed. J. L. Gillespie (Stroud, 1997), pp. 165–89.

political elite over the previous two years. The appeal of treason (a public allegation delivered by an individual or group against another individual or group, in full parliament) had been one of the most destructive political phenomena of the previous reign.[5] The appeal had first been used in a political context by Richard II's enemies to procure the forfeiture, execution and exile of several ministers and courtiers in the Merciless Parliament of 1388. Nine years later, in the Revenge Parliament of 1397, Richard II turned the appeal of treason against its inventors, the duke of Gloucester and the earls of Arundel and Warwick.[6] Henry IV was quick to recognise that the appeal of treason was a dangerous mutation of legal process and, in October 1399, it was formally abolished. Henceforth, all allegations of treason would be within the cognisance of the court of the constable and marshal of England.[7]

In the Deposition Parliament of September 1399, Sir William Bagot, who had turned his coat with remarkable celerity, accused Edward, earl of Rutland, of having conspired to murder the duke of Gloucester and the earls of Arundel and Warwick. Rutland offered to prove himself with his body and cast down his hood, but the king intervened to prevent any further confrontations. However, Rutland was a man with many enemies, and was appealed again, by Walter, lord Fitzwalter, of complicity in the death of his late lord, Thomas, duke of Gloucester. The Fitzwalter appeal depended on testimony from Thomas Mowbray, duke of Norfolk, news of whose death had yet to reach England from his Venetian exile. Once Henry had become aware of Norfolk's death he appears to have persuaded Fitzwalter to withdraw his appeal.[8]

The former retainers of Thomas of Woodstock did not abandon their efforts to punish the men they held responsible for his death. The appeal moved by Thomas, lord Morley,[9] against John Montagu, earl of Salisbury, was the most significant private proceeding of the entire Lancastrian revolution.[10] Morley's charges were numerous, but centred on the allegation that Salisbury had betrayed the confidential deliberations of Thomas of Woodstock's council to Richard II. Montagu had subsequently served Richard II as one of the Counter-Appellants against Duke Thomas, who was convicted as a notorious traitor in parliament on 24 September 1397, after his apparent secret murder in a Calais inn.[11]

---

[5]   The large, and mainly technical, literature on appeals of treason includes S. Rezneck, 'The Early History of the Parliamentary Declaration of Treason', *EHR* xlii (1927), pp. 497–513; M. V. Clarke, *Fourteenth Century Studies* (Oxford, 1937), pp. 242–71; T. F. T. Plucknett, 'State Trials Under Richard II', *TRHS* 5th ser. ii (1952), pp. 159–71; T. F. T. Plucknett, 'Impeachment and Attainder', *TRHS* 5th ser. iii (1953), pp. 145–58; C. D. Ross, 'Forfeiture for Treason in the Reign of Richard II', *EHR* lxxi (1956), pp. 560–75; J. G. Bellamy, *The Law of Treason in England in the Later Middle Ages* (Cambridge, 1970), chapter 7.

[6]   For narrative of the appeals of 1388 and 1397, see N. Saul, *Richard II* (London, 1997), pp. 191–6, 375–9.

[7]   *RP*, III, pp. 426, 442. Proceedings before the court of the constable and marshal are described in M. H. Keen, 'Treason Trials Under the Law of Arms', *TRHS* 5th ser. xii (1962), pp. 85–103, and R. I. Jack, 'Entail and Descent: The Hastings Inheritance, 1370 to 1406', *BIHR* xxxviii (1965), pp. 1–19.

[8]   *Chronicles of the Revolution, 1397–1400*, ed. Chris Given-Wilson (Manchester, 1993), p. 46.

[9]   The connections between Thomas of Woodstock and the Fitzwalter and Morley families are discussed in A. Goodman, *The Loyal Conspiracy: The Lords Appellant under Richard II* (London, 1971), pp. 123–5.

[10]   'Morley vs. Montagu (1399): A Case in the Court of Chivalry', ed. M. H. Keen and M. Warner, *Camden Miscellany XXXIV* (Camden Society 5th ser. x, London, 1997), pp. 141–95.

[11]   *RP*, III, pp. 377–8.

Unlike Fitzwalter's appeal, that of Morley proceeded to the court of chivalry. In the presence of the appellant and defendant, in the king's bedchamber at Kennington on 5 December 1399, Henry Percy, earl of Northumberland and constable of England, adjudged trial by battle for Newcastle upon Tyne on 14 February following.[12] However, the death of the defendant, Salisbury, during the Epiphany Rising of January 1400, ensured that the appointment was never kept.[13]

Had there been any substance to John Kighley's allegations of Stephen's involvement in the 1400 conspiracy, it would add a further layer of complexity to a phase of Henry IV's reign that remains still only partially understood. Although the principal events of the rising occurred in the Thames Valley along the axis of London, Windsor and Cirencester, the inquisitions conducted in its aftermath uncovered extensive preparations on the Devon estates of John Holand, earl of Huntingdon.[14] Geoffrey Penriche, bailiff of Trematon, and Thomas Porter were alleged to have threatened to behead those men of Saltash who would not ride with them, and robbed six marks from the 'common box' for good measure.[15] Further evidence of the degree of John Holand's advanced planning is apparent from his recruitment, for life, of two new esquires, Thomas Trenarke and Thomas Proudfoot, on 22 and 24 September 1399.[16] Similar suspicious activity was apparent on the estates of Thomas, lord Despenser. When the royal escheators came to Hanley Castle in the aftermath of the Epiphany Rising, they found that Despenser's steward, William Pottleswith, his attorney, William Canel, and his bailiff, Robert Stephens, had colluded to conceal, and possibly destroy, his papers in anticipation of their arrival.[17]

While his father Richard is renowned for his famous dispute with Sir Robert Grosvenor over the armorial bearings *azure a bend or*, and his brother William became infamous for his complicity in Richard II's worst excesses, Stephen Scrope has attracted remarkably little attention.[18] In many respects, however, the career of Stephen Scrope was far more representative of the dilemmas of personal and political loyalty facing the men of knightly and gentle rank in the political community at the time of the Lancastrian revolution. Stephen was the third son of the eminent – and apparently popular – Richard, first lord Scrope of Bolton in Wensleydale.[19] Richard Scrope had combined long careers in arms (in the service of the Black Prince), and national government (as treasurer from 1371 to 1375, and chancellor from 1378 to 1380, and again from 1381 to 1382) with a devoted patronage of monasteries, friaries and hospitals in his native Yorkshire.[20] In spite of Richard

---

12 'Morley vs. Montagu', p. 165.

13 The role of popular violence in the deaths of the leading conspirators in the Epiphany rising is considered by A. J. Dunn, 'Henry IV and the Politics of Resistance in Early Lancastrian England', *The Fifteenth Century III: Authority and Subversion*, ed. Linda Clark (Woodbridge, 2003), pp. 000–000.

14 *CIM 1399–1422*, pp. 54, 55 (nos. 88, 89).

15 *CIM 1399–1422*, pp. 57–8 (no. 99).

16 J. M. W. Bean, *From Lord to Patron: Lordship in Late Medieval England* (Manchester, 1989), p. 93.

17 PRO, E 159/178, m. 3 (Hilary Term, 1401–2).

18 For Scrope vs. Grosvenor, see *The Controversy between Sir Richard Scrope and Sir Robert Grosvenor in the Court of Chivalry*, ed. N. H. Nicolas (2 vols, London, 1832).

19 His elder brothers were William (executed 1399) and Roger (d. 1403). Walsingham claimed that Richard Scrope had been 'the choice of all the nobility and common people of the kingdom' when appointed chancellor in 1379: *Historia Anglicana*, ed. H. T. Riley (2 vols, Rolls Series, London, 1863–4), II, pp. 224, 226.

20 Richard, first lord Scrope's career is summarised in *Complete Peerage*, XI, p. 540. Lord Scrope's

Scrope's loyal service, his relationship with Richard II had been far from harmonious. Famously, in 1382, Scrope was ejected from the chancellorship for his opposition to Richard's attempts to farm out the Mortimer inheritance, and, on 29 November 1397, he was forced to admit that his earlier adherence to the Lords Appellant had been treasonable.[21]

After his exclusion from government in 1382, Richard Scrope devoted the remaining three decades of his life to consolidating the power and landed wealth of his dynasty. In 1379 he had commenced the building of Bolton Castle, which took eighteen years and absorbed £12,000.[22] He had also been investing in land throughout Richmondshire and elsewhere in England at this time.[23] This considerable landed wealth enabled him to channel substantial resources into the endowment of his eldest son, William, especially as Roger and Stephen had already been provided for by a double marriage to the heiresses of Robert, lord Tiptoft (d.1372). In 1392 Richard Scrope was able to furnish his eldest son with a remarkable landed endowment, the Isle of Man, purchased from the earl of Salisbury for 10,000 marks.[24]

The third of four sons, Stephen Scrope inherited only one of his father's properties, the Yorkshire manor of Wighton. His father's bequest to him of his 'second sword' was an apt metaphor for the many years that Stephen spent in the shadow of his eldest brother in the 1380s and 1390s.[25] Stephen Scrope's principal source of income is likely to have been the properties brought to him by his wife, Milicent, daughter and co-heiress of Robert Tiptoft, whom he had married at some point in the 1370s. In 1372 lord Scrope had been granted the custody of Milicent and her sister Margaret, who was married to Roger Scrope, Stephen's elder brother.[26] Although Stephen received the lesser share of the spoils of this double marriage, he did gain the lordships of Bentley, near Doncaster, and of Castle Combe, the Wiltshire seat of his wife's Dunstanville ancestors.[27] For the first years of his royal service, Stephen Scrope undoubtedly rode on the coat-tails of his increasingly infamous eldest brother, William.[28] When Richard II's army crossed to Ireland in

remarkable will included more than thirty separate bequests to religious houses, corporations and hospitals. *Testamenta Eboracensia I*, ed. J. Raine (Surtees Society, iv, Durham, 1836), pp. 272–8.

[21] *Chronicon Angliae, 1382–1388*, ed. E. M. Thompson (Rolls Series, London, 1874), p. 353; *CPR 1396–9*, p. 244; Chris Given-Wilson, 'Richard II and the Higher Nobility', *Richard II: The Art of Kingship*, ed. A. Goodman and J. L. Gillespie (Oxford, 1999), p. 113; A. Dunn, 'Richard II and the Mortimer Inheritance', *Fourteenth Century England II*, ed. Chris Given-Wilson (Woodbridge, 2002), p. 160.

[22] *CPR 1377–81*, pp. 272, 369 (licence to crenellate, 4 July 1379); K. B. McFarlane, *The Nobility of Later Medieval England* (Oxford, 1973), p. 93.

[23] B. Vale, 'The Scropes of Bolton and Masham c. 1300–1450: A Study of a Northern Noble Family' (unpublished DPhil thesis, University of York, 1987), pp. 70–88, 131–5.

[24] *CCR 1389–92*, p. 28. William Scrope used the Isle of Man's achievement of three joined armoured legs (*Triskele*) on his arms. G. H. Clucas, 'Sir William Le Scrope', *Mannin* iii (1915), p. 257; M. J. Bennett, 'Richard II and the Wider Realm', *The Age of Richard II*, ed. Goodman and Gillespie, p. 196.

[25] *Testamenta Eboracensia I*, p. 275; J. Hughes, 'Stephen Scrope and the Circle of Sir John Fastolf: Moral and Intellectual Outlooks', *Medieval Knighthood IV*, ed. C. Harper-Bill and R. Harvey (Woodbridge, 1992), p. 110.

[26] *Complete Peerage*, XI, p. 541.

[27] *DNB*, XVII, pp. 1083–3; *CIPM 1370–3*, no. 212, pp. 192–5. Unfortunately, there were no values given in Robert Tiptoft's inquisition post mortem, and so it is not possible even to ascribe a nominal income for Milicent Scrope's share of the inheritance.

[28] *Annales Ricardi Secundi et Henrici Quarti*, ed. H. T. Riley (Rolls Series, London, 1866), pp. 156–7. For a narrative of William Scrope's subsequent career as chamberlain (1394) and justiciar of Ireland (1395), earl of Wiltshire (1397), justiciar of Chester and North Wales (1398), and treasurer of England

October 1394, Stephen was a member of William's retinue.[29] William Scrope remained in Ireland after the king's return to England in the spring of 1395, adding (on 25 April) the justiciarship to a growing portfolio of offices that he held in the lordship.[30] Although nominally the subordinate of Roger Mortimer, earl of March and Ulster, and lieutenant of Ireland, William Scrope was effectively his equal, and enjoyed absolute jurisdiction in Leinster, Munster and Louth.[31]

On the very day that he became justiciar, William Scrope appointed Stephen as his lieutenant, an office that the latter held for two years at a daily wage of 4s, earning him the substantial sum of £146.[32] Eventually the exchequer caught up with the fact that William Scrope's appointment of his brother had not been sanctioned by his original indenture as justiciar, and, in a unique instance of criticism of his favourite, Richard II sent William a rebuking privy seal letter from Shrewsbury on 29 January 1398.[33] In spite of the irregularity of his appointment, however, Stephen Scrope soon came to be trusted with sensitive work. In August 1396 he escorted Donough O'Byrne and eleven of his kinsmen (and one hundred horses) to pay homage to the king at Westminster.[34] Stephen's importance was officially recognised on 13 September 1396, when he was appointed to replace his brother as justiciar in Leinster, Munster and Louth, until the following Easter.[35]

In the summer of 1397, Stephen benefited from the escalation in Richard II's retaining,[36] and on 21 July he became a king's knight, with the substantial annual fee of 100 marks.[37] Later that autumn he replaced his brother William as keeper of Bamburgh Castle for life, indicating the king's growing trust in his capabilities.[38] The prominence at court of Stephen's brother, William, brought the family increasingly close to the heart of Ricardian rule. William's many rewards for service as a Counter-Appellant in 1397 included the earldom of Wiltshire, granted on 29 September, supported by a substantial landed endowment (comprising a mixture of alienations from forfeited estates and custodies of crown lands) and, on 17 September 1398, the treasurership of England.[39] By the beginning of 1398, Stephen Scrope had returned to England and, on the day of his brother's promotion to the treasurership, he filled his shoes in the office of chamberlain of the royal house-

---

(1398), see A. J. Dunn, 'The Endowment and Disendowment of Lay Magnates in England and the Welsh Marches, 1396–1408' (unpublished DPhil thesis, University of Oxford, 1999), pp. 187–94.

29   PRO, E 101/69/1/286 (indenture of 1 June 1394).

30   *Rotulorum Patentium et Clausorum Cancellariae Hiberniae Calendarium, Hen. II–Hen. VII*, ed. E. Tresham (Dublin, 1828), pp. 152–3; *CPR 1396–9*, p. 174 (inspeximus and confirmation of 14 July 1397); D. B. Johnston, 'The Interim Years: Richard II and Ireland, 1395–1399', *England and Ireland In the Later Middle Ages: Essays In Honour of Jocelyn Otway-Ruthven*, ed. J. F. Lydon (Dublin, 1981), p. 176.

31   *CPR 1396–9*, p. 715.

32   PRO, E 101/43/4, m. 1 (pardon of account to William Scrope, justiciar of Ireland, 1395–7).

33   PRO, E 101/69/1/286 (indenture of William Scrope, justiciar of Ireland); E 404/19/26, no. 25.

34   PRO, E 101/41/34, m. 2.

35   *CPR 1396–9*, p. 23.

36   For the political context to the growth of the royal affinity, see Chris Given-Wilson, *The Royal Household and the King's Affinity: Service, Politics and Finance in England, 1360–1413* (London, 1986), pp. 215–17.

37   *CPR 1396–9*, p. 171; PRO, E 404/14/96, no. 101.

38   *CPR 1396–9*, p. 251 (12 October 1397).

39   *RP*, III, p. 355; *CPR 1396–9*, pp. 200, 209, 535; *CFR 1391–9*, p. 280. The instrument creating the earldom of Wiltshire did not limit its descent to the issue of the *body* of William Scrope. G. H. Ellis, *Earldoms in Fee* (London, 1961), p. 54.

hold.[40] This latter appointment has attracted surprisingly little attention, considering the acute political sensitivity of the office at a time of mounting crisis, and the daily access it afforded to the king.

Richard II's faith in Stephen was not misplaced, as he showed absolute loyalty until the end of the reign. When Richard abandoned his army at Caermarthen during the night of 31 July 1399, Stephen Scrope was one of the handful of men who accompanied him on his flight into north Wales.[41] When compared to the conduct of Thomas Percy, the steward of the household, and Edward, earl of Rutland, constable of England, Scrope's fidelity was remarkable – especially as news may already have reached him of his brother's execution at Bristol, two days previously.[42]

Little is heard of Stephen Scrope in the immediate aftermath of Richard II's capture, but it seems certain that he was in the king's company at the time of his arrest by Northumberland, and, presumably, was brought back to London in August. This was a perilous time for the Scrope family, as two of its sons had been closely bound up with Richard II's regime. On 19 November 1399 William Scrope was sentenced to posthumous forfeiture, even though he had been killed without any process.[43] William and the two other principal victims of the Lancastrian revolution – Sir John Bussy and Sir Henry Green – served as useful scapegoats for crimes that, in reality, had required the complaisance of a broad cross-section of the political community. But Richard Scrope feared that this was the preliminary to a broader assault on his family, and 'rising with great humility and humble pleading prayed to the king, that nothing be done in the said parliament touching the disinheritance of the said Richard or his children', later adding that he had been 'most distressed' by his son's actions. Henry IV's famous reply is emblematic of his attitude to those who had remained loyal to Richard without actively resisting his usurpation. 'The king said to the said Richard that he had no wish to have any of his lands or those of his relatives then living, but that he held him as a true knight, and had always done so.'[44]

Henry IV's undertaking notwithstanding, the Scropes of Bolton suffered serious blows to their wealth and status after the fall of Richard II. Perhaps the most financially painful loss was that of the Isle of Man, which the family had purchased at such expense only seven years previously. In the spring of 1399 Roger Scrope, younger brother of William, had been in charge of the island, and it is possible that Richard II had envisaged for him a longer-term role as the governor of this strategically vital staging post between Wales, Chester and Ireland.[45] Where the Scrope family lost out, the Percys gained, and on 19 October 1399 the island and lordship

[40] Given-Wilson, *Royal Household*, p. 283. I am grateful to Chris Given-Wilson for confirming 17 September 1398 as the date of Stephen Scrope's appointment. For the wages he received in this office, see PRO, E 403/563, m. 10 (payment of £100 to Stephen Scrope, under-chamberlain, 10 May 1399).

[41] *Chronicque de la traïson et mort de Richart Deux roy Dengleterre*, ed. Benjamin Williams (London, 1846), p. 196; *Chronicles of the Revolution*, p. 140; Walker, 'Janico Dartasso', p. 31. According to the author of the *Traïson et mort* and Jean Creton, the other members of the group consisted of Thomas Merks, bishop of Carlisle, the earl of Salisbury, William Ferriby, Alan Buxhill the younger and Janico Dartasso.

[42] *Annales Ricardi Secundi*, pp. 240, 246–7; *The Chronicle of Adam Usk, 1377–1421*, ed. C. Given-Wilson (Oxford, 1995), pp. 52–3.

[43] For accounts of William Scrope's death, see *Chronicles of the Revolution*, pp. 120–1, 128–9.

[44] *RP*, III, p. 453.

[45] *CCR 1389–92*, p. 559 (purchase of 1392); *CPR 1396–9*, p. 498.

were granted to the earl of Northumberland, for the service of bearing 'Lancaster sword' at the coronation.[46]

The posthumous forfeiture of William Scrope also cost the dynasty an earldom. When the earldom of Wiltshire had been created in September 1397, its transmission had *not* been confined to the issue of the bodies of the childless William Scrope and Isabella Russell. Had the Scrope family been rehabilitated to the same degree as the Holands or Montagus in the later years of Henry IV's reign and the early years of his successor, the earldom of Wiltshire (as well as the family barony) would have descended to Roger Scrope and his issue.[47] On 29 September 1397 William Scrope had also been granted the forfeited Beauchamp lordship of Barnard Castle, which lay within easy riding distance of the paternal estates in Richmondshire and Swaledale.[48] His tenure of Barnard Castle (which was restored to the earl of Warwick in October 1399) had afforded a fleeting glimpse of a remodelled territorial order in the north, where the Scropes of Bolton would have become key agents of Richard II's kingship.

The most disadvantaged member of the family was Isabella Russell, formerly countess of Wiltshire and widow of William Scrope. On 5 May 1400 Isabella successfully petitioned Henry IV for an exchequer annuity of 200 marks.[49] However, over the following years the widow of the hated Scrope was hardly a priority for Henry IV's scarce resources. In 1404 she petitioned parliament again:

> That as her said lord at the time of his death had had neither time nor space, on account of his hasty death, to ordain for the said supplicant anything from which she might live or sustain herself, and that after the death of the said William his lands, tenements, goods and chattels were seized into the hands of our lord the king, on account of the judgment that was made against the said William, with the result that the said supplicant was left so poor and so dissolute that she had next to nothing of her own. And afterwards, our very redoubtable and sovereign lord the king, considering the poor estate of the said supplicant, and that she had no lands, nor tenements, nor goods nor chattels, nor dower nor joint estate, nor any others means by which she might live, and of your special grace and by your letters patent granted to the said supplicant 200 marks, for the term of her life, to be taken annually from your exchequer, of which 200 marks nothing has been paid for an entire year.[50]

Isabella's claims are supported by the exchequer issue rolls, which show that the only payment that she had received was a one-off grant, authorised on 13 December 1399, of £100 of her late husband's goods, which were released to her on the

---

[46] *CPR 1399–1401*, p. 27.

[47] *Report from the Lords' Committees . . . for All Matters Touching the Dignity of a Peer* (5 vols, London, 1820–9), V, p. 117. Had Roger Scrope inherited the earldom of Wiltshire, he would have been the first northern-based magnate with a southern title, predating Richard Neville, earl of Salisbury by several decades. B. Vale suggests that the new earldom had been intended to counterbalance the power of the Nevilles and Percys in the north: Vale 'Scropes of Bolton and Masham', p. 87.

[48] *CPR 1396–9*, p. 207 (29 September 1397). Warwick's public assertion of his family's title to Barnard Castle is clear from his enfeoffment of his son and heir, Richard, on 28 October 1399: *Catalogue of Ancient Deeds*, I, p. 77.

[49] PRO, SC 8/22/1076; *CPR 1399–1401*, p. 285.

[50] *RP*, III, p. 483.

following 27 January.[51] Indeed, the warrants for issue record that her annuity was in arrears on eight occasions between 1400 and 1404.[52] Isabella concluded her petition by demanding not only that a secure source of income be found to vouchsafe her annuity, but also that she be enfeoffed with all of her late husband's lands.[53]

Henry IV responded to these strident claims with the award of an additional £100 annuity, granted on 12 November 1404.[54] But Isabella had no better luck with this new annuity, as it fell into arrears on seven occasions between 1404 and 1408.[55] Of the £234 that she was due to receive, annually, from 1404, she had received only £191, in total, by the end of 1408.[56] Payments continued to be highly irregular until the annuity was re-granted by Henry V on 20 November 1413.[57] Most significantly, Henry IV completely ignored her naive plea for her late husband's forfeited estates, the majority of which had been crown custodies or the proceeds of forfeitures and which had long since been granted out or restored to their rightful occupiers. Remarkably, Isabella Russell embarked on three subsequent marriages before her death in 1437, and was survived by twenty-four years by her fourth husband, Stephen Hatfield.[58]

Sir Stephen Scrope's loss of the chamberlainship of the royal household to a dedicated Lancastrian, Sir Thomas Erpingham,[59] was to have been expected, but Henry appears to have had no desire to make an enemy out of him, and confirmed his 100 mark annuity on 8 November 1399.[60] Two months later, Henry IV and his family narrowly escaped assassination in the Epiphany Rising, the failure of which threatened disaster for Stephen Scrope and his kin. The position of known former servants of Richard II in the spring of 1400 prefigured that of the Catholic peers and gentry in the aftermath of the 1605 Gunpowder Plot: regardless of the degree of their actual participation, they were tainted with the guilt of presumed sympathy with the plotters.

One of the chief suspects in 1400 was Henry Despenser, bishop of Norwich, who was so exercised by rumours of his alleged complicity that he wrote a long letter to his nephew at court (possibly Sir Hugh Despenser), claiming that his entire knowledge of the Epiphany Rising derived from news brought to him by Robert, lord Scales at three o'clock on Tuesday 12 January, and that throughout the period he had

[51] *CPR 1399–1401*, p. 150; PRO, E 404/15/134; E 403/564, m. 9.

[52] PRO, E 404/16/12 (3 October 1400); E 404/16/518 (20 April 1401); E 404/17/179 (14 October 1401); E 404/17/655 (17 April 1402); E 404/18/126 (14 October 1402); E 404/18/371 (25 April 1403); E 404/19/95 (17 October 1403); E 404/19/354 (15 April 1404).

[53] *RP*, III, p. 483.

[54] *CPR 1401–5*, p. 466.

[55] PRO, E 404/20/272 (15 May 1405); E 404/21/230 (22 May 1406); E 404/21/345 (22 October 1406); E 404/22/101 (16 October 1406); E 404/22/391 (20 April 1407); E 404/23/45 (3 October 1407); E 404/23/331 (24 April 1408).

[56] PRO, E 403/582, m. 4, £66 13 4d (15 May 1405); £38 1s 2d; E 403/585, m. 7, £50 (6 November 1405); E 403/585, m. 12, £16 1s 7d (10 December 1405); E 403/595, m. 1, £13 6s 8d (25 April 1408); E 403/596, m. 7, £6 13s 4d (4 December 1408). Total: £190 16s 6d.

[57] *CPR 1413–16*, p. 142.

[58] *Complete Peerage*, XII, p. 734. She subsequently married Sir Thomas de la Riviere of Westrop, Wiltshire, Sir John Drayton of Oxfordshire, and Stephen Hatfield, who survived her, dying in 1461.

[59] Given-Wilson, *Royal Household*, p. 190; PRO, C 53/168, m. 53 (no. 22) (Erpingham as chamberlain, 27 October 1399).

[60] *CPR 1399–1401*, p. 75. For payments see PRO, E 403/569, m. 8 (7 December 1399); E 403/571, m. 8 (17 November 1401).

not left the manor of South Elmham other than to attend the burial of one of his servants in the parish church. Bishop Despenser's letter concluded with a lengthy and sophisticated defence of his loyalty. But this went beyond a mere apologia for his own conduct, and was an elaborate articulation of his own construction of the relationship between rank and personal honour, in the context of political insurrection:

> And should anyone speak to the contrary of that which is written above, that we are, or have ever been, disloyal to my liege lord, or in any other way to my liege lord, whatever it should be, outside my liegeance, if he should be so a high a lord of such estate to whom we owe reverence by law, we say, saving our reverence, he does not know nor see correctly with regard to us, for he says other than what he sees. And if he should be our equal or any other person, our open response is that he conceives this falsely, and we will be ready to maintain this as long as the spirit remains in our body, in whatever manner that our most redoubtable lord the king and my lord of Canterbury should ordain me so to do. And in witness of these letters we have appended the seal of our arms. About which matter, very dear and beloved nephew we pray you with all our heart, as much as we think or can conceive, and we require you by virtue of blood and your obligations as nephew, that if you hear anyone say anything against anything that we have affirmed in this letter, to respond for us, and to speak in such a manner as you would, which we would do for you in your absence, if we were a temporal man like you are, showing him this present letter. And should you hear no one speak of such matters, please it you to keep this letter secret, and do not show it, because we want to let sleeping dogs lie.[61]

Despenser's letter is a powerful articulation of the political limbo into which known Ricardians had descended. Edward, earl of Rutland was in a similarly tenuous position at this time. Although the full extent of his participation in the Epiphany Rising may never be known, his enemies were not slow to credit him with a leading role. For the author of the *Traison et Mort*, Rutland was not merely the betrayer of the plot to Henry IV, but also a double-dealer, who then returned to his fellow-rebels at Colnbrook and counselled them to ride into Cheshire to link up with supporters of the captive Richard II.[62]

The fact that Stephen Scrope's enemies were able to locate his political orientation in this caucus of suspected traitors and known trimmers pointed to the very real dangers that he faced in 1400. Anonymous reports that he had been riding with the Epiphany rebels were readily accepted by the sheriffs of London, who seized his inn in the city. However, on 23 January, Mayor Thomas Knolles was ordered to restore Scrope's possessions, as he had in fact been with the king 'and not in the company of the rebels'.[63]

This was only the beginning of Scrope's difficulties. Later that year he was appealed by a royal esquire, John Kighley, on the following charge:

---

61 For a full transcription of the letter, see *Anglo-Norman Letters and Petitions*, ed. M. D. Legge (Anglo-Norman Text Society iii, Oxford, 1941), pp. 110–12.
62 *Chronicles of the Revolution*, pp. 230–2.
63 *CCR 1399–1402*, p. 36. This may have been the Scrope Inn that featured prominently in the Scrope vs. Grosvenor controversy.

> I, John Kighley, esquire, accuse and appeal you Stephen Scrope, knight, and say that in the first year of our lord the king who now is, in the month of December, at the manor of Bingbery in the county of Kent, and in other places, had very great treasonable purposes against the king and his kingdom, that is to say that our said lord the king be destroyed, and that Richard, lately king, his predecessor, be restored to the said kingdom of England.[64]

Grave though these charges were, they lacked essential details. Not only was Kighley unable to elaborate on the identities of Stephen Scrope's alleged co-plotters, but he also failed to provide any details about the way in which the assassination was to have been effected. Therefore, it would seem that Kighley was attempting to implicate Stephen Scrope, in a vague way, with the recent Epiphany Rising. Compared to the lengthy charges brought by lord Morley against the earl of Salisbury, which had included details of names, places and dates,[65] Kighley's testimony was threadbare. The weakness of his case notwithstanding, Kighley offered his challenge:

> And I the said John say that you are a false traitor, and I have shown your falsehood by this same appeal and accusation pursued loyally, and that by my body on yours I offer and promise myself by the aid of God, according to the law and the custom of arms.[66]

John Kighley was the younger brother of Sir Gilbert Kighley, and the son of Nicholas Kighley. Although an established Lancashire gentry dynasty, the Kighleys had not enjoyed any connections to John of Gaunt.[67] Their exclusion from the Lancastrian affinity may have owed something to John Kighley's dangerous reputation. On 7 December 1397, Henry of Lancaster (Gaunt's son and the future Henry IV) had succeeded in obtaining for Kighley a royal pardon for a catalogue of serious trespasses and felonies. Kighley's principal victim had been John Tounlay of Clivacher, whose property he had broken and ransacked and whose servants he had beaten on four successive occasions in 1393–4.[68] How Kighley had acquired such a powerful patron is unknown, as he does not feature in any of the lists of men in receipt of the livery of Henry of Lancaster in the 1390s.[69] However, by November 1399 he was described as 'king's esquire' and was appointed as bailiff for life of the skivinage of Calais and of the Isle of Colne, most probably a sinecure.[70] Although the reasons for the grant are not elaborated, it may well be the case that Kighley was reaping the benefits of a conspicuous display of Lancastrian loyalty during the 1399 revolution. But, as before, there is no mention of Kighley among the lists of men who were rewarded for serving Henry of Lancaster during this period.[71] Therefore,

[64] BL, MS Additional 9021, fols 240–1.
[65] 'Morley vs. Montagu'.
[66] BL, MS Additional 9021, fol. 241.
[67] Simon Walker, *The Lancastrian* Affinity, *1361–1399* (Oxford, 1990), p. 146.
[68] *CPR 1396–9*, p. 275. Thursday 23 October 1393, Monday 12 January 1394, Thursday and Friday 27–28 March 1394, Wednesday 29 July 1394.
[69] I am grateful to Simon Walker for checking his notes on the palatinate of Lancaster records.
[70] *CPR 1399–1401*, p. 78.
[71] PRO, DL 29/728/11987–90; A. J. Dunn, 'Exploitation and Control: The Royal Administration of Magnate Estates, 1397–1405', *Revolution and Consumption in Late Medieval England*, ed. M. Hicks (Woodbridge, 2002), pp. 41–2.

although the evidence is tenuous, it would seem that the Lancastrian revolution brought John Kighley from the unstable margins of county society, where he had acquired an unsavoury reputation, into the lower rungs of the royal affinity.

Although part of a continuum of political rivalry played out in the court of chivalry, the appeal of John Kighley against Stephen Scrope differs from the cases discussed earlier in this article in many key respects. Whereas the earlier appeals had related to the events of the summer of 1399, Kighley vs. Scrope casts new light on the interplay of high politics and personal rivalries surrounding the failed Ricardian re-adeption of the following January.

For all of his vulnerability, Stephen Scrope was very confident in the defence that he gave on 2 August 1400:

> To the most honourable lords the constable and marshal, Stephen Scrope, lately appealed by John Kighley of very high treasons, on which I place my responses and defence on other matters as well as the said appeal, surmised against me as a slander on account of certain debates between us over certain lands. And on this matter of my defence I have produced certain witnesses and notices by me, Stephen, of what the same John Kighley, appellant, has done to have me murdered in my chamber in the manor of Bingbery in the county of Kent in the month of June in the first year of our most redoubtable lord King Henry IV who now is [1400].

After re-iterating the false nature of Kighley's appeal, Scrope concluded:

> that it seems well that the said John knew well that his appeal had been false, and that he had great power to exploit his appeal by having me murdered before the determination of the said appeal, which things are public, notorious, manifest and infamous in the county of Kent, as well as in London and other parts of England, as well as before the council of our most redoubtable lord the king, of which accusation in the said cause has been fully presented to our most redoubtable lord the king, and certified by his council. The which matters I offer to prove by myself according to the law and customs of arms, and to prove these things I Stephen demand that the said John Kighley should be punished in accordance with what this case requires and demands, according to the law and custom of arms, and for it to be declared that I have fully proven by my defence how the appeal of the said John Kighley is false.[72]

It is clear from Scrope's testimony that Anstis' transcription only offers a partial view of the case, as testimony had also been given outside the cognisance of the court of chivalry. Above all, the loss of the depositions given by Stephen Scrope and his witnesses before the royal council prevents a full understanding of his defence and of the origins of the Bingbery manor dispute. However, the survival of both parties' depositions given at Newcastle, and of the eventual verdict of the court, offers a fascinating insight into how a private dispute became entangled in the politics of the Lancastrian revolution.

The Scropes had had no inherited connections with Kent, and their interests in the county had been due entirely to the patronage of Richard II. On 1 May 1389, William Scrope had been appointed constable of Queenborough Castle – the

---

72 BL, MS Additional 9021, fols 242–3.

state-of-the art fortress on the Isle of Sheppey built during the later years of the reign of Edward III.[73] On 15 June 1397 William Scrope received a supplementary annuity of £20 to be drawn from the issues of Kent 'in consideration of his great charge in keeping Queenborough Castle without any fee'. Richard II was clearly attempting to build up the power of William Scrope in Kent, and this was further perpetuated during the emergency of July 1399, when he was made constable of the castles of Leeds and Rochester.[74]

Kent may have been far removed from their inherited concentrations of estates, but the Scrope family had shown themselves to be avid investors in land throughout the kingdom. Although Man was the Scropes' most spectacular acquisition, in 1393 they had purchased six Hertfordshire manors from the feoffees of Sir William and Sir Robert Lisle, including Pishobury, where Richard, lord Scrope would later date his will.[75] Sir Stephen continued his family's policy of expansion by taking out a lease of the manor of Northwood Sheppey (conveniently near to Queenborough Castle) from Sir Roger Northwood and his feoffees, for 50 marks annually, on 26 January 1398.[76] (Although Bingbery was not mentioned explicitly in the lease, it later became clear that it was a parcel of this transaction.) Stephen was joined as feoffee in the transaction by John Tibbay, a clerk in the Scrope family's service, who would later serve as one of his attorneys on his appointment as justiciar of Ireland in 1401.[77] Tibbay played a central role in the life of the Scrope family, and would later be remembered by Richard, lord Scrope, in his will of 2 August 1400, with a handsome bequest of silver plate and precious furnishings.[78] Richard Scrope's second son, Roger, who survived him by only three months, would also nominate Tibbay as an executor for his own will of 23 September 1403. [79] Significantly, Tibbay had also acted as a feoffee in 1393 in Richard Scrope's purchase of the Lisles' Hertfordshire manors.[80] Therefore, Tibbay's service as Stephen Scrope's feoffee in the Sheppey leases of 1398 suggests that these may have been the preliminaries to an eventual purchase by the Scrope family.

Other than his evident desire to wrest them from Stephen Scrope's control, the precise nature of John Kighley's interest in Northwood Sheppey and Bingbery remains unclear. In 1372 Sir John Northwood had entailed Northwood Sheppey on his son, Sir Roger, and daughter-in-law, Eleanor Savage, with remainder to the male issues of their bodies. There was no mention of Kighley in the 1372 entail; nor did

---

[73] *CPR 1388–92*, p. 13; J. Newman, *Buildings of England and Wales: North and East Kent* (London, 1969), pp. 403–4.

[74] *CPR 1396–9,* pp. 89, 591.

[75] *CCR 1392–6*, pp. 123, 373; *Testamenta Eboracensia I*, p. 273.

[76] *CCR 1396–9*, p. 281. Although Bingbery is not specifically mentioned in the enrolled version of the January 1398 Northwood Sheppey lease, it seems most likely that it did form a parcel of the original feoffment between Sir Roger Northwood and Sir Stephen Scrope.

[77] *CPR 1399–1401*, p. 507 (7 July 1401).

[78] *Testamenta Eboracensia I*, p. 277. 'Item to Lord John de Tibbay I bequeath six silver plates, and six silver salt sellers, one covered cup of silver with my arms and those of Lord Brian de Stapleton, engraved on the handle, one seller of worked silver, and twenty-four silver spoons. Item I bequeath to the same John my ruby coloured bed, with butterflies, embroidered with my arms, with testers, coasters and curtains, all pertaining to the same bed.'

[79] Ibid., pp. 330–1. Tibbay was later murdered by John Nixander, suitor to Margaret Scrope, in the struggle for control of the family's estates that followed Sir Stephen's death: Hughes, 'Stephen Scrope', p. 111.

[80] *CCR 1392–6*, p. 123.

he feature in the 1398 lease to Scrope.[81] But in his enrolled quitclaims to Stephen Scrope for Bingery and Northwood Sheppey, which he conceded on 8 and 18 April 1402 respectively, Kighley was mentioned with two of the deceased original feoffees, Sir Roger Northwood and William Periare.[82] Therefore, the absence of an explicit reference to Kighley in the 1398 lease, and his lack of a defence to Stephen Scrope's counter-allegations of malicious appeal, suggests that he had no valid title or reversionary interest.

What remains unclear is why Kighley had apparently resorted to the extreme measure of attempted murder to take possession of these properties. Tenurial disputes were endemic to landed society, but were usually resolved through litigation or frequently (and with less cost and more fruitful results) through private arbitration. Often in these instances a great magnate, or the king himself, would play the role of honest broker. But who could have filled this role in Kent during the final months of Richard II's reign? Both Thomas Arundel, archbishop of Canterbury, and the principal lay magnate, John, lord Cobham, had been exiled by Richard II (the latter in January 1398). Richard II's recently appointed archbishop, Roger Walden, would scarcely have inspired confidence, while Cobham's interests were represented by a newcomer to the county, Sir Reginald Braybrook, the husband of Cobham's granddaughter.[83]

In 1978, J. B. Post highlighted the ways in which the forfeiture of the earl of Warwick and the intrusion into his lordship of Thomas Holand, duke of Surrey, diminished the potential for disinterested arbitration in the long-running dispute over Ladbroke Manor. In spite of repeated judgements in favour of the defendant and holder of the manor, John Catesby, the duke of Surrey took seisin of Ladbroke Manor himself, at the supplication of the complainants, the Cardian family, in January 1399.[84] The extreme dislocation of political society during these months, combined with the deaths or exiles of leading figures in the political community, were hardly conducive to an equitable outcome to arbitration. Perhaps, as Scrope argued, Kighley saw this as a window of opportunity to kill his rival, while the attentions of the new king, his council and justices were directed towards the suppression of political insurrection.

Given the weakness of Kighley's appeal, and the transparency of his ambitions to destroy Scrope, it is not surprising that Northumberland and Westmorland took cognisance of the charges themselves, and found for Scrope, without a single blow having been exchanged.[85] However, when the political position of the Scrope family is considered, as well as the reality of ongoing conspiracies against Henry IV, the outcome seems to have been far less certain. On the very day that Scrope was giving his testimony in the Moot Hall in Newcastle on 2 August, his father was writing his

[81] S. Payling, 'Late Medieval Marriage Contracts', *The McFarlane Legacy: Studies in Late Medieval Politics and Society*, ed. R. H. Britnell and A. J. Pollard (Stroud, 1995), p. 40.

[82] *CCR 1396–9*, p. 281; *CCR 1399–1402*, pp. 519, 555.

[83] R. G. Davies, 'Richard II and the Church in the Years of Tyranny', *Journal of Medieval History* i (1975), pp. 342–3; Saul, *Richard II*, p. 381.

[84] J. B. Post, 'Courts, Councils and Arbitrators in the Ladbroke Manor Dispute, 1380–1400', *Medieval Legal Records Edited in Memory of C. A. F. Meekings*, ed. R. F. Hunnisett and J. B. Post (London, 1978), pp. 293–4.

[85] BL, MS Additional 9021, fol. 244.

will in his chamber at Pishobury in Hertfordshire.[86] Although this dating may have been purely coincidental, it is of course possible that Richard Scrope feared a new onslaught against his family, particularly if Kighley's appeal had been proven.

The fact that the court had found for Scrope should have had the gravest of consequences for the appellant. Bringing a malicious appeal of treason commanded the penalty of death. In his verdict of 4 August 1400 Northumberland stated:

> We judge and determine that the said John Kighley should have the same pain that the said Sir Stephen would have sustained had he been convicted of the said appeal and accusation, and also that the said John Kighley, in the party of appellant or accuser, be adjudged and determined to have lost and forfeited the surety of the fees that he had been obliged to our lord the king.[87]

However, nothing was heard of the failed (and now condemned) appellant until 6 February 1401, when he was fully pardoned the execution of the sentence, and restored to his liberty and all his forfeited lands, goods and chattels.[88] Beyond this statement of royal grace, no further explanation was given for Kighley's pardon.

The reasons for Kighley's escape are likely to have lain in the broader political considerations confronting Henry IV. In the face of the threat of further insurrections and conspiracies, Henry could not afford to be too selective in his choice of allies.[89] Notwithstanding Kighley's liabilities as a former criminal and a condemned appellant, he was unswervingly Lancastrian in his political sympathies. Thus, Kighley embodied one of the broader problems facing Henry IV – what Helen Castor has identified as the conflict between his 'public' and 'private' responsibilities, as king and duke.[90] In Kighley's case Henry's instincts as 'good lord' prevailed over his broader obligations as the impartial upholder of justice.

By 1412 Kighley had extended his interests southwards from his Lancashire heartland to Anglesey, where he was farming the lands late of a certain Richard Golding. Griffiths notes that Kighley was one of many in that region who quarrelled with the corrupt royal chamberlain, Thomas Barneby, although the origins of this feud remain obscure.[91] But Kighley eventually showed his utility to the House of Lancaster during Henry V's wars: he was one of ten Lancashire gentlemen who brought companies of archers to France in 1415, and his kinsman Sir Richard was slain at Agincourt.[92] John Kighley himself played a leading role in the capture of Lisieux in September 1417, and later served as bailli of Rouen and captain of Louviers in the 1420s.[93]

The implications of the appeal were no less dramatic for Stephen Scrope. Although Stephen was officially cleared of any treasonable designs, and was shown

---

[86] *Testamenta Eboracensia I*, p. 273.
[87] BL, MS Additional 9021, fols 244–5; *CPR 1399–1401*, p. 401 (enrolment of verdict, 16 December 1400).
[88] BL, MS Additional 9021, f. 250; *CPR 1399–1401*, p. 431.
[89] *Annales Ricardi Secundi*, pp. 337–8.
[90] Helen Castor, *The King, the Crown and the Duchy of Lancaster: Public Authority and Private Power, 1399–1461* (Oxford, 2000), pp. 16–21.
[91] R. A. Griffiths, *Conquerors and Conquered in Medieval Wales* (Stroud, 1994), pp. 131, 132, 137n.
[92] J. H. Wylie and W. T. Waugh, *The Reign of Henry V, II, 1415–1416* (Cambridge, 1919), p. 188n.
[93] Ibid., *III, 1415–1422* (Cambridge, 1929), p. 55; M. J. Bennett, *Community, Class and Careerism: Cheshire and Lancashire Society in the Age of Sir Gawain and the Green Knight* (Cambridge, 1983), p. 172.

to have been a victim of a conspiracy against his life and property, his position within the new political order remained unclear. Some former Ricardians such as Sir Richard Abberbury and Sir Simon Felbrigg remained outside Lancastrian government (through a mixture of exclusion and choice), while others, such as Sir William Bagot embraced new opportunities to recover their lost status and position through royal service.

The scale and speed of Sir Stephen Scrope's political rehabilitation suggests a degree of personal affection and trust on the part of Henry IV. Scrope's first employment was in the north, where he served as joint keeper of Roxburgh Castle with Sir Richard Grey, from some point in 1400 until the end of 1401, although there is no evidence to suggest that he resided on the northern Marches in person.[94] But this position merely prefigured a much more significant role on the peripheries of Lancastrian rule. On 18 May 1401, Henry IV's second son, Thomas of Lancaster, then aged about twelve, was appointed lieutenant of Ireland, and Stephen Scrope was made his deputy.[95]

A Lancastrian precursor to Robert Devereux, earl of Essex, and to Thomas Wentworth, earl of Strafford, Stephen Scrope was sent to Ireland by his king to test his loyalty against the malicious whisperings of his enemies back home.[96] But Stephen was also the obvious choice for this position, given the experience that he had gained in 1394–7, and it is to Henry IV's credit that he chose Scrope over others with a record of Lancastrian service. Another erstwhile Ricardian and close friend of Stephen who also found political redemption through service in Ireland was Janico Dartasso, and the two men campaigned together throughout the period from 1401 to 1407.[97]

On 23 August 1401, Stephen Scrope returned to Dublin after an absence of more than four years. The lieutenant's youth rendered Stephen the *de facto* governor of the lordship from the moment of his return.[98] Throughout the autumn of 1401 he secured the allegiance of several leading chiefs, including O'Connor Faly, O'Byrne (with whom he had travelled to London in 1396) and MacMahon. In the following February, O'Reilly also came to Scrope to recognise the overlordship of Henry IV. As was so often the case, however, the submissions of chiefs did little to prevent bitter conflicts and feuding between the princes of the north and west of Ireland. Thomas of Lancaster and Stephen Scrope were also seriously hindered by acute shortages of funds for the payment of their soldiers and the purchase of victuals.[99] The costs of resisting the ongoing insurrections in England throughout 1401–3 ensured that Ireland was near the bottom of Henry IV's financial priorities. In November 1403 Prince Thomas's departure left Scrope in sole command, until the

---

[94] *Proceedings and Ordinances of the Privy Council of England*, ed. N. H. Nicolas (7 vols, London, 1834–7), I, p. 125. Wages of Stephen Scrope as keeper of Roxburgh Castle, PRO, E 403/571, m. 8 (17 November 1401), 573, m. 1 (8 April 1402).

[95] Stephen Scrope appears to have held the office of deputy justiciar from at least 12 March 1401, when he confirmed letters issued by the late earl of March. *CPR 1401–5*, p. 86.

[96] For comparisons, see R. F. Foster, *Modern Ireland, 1600–1972* (London, 1989).

[97] Walker, 'Janico Dartasso', p. 43.

[98] *CPR 1399–1401*, p. 507; *CCR 1399–1402*, p. 338, 342; A. J. Otway-Ruthven, *History of Medieval Ireland* (London, 1968), p. 341.

[99] Ibid., p. 342.

latter too returned to England in the following February.[100] In Scrope's absence, the earl of Ormond was appointed by a great council as emergency governor, and the following months were characterised by sustained violence and destruction in Ulster.[101]

Scrope returned to Ireland in October 1404, and remained there a further eight months, until June 1405. He did not return again until the autumn of 1406. Throughout this period the weakness and poverty of the English administration could do little to resist sustained and high levels of local conflict. However, Scrope did achieve a local victory near Callan in 1407, when he led a force that slew Tadhg O'Cearbhill of Ely, whose men had been harrying Kilkenny.[102] Scrope returned to England shortly after 8 December 1407, when he appointed the earl of Desmond as his deputy. Stephen Scrope made one last journey to Ireland, where he died from the plague at Castledermot on 4 September 1408, possibly with Milicent at his side.[103]

On 13 January 1409, in Ireland, Milicent Scrope married Sir John Fastolf, who would become one of the greatest men of Lancastrian England. The enduring connection between the Scropes and other former Ricardians is clear from the presence of Janico Dartasso as a witness to the financial settlement whereby Fastolf promised Milicent £100 *per annum* for the expenses of her chamber.[104] But Fastolf appeared to have had little affection for his Scrope stepchildren, and, as Clarke and Galbraith noted, he sold the wardship and marriage of the younger Stephen to Sir William Gascoigne. Jonathan Hughes has detailed the decades of humiliation endured by the younger Stephen at the hands of Fastolf, which eventually resulted in the loss of many of his estates through sales and enfeoffments. He later claimed that Fastolf 'bought me and solde me as a beste, ayens al right and lawe'. Forced by poverty and chronic illness to abjure his father's life of action and military service, the younger Stephen Scrope gave himself to study, and his works included a translation of Christine de Pisan's *Epistle of Othea*.[105] It was only after the death of his stepfather in 1459 that Stephen was able to enter into his inheritance, and soon after this the legacy of Fastolf's mismanagement compelled him to sell the remainder of his inheritance apart from Castle Combe, which remained in the hands of his descendants (and who, outliving the more famous Bolton and Masham branches of the Scrope clan, survived until 1852).[106]

The most convincing explanation for the survival of the Scropes of Castle Combe surely lies in Sir Stephen's willingness to adapt to the dramatically altered political climate that followed the 1399 revolution. With estates in Yorkshire, Wiltshire and

---

[100] *A New History of Ireland II*, ed. Art Cosgrove (Oxford, 1987), p. 538. For Scrope acting in the absence of Thomas of Lancaster in 1404, see *CPR 1401–5*, pp. 377, 419.

[101] Roll of the Proceedings of the King's Council in Ireland for a Portion of the 16th year of the Reign of Richard II, 1392–1393, ed. J. Graves (Rolls Series, London, 1877), pp. 269–72.

[102] *New History of Ireland II*, p. 581.

[103] Otway-Ruthven, *History of Medieval Ireland*, p. 346. When Milicent married Sir John Fastolf the following year, the ceremony was held in Ireland. Perhaps Milicent had remained there in the months following her husband's death. William Worcestre, *Itineraries*, ed. J. H. Harvey (Oxford, 1969), p. 349.

[104] Ibid.

[105] M. V. Clarke and V. H. Galbraith, 'The Deposition of Richard II', *Bulletin of the John Rylands Library* xiv (1930), pp. 152–3; *The Epistle of Othea*, ed. C. F. Buhler (Early English Text Society original ser. cclxiv, Oxford, 1970). Christine de Pisan's son had been educated in the household of the earl of Salisbury (d.1400), a friend of the elder Stephen Scrope, with whom he may have shared books. Hughes, 'Stephen Scrope', pp. 123–4.

[106] *DNB*, XVII, pp. 1081–2; Hughes, 'Stephen Scrope', pp. 119–20.

Kent, Sir Stephen Scrope could well have retired to a comfortable private life – albeit not on the lavish scale enjoyed by his father and elder brothers.[107] But the reasons for Sir Stephen's return to public life may well have been driven by a more hard-headed political calculation: the need to demonstrate not merely an accommodation with Lancastrian rule, but also an active and palpable loyalty.[108] By returning to Ireland, Scrope was accepting a dispiriting and under-resourced posting and one that repeatedly exposed him to danger and sickness. Perhaps Scrope, like Dartasso, had no real choice but to accept a role that few would have wanted, but which would test his loyalty in the most extreme conditions.[109]

Although long overshadowed by that of his eldest brother, the career of Stephen Scrope offers further evidence about personal responses to the challenge of a new political order. Whereas Rutland, Bagot and Thomas Percy had turned their coats shamelessly, men such as Dartasso and Stephen Scrope faced agonising personal choices, as the margins of loyalty were repeatedly redrawn. What also of Rawlyn Govely, the squire of John Holand, who refused to remove his master's livery even *after* the failure of the Epiphany Rising?[110] Kighley's appeal of treason was one more challenge to Scrope in his efforts to weather the storm of 1399. Indeed, Kighley's calculation that few would mourn the brother of the hated William Scrope may not have been wide of the mark. But, like many others in the political community, Stephen Scrope embraced the Lancastrian ethos of redemption through service, while remaining, in the words of Henry IV's description of his father, 'a true knight'.[111]

---

107 *CIPM 1370–3*, no. 212.

108 In the autumn of 1403 Sir William Bagot allowed his castle of Baginton (Warwickshire) to be used for the imprisonment of the earl of Northumberland. (*Proceedings and Ordinances of the Privy Council*, I, p. 217.)

109 Walker, 'Janico Dartasso', p. 43.

110 *CIM 1399–1422*, pp. 54, 55 (nos. 88, 89).

111 *RP*, III, p. 453.

THE FURNISHING OF ROYAL CLOSETS AND THE USE OF SMALL DEVOTIONAL IMAGES IN THE REIGN OF RICHARD II: THE SETTING OF THE WILTON DIPTYCH RECONSIDERED

Lisa Monnas

Today, the Wilton Diptych (Plates 1, 2) is a lone survivor in England of a class of portable devotional paintings that once formed a normal part of royal worship. During the late fourteenth century, Richard II, like other contemporary rulers, led a peripatetic existence, travelling between his various residences as well as making specific journeys for military campaigns or for pilgrimages.[1] As he progressed, his furnishings would have preceded him, including chapel ornaments, comprising vestments, plate, books and, in all likelihood, some portable devotional images. Theories surrounding the intended purpose and location of the Wilton Diptych[2] have in the past included the suggestions that it could have been the focus of a secret brotherhood[3] or even a posthumous image created in the reign of Henry IV.[4] Currently, the most widely accepted view seems to be that this painting was created for Richard II's personal devotions, for use in his private oratories.[5] This article will explore the importance of the private oratory or 'closet' as a setting for small devotional images, and will reconsider the chapel of St Mary of the Pew at Westminster Abbey as one of several possible settings for the Wilton Diptych.

From an entry in Henry III's accounts published by Colvin, it is evident that the Wilton Diptych was not the first small painted diptych to be owned by an English monarch. In 1235, a painting was purchased for Henry III's chapel at Guildford at a cost of just under 10s, described as 'una parva tabula . . . et alia parva tabula eidem respondenti . . . Et eisdem tabulis coniungendis ita quod claudi et aperiri possint' ('a small panel, and another small panel corresponding to it, and those panels joined in such a way that they can be closed and opened'). The panels were painted with the Crucifixion with Mary and John on one side and, on the opposite panel, Our Lord in

---

[1] N. Saul, *Richard II* (London, 1997), p. 336. I should like to thank John Goodall, Dillian Gordon, Fiona Kisby, Shelagh Mitchell, Richard Mortimer and Tony Trowles for their kind help in the preparation of this article.

[2] Many of the theories surrounding the Diptych are discussed by D. Gordon, *Making and Meaning: The Wilton Diptych* (London, 1993) and are summarised by D. Gordon, 'The Wilton Diptych: An Introduction', *The Regal Image of Richard II and the Wilton Diptych*, ed. D. Gordon, L. Monnas and C. Elam (London, 1997), pp. 19–26.

[3] J. Harvey, 'The Wilton Diptych – a Re-examination', *Archaeologia* xcviii (1961), pp. 1–28 (esp. pp. 16ff). See also C. M. Barron, 'Introduction', *Regal Image*, ed. Gordon, Monnas and Elam, p. 13.

[4] This idea is discussed by Gordon in *Making and Meaning*, p. 59; see also F. Wormald, 'The Wilton Diptych', *Journal of the Warburg and Courtauld Institutes* xvii (1954), pp. 191–207.

[5] Gordon, *Making and Meaning*, p. 21; U. Ilg, *Das Wiltondiptychon Stil und Ikonographie* (Berlin, 1996), pp. 139–42; N. Morgan, 'The Signification of the Banner in the Wilton Diptych', *Regal Image*, ed. Gordon, Monnas and Elam, pp. 179–88 (esp. p. 181).

Plate 1. The Wilton Diptych, interior; tempera on oak panel. London, National Gallery

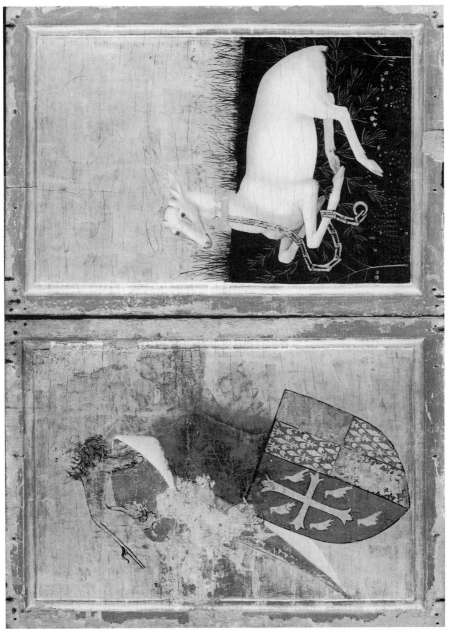

Plate 2. The Wilton Diptych, exterior, tempera on oak panel. London, National Gallery

Majesty and the four Evangelists.[6] During his long reign, Henry III commissioned several panel paintings, including, in 1258, another diptych, of unspecified size, for the Lady Chapel in Westminster Abbey.[7]

In the next century, Queen Isabella, wife of Edward II, numbered among her chapel goods four *tabulae depictae*, recorded in a list taken at her death in 1358 published by Palgrave.[8] Two of these paintings, composed of seven and six panels respectively, were estimated at £3 each. The third of four panels was estimated at £2; and the last, a triptych, showing the Virgin Mary, was valued at £1 6s 8d. Their size is not indicated, but it may be possible to get some idea by comparing their estimated worth with the cost of the large carved and painted reredos ordered in 1360s by Edward III for St George's Chapel, Windsor. The carving alone totalled £50, and the cost of painting exceeded even this sum.[9] The comparison suggests that Queen Isabella's paintings, especially the triptych showing the Virgin, were considerably smaller, perhaps portable images.[10]

In 1332, Edward III's great wardrobe contained nine panel paintings.[11] Stored in leather cases, among assorted chapel furnishings, they seem to have been destined to be moved around. Not all were of English origin. One, a triptych with folding wings ('j tabula depicta cu[m] ij foliis plicat[is]'), was specified as a gift of the king of France. Although this example was most probably French, it may have been similar in form to the triptychs from the workshops of Duccio or Bernardo Daddi produced in Italy during the first half of the fourteenth century (Plate 3: maximum height 87.5cm, open width c.78.7cm).[12] Italian paintings were certainly coming into England by Edward III's reign: by 1357, that king's chapel goods included three Italian panel paintings, described as 'tabul[a]e de opere lombardorum'.[13] In his will of 1361, Hugh of St Albans, the painter of St Stephen's Chapel, bequeathed to his wife a six-piece 'Lombard' panel painting, which had cost him the enormous sum of £20 when still unfinished and unframed.[14]

Members of the chapel royal and a selection of liturgical furnishings – including devotional objects – routinely moved with the king. One well-known example is the Neath Cross – a jewelled cross containing a prized splinter of the True Cross –

---

[6]   R. A. Brown, H. M. Colvin and A. J. Taylor, *The History of the King's Works: The Middle Ages* (2 vols, London, 1963), I, p. 952.

[7]   P. Binski, *Westminster Abbey and the Plantagenets: Kingship and the Representation of Power, 1200–1400* (London, 1995), p. 153.

[8]   *The Antient Kalendars and Inventories of His Majesty's Exchequer*, ed. F. Palgrave (3 vols, London, 1836), III, pp. 235–44: indenture between John de Newbury, treasurer of Queen Isabella (deceased) and the treasurer and chamberlains of the exchequer. See p. 238, items 66–9.

[9]   The documents have partly been published in *Issues of the Exchequer, Henry III to Henry VI*, ed. F. Devon (London, 1837), pp. 160, 185, 187, 188; further evidence concerning the reredos is discussed by C. Wilson, 'The Royal Lodgings of Edward III at Windsor Castle: Form, Function, Representation', *Windsor: Medieval Archaeology, Art and Architecture of the Thames Valley*, ed. L. Keen and E. Scarff (British Archaeological Association Conference Transactions xxv, Leeds, 2002), p. 38.

[10] For an example of a small folding altarpiece in four panels of c.1400, see H. Nieuwdorp, 'The Antwerp Baltimore Polyptych: A Portable Altarpiece Belonging to Philip the Bold, Duke of Burgundy', *The Art of Devotion in the Late Middle Ages in Europe*, ed. H. van Os (London, 1994), pp. 137–50.

[11] PRO, E 101/386/3, fol. 3r.

[12] For an alternative form of triptych, see D. Hemsoll, 'Simone Martini's St John the Evangelist Re-examined: A Panel from an Early Portable Triptych', *Apollo* cxlvii (1998), pp. 3–10 (esp. figs. 7, 8).

[13] PRO, E 101/393/4.

[14] P. Binski, *Medieval Craftsmen: Painters* (London, 1991), pp. 12–13; Binski, *Westminster Abbey*, p. 182.

Plate 3. Bernardo Daddi (active 1312; d.1348), triptych, interior: the Virgin and Child enthroned with saints and angels (centre); the Nativity, the Crucifixion (wings); the Redeemer (above, centre), the Annunciation (above, wings); dated on plinth, 1338; tempera on panel. London, Courtauld Gallery, Princes Gate Collection (P. 1978.PG.81)

which moved with Edward III to wherever he happened to celebrate Easter.[15] Sixteenth-century sources describing the ordering of the king's chapel stress the frequency of worship and the way in which the place of worship was arranged according to the king's pleasure: when he had made it known where and when he would attend mass.[16] These later manuscripts describe elaborate preparations for royal worship which show that the various royal chapels were naturally not kept in a permanent state of readiness, but were vested as need arose. A recent study of the early Tudor chapel royal has emphasised the way in which royal public worship punctuated the calendar in a spectacular fashion for a limited number of days each year, while private worship within the royal closets continued on a daily basis.[17] Because the early Tudor court derived much of its religious ceremonial from an unbroken tradition of medieval worship, many observations concerning the organisation of royal worship in the early sixteenth century are applicable to the way in which Richard II made his devotions.

The descriptions in contemporary chronicles of Richard II worshipping usually describe only significant public occasions. Shelagh Mitchell has shown that these selective descriptions can be augmented by a study of the accounts of the wardrobe of the household, which contain comprehensive lists of the feasts attended by the king in person.[18] Feasts regularly attended by Richard II included those of St George (23 April), the nativity and decollation of St John the Baptist (24 June, 29 August), St Edmund (death 20 November, translation 29 April) and St Edward the Confessor (death 5 January, translation 13 October), as well as the four days on which the king offered gold: the feast of St John the Evangelist (27 December), Epiphany (6 January), the Purification of the Virgin (2 February) and Good Friday. Other important dates in Richard II's religious calendar were the anniversary masses for his deceased relatives: for his parents and grandparents, for his brother Edward, for his wife, Anne of Bohemia, and for the empress, his wife's mother.[19] These anniversaries were celebrated with considerable splendour: both the vigil and the day were attended by paupers liveried in black holding blazing torches, in a church draped in

---

[15] The Neath Cross or 'Croes Neith' had been among the most treasured regalia of the Welsh princes, until it was presented to Edward I at Conway, 1 June 1283; the cross accompanied Edward I on his travels, and was eventually given by Edward III to St George's Chapel, Windsor, by 1352, following the foundation of the Order of the Garter (1348). A. Taylor, 'Royal Arms and Oblations in the Later Thirteenth Century: An Analysis of the Alms Rolls of 12 Edward I (1283–4)', *Tribute to an Antiquary: Essays Presented to Marc Fitch*, ed. F. G. Emmison and R. Stephens (London, 1976), pp. 119–20. For Edward III and the Neath Cross, see W. M. Ormrod, 'The Personal Religion of Edward III', *Speculum* lxiv (1989), p. 856, citing PRO E 36/204, fols 72r, 72v. See also, M. Bond, *The Inventories of St George's Chapel, Windsor Castle, 1384–1667* (Windsor, 1947), p. 50, item no. 116 and n. 2, and text accompanying Plate III. Richard II is recorded adoring the Neath Cross in St George's Chapel on the Feast of St Hadrian, 8 September 1395: PRO, E 101/403/10, fol. 37r.

[16] BL, MS Sloane 1494; MS Additional 71009 (see below, n. 17).

[17] F. Kisby, 'The Early-Tudor Royal Household Chapel in London, 1485–1547' (unpublished PhD thesis, Royal Holloway, University of London, 1996); F. Kisby, 'Ceremonies and Services at the Tudor Court: Extracts from British Library, Additional Manuscript 71009', in *Religion, Politics and Society in Tudor England*, ed. S. Adams *et al.* (forthcoming); F. Kisby, ' "When the King goeth a Procession": Chapel Ceremonies and Services, the Ritual Year, and Religious Reforms at the Early Tudor Court, 1485–1547', *Journal of British Studies* xl (2001), pp. 44–75.

[18] S. Mitchell, 'Richard II: Kingship and the Cult of Saints', *Regal Image*, ed. Gordon, Monnas and Elam, pp. 115–24.

[19] PRO, E 101/401/2, fols 37r–38v; E 101/402/5, fols 26r–27r; E 101/402/10, fol. 33v; E 101/403/10, fols 36r–37v.

suitable hangings.[20] Each year at Christchurch, Canterbury, for example, the Black Prince's anniversary was dignified by a set of impressive liturgical furnishings bequeathed by the prince, made from a set of his own secular furnishings of black tapestry woven with a design of his personal badge of ostrich feathers, and red borders displaying swans with women's faces.[21] When Richard II could not attend the services at Canterbury and Westminster in person, he sent the traditional offering of cloth of gold with a proxy and attended a service of requiem wherever he happened to be.[22]

Richard II's palaces, like those of his royal predecessors and those of contemporary rulers in France, were equipped with both domestic chapels and private oratories ('closets') for the king and queen.[23] Small closets, accommodating the king and his chaplain, led off the royal bedchambers, and larger closets, capable of holding the king, his chaplain and select guests, looked onto the domestic chapels. Some of these chapels, like St Stephen's in Westminster Palace, had an oratory set high into a wall so that the king could view the mass from an elevated position.[24] These closets overlooking the chapel were equipped with glass windows, normally displaying the royal arms or badges. There is a reference to the repair of the glass windows in the king's closets at Kings Langley[25] and at Sheen[26] in the 1380s. At Eltham, expenses were recorded in the 1380s for glass with heraldic decoration to be inserted for a new 'oriel' for the queen in the king's private chapel.[27]

In the late fifteenth century, during the reign of Edward IV, when the Black Book of the Household was compiled, the royal chapel staff were assigned to various apparently well-defined offices: the dean of the chapel royal organised the liturgical content of the services, the sergeant of the vestry oversaw the physical appointment

---

[20] For the accounts of the anniversaries of Isabella, wife of Edward II, and Philippa of Hainault (PRO, E 101/397/1; E 101/397/7), see J. Catto, 'Religion and the English Nobility in the Later Fourteenth Century', *History and Imagination: Essays in Honour of Hugh Trevor-Roper*, ed. H. Lloyd Jones, V. Pear and B. Worden (London, 1981), p. 47.

[21] The furnishings, described in the will as *notre sale des plumes d'ostruce*, consisted of a *dorser* (a large cloth of estate), eight *costers* (wall hangings) and four *bankers* (large draped seat covers). The will stipulates that the dorser was to be cut to serve 'before and around' the high altar; the fabric remaining from the dorser and the bankers were to be adapted to serve at the altar of St Thomas' shrine, the altar of his skull, the altar of the point of the sword which killed St Thomas, and around the body of the Black Prince in the chapel of Our Lady of the Undercroft. The costers were to form hangings for the choir above the stalls. These were to be used on the feast of the Trinity, and on all the principal feasts of the year, including the feasts of St Thomas Becket and the feasts of Our Lady, and at the anniversary of the Black Prince. *Royal Wills*, pp. 69–70. These furnishings might have been deployed when Richard visited Canterbury on 16 February 1385, when he made offerings to the shrine of St Thomas, to the altars of the saint's head and of the point of the sword and to the image of Our Lady of the Undercroft, making further offerings at the altar before St Thomas's shrine during a mass for the saint and when he attended a requiem mass sung for the Black Prince. (On leaving Canterbury, on 20 February, he made three further offerings in Christchurch.) PRO, E 101/401/2, fol. 37.

[22] PRO, E 101/406/6, mm. 20, 24.

[23] Closets owned by Richard II's predecessors are discussed by Brown, Colvin and Taylor, *King's Works*: for example, Henry III's closet in his palace at Woodstock (*King's Works*, II, p. 960); construction of a closet for Edward III adjoining his chapel in the manor of Henley: this closet looked onto the chapel from a first floor level, it contained an altar and had glass windows with heraldic decoration (ibid., II, p. 1013).

[24] Ibid., I, p. 517.

[25] Ibid., II, p. 975.

[26] PRO, E 101/473/2, m. 7.This records 2s paid to a 'master of glass' for repairing the windows of the king's chapel and closet at Sheen.

[27] Brown, Colvin and Taylor, *King's Works*, II, p. 934.

of the chapel and the clerk of the closet was charged with the appointment of the king's closet; the queen was served by her own chapel staff, including her own clerk of the closet.[28] During the reign of Richard II, individual entries in the enrolled great wardrobe accounts attribute the charge of all of the physical aspects of worship to one person, the dean of the chapel royal.[29] There were successive issues to the dean of vestments and of a steady stream of rich silk fabrics used to create or mend existing vestments. There were also issues of cotton wool, coffers, cloth sacks and leather cases for packing assorted chapel goods, such as the silver gilt image of the Blessed Virgin packed in a leather case of *cuir bouilli* in 1388.[30] Yet there was undoubtedly a more complex infrastructure than these summary accounts betray: an individual warrant records a payment in arrears in February 1394, to John Pevense, one of the clerks of the king's chapel, for his services to Anne of Bohemia as 'clerk of her closet'.[31] This seems to be the earliest known reference to a clerk of the closet in the English royal household.

Sixteenth-century texts describe how the royal closet should be furnished with a screening curtain or 'traverse', with a carpet and cushion for the king to kneel upon and with a cloth to cover his lectern.[32] A text from the late 1440s which enumerates things 'needful' for Henry VI's closet included references to upper and lower altar frontals of cloth of gold, a corporal case, a chasuble of blue satin powdered with gold ostrich feathers, with all its apparel, linen towels for the altar and for washing, a traverse of 'good' satin, three cushions, a kneeling *tapet* and two further *tapets*, presumably for hanging, matching the traverse in colour.[33] Fourteenth-century closets seem to have been equally luxuriously appointed. The inventory of Charles V of France (d.1380), published by Labarte, records sets of curtains for *oratoires* stored together with altar curtains. One set of altar curtains, of red silk samite with gold stripes, had matching oratory curtains (item 1147 in Labarte's edition).[34] Two carpets woven with heraldic decoration, perhaps destined for Charles V's closet, were found stored in his oratory in his chateau in the Bois de Vincennes. One (item 2602) had golden lions holding scrolls inscribed with *Karolus Dei gracia Francorum rex* and KL crowned. Further precious objects were recorded in the same oratory, before the chapel next to his chamber (items 2574–2634). These included a magnificent book of hours and psalter (item 2599), altar furnishings for the oratory, a curtained enclosure (*pavillion*), and two cushions (item 2604).

---

[28] A. R. Myers, *The Household of Edward IV: The Black Book and the Ordinance of 1478* (Manchester, 1959), pp. 133–5, 137–9. For Richard II's chapel staff, see C. Given-Wilson, *The Royal Household and the King's Affinity: Service, Politics and Finance in England, 1360–1413* (London, 1986), pp. 67–9.

[29] Two deans of the chapel royal served under Richard II: Thomas of Lynton (1377–89) and John Boor (1389–99). Ilg, *Das Wiltondiptychon*, p. 151.

[30] PRO, E 361/5, mm. 2r, 3r, 4v, etc. For the image of the Virgin, see PRO, E 101/401/16, m. 25.

[31] PRO, SC 1/ 51/ 21, dated 5 February 1394; the letter has been published, translated from the French in A. Crawford, *Letters of the Queens of England 1100–1547* (Stroud, 1994), p. 105. For the career of John Pevense, see also *CPR 1381–5*, pp. 242, 462; *CPR 1385–9*, pp. 365, 382, 519. For livery issued to John Pevense, see PRO, E 101/401/16, mm. 21, 22. For the office of clerk of the closet, see J. Bickersteth and R. W. Dunning, *Clerks of the Closet in the Royal Household* (Wolfeboro Falls, 1991).

[32] See texts cited above, n. 16. See also *The Inventory of King Henry VIII*, ed. D. Starkey (London, 1998), items 12464–8 (closet stuff for the king, in the jewel house at Hampton Court), 12469–72 (closet stuff for the Queen, same location).

[33] PRO, E 101/409/19, m. 38.

[34] *Inventaire du mobilier de Charles V, roi de France*, ed. J. Labarte (Paris, 1879).

Richard II's great wardrobe accounts present a similarly lavish picture of his closet furnishings. Among the items ordered for his closet were a worsted carpet and missals and primers covered in velvet and cloth of gold.[35] A set of vestments left to Richard by the Black Prince was perhaps intended to serve in a closet adjoining a bedchamber, as this set was described together with a matching bed 'que nous avons de mesme la sute [sic]'.[36] Some of the chapel and closet furnishings were also ordered in matching sets. In 1385–6, two matching sets of vestments were made out of blue and white *baldekin* silk 'paned' with blue *camacas* silk, embellished with chains made of applied red satin embroidered in coloured silk, and with applied letters embroidered in cyprus gold.[37] These included furnishings for two altars, and the document explicitly states that they were to serve the altar in the chapel and the altar in the king's closet within the household.[38] Books intended for the chapel and closet respectively were also bound to match the altar furnishings in covers of blue and white satin.[39] Other liturgical textiles were variously ordered for the chapel in the king's household, for the two chapels in the palace of Westminster, for the *privat' capell' camere regis* and for the *closett' private capelle camere*.[40] The taste for heraldic decoration and the use of personal badges was all pervading. Both the royal chapel plate and the liturgical vestments were frequently decorated with the royal arms and or badges.[41] After Richard's deposition, among various items found at Haverford Castle there was a spectacular set of high mass vestments made of white cloth of gold woven with Richard II's distinctive badge of harts.[42]

The king would have worshipped privately more than once every day – usually in the closet adjoining his chamber – only venturing into the body of a chapel or church for important liturgical feasts.[43] Even this 'public' worship involved the use of a closet, as the king would have spent a part of the lengthy service within his closet overlooking the chapel, emerging only for the key moments of the ceremony in which he processed or took communion or made his offering, or healed the sick and gave alms. When the king attended mass in a church or cathedral in which he

---

35 PRO, E 101/400/4, mm. 9–10, describes a variety of liturgical texts being covered with precious remnants of silk *baudekyn* from the *officium cissoris magne garderobe'*. PRO, E 101/401/6, m. 18, for the carpet, issued to Thomas of Lynton 'ad ponend' sub ped' regis in closett' priuate capelle camere' by letter under privy seal dated 26 March 1384.

36 *Royal Wills*, p. 74: the vestment is described as 'blu avec roses d'or à plumes dostruce'.

37 A low mass set of vestments of similar design was found at Haverford after Richard's deposition: *Antient Kalendars*, p. 359.

38 PRO, E 101/401/16, m. 13.

39 PRO, E 101/401/15; E 101/401/16 m. 4. The books were stored in protective linen bags: see also PRO, E 101/400/4. The colour and design of these liturgical ornaments may have conformed to a royal livery: in 1384/5, the king had ordered three long gowns with the left sleeve in blue, with chains and letters embroidered in gold, for the feast of Pentecost, and another similar gown and hood for the feast of the Purification: see PRO, E 101/401/6. In the same livery roll, John de Strawesburgh, the king's embroiderer, was paid for embroidering eight chains with the letters A R P H on chains, embroidered in silk, gold and silver of cyprus to place on the left sleeve of eight gowns, four of blue cloth and four of unspecified colour. The chains were to be sewn to the left sleeve, of white cloth. In the same account, another garment in black, embroidered with chains and letters, was made for the feast of St John the Baptist. See Mitchell, 'Richard II: Kingship', p. 120.

40 Other vestments and furnishings for the chapel and closet: PRO, E 101/400/4.

41 For plate decorated with the white hart belonging to Richard II, see Gordon, *Making and Meaning*, p. 50, esp. n. 31.

42 PRO, E 101/335/3, printed in *Antient Kalendars*, p. 360.

43 See Given-Wilson, *Royal Household*, p. 67.

Plate 4. The Duke of Burgundy attending Christmas mass, from the Très Riches
Heures of the Duc de Berry. Chantilly, Musée Condé, MS 65, fol. 158

did not have a permanent oratory, a temporary closet, consisting of a curtained enclosure, sometimes called a 'traverse', attached to a timber frame would have been set up for him in a privileged position, normally on the right of the high altar.[44] Unlike the permanent closets, these temporary enclosures did not contain an altar, as their purpose was to allow the royal worshipper to participate in the main service at the high altar, separate and yet included. Richard II inherited two sets of furnishings called 'closets' from Edward III, one described as 'a large closet of red cendal' and one in black, stored with a set of black vestments, described as 'a closet (*clotet*) for the king'.[45] In an undated inventory from the reign of Richard II, after a vestment of black *baudekyn* silk, a traverse of blue *tartaryn* silk is listed.[46] Both the 'closets' and the traverse may have been curtains intended for temporary closets. When Richard II attended mass celebrated at the high altar in Westminster Abbey, a temporary closet would have been arranged for him. In the 1388 inventory of Westminster Abbey, there is a reference to a 'pannus de diversis coloribus stragulat' vocat' kanope ad coperiendum cawagium regis iuxta magna altare' ('a cloth striped with diverse colours called "canopy" to cover the *cawagium* of the king next to the high altar'). The *cawagium* has been interpreted elsewhere to indicate a royal pew.[47] Next to the high altar within the Abbey, this is likely to have been a curtained enclosure supported by a temporary timber frame, hence the need for a stored canopy.

In the great wardrobe accounts, distinctions were made between the books destined for Richard II's chapel and those for his private consumption in the closet.[48] Illuminated manuscripts of the fourteenth and fifteenth centuries often show noble and royal worshippers kneeling in the oratories that these texts were destined to serve. An elaborate depiction in the Très Riches Heures of the Duc de Berry showing the duke attending the celebration of high mass (Plate 4) illustrates the privileged position of the closet in which the duke kneels near to the high altar, giving him an intimate view of the mass.[49] It is noticeable that the cover of his

---

[44] For Richard II's coronation, a temporary closet was arranged for his mother in the gallery looking down onto the sanctuary: 'la princes, meir au roy, fuist assis ovesque ses damoisels en une bele closett fuit en la haut alée pour vere la sollempnitée', *The Anonimalle Chronicle, 1333–1381*, ed. V. H. Galbraith (Manchester, 1927), p. 115.

[45] PRO, E 101/400/2 (1, 2). See the provision of two closets, one of *sindon afforc'* and one of *sindon de tripl'* for the chapel of Edward III in 1345: PRO, E 101/389/14. See also the provision of a closet of triple *sindon* as part of the chapel furnishings for Princess Joan, daughter of Edward III, included in her trousseau for her marriage to Peter, son of King Alphonso of Castile: N. H. Nicolas, 'Observations on the Institution of the Most Noble Order of the Garter', *Archaeologia* xxxi (1846), pp. 145, 153.

[46] For the traverse of blue *tartaryn*, see PRO, E 101/403/24. During this period, and into the sixteenth century, 'traverses', or screening curtains, were also part of the furnishings of a bedchamber: see, e.g., PRO, E 361/5, m. 6.

[47] A *cawagium* may simply have meant an enclosed space, as it was not exclusively used in a liturgical context. During the fourteenth century, the monks' refectory at Westminster had a *cawagium* – a two-storey chamber – at one end, and the Abbey bakery also included a *cawagium* of unspecified form. See B. Harvey, *Westminster Abbey and its Estates in the Middle Ages* (Oxford, 1977), p. 41; and for the interpretation of the *cawagium* in the Westminster Abbey inventory of 1388 as a royal pew, see J. J. G. Alexander, 'The Portrait of Richard II in Westminster Abbey', *Regal Image*, ed. Gordon, Monnas and Elam, p. 197.

[48] PRO, E 101/401/6, m. 2; E 101/401/15; E 101/401/16, mm. 4, 13.

[49] The dating and attribution of the illustration of the Christmas mass in the Très Riches Heures is not straightforward: Millard Meiss has argued that the scene had been designed by the Limbourg brothers 1413–16 and completed by the workshop of Jean Colombe in the 1480s. M. Meiss, *Les Très Riches Heures du Duc de Berry* (London, 1969), text accompanying Figure 120.

Plate 5. The Duke of Berry praying, initial below an illustration of the Annunciation, book of hours (use of Paris), French with Burgundian additions. Cambridge, Fitzwilliam Museum MS 3–1954, fol. 13

lectern matches the frontals of the altar, a coordinated effect reminiscent of Richard II's documented closet and chapel furnishings. A secular attendant bearing a mace draws back the curtain for the duke to allow him a good view of the celebration.[50] Plate 5 shows another depiction of Jean de Berry attending mass, framed by simple curtains with no ceiling, typical of many illustrations of temporary closets from the fourteenth century.[51] Apart from the reference to the *kanope* in the Westminster inventory of 1388, it is impossible to tell whether the 'closets' which Richard II inherited from Edward III referred to the simple curtains shown in fourteenth-century depictions or whether they resembled the more elaborate ceilinged enclo-

---

[50] As in this French example, the English king would always have had the curtain drawn for him: sixteenth-century English texts stress the need for a yeoman usher to give attendance at the king's traverse, ready to draw the curtain for the king. See, e.g., BL, MS Additional 71009, fol. 7.

[51] See also the manuscript illuminations showing figures kneeling within oratories/closets consisting of curtains without ceilings in the Grandes Heures of Philip the Bold of Burgundy, of 1376–8: Cambridge, Fitzwilliam Museum MS 3–1954, illustrated in P. M. de Winter, *La bibliothèque de Philippe le Hardi Duc de Bourgogne 1364–1404: Étude sur les manuscrits à peintures d'une collection princière a l'époque du 'style Gothique Internationale'* (Paris, 1985), figs 122, 123, 126, etc.

Plate 6. Jean le Tavernier (active in Oudenaarde, c.1434–69), Duke Philip the Good of Burgundy attending mass, from Jean Miélot, Treatise on the *Oraison Dominicale*. Brussels, Bibliothèque Royal de Belgique MS 9092, fol. 9

sures which appear in fifteenth-century illustrations such as Plate 6. This shows Duke Philip the Good of Burgundy attending mass in a closet equipped with a ceiling. Unlike the more elaborate permanent closets which contained an altar, these temporary closets did not contain an altar, as their purpose was to allow the royal worshipper to participate in the main services at the high altar. Illustrations of small devotional objects within this type of closet are rare, but the miniature showing Philip the Good features a tiny diptych suspended from the curtain of his closet. It is just possible to discern on the diptych the black-clothed figure of the duke, kneeling before the Virgin, who is wearing blue.[52]

[52] The kneeling figures in the diptych have been identified by Delaissé, who cites a portable diptych formerly the possession of Charles the Bold: see L. M. J. Delaissé, *Miniatures médiévales de la librairie de Bourgogne au Cabinet des manuscrits de la Bibliothèque Royale de Belgique* (Cologne, 1959) pp.

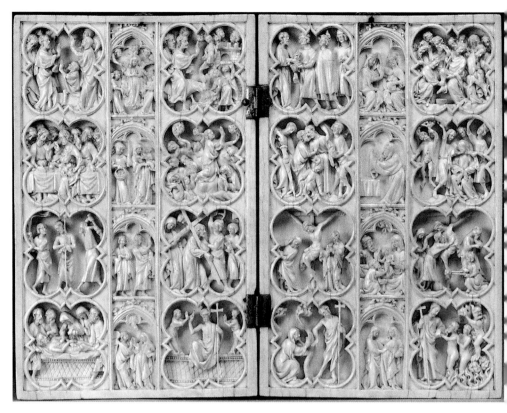

Plate 7. Diptych showing scenes from the Passion of Christ, Paris, c.1370–80, ivory. Paris, Musée du Louvre OA 4089

Fourteenth-century monarchs seem to have owned a range of small, devotional objects, including ivory carvings, relics encased in elaborate metalwork and small panel paintings which were ideally suited for contemplation in their closets (Plate 7: height 20.3cm, width 22.5cm). The list of Edward III's goods drawn up in 1332 (referred to earlier) included, besides vestments, plate and panel paintings, some precious reliquaries and ivory carvings.[53] The inventory of Charles V of France describes a selection of small devotional items found in the chapel of the chateau of Bois de Vincennes, in the bastion of the donjon (items 2459–2516). Among these, item 2512 comprised 'les verges dudit oratoire, à pilliers, ou pendent lesditz réliquaires, et sont d'argent'. In the oratory above, there were a number of small devotional objects – 'une petite croisette d'or' (item 2565), 'ung petit réliquaire d'or bellong' (item 2567) and 'ung petit "Agnus Dei" d'argent doré' (item 2568),

173–5. The words *Pater Noster* are written in gold on the curtain above the diptych, indicating that the duke was saying this prayer.
[53] PRO, E 101/386/3.

together with 'les fers ou pendent lesdictes réliques . . . de laton doré' (item 2572).[54] Some of the small, devotional objects owned by Richard II could also have been used in his closets.[55] These would have included not only the framed, embroidered picture of the Virgin recorded in the great wardrobe accounts during his reign, but also the many precious metalwork tablets – featuring St George, St Christopher and St John the Baptist among others – listed in his inventory of 1399.[56]

The only small devotional painting directly associated with Richard II to survive is the Wilton Diptych (Plates 1, 2). The diptych is composed of two oak panels painted on both sides, and each wing measures 53 x 37cm. On the outside, the white hart lodged, gorged with a crown and chained – the badge of Richard II – lies on a bed of lush vegetation. On the opposite panel, a lion *passant guardant* surmounts the helm and coat of arms of Richard II impaled with the mythical arms of the Confessor. Inside, Richard is shown kneeling in front of Sts Edmund, Edward the Confessor and John the Baptist. The Baptist, Richard II's patron saint, places a hand on Richard as his sponsor, introducing him to the Virgin.[57] In the opposite panel, the Virgin stands holding the Child, accompanied by eleven angels. One of the angels holds a banner with a red cross upon a white ground surmounted by an orb. Richard wears a gold collar composed of broom cods, with a badge of the white hart; the eleven angels also wear broom cod collars and white harts. Because of the inclusion of Edward the Confessor's mythical arms (which Richard II impaled with his own in c.1395) and the broom cod livery (adopted from the time of Richard II's marriage to Isabelle, daughter of Charles VI of France, in 1396), the painting is thought to date from between 1396 and 1399, the year of Richard's deposition.[58] The fact that Richard II, already married for the second time, is portrayed kneeling alone does not

---

[54] For Charles V's inventory, see *Inventaire de Charles V.*

[55] In 1385, a small, portable altar or altarpiece (*altare portatile*) made of wood was ordered for the king to carry with him to Scotland. PRO, E 101/401/5, the expenses roll of Alan de Stokes, lists the expenditure of 17s 4d upon 'merem' tabul' ac p[ro] gemell hokes et anul' de fer' unius altar' portatil' ordin' ad cariand' cu[m] d[omi]no rege cont[r]a viag' su'm ad p[ar]tes scoc': Gordon, *Making and Meaning*, p. 62 and n. 148. As part of the commission, twin hooks and rings were ordered; Gordon, *Making and Meaning*, p. 62 suggests that these could have been hinges and fastenings for opening and closing two panels. An alternative suggestion – if this indeed refers to an altarpiece – is that these metal rings and hooks could have been intended to suspend the painting in the king's closet in the same way as Philip the Good's diptych (Plate 6). After its completion, Thomas de Lynton was entrusted with overseeing the altarpiece's packing along with the surplices and vestments, for the Scottish campaign. PRO, E 101/401/6, the livery roll of Alan de Stokes, records, 'D[omi]no Thom[as]e de Lynton decano capell' infra hospic' d[omin]i n[ost]ri regi p[ro] sc' & socii p[ro] capellanis et al' minoribus cl[er]ici eiusd[em] capel' ad induend' & utend' tempore ministrac[i]o[n]is divini s[er]vicii in ead[em] xij supellic' de tel' lin' brabant' & x supellic' de tel' lin' flandr' ac p[ro] vestiment' & al' ornament' eiusd[em] capell' imponend' & trusand' ac p[ro] uno altari portatil' ordinat' ad cariand' us[que] p[ar]tes scoc' imponend' & truss[and'] & p[ro] quibus defect' vestiment' & al' ornament' eiusde[m] capelle emend' & reparand' . . . iiij coffr' standard, j par' coffr' trussabil', ij sacc' ad panni, j mantica, j uns s[er]icum, ij lb filum, iij lb cord fili'.

[56] The embroidered image of the Virgin is listed in the great wardrobe from the beginning of Richard II's reign into that of Henry IV: see PRO, E 361/5, mm. 2r, 3r, 4d, 6r, 10r, 10d, 12r. For the 1399 inventory, see U. Ilg, 'Ein wiederendecktes Inventar der Goldschmiedarbeiten Richards II von England und seine Bedeutung für die Ikonographie des Wiltondiptychons', *Pantheon* lii (1994), pp. 10–16. An edition of this inventory (PRO, E 101/411/9) is currently being prepared for publication by Jenny Stratford.

[57] For the Baptist as Richard II's patron saint, see Gordon, *Making and Meaning*, pp. 55–56; Mitchell, 'Richard II: Kingship', pp. 119–22.

[58] For the dating of the Wilton Diptych, see Gordon, 'The Wilton Diptych: An Introduction', pp. 20–3, who cites the two seminal articles: M. V. Clarke, 'The Wilton Diptych', *Burlington Magazine* lviii (1931), pp. 283–94, reprinted in M. V. Clarke, *Fourteenth Century Studies*, ed. L. S. Sutherland and M. McKisack

present a problem if the Wilton Diptych is perceived as an image destined for his closet, where he would have knelt at his priedieu, contemplating this image set up on a small altar. The queen would have had her own devotional images for use in her closet.[59]

During recent cleaning undertaken by the National Gallery, it was discovered that the tiny orb surmounting the banner in the Wilton Diptych contains a minute landscape depicting a ship sailing upon a silver sea, before an island with a castle and trees.[60] This has been interpreted by Dillian Gordon to represent a map of England, alluding to the concept of England as the Virgin's dowry. She has pointed to a connection between this image and a lost Ricardian altarpiece formerly in the English College in Rome. In that large altarpiece, known only through seventeenth-century engravings and descriptions, Richard and his queen, Anne of Bohemia, accompanied by standing saints, knelt before the Virgin offering to the Virgin the 'globe or patterne of England', referring to it as the Virgin's dowry.[61] Dr Gordon has stressed the personal nature of the iconography of the Wilton Diptych, and especially of the map upon the orb, which would 'have been obvious only to those who knew it was there, that is the king, the painter and whoever devised the iconographic programme, if indeed there was a third party'.[62]

The heraldry and idiosyncratic iconography of the Wilton Diptych proclaim it as the personal possession of the king. It has been suggested that the diptych could have been designed to accompany Richard on his expedition to Ireland in 1394–5.[63] Quite apart from the heraldic objections to such an early date, the portable nature of this object does not necessarily mean that it was designed for campaign or even for a specific journey. The peripatetic existence of medieval kings meant that portable devotional objects were needed on a regular basis.[64] Furthermore, the concept of 'portable' images need not even have implied a journey as Richard II could have worshipped in more than one location within a particular residence. The dynastic complex of Westminster Palace and Westminster Abbey, for example, offered several possible locations for the diptych. During Richard II's reign, the palace contained, besides the oratory overlooking St Stephen's Chapel,[65] a lower oratory or chapel of St Mary of the Pew[66] and a closet adjoining the Painted Chamber.[67] It will

(Oxford, 1937), pp. 272–92; and Harvey, 'Wilton Diptych'. For a detailed discussion of Richard II's use of the broomcod, see S. Mitchell, 'Richard II and the Broomcod Collar: New Evidence from the Issue Rolls', *Fourteenth Century England II*, ed. C. Given-Wilson (Woodbridge, 2002), pp. 171–80.

[59] Shelagh Mitchell has independently reached the same conclusion.

[60] D. Gordon, 'A New Discovery in the Wilton Diptych', *Burlington Magazine* cxxxiv (1992), p. 664.

[61] Gordon, 'A New Discovery'. For the Rome altarpiece and the concept of the Virgin's dowry, see also Harvey, 'Wilton Diptych', pp. 20–1.

[62] Gordon, 'A New Discovery', p. 667.

[63] P. Tudor-Craig, 'The Wilton Diptych in the Context of Contemporary English Panel and Wall Painting', *Regal Image*, ed. Gordon, Monnas and Elam, pp. 220–1.

[64] Saul, *Richard II*, pp. 468–74; Mitchell, 'Richard II: Kingship'.

[65] According to Brown, Colvin and Taylor, *King's Works*, I, p. 517, the closet projected from the south wall of St Stephen's Chapel, close to the high altar, and was entered from the gallery connecting the Painted Chamber to the chapel.

[66] For St Mary of the Pew in Westminster Palace, see C. L. Kingsford, 'The King's Oratory or Closet in the Palace of Westminster', *Archaeologia* lxviii (1917), pp. 1–20, cited by Gordon, *Making and Meaning*, p. 62, who suggests this as a possible location for the diptych.

[67] The closet adjoining the Painted Chamber had a quatrefoil window looked on to a depiction of St Edward and the Ring. The chamber had a thirteenth-century mural of the Coronation of St Edward

be argued that the Wilton Diptych was not designed to be used in only one setting, even though it is possible to point to iconographic links with at least two Westminster chapels.

Gervase Rosser has proposed that the Virgin in the Diptych could have been made as an *ex voto* tribute to a lost miracle-working sculpture of the Virgin located in the Abbey or Palace of Westminster.[68] This attractive suggestion is hard to prove, but it is evident that the textile furnishings for the royal closet and chapel were sometimes coordinated. There would certainly have been scope for visual interplay between the iconography of a small image within a closet and that of larger sculptural or pictorial decoration in a chapel. St Stephen's Chapel, for example, had been lavishly decorated during the reign of Edward III, with murals that included, among other subjects, a depiction of St George introducing Edward III and his sons kneeling in arcades beneath an Epiphany scene (Plate 8).[69] In the Wilton Diptych, the presence of three crowned kings (Richard II and the two royal saints) before the Virgin evokes an Epiphany scene, with Richard kneeling as the youngest magus, an appropriate choice for Richard who had been born on the feast of the Epiphany. This was an important feast for the English kings, who, in a public affirmation of their regality, attended the service crowned and wearing robes of estate, offering gold, frankincense and myrrh to the altar in a solemn reference to the presentation of these gifts to Christ.[70] When Richard II attended mass in St Stephen's Chapel, he would have spent part of the service in the oratory looking onto the chapel. If, on such an occasion, the Wilton Diptych had been set out in that oratory, the resonances between the Epiphany symbolism of the diptych and of the mural decoration in the chapel would have been clear to the king and privileged guests.

Close links with Westminster Abbey suggested by the iconography of the Wilton Diptych have already been pointed out by Francis Wormald and by other authors.[71] The Virgin, St John the Baptist and St Edmund as represented in the diptych correspond to the saints represented in the radiating chapels surrounding the shrine of the Confessor. Adjacent to the Baptist's chapel is the small chapel of St Mary of the Pew. This chapel retains traces of rich ornament from the reign of Richard II. These include a white hart painted on the east wall and two angels carved in stone at the entrance to the chapel, each bearing a shield, one charged with the arms of France

dating from the reign of Henry III. See P. Binski, *The Painted Chamber at Westminster* (London, 1986), pp. 13, 17, 45, col. pl. 1 (showing a copy by Stothard), fig. 1 (showing the quatrefoil outline of the window).

[68] G. Rosser, review of *The Regal Image of Richard II and The Wilton Diptych*, *Apollo* cxlviii (1999), pp. 60–1 (esp. p. 61), relates that Everard Greene had suggested that the diptych could have been an offering made at the altar of Our Lady of the Pew, but that he thought that it had been made at the time of the coronation of 1377, which is impossible on heraldic grounds (see text accompanying n. 58 above for the dating of the Wilton Diptych).

[69] For the murals in St Stephen's Chapel, see E. W. Tristram, *English Wall Painting of the Fourteenth Century* (London, 1955), pp. 206–19; and for the depictions of Edward III and Philippa of Hainault, see ibid., esp. pp. 207–10.

[70] For the Epiphany iconography of the Wilton Diptych, see Gordon, 'The Wilton Diptych: An Introduction', p. 22. I am indebted to Olga Pujmanova for drawing my attention to the relevance of the English royal Epiphany ceremony in the Wilton Diptych. See O. Pujmanova, 'Portraits of Kings depicted as Magi in Bohemian Painting', *Regal Image*, ed. Gordon, Monnas and Elam, pp. 247–66 (esp. pp. 262–4). For Richard portrayed as the youngest magus in the Wilton Diptych, see Mitchell, 'Richard II and the Broomcod Collar', p. 179.

[71] Wormald, 'Wilton Diptych', pp. 191–203; Gordon, *Making and Meaning*, p. 61.

Plate 8. Edward III and his sons kneeling below an Epiphany scene, drawing by R. Smirke after the mural decoration of St Stephen's Chapel, Palace of Wesminster. London, Society of Antiquaries Red Portfolio, Westminster: XVI

Ancient and England quarterly and the other with the Confessor's mythical arms.[72] Dillian Gordon and Nigel Saul have both proposed the chapel of St Mary of the Pew as a possible location for the diptych. Dr Gordon has suggested that this tiny chapel in the heart of the Abbey could have functioned as a closet (or royal 'pew') for the king, pointing out that the wide ledge of the altar niche could easily have accommodated the Wilton Diptych.[73]

The king could not have attended a mass celebrated at the high altar of Westminster Abbey from the vantage point of the chapel of St Mary of the Pew.[74] This chapel could, however, have served as a royal pew for services held in the adjoining chapel of St John the Baptist. Richard II would have had good reason to attend services in the chapel of the Baptist, the patron saint to whom he was especially devoted and whose intercession he sought in the inscription on his tomb.[75] During the 1390s, Richard II favoured the Baptist's chapel with his patronage, endowing it as a chantry chapel for himself and Anne of Bohemia. In 1391, he endowed an elaborate mass to be celebrated in the chapel of the Baptist every year on 16 July, the anniversary of his coronation, which coincided with the Feast of the Relics.[76] The anniversary mass was to be held 'for the good estate of the king and Queen Anne, while they live, and for observing an obit for each of them every year after their death'. Anne of Bohemia died on 7 June 1394, and, following her death, the first foundation was superseded by a generous endowment of £200 for a weekly and yearly anniversary for Queen Anne on 7 June and for the king 'when he should die'.[77]

Richard II was punctilious in attending the requiem masses held annually for his relations and he would certainly have attended, whenever circumstances permitted, the anniversary mass for his beloved wife. It can be demonstrated from the Westminster Abbey sacrist's rolls and from the accounts of the wardrobe of the household that the king did attend the mass held for Queen Anne at Westminster Abbey on 7 June 1395 and again in 1396.[78] He was at Westminster from 1 to 20 June 1397 and, although his presence at the anniversary mass is not specifically recorded, it

---

[72] Illustrated in Gordon, *Making and Meaning*, fig. 20.

[73] Ibid., p. 62.

[74] Noted by Gordon, who stressed that the chapel of St Mary of the Pew was used by Richard II, 'as his oratory for private devotions': ibid., p. 62.

[75] Richard II was born on 6 January 1367, the feast of the Baptism of Christ (as well as of the Epiphany) and succeeded to the throne on 22 June 1377, the eve of the vigil of the feast of St John the Baptist: Gordon, *Making and Meaning*, pp. 55–6; Mitchell, 'Richard II: Kingship', pp. 119–22. There is, however, some doubt that the feast of the Baptism was celebrated in the Western Church during the fourteenth century, which principally celebrated the Epiphany on that day (verbal communication, Shelagh Mitchell). For the inscription on Richard II's tomb, see P. Lindley, 'Absolutism and Regal Image in Ricardian Sculpture', *Regal Image*, ed. Gordon, Monnas and Elam, p. 62.

[76] Tristram, *English Wall Paintings*, p. 22; the feast of the relics was nominally held upon the first Sunday after 7 July, but some churches had their own days, and that of Westminster Abbey was held upon the eve of the feast of St Kenelm, King and Martyr. See C. R. Cheney, *A Handbook of Dates for Students of English History* (London, 1978) pp. 54, 59–60.

[77] Harvey, *Westminster Abbey*, p. 397. The endowment of 1391 is noted by Mitchell, 'Richard II: Kingship', p. 120, in her discussion of Richard II's devotion to the Baptist.

[78] 1395: WAM 19654, 'Cont' in expn' in j iantaculo p[ro] eodem d[omi]no rege & alio[rum] d[omi]no[rum] cu[m] eo veniente in anniversar' Anne regine xlijs. In vino eod[em] die xs.' 1396: PRO, E 101/403/10, p. 36r. I owe thanks to Richard Mortimer for helping me to decipher the meaning of *iantaculo* as a collation offered to the king and his retinue by the Abbey.

seems likely that he would have attended Queen Anne's mass in the Abbey.[79] The
chapel of the Baptist seems rather small to have accommodated the king together
with his chosen retinue as well as members of the clergy and an array of paupers.
The king could perhaps have attended the requiem service for Anne of Bohemia in
part from the chapel of Our Lady of the Pew, with the Wilton Diptych serving as an
altarpiece for him there.

The iconography of the diptych would have suited both the location and the occasion: not only does it feature the Baptist in company with the dynastic saints whose
cult was celebrated in Westminster Abbey, but it also contains symbolic references
to Queen Anne. Inside the diptych, Richard is depicted wearing a robe woven with
his livery badge of the white hart encircled by broom cod collars, which refer to his
second wife, interspersed with eagles, denoting the imperial lineage of Anne of
Bohemia. On the outer panel the white hart lies amidst vegetation containing yellow
irises, underlining the English crown's connection with the royal house of France,
alongside Anne of Bohemia's personal emblems of ferns and rosemary.[80] Rosemary
may have carried a specific connotation of remembrance,[81] and the inner panels
showing Richard kneeling before the Virgin in Paradise would have provided a suitable meditational focus for the king during the anniversary masses. The painting
would not have been ready for use in June 1395 since (as mentioned above) the
display of the broom cod indicates a date of 1396 at the earliest for its completion.[82]

It is important to recognise, however, that the chapel of St Mary of the Pew with
its doorway leading into the Baptist's chapel is not in its original state. At the beginning of Richard II's reign, the chapel was even smaller, measuring just over 1.5m
square. The chapel was subsequently expanded to its present measurement of 1.83m
by 2.74m, and a bracket with its image was moved back onto the new north wall. A
new doorway was opened providing an entrance into the Baptist's chapel through the
enlarged chapel of Our Lady of the Pew. Documentary evidence points to considerable alteration to the chapel of St Mary of the Pew in the early sixteenth century:
payments for the 'taking down of the chapels of the Blessed St Erasmus and St Mary
of the Pew' and for the removal of masonry suggest that both the enlargement and
the opening of the door may have taken place then.[83] In support of this, it has been

---

[79] Saul, *Richard II*, p. 473, records Richard II's presence at Westminster 1–20 June 1397. The sacristan's
roll for 1397, WAM 19655, simply contains a blanket payment of £7 10s 'in exp'n' d[omi]ni regis &
familiae suae ven . . . p' div[er]s' vices'.

[80] For rosemary, see Harvey, 'Wilton Diptych', p. 10; for irises, see C. Fisher, 'A Study of the Plants and
Flowers in the Wilton Diptych', *Regal Image*, ed. Gordon, Monnas and Elam, p. 162; for ferns, see Ilg,
'Ein wiederendecktes Inventar', p. 14.

[81] Harvey, 'Wilton Diptych', p. 10, has reservations about whether rosemary was a herb of remembrance
in 1390s or whether it acquired this connotation later.

[82] See Gordon, *Making and Meaning*, p. 51.

[83] The alteration to the chapel is mentioned in the account of John Islipp, warden of the new work at
Westminster Abbey, for 1502–3 (WAM 23581), referring to the chapel by its later dedication to St
Erasmus as well as to the Virgin: under Vadia & stipend', 'Et in st'rp' Ric'i Russell' carp' op'ant' c'ca le'z
scaffold' novi op'is de deponend' capell' s'c'i erasmi p' lxxiij dies, cap' p' diem viijd . . . xlviijs' also in
the same paragraph, 'Et sol' laborat' laborandu' c'ca p[ro]st[er]nat[ionem] capelle beate marie & s'c'i
erasmi in cariag' pet[r]a[rum] ad div's' loca monast[er]ii ut pat[et] p' lib' fr's Ric'i Nub'y . . . xiij li' iiijs
vjd.' I am most grateful to Richard Mortimer and Tony Trowles for their kind advice on the dating of the
enlargement of the chapel of St Mary of the Pew, and for Richard Mortimer's help in finding and deci-
phering these references.

pointed out that the crude vaulting of the ceiling in the extension appears at odds with the fine details of the original chapel. Yet the painted mural decoration of the extension, including palmettes containing fleurs de lys and a white hart painted on the 'new' altar wall appear more likely to date from the time of Richard II than from the early Tudor period. This leads to the conclusion that the chapel had already been enlarged during Richard's reign, and that only the doorway into the Baptist's chapel was opened in the sixteenth century.[84] Before this date, the two chapels could have been connected by a squint. There is at present a small opening (c.38cm x c.20cm) cut into the blind arcading of the chapel of St Mary of the Pew, offering an oblique view of the Baptist's chapel. This aperture does not function as a squint, but another, similar opening could originally have penetrated straight through the wall of the extended chapel to afford Richard II a view of the services held in the Baptist's chapel.[85]

This examination of two possible locations for the Wilton Diptych (the oratory of St Stephen's chapel, and the chapel of St Mary of the Pew) need not be taken as evidence that the painting was designed for a specific Westminster setting. The complex iconography of the diptych, drawing together so many strands of Richard II's personal religion, meant in practical terms that this versatile image was equally appropriate for a variety of services which he would have attended: to name the most obvious, the feasts of the Virgin, the Baptist, the Confessor, St Edmund and the Epiphany, and the anniversary masses for Anne of Bohemia. The royal cult at Westminster was central to Richard II's religious beliefs and to his ideals of kingship and it is natural that the dynastic saints should appear so prominently in the iconography of his personal travelling altarpiece. It seems likely that some of this imagery (for example, the use of personal badges or the depiction of Sts Edmund and Edward) would have been echoed in the domestic chapels in Richard II's other residences, such as Eltham or Kings Langley; but we have no detailed evidence for their decoration during his reign.

If the practice of royal worship within the various closets is understood, then any idea of the Wilton Diptych being the focal point of a secret brotherhood, let alone a posthumous painting, seems far less likely than the widely accepted view that this exquisite image was an object for Richard II's private devotions. There is no physical evidence to show that the Wilton Diptych was ever suspended from hooks in a temporary closet, and it does seem too large to have been used in this fashion. It should, perhaps, simply be regarded as one of a series of devotional objects which would have been set out, at the king's pleasure, for his contemplation upon an altar within his several permanent closets, travelling with him during his gyrations. Our

---

[84] The opening of a doorway had become necessary when the original entrance to the Baptist's chapel, through a screen from the ambulatory, was blocked first by the tomb of George Fascet, abbot of Westminster (1498–1500) and then by that of Thomas Ruthall, bishop of Durham (d.1523). See Royal Commission for Historical Monuments, *An Inventory of the Historical Monuments in London, I: Westminster Abbey* (London, 1924), pp. 34, 73–4, plates 141–3; *Westminster Abbey: Official Guide*, ed. T. Trowles (London, 1997), p. 60.

[85] I am indebted to John Goodall for his kind advice on the construction of the chapel of St Mary of the Pew, and I owe to him the suggestion of the squint. See J. Goodall, 'The Chantry of Humphrey, Duke of Gloucester', *Alban and St Albans: Roman and Medieval Architecture, Art and Archaeology*, ed. M. Henig and P. Lindley (British Archaeological Association Conference Transactions xxiv, Leeds, 2001), pp. 231–55, esp. p. 242 n. 36 and p. 244.

understanding of the use of small devotional images in the later Middle Ages is generally enhanced by imagining them within the setting of a closet. In the richly appointed permanent closets, the fixed heraldic decorations of the mural paintings, applied sculpture and stained glass, would have complemented the devices displayed upon moveable items: the textiles, plate, illuminated manuscripts and portable images.

'WEEP THOU FOR ME IN FRANCE':
FRENCH VIEWS OF THE DEPOSITION OF RICHARD II

Craig Taylor

On 30 September 1399 Richard II was deposed by his cousin Henry Bolingbroke. Within five months, Richard was dead, almost certainly murdered after the Earls' Revolt had demonstrated how much of a risk he still posed to the new regime.[1] These events had a strong impact on the other side of the English Channel, where the Valois court enjoyed particularly close ties with Richard II and his government. Decades of close diplomatic negotiations, involving princes of the blood on both sides, had culminated in 1396 in a marriage between the English king and Isabelle, daughter of the French king, Charles VI.[2] These political links between the courts were reinforced by the cultural links fostered by individuals such as Geoffrey Chaucer, Oton de Grandson, Eustache Deschamps and Philippe de Mézières.[3] Indeed, four Frenchmen attended the court of Richard II in the 1390s and wrote accounts of the events leading up to the deposition. The most famous of these was the Hainaulter, Jean Froissart, who discussed the deposition of Richard II in Book IV of the *Chroniques*; he had travelled to England in 1395 to present the king with a book on 'matters of love', no doubt recognising the value of such a theme in the context of the marriage negotiations.[4] Less well known to English scholars is the French royal notary and secretary, Pierre Salmon, who accompanied Isabelle of France to Calais for the marriage to Richard II in 1396 and then travelled on to England. In his *Dialogues*, written in 1409 and revised between 1412 and 1415, Salmon offered an account of his hectic diplomatic missions, travelling backwards and forwards between Paris, London and other European cities during the last years of Richard II's reign.[5] Jean Creton, *valet de chambre* of the king of France and the duke of Burgundy, was almost certainly the author of the *French metrical history of the deposition of King Richard the Second*, a verse chronicle written during the winter of 1401–2; the writer had been in England from the spring of 1399, and

---

[1]   The quotation in the title to this article comes from William Shakespeare, *Richard II*, Act V, Scene 1, l. 87.

[2]   J. J. N. Palmer, *England, France and Christendom, 1377–99* (London, 1972), together with the review by M. G. A. Vale in *English Historical Review* lxxxviii (1973), pp. 848–53; Anthony Tuck, 'Richard II and the Hundred Years War', *Politics and Crisis in Fourteenth-Century England*, ed. J. Taylor and W. Childs (Gloucester, 1990), pp. 117–31.

[3]   See, for example, Ardis Butterfield, 'French Culture and the Ricardian Court', *Essays on Ricardian Literature in Honour of J. A. Burrow*, ed. A. J. Minnis, C. C. Morse and T. Turville-Petre (Oxford, 1997), pp. 82–120; Michael Hanly, 'Courtiers and Poets: An International System of Literary Exchange in Late Fourteenth Century Italy, France and England', *Viator* xxviii (1997), pp. 305–32.

[4]   Jean Froissart, *Oeuvres*, ed. Kervyn de Lettenhove (26 vols, Brussels, 1867–77), XV, pp. 142, 167–8.

[5]   Pierre le Fruictier, dit Salmon, *Les demandes faites par le roi Charles VI touchant son état et le gouvernement de sa personne, avec les réponses de Pierre Salmon, son secrétaire et familier*, ed. G.-A. Crapelet (Paris, 1833), pp. 41–62. This work is now more commonly known as the *Dialogues*.

enjoyed a remarkable eyewitness perspective on most of the key events culminating in the deposition of Richard II.[6] Finally the *Chronicque de la traïson et mort de Richard Deux* was written at about the same time by an anonymous Frenchman, perhaps a subject of the duke of Burgundy from Artois or west Flanders, who had travelled to England in the household of queen Isabelle during her brief sojourn in England and probably served as an herald in the household of John Holand, duke of Exeter.[7]

These French accounts are essentially free of the controlling influence of Lancastrian propaganda, presenting the revolution of 1399 as 'a story of opportunistic rebellion, treason, betrayal and, ultimately, regicide'.[8] In practice only Jean Creton's *French metrical history* is a particularly useful source for the actual study of the usurpation.[9] Jean Froissart was not an eyewitness to the events leading up to the deposition; his account of the final years of the reign of Richard II is often wildly inaccurate and sheds little light on the motivations of the protagonists.[10] Pierre Salmon was in England during the crucial years but gives little direct testimony on the domestic political concerns of Richard II. In contrast, Jean Creton offers a virtually unique perspective in the *French metrical history* because he was present at most of the crucial events that he described, and was generally honest about the sources of his information for incidents that he had not personally witnessed. Unfortunately the *Traïson et mort* is less reliable. The anonymous author rarely saw anything important and so invented the majority of the scenes that he described with such panache; and even though the chronicle was revised on up to three subsequent occasions, these changes drew to an increasing degree upon the existing work of Jean Creton.[11]

Whether or not the *French metrical history* and the *Traïson et mort* provide a 'true' account of the events in question, it is clear that their construction of the deposition of Richard II shaped contemporary French views of the Lancastrian revolution. These two chronicles were medieval 'bestsellers' in France: there are seven surviving copies of the *Metrical history*, including ones owned by Charles III of Anjou and Philip the Bold, duke of Burgundy, and thirty-nine copies of the more dramatic and entertaining *Traïson et mort*.[12] Moreover the *Traïson et mort* was used as the main source by the majority of contemporary French chronicles that discussed the deposition of Richard II, including the *Chronique du Religieux de Saint-Denis* by Michel Pintouin, the *Histoire du roy Charles VI* attributed to Jean Juvénal des

---

[6] J. J. N. Palmer, 'The Authorship, Date and Historical Value of the French Chronicles of the Lancastrian Revolution', *Bulletin of the John Rylands Library* lxi (1978–9), pp. 145–54.

[7] Ibid., pp. 154–72.

[8] Michael J. Bennett, *Richard II and the Revolution of 1399* (Stroud, 1999), p. 8.

[9] Palmer, 'The Authorship, Date and Historical Value of the French Chronicles of the Lancastrian Revolution', pp. 145–81, 398–421; Antonia Gransden, *Historical Writing in England, c.1307 to the Early Sixteenth Century* (London, 1982), pp. 157–93; *Chronicles of the Revolution, 1397–1400*, ed. Chris Given-Wilson (Manchester, 1993), pp. 3–10.

[10] Froissart, *Oeuvres*, XV, pp. 142, 167–8. In general, see James W. Sherborne, *War, Politics and Culture in Fourteenth-Century England* (London, 1994), pp. 169–70; George B. Stow, 'Richard II in Jean Froissart's *Chroniques*', *Journal of Medieval History* xi (1985), pp. 333–45.

[11] Palmer, 'The Authorship, Date and Historical Value of the French Chronicles of the Lancastrian Revolution', pp. 398–421.

[12] Ibid., pp. 180–1; to which should be added the copies of the *Traïson et mort* in Brussels (Bibliothèque royale, MSS 12192–4) and Vienna (Osterreichische Nationalbibliothek MS 3392).

Ursins, the *Chronique* of Jean Brandon, the *Chronique des Pays-Bas*, the *Chronographia regum Francorum*, the *Cronique martiniane*, the *Recueil des croniques et anciennes istoires de la Grant Bretaigne* by Jean de Wavrin and even the *Recueil des plus celebres astrologues* of Simon de Phares.[13] In the hands of these chroniclers as well as those of the polemical writers of Valois France, the story of the deposition of Richard II was used to explore the legitimacy of tyrannicide and the vagaries of fortune, to attack the Lancastrian government, and as an argument with which to attack either side in the mounting civil war between Armagnacs and Burgundians.

Tyranny and tyrannicide

The fourteenth century witnessed a series of depositions and assassinations of reigning sovereigns across Europe. In 1327 Edward II king of England was forced to abdicate and was then murdered. In 1345 the son of the king of Hungary was stran-gled on the order of his wife, Joanna, queen of Naples; almost thirty years later Joanna herself was murdered on the orders of Charles of Durazzo, who was in turn assassinated in 1386. In 1369, Peter I king of Castile was murdered, as was Peter I king of Cyprus, the exemplar of chivalry and crusading élan. The most famous chronicler of the age, Jean Froissart, concluded his *Chroniques* by describing the assassinations of the ruler of Milan, Bernabo Visconti, by his nephew Giangaleazzo, the withdrawal of French support from the Avignonese pope, Benedict XIII, in 1398, and the depositions of Richard II in 1399 and of the emperor Wenzel IV in 1400. Even in France, the apparent stability of the Valois dynasty was something of an illusion, given that the kings were never entirely secure in the face of challenges from rivals such as the Plantagenet kings of England and Charles of Navarre, not to mention the very real prospect of 'elective' monarchy following the precedents set in 1317 and 1328 when public assemblies had resolved disputes over the royal succes-sion.[14] Even more worryingly, the political vacuum created by Charles VI's constant battles with mental instability after 1392 slowly created the very real prospect of dramatic political upheaval – which became a frightening reality in 1420 when the Burgundians allied with the English to replace the legitimate heir to the throne. In short, the stability and security of sovereign power across Europe, and even in France, was severely threatened by the realities of contemporary politics.

In this context, it is hardly surprising that most late medieval French writers were essentially conservative when discussing the topic of royal deposition in general, and the story of Richard II in particular.[15] The deposition of that English king could

---

[13] Palmer, 'The Authorship, Date and Historical Value of the French Chronicles of the Lancastrian Revolution', pp. 173–4; Simon de Phares, *Le recueil des plus celebres astrologues de Simon de Phares*, ed. Jean-Patrice Boudet (2 vols, Paris, 1997–9), I, pp. 506, 511–8, 530–8.

[14] The suitability of Jean to succeed to Philip of Valois was contested during the reign of his father, and following the death of Jean, there was an interregnum before the accession of his son Charles. Raymond Cazelles, *La société politique et la crise de la royauté sous Philippe de Valois* (Paris, 1958), pp. 72–3; Raymond Cazelles, *Société politique, noblesse et couronne sous Jean le Bon et Charles V* (Paris, 1982), pp. 455–60.

[15] See Alfred Coville, *Jean Petit et la question de tyrannicide au commencement du XVe siècle* (Paris, 1932), pp. 179–206; P. S. Lewis, *Essays in Later Medieval French History* (London, 1985), pp. 169–87; Jean-Claude Mühlethaler, 'Le tyran à table: Intertextualité et référence dans l'invective politique à l'époque de Charles VI', *Représentation, pouvoir et royauté à la fin du moyen âge*, ed. Joël Blanchard

have been employed as an *exemplum*, highlighting the dangers of bad and even tyrannical kingship and thereby providing an object lesson for French kings and princes.[16] Yet French scholars were essentially unwilling to countenance active tyrannicide at this vulnerable time for the Valois monarchy; most argued that the good subject would not rebel, preferring to see the bad ruler as a punishment deserved by a bad people, and to believe that the wicked prince would ultimately be subject to the wrath of God.[17] Thus in *Tres crestien, tres hault, tres puissant roy*, written in 1444, Jean Juvénal des Ursins rehearsed in limited detail the Lancastrian charges against Richard II but concluded that

> [Even] supposing that Richard [II] had failed and acted very badly, still it was not for Henry nor for the people of England to do what they did; and for a people to judge the sovereign is like a monster in nature. And Seneca says that if a sovereign prince offers a criminal punishment or kills someone, if that man has deserved it, this is justice, and if that man does not deserve it, this is fortune. And it is necessary to dissimulate, because [the king's] will alone is reputed as law and reason, and his only judge is God.[18]

As Jean Juvénal demonstrated, the French writers were under no illusions about the quality of Richard II's rule. Jean Froissart emphasised the king's lack of political judgment, particularly under the influence of evil counsellors, and his mounting unpopularity.[19] The *French metrical history* and the *Traïson et mort* jumped into the story at the very end, missing out most of the crucial background of Richard's reign, but nevertheless were quite aware of the mounting unpopularity of the English king, even if this was partially due to the effective propaganda of his opponents. Moreover, both admitted that the king had been planning to turn the tables on Henry of Lancaster and kill him, while the *Traïson et mort* also showed how the initial stoicism of Richard in the face of his capture slowly broke down as he degenerated into a weeping wreck.[20] Drawing upon the *Traïson et mort*, the monk of St Denis, Michel Pintouin, observed that Richard had not been open to the counsel of his natural advisors, the nobility, that his taxes had been oppressive and that the king had often failed to keep his word.[21]

(Paris, 1995), pp. 49–62; Jeanine Quillet, 'Tyrannie et tyrannicide dans la pensée medievale tardive (XIVe–XVe siècles)', *D'une cité l'autre: Problèmes de philosophie politique médiévale* (Paris, 2001), pp. 147–57.

[16] John of Salisbury's famous set of *exempla* of tyrannicides in *Policraticus* was translated into French by Denis Foulechat in 1372. Charles Brucker, 'Denis Foulechat, tyrans, princes et prêtres (Jean de Salisbury, *Policraticus* IV et VIII)', *Le moyen français* xxi (1987), pp. 105–10.

[17] A rare exception was the voice of Sedition in Jean Gerson's sermon *Vivat rex* (1405), though this famous theologian took a more conservative position as one of the chief opponents of Jean Petit's discussion of tyrannicide in the *Justification de monseigneur le duc de Bourgogne* (1408). Jean Gerson, *Oeuvres complètes*, ed. P. Glorieux (10 vols, Paris-Tournai, 1960–73), VII,ii, pp. 1137–85; and see below, pp. 219–20.

[18] Jean Juvénal des Ursins, *Les écrits politiques de Jean Juvénal des Ursins*, ed. P. S. Lewis (3 vols, Paris, 1978–93), II, pp. 152–3.

[19] Stow, 'Richard II in Jean Froissart's *Chroniques*', pp. 333–45; Michel Zink, *Froissart et le temps* (Paris, 1998), pp. 89–110.

[20] J. Webb, 'Translation of a French Metrical History of the Deposition of King Richard the Second', *Archaeologia* xx (1824), pp. 357–9; *Chronicque de la traïson et mort de Richart Deux roy Dengleterre*, ed. Benjamin Williams (London, 1846), pp. 34–7, 49–67.

[21] *Chronique du religieux de Saint-Denis contenant le règne de Charles VI, de 1380 à 1422*, ed. Louis Bellaguet (6 vols., Paris, 1839–52; repr. Paris, 1994), I, pp. 494–6; II, pp. 670, 674–6. These themes were

Nevertheless, the French chroniclers did not accept the Lancastrian view that Richard II had been a tyrant who was justly removed from the throne. Their Richard was a flawed but ultimately courageous figure, as seen in his military enterprises in Ireland, his compassion and loyalty towards his supporters, and his strength and resolution in the face of his ultimate fate. At the very end, according to the *Traïson et mort*, the king fought against Sir Peter Exton and the assassins with vigour and courage, 'like a good and loyal knight'; the account may be historically unreliable but it powerfully evokes the nobility of Richard and the horror of his fate.[22] Richard II's French wife became a key figure in locating sympathy in the narrative. As the daughter of Charles VI, she was the natural focus for French interest in these events and the chroniclers used her to direct the audience's sympathies, giving them a much more personal stake in these events. In the *Traïson et mort*, Richard's primary concern in the face of his doom is to ensure the safety of his wife: he calls upon the French royal family to protect her, now that she is 'like the lamb amongst the wolves'.[23]

These writers attributed Richard's deposition to English hostility to the prospect of peace between England and France. The marriage of Richard II and the French princess, Isabelle, in 1396 had been widely celebrated in France as a crucial step towards the resolution of the long-standing conflict between the two nations; Eustache Deschamps wrote two poems in support of the marriage, celebrating the event with the refrain 'All peaces comes through a holy marriage.'[24] Yet according to Jean Creton, this amity between Richard II and his father-in-law created great resentment amongst the war-mongering English.[25] Similarly, both Froissart and the *Traïson et mort* argued that Richard's peace proposals and amity with France incited Gloucester to rebel.[26] This became the standard perspective of the Valois writers. For example, in 1449, Robert Blondel argued in the *Oratio historialis* that the English were worse than Saracens for their actions against a divinely instituted king who was no tyrant, but only guilty of wanting to make peace and fulfil his sworn oath of office. The French translator of this work emphasised the hostility of Richard II's enemies to his supposed plans to make the kingdom of England subject to the French crown, as seen when he returned Cherbourg to the French king and Brest to the duke of Brittany.[27]

Thus, the French writers preferred to view the treatment of Richard II as

---

echoed, for example, in the *Histoire de Charles VI*, attributed to Jean Juvénal des Ursins: 'Histoire de Charles VI, roy de France, et des choses mémorables advenues durant quarante-deux années de son règne depuis 1380 jusques à 1422', *Nouvelle collection des mémoires pour servir à l'histoire de France*, ed. J. F. Michaud (Paris, 1836), II, pp. 343, 411.

[22] Webb, 'Translation of a French Metrical History', pp. 316, 337–40, 372, 406–8; *Chronicque de le traïson et mort*, pp. 27–33, 95.

[23] *Chronicque de la traïson et mort*, pp. 53–5.

[24] Eustache Deschamps, *Oeuvres*, ed. Marquis de Queux de Saint Hilaire and G. Raynaud (11 vols, Paris, 1878–1903), I, pp. 199–201 (ballad no. 93); VI, pp. 133–4 (ballad no. 1181).

[25] Webb, 'Translation of a French Metrical History', pp. 373–4, 409–10.

[26] Froissart, *Oeuvres*, XVI, pp. 4–5; *Chronicque de la traïson et mort*, pp. 1–2. In two of the surviving manuscripts of the *Traïson et mort*, Jean le Beau, canon of Liège, added passages which highlighted the bellicosity of the English: Palmer, 'The Authorship, Date and Historical Value of the French Chronicles of the Lancastrian Revolution', p. 156.

[27] Robert Blondel, *Oeuvres de Robert Blondel*, ed. A. Héron (2 vols, Rouen, 1891–3), I, pp. 258–9, 272 (*Oratio historialis*), 439–40, 456–7 (*Des droiz de la couronne de France*, composed in 1460). The same argument had appeared in Jean Juvénal des Ursins, *Les écrits politiques*, II, p. 152.

evidence of the regicidal proclivities of the English, which in turn emphasised the apparent loyalty and stability of the French polity. In the *Traïson and mort*, Richard II advised the nobility of France 'to preserve the honour of chivalry as you have done, for never was it known that such treason was committed against any of the noble kings of France as my own cousins and kin have committed against me'.[28] In the *French metrical history*, Jean Creton drew wider conclusions from the actions of the English against Richard II:

> As regards their origin and nature, they are readily disposed towards betrayal, always supporting the very powerful and the best prepared, without regard for right, law, reason or justice. This is not just the case now, because many times they have defeated and destroyed their king and lord, as may be seen in many histories and chronicles.[29]

This notion that 'the English kill their lords and kings' was later developed by Valois writers as part of a wider rhetorical strategy to rally support against the very real threat that Henry V and the duke of Burgundy would successfully disinherit the dauphin Charles; the English killed their kings but the French were a naturally loyal race who would support the rightful heir to the throne against the English usurper and his Burgundian allies. Thus the anonymous pamphlet *Debats et appointements*, written around 1419, reported that the English were

> a sect of evil men, speaking against all good and all reason, hungry wolves, proud, pompous, schismatics, deceivers without conscience, tyrants and persecutors of Christians, and they drink and bathe in human blood, resembling in nature the birds of prey who live on slaughter at the expense of their simple and affable neighbours. And it is good to recognise that they cannot behave well towards others when they have betrayed and destroyed their kings and sovereign lords, as seen with King Richard [II] and many other kings, up to the number of twenty-two who have been deposed, falsely betrayed and killed in past times by their false and evil treasons.[30]

Similarly, in the pamphlet *Fluxo biennali spacio*, probably written between 1422 and 1429, France charged England with the murder of the French king, Jean II, while he was a hostage in England and declared that 'you [English] are the enemies of peace, accustomed to killing your lords and kings'. The anonymous author went on to cite not just the murder of Richard II but also those of King Cnut and of six Anglo-Saxon kings. In response, England could only respond, 'I am silent.'[31] In 1444, Jean Juvénal des Ursins simply declared, 'They have a manner in England, of

[28] *Chronicque de la traïson et mort*, p. 205.

[29] Webb, 'Translation of a French Metrical History', pp. 369–70.

[30] *L'honneur de la couronne de France: quatre libelles contre les Anglais, vers 1418–vers 1429*, ed. Nicole Pons (Paris, 1990), pp. 66–7. The *Genealogies des rois d'Angleterre*, accompanying the text in the manuscripts, states that seven kings destroyed each other in the context of events of the sixth century, so that it is possible that the '.xxii.' deposed English kings represent in fact a palaeographic corruption of the number '.vii.'.

[31] *L'honneur de la couronne de France*, pp. 194–7. This list was subsequently repeated by the chronicler Noël de Fribois in his *Cest chose profitable*, written in the 1450s; and in 1484, the chancellor of France claimed that there had been twenty-six changes of dynasty since the start of the English monarchy. Lewis, *Essays in Later Medieval History*, pp. 188–92 ; Jean Masselin, *Journal des Etats généraux de France tenus à Tours en 1484, sous le règne de Charles VIII*, ed. J. Bernier (Paris, 1835), p. 38.

thinking nothing of changing their king whenever they wish, seeing that they kill and put them to death evilly.' In support of this argument, he cited the murder of Richard II, as well as other examples both from the Anglo-Saxon period but also more recent such as king John's murder of his nephew Arthur of Brittany and the deposition of Edward II.[32]

Thus French writers generally avoided using Richard II as a contemporary example of tyranny and hence as a moral lesson to persuade a French king to rule properly. Nevertheless, the tragic dimensions of Richard's fall and the moral lessons that this offered could be presented to a French audience in a more acceptable manner through the device of fortune.[33] In the *French metrical history*, Creton described Richard's last moments of freedom as he travelled towards Conway with his closest allies:

> Now consider the power, the possessions and the grandeur of King Richard, who was such a great lord, and what remains to him now by favour, treason and fortune, who at all times has power and domination to defeat those who are selected. She is a cruel, powerful and proud mistress, most changeable and very impetuous. . . . She has no care for kings and princes, because all is one to her, as she demonstrates, for as everyone says, she has entirely stripped a powerful Christian king of all that he had. She raises one and throws down another.[34]

At the very end of the *Livre de la mutacion de fortune*, completed in November 1403, Christine de Pizan offered a list of the outstanding people of her own age who had been the victims of fortune, including Peter I of Cyprus, Peter I of Castile, Queen Joanna I of Naples and Richard II. She concluded by wishing that fortune's continuing favour be granted to the French princes who were still living, offering a clear moral warning to her audience.[35] In the *Avision Christine*, written in November 1406, she offered a more personal perspective on the evil fortune that had befallen Richard II and his allies. She had met the earl of Salisbury while he was in Paris on a diplomatic mission in late 1398 and persuaded him to take her son into his household.

> But that woman (or adverse Fortune) who so often injured me did not intend to suffer this benefit for long; as everyone knows, not long thereafter she brought the cruel pestilence against the said King Richard in the aforesaid country of England, because of which, the good count was later most unjustly beheaded for his great loyalty to the rightful lord.[36]

---

32 Jean Juvénal des Ursins, *Les écrits politiques*, II, p. 138, and in general see pp. 134, 138–59.

33 The theme of Fortune had been given new popularity by the French translations of Petrarch's *De remediis utriusque fortunae* by Jean Daudin in 1378 and of Boccaccio's *De casibus virorum illustrium*, completed by Laurent de Premierfait in November 1400. See, for example, Nicholas Mann, 'La fortune de Pétrarque en France: Recherches sur le *De remediis*', *Studi Francesi* xxxvii (1969), pp. 1–15.

34 Within the narrative, Richard himself was quite aware of the wider forces at work, calling out to the Virgin Mary that 'fortune is treating me most harshly'. Webb, 'Translation of a French Metrical History', pp. 334–5, 337.

35 Christine de Pizan, *Le livre de la mutacion de fortune*, ed. S. Solente (4 vols, Paris, 1959–66), IV, pp. 75–6 (ll. 23501–12). Earlier, she had alluded to the role of the 'counsellors of England' in Richard's downfall, no doubt meaning parliament, and had praised the courage and exploits of Richard II before he was imprisoned. Ibid, II, p. 7 (ll. 4401–2), 12 (ll. 4541–54).

36 Christine de Pizan, *Christine's Vision*, trans. G. K. McLeod (New York, 1993), pp. 120–1.

When Henry IV tried to lure her to the English court, it is perhaps not surprising that Christine refused to serve such a disloyal and treacherous man.[37]

Yet the discussion of fortune was more than just a literary device to emphasise the tragic dimensions of the rise and fall of great men; it could also serve as a politically safe way of conveying advice to a ruler. Thus Pierre Salmon presented Richard II and Louis, duke of Orléans, who was murdered in 1407, as examples for Charles VI:

> by the most sorrowful and pitiful fortunes that have happened to these two lord of whom I have just spoken, who during their lives were so great and powerful that it has been impossible to believe that such great and marvellous fortunes might happen to them . . . you can well learn and recognise that the power of God is very great and his judgments are very marvellous and most obscure for the understanding of men.[38]

But Salmon did not wish to suggest that Charles VI was helpless in the face of fortune: if he listened to good counsel he might evade the fates of his relatives.[39] Similarly, in 1419 the anonymous author of the pamphlet *Debats et appointements* concluded his lengthy examination of the moral and legal dimensions of the war with England by calling upon the reader to 'fear evil fortune, because I know and believe what it has done to others in times past'. This was demonstrated through a long inventory of those from classical and more recent times who had suffered at fortune's hand, including not just Richard II, 'whose subjects deposed and killed him', but also French princes such as the duke of Burgundy who had just been murdered at the bridge of Montereau in September. This litany of ill-fortune served to give authority to the anonymous author's practical advice: the leaders of France should not only to have faith in God, but also take active steps to rule well by making sound laws, paying and disciplining the army properly, and ensuring that government servants were honest and worthy.[40]

Diplomacy and propaganda

The deposition of Richard II clearly had a direct impact on diplomatic relations between the two governments. The Valois monarchy had no choice but to negotiate with the new regime in England, especially after the news of Richard's death filtered through to France. The first priority was to secure the return of the princess Isabelle, virtually a hostage in the hands of Henry IV, and this in turn required the resumption of diplomatic contact with the Lancastrians; in June 1400, the twenty-eight year truce was confirmed and remained in force until Henry V invaded Normandy in 1415.[41] Nevertheless, the Lancastrian usurpation clearly increased the

---

[37] Pizan went on to say that she had to buy her son back from Henry IV by giving copies of at least two of her works. See Charity Cannon Willard, *Christine de Pisan: Her Life and Works* (New York, 1984), pp. 42–3, 78, 164–5.

[38] Salmon reproduced a letter that he had written to the king on 1 November 1408 in his mirror of princes, the *Dialogues*, in 1409. Salmon, *Les demandes faites par le roi Charles VI*, pp. 98–9.

[39] See below, p. 220.

[40] *L'honneur de la couronne de France*, pp. 68–79.

[41] S. P. Pistono, 'Henry IV and Charles VI: The Confirmation of the Twenty-Eight Year Truce', *Journal*

tension in these diplomatic negotiations. According to Jean Froissart, Charles VI was so shocked by the news of the deposition of Richard II that he suffered a recurrence of the madness that had afflicted him irregularly since 1392, while the monk of St Denis reported that Charles was not shown letters from his daughter Isabelle because of his weakened mental condition.[42] Whether these accounts are true or not, the French king did initially refuse to receive the ambassadors of Henry IV and even imprisoned the herald who had requested a safe conduct on their behalf, subsequently stating that he had not wished 'that anyone might imagine that he tacitly or openly approved of the title of the duke [Henry] who called himself king'.[43] Thereafter Charles VI continued to deny that the Lancastrian was the rightful king of England and appointed his eldest son to the 'vacant' duchy of Guyenne in January 1401, implying that he intended to enforce the confiscation of the duchy.[44] Moreover the French king resolutely refused to consider the possibility of a marriage alliance, particularly between Richard II's widow Isabelle and one of the sons of Henry IV. In early 1402, Charles even sent Jean Creton to Scotland on a wild-goose chase to check whether rumours of Richard's survival were accurate, and Creton subsequently reported in the *French metrical history* that the body that had been displayed publicly in 1400 was in fact that of a priest named Maudelyn who resembled Richard II.[45] The French government also took practical measures to undermine the Lancastrian regime. In 1399, they put their garrisons on the frontiers in the south-west and in Picardy on alert, and then sent representatives to negotiate with disaffected Gascon nobles.[46] In the ensuing years, both sides turned a blind eye to the actions of privateers in the English Channel, while the French provided aid for Robert III of Scotland and Owain Glyn Dwr's Welsh rebels against Henry IV, co-ordinated raids on the south coast of England and launched an unsuccessful campaign against Guyenne in 1406.[47] Moreover, both Louis, duke of Orléans, and Waleran, count of St Pol, demonstrated their opposition to Henry IV by issuing personal letters of defiance, seeking revenge against him for his actions against

---

of Medieval History iii (1977), pp. 357–63; Christopher J. Phillpotts, 'The Fate of the Truce of Paris, 1396–1415', *Journal of Medieval History* xxiv (1998), pp. 67–80.

[42] Froissart, *Oeuvres*, XVI, pp. 189–90, 211–2; *Chronique du religieux de Saint-Denis*, II, p. 720.

[43] 'Minutes de pièces diplomatiques concernant la restitution de la reine Isabelle, et l'ambassade envoyée en Écosse (août 1400)', *Choix de pièces inédites relatives au règne de Charles VI*, ed. L. Douët d'Arcq (2 vols, Paris, 1863–4), I, p. 188.

[44] Pistono, 'Henry IV and Charles VI', pp. 357–63; Anthony Tuck, 'Henry IV and Europe: A Dynasty's Search for Recognition', *The McFarlane Legacy: Studies in Late Medieval Politics and Society*, ed. R. H. Britnell and A. J. Pollard (Stroud, 1995), pp. 107–9; Phillpotts, 'The Fate of the Truce of Paris, 1396–1415', pp. 67–9.

[45] Webb, 'Translation of a French Metrical History', pp. 220–1; Palmer, 'The Authorship, Date and Historical Value of the French Chronicles of the Lancastrian Revolution', pp. 151–4.

[46] M. G. A. Vale, *English Gascony, 1399–1453: A Study of War, Government and Politics During the Later Stages of the Hundred Years War* (Oxford, 1970), pp. 27–42; Pistono, 'Henry IV and Charles VI', pp. 353, 356–7. Henry IV certainly feared an invasion of England in the early months of 1400: Pistono, 'Henry IV and Charles VI', p. 361.

[47] C. J. Ford, 'Piracy or Policy: The Crisis in the Channel, 1400–1403', *TRHS* 5th ser. xxix (1979), pp. 63–77; R. R. Davies, *The Revolt of Owain Glyn Dwr* (Oxford, 1995), pp. 193–5; Tuck, 'Henry IV and Europe', pp. 107–25; Philip Morgan, 'Henry IV and the Shadow of Richard II', *Crown, Government and People in the Fifteenth Century*, ed. Rowena Archer (Stroud, 1995), pp. 16–23; Phillpotts, 'The Fate of the Truce of Paris, 1396–1415', pp. 71–3.

Richard II and Isabelle.[48] In short, Charles VI and the French royal family waged a 'personal vendetta' against the Lancastrians.[49]

In this context, the deposition and murder of Richard II provided a powerful rhetorical weapon for the French diplomats, and for the notaries and secretaries who provided the legal and moral framework within which negotiations were conducted.[50] Rhetorically, these French writers were able to present the Lancastrians as the enemies of peace, a position that may not have seemed far from the truth to the Valois court: immediately after the deposition, Jean, duke of Berry, wrote to the duke of Burgundy, expressing his concern that Henry of Lancaster was controlled by the commons of England who desired war.[51] Indeed, the notion that the English were warlike was widespread in Europe. In 1402, a Veronese agent described the English as 'a most warlike race', and in the middle of the fifteenth century the Castilian chronicle of Don Pero Nino, *El victorial*, reported in passing that the English had killed Richard II because he had agreed a perpetual peace with France: 'they have no wish to live in peace with any other nation, for peace suits them not, seeing that they are so numerous that they cannot keep within their country.'[52]

Thus, in *Le livre des fais et bonnes meurs du sage roy Charles V*, written in November 1404, Christine de Pizan reported that the marriage of Richard II and Isabelle of France would have led to a perpetual peace:

> if fortune had not smiled upon the treason plotted by Henry of Lancaster, who captured this King Richard by means of a false and disloyal trap and put him to death. It was to avenge this treason and this odious crime . . . that the present war between the French and English arose.[53]

Similarly a pamphlet entitled *Réponse d'un bon et loyal François*, written in 1419, attacked the proposed treaty of Troyes, arguing that Henry V would never bring peace to France, especially in light of previous Lancastrians crimes such as those against Richard II and his French wife.[54] In the later pamphlet *Fluxo biennali spacio*, written between 1422 and 1429, the anonymous author berated the English, demanding 'By what means do you lament over peace, when you will always be enemies and thieves to it?', before citing the murder of Richard II, 'by whose means you might have sought perpetual peace, if you had been worthy'.[55]

At the same time, the treachery of Henry of Lancaster provided a direct justifica-

---

[48] For Count Waleran, brother of Isabelle, see Enguerran[d] de Monstrelet, *La chronique d'Enguerran de Monstrelet, avec pièces justicatives, 1400–44*, ed. L. Douët d'Arcq (6 vols, Paris, 1857–62), I, pp. 43–5, 52–7. For Orléans, see below, p. 219.

[49] Phillpotts, 'The Fate of the Truce of Paris, 1396–1415', p. 72.

[50] Craig Taylor, 'War, Propaganda and Diplomacy in Fifteenth-Century France and England', *War, Government and Power in Late Medieval France*, ed. C. T. Allmand (Liverpool, 2000), pp. 70–91.

[51] Françoise Lehoux, *Jean de France, duc de Berri: Sa vie, son action politique, 1340–1416* (4 vols, Paris, 1966–8), II, pp. 420–1.

[52] Gutierre Díaz de Gámez, *The Unconquered Knight: A Chronicle of the Deeds of Don Pero Niño, El Vitorial*, trans. Joan Evans (London, 1928), p. 104; Tuck, 'Henry IV and Europe', p. 110.

[53] Christine de Pizan, *Le livre des fais et bonnes meurs du sage roy Charles V*, ed. S. Solente (2 vols, Paris, 1936–40), I, pp. 147–8.

[54] *L'honneur de la couronne de France*, pp. 128–9.

[55] Ibid., p. 194.

tion and indeed rallying cry for the resumption of warfare.[56] In his instructions to one of the agents sent to stir up trouble in Guyenne in late 1399, Charles VI directly cited the usurpation of the English throne by Henry of Lancaster, who had broken his feudal obligations to his king and acting in a way that all noble men of true chivalric sensibilities could only condemn as dishonourable, offensive and unparalleled even in ancient Scriptures.[57] Jean Creton was the first writer to call for vengeance upon those who had deposed Richard II, concluding the *French metrical history* by declaring, 'Princes and kings, knights and barons, French, Flemings, Germans and Bretons should attack you [the English] for you have done the most horrible deed that ever man committed.' At the time that he wrote these words, Creton still believed that Richard was alive, but the realisation that the king was in fact dead simply increased Creton's appetite for revenge: he called upon Philip the Bold and the French nobility to take action in a letter addressed to the duke of Burgundy.[58] The *Traïson et mort* dramatised the point by having Richard call upon the dukes of Berry, Burgundy, Brittany and his brothers-in-law, the dauphin of Viennois and the count of St Pol, as well as other European princes such as Sigismund of Hungary, the duke of Guelders and the king of Scotland, to avenge him after his capture by the Lancastrians:

> All you noble lords of France, dukes, counts, princes and other noble knights, just as in truth I have never forfeited my knighthood, so I call upon you to protect the honour of chivalry loyally, as you have done. For it has never been known that such treason was committed against any of the noble kings of France as my own cousins and kin have committed against me. Thus I humbly beg that you might be willing to aid and support my dear father, the lord and noble king of France, whenever he chooses to seek vengeance.[59]

Robert Blondel simply declared that all Christian knights had a just title to avenge the murder of Richard II, while during the 1450s, the anonymous *Debate between the heralds* argued that France had a just quarrel with England for a number of reasons, the first of which was the murder of Richard II, husband of the 'daughter of France', a shameful act that all kings and princes had every right to try to avenge.[60]

At the same time, the French writers were certain that the Lancastrians were already reaping their just deserts. Writing in 1406, Christine de Pizan observed that Henry IV 'had stolen the crown' and declared, 'I could not believe that a traitor

---

[56] A marginal note in a contemporary manuscript noted the ironic contrast between King Demaratus, who went into exile at the court of Xerxes but still warned his own country of an impending attack, and Henry of Lancaster, who returned home to kill his own lord and usurp the throne. See Manchester, John Rylands University Library MS French 63, fol. 56r, containing Simon de Hesdin and Nicolas de Gonesse's translation of Valerius Maximus' *Facta et dicta memorabilia*, written between 1375 and 1402 for Charles VI and the duke of Berry. Cited in Morgan, 'Henry IV and the Shadow of Richard II', p. 15.

[57] J. de la Martinière, 'Instructions secrèts données par Charles VI au sire d'Albret pour soulever la Guyenne contre Henri IV', *Bibliothèque de l'Ecole des Chartes* lxxiv (1913), pp. 329–40. Ironically, Henry IV enjoyed an international reputation for his chivalric conduct, particularly crusading in Prussia: Anthony Tuck, 'Henry IV and Chivalry', *Henry IV: The Establishment of the Regime, 1399–1406*, ed. Gwilym Dodd and Douglas Biggs (York, 2003), pp. 55–71.

[58] Webb, 'Translation of a French Metrical History', pp. 421–2, 452.

[59] *Chronicque de la traïson et mort*, pp. 53–6.

[60] Robert Blondel, *Oeuvres*, I, pp. 259, 440–1; *Débat des hérauts d'armes de France et d'Angleterre, suivi de 'The debate between the heralds of England and France' by John Coke*, ed. Léopold Pannier and Paul Meyer (Paris, 1887), pp. 49–50.

would come to a good end.'[61] Her prediction appeared to come true and so the anonymous author of *Debats et appointements*, writing around 1419, referred to 'Henry [IV] who traitorously murdered the said Richard and wrongly usurped the crown of England, and then died of the sickness of leprosy.'[62] A French memorandum prepared for diplomats appearing before the papacy in the 1420s reported that Henry IV died after a brief reign 'by divine sentence', as did his son Henry who passed away 'in the flower of his youth and strength'.[63] In 1435, Jean Juvénal des Ursins observed that divine punishment had also extended to Henry IV's other sons, Clarence, Bedford and Gloucester, and then went on to argue that military defeats were divine judgment for French failure to avenge the murder and usurpation of power from King Richard; thus he too called upon Charles VII and the dauphin, Louis, to avenge the murder.[64] In the 1470s, the Burgundian chronicler, Georges Chastellain, argued that the usurpation had brought down divine retribution upon the Lancastrians, manifested in the exile of Henry VI, which forced his queen, Margaret of Anjou, to come cap in hand to Philip the Good for support.[65]

But, of course, French diplomats were also quick to identify a more practical legal consequence of the deposition of Richard II: Henry IV could not call himself king of France because he was a usurper and hence could not have rightfully inherited such a title, even supposing that any English king had ever had a rightful claim to the French throne. In 1408, Jean de Montreuil was the first French writer to make the point that Henry IV's position as a usurper destroyed any legitimate claim to either the English or the French throne.[66] In 1444, Jean Juvénal des Ursins declared that Henry IV and his Lancastrian heirs 'might not have any right to the crown and realm of England . . . [because] it would be a very strange and marvellous thing if the one who tyrannically and evilly put to death his own sovereign lord might then succeed in his place'; thus the Lancastrians certainly could not claim the French throne.[67] In 1449, Robert Blondel declared that Henry IV had tyrannically usurped the throne of England, and because of the immense horror of his crime, none of the Lancastrians could have any claim, right or title either to the kingdom of England or to that of France: 'the crime of lèse-majesté and patricide is so execrable that that man and his posterity and lineage were deprived of all majesty and lordship'. Indeed, he argued that all of the English people were culpable for this crime, and concluded that the political body deserved to be cut up and amputated, just as a doctor would treat any body that was infected.[68]

---

[61] Christine de Pizan, *Christine's Vision*, p. 121.

[62] *L'honneur de la couronne de France*, p. 65.

[63] Ibid., pp. 66–7, 195–6, 261–2.

[64] Jean Juvénal des Ursins, *Les écrits politiques*, I, p. 183; II, pp. 134, 138–160.

[65] Georges Chastellain, *Oeuvres de Georges Chastellain*, IV, ed. Kervyn de Lettenhove (Brussels, 1864), pp. 295–6 (and also see pp. 285–94).

[66] Jean de Montreuil, *Opera*, ed. N. Grévy-Pons, E. Ornato and G. Ouy (4 vols, Turin-Paris, 1963–86), II, pp. 79, 106, 196–7, 208, 250–1, 304.

[67] Jean Juvénal des Ursins, *Les écrits politiques*, I, pp. 178–9, 215; II, pp. 100, 158–9, 164.

[68] Robert Blondel, *Oeuvres*, I, pp. 258–9, 272–3 (*Oratio historialis*), 440, 456–7 (*Des droiz de la couronne de France*). Also see the *De complanctu bonorum Galicorum* and its French translation by the clerk Robinet, in ibid., I, pp. 35–6, 130–1.

Armagnacs and Burgundians

The deposition of Richard II also had a direct impact on the internal politics of France, and in particular on the mounting tensions between the Armagnac supporters of the duke of Orléans and the Burgundians. Both factions condemned the murder of Richard II, but the Burgundians claimed that Louis, duke of Orléans, had been complicit in the actions of Henry of Lancaster, while Armagnac writers attacked the duke of Burgundy for acting just like Henry of Lancaster when he murdered the duke of Orléans in 1407.

Immediately before the usurpation of 1399, Henry of Lancaster was warmly welcomed into the French royal court during a brief period of exile, taking up residence in the Hôtel de Clisson. He clearly charmed the French princes, so much so that Jean, duke of Berry, offered his daughter to Henry in marriage and Louis, duke of Orléans, signed a treaty of friendship and support with the English duke.[69] Following the deposition and murder of Richard II, this personal alliance with Henry was a particular embarrassment to Orléans, and so the French duke went out of his way to demonstrate his anger at the treatment of Richard II and his French widow.[70] Orléans played a leading role in organising the military actions against the Lancastrians: he assisted David Lindsay, earl of Crawford, in assembling a fleet with which to harass English shipping in 1402; and in May of that year, seven of the duke's knights and officers defeated seven English knights in single combat, declaring that, during a truce, this was the only legitimate and honourable way that they might avenge the murder of Richard II and the treatment of his widow Isabelle. On three occasions during the next eighteen months, Orléans personally challenged Henry IV to single combat, charging Henry with the responsibility for the death of Richard II and the harm done to Queen Isabelle.[71]

Nevertheless, Orléans' association with the treacherous Henry of Lancaster offered a powerful weapon for his political opponents in France. On 23 November 1407, Louis, duke of Orléans, was assassinated on the instructions of John the Fearless, duke of Burgundy. In March of the following year, the theologian, Jean Petit, delivered a four-hour defence of the murder at the royal residence at St Pol, the *Justification de monseigneur le duc de Bourgogne*. Petit argued that Burgundy had acted in a virtuous manner, killing a traitor and tyrant who had planned to kill the king and his heirs, and to seize the throne for himself.[72] One aspect of Orléans' treason, according to Petit, was that the French duke had conspired with Henry of Lancaster, an infamous traitor, to murder Richard II and Charles VI; Petit claimed that

---

[69] *Chronique du religieux de Saint-Denis*, II, pp. 674–6, 697–708; and the alliance signed between Orleans and Lancaster in June 1399 in *Chronicles of the Revolution*, pp. 105–6, 109–14.

[70] In June 1406, Isabelle married Louis's son Charles and her dowry included the claim for the repayment of the 200,000 francs originally paid as dowry for her marriage to Richard II and now due for repayment by Henry IV. Phillpotts, 'The Fate of the Truce of Paris, 1396–1415', p. 71.

[71] *Chronique du religieux de Saint-Denis*, III, pp. 30–4, 54–60; Bertrand Schnerb, *Les Armagnacs et les Bourguignons: La maudite guerre* (Paris, 1988), pp. 64–7; Morgan, 'Henry IV and the Shadow of Richard II', pp. 17–18. Christine de Pizan regarded these challenges as testimony to the chivalrous courage of the duke, in *Le livre des fais et bonnes meurs du sage roy Charles V*, I, pp. 170–1.

[72] This public address was widely distributed, particularly through countless paper copies produced by a veritable production line. Charity Cannon Willard, 'The Manuscripts of Jean Petit's *Justification*: Some Burgundian Propaganda Methods of the Early Fifteenth Century', *Studii Francesi* xlviii (1969), pp. 271–280.

Richard II had even denounced Orléans to Charles VI during their famous meeting at Ardres in 1396. Thus the Burgundians sought to put a sinister spin on the friendship and alliance between Orléans and Henry of Lancaster, clearly seeking to play upon the paranoid fears of Charles VI.[73]

A similar theme appeared just a year later, in the third part of *Dialogues* of Pierre Salmon. In the course of a complex narrative of his diplomatic missions to the English royal court following the wedding of Richard II and Isabelle of France, Salmon reported that the English king feared for the safety of his father-in-law, Charles VI, whose health and even life were at risk because of the diabolical arts of Louis of Orléans. According to Salmon, the evidence for these accusations was provided by a Burgundian cleric who denounced Orléans to Richard II. In retrospect, such a source would appear to be unreliable, but Salmon said that the information was confirmed much later, when he met with the merchant Giovanni Rapondi in Lucca and learned that Orléans' father-in-law, Giangaleazzo Visconti, owned a silver image that kept Charles VI in subjugation.[74] Clearly these charges against Orléans tied in with the accusations voiced by Jean Petit in March 1408, leading most modern scholars to identify Salmon as a Burgundian sympathiser.[75] Yet Salmon may have been pursuing a more sophisticated strategy than simply attacking the duke of Orléans. The French duke was presented as an example of a prince who refused to listen to counsel; he had ignored Salmon's three correct warnings of impending disaster, and therefore served as a mechanism to persuade King Charles VI to listen to the advice offered by Salmon. Hedeman has noted that the same message was offered through the association of Orléans and Richard II in a prophecy of doom offered by a Carthusian monk and in the pair of miniatures accompanying this passage, where Salmon himself guides Charles VI, Richard II and Orléans away from a devil-infested river.[76] Moreover it is hard to see Salmon as an advocate of political assassination and tyrannicide: when Richard II indicated to Salmon that he wanted to assassinate the duke of Orléans and thereby protect his father-in-law, the king of France, Salmon proudly declared:

> that my lord the duke of Orléans was the brother of the king of France, my sovereign lord, and moreover that he was my natural lord, and that I was his man; and that if he was the case that he had been disloyal like [Richard II] said, even so I was not the one who should correct him; and that with regard to anything that might cause inconvenience to his person, for whatever good that might come to be, I would not be the cause nor would I consent.[77]

This was a typically submissive response to tyranny amongst the fifteenth-century French, and in this context it is hardly surprising that Jean Petit's campaign to exonerate Jean Petit for the crime of tyrannicide failed. In September 1413, Jean

---

[73] Enguerran[d] de Monstrelet, *La chronique*, I, pp. 178–242; Coville, *Jean Petit et la question de tyrannicide*, pp. 337–42.

[74] Pierre Salmon, *Les demandes faites par le roi Charles VI*, pp. 43–71, 84–5.

[75] See for example Willard, 'The Manuscripts of Jean Petit's *Justification*', p. 273; Bernard Guenée, *Un meurtre, une société : L'assassinat du duc d'Orléans, 23 Novembre 1407* (Paris, 1992), pp. 210–23.

[76] Pierre Salmon, *Les demandes faites par le roi Charles VI*, pp. 64, 115–6, together with the miniatures in Paris, Bibliothèque Nationale MS français 23279, fols 64v-65r, discussed in Anne D. Hedeman, *Of Counselors and Kings: The Three Versions of Pierre Salmon's 'Dialogues'* (Urbana-Champaign, 2001), pp. 17–25.

[77] Pierre Salmon, *Les demandes faites par le roi Charles VI*, p. 56.

Gerson, chancellor of Notre-Dame, preached a thinly veiled attack on the king's decision to allow Burgundy to go unpunished for the murder of Orléans, stressing the commandment 'Thou shalt not kill.' When some of Gerson's arguments were in turn challenged within the university by those with Burgundian sympathies, Charles of Orléans used the opportunity to launch an investigation into Jean Petit's *Justification* that led to its condemnation by the bishop of Paris and the council of Constance.[78] Shortly afterwards, the example of the deposition of Richard II was turned back against the duke of Burgundy. In the poem, the *De complanctu bonorum Gallicorum*, written in May 1418, Robert Blondel attacked the duke of Burgundy for being a traitor and perjurer who had murdered Louis duke of Orléans; Blondel was keen to highlight the parallels between the crimes committed by Henry IV against Richard II and the actions of John the Fearless against Louis of Orléans.[79]

Epilogue

Most French writers during the first half of the fifteenth century were united in condemning the murder and deposition of Richard II, using it as an *exemplum* with which to emphasise the horrors of usurpation rather than the problems of misgovernment and tyranny. As a result, French reactions to the Lancastrian revolution offer a valuable case study of the Valois rhetorical campaign against the notion of active resistance to a king, given momentum by sheer fatigue after such a sustained period of civil and international conflict and because it became increasingly clear that only the monarch could provide a solution to the woes besetting France.

This fragile French consensus regarding the deposition of Richard II was challenged by the Yorkist usurpation of the English throne in 1461. French propagandists had long championed the claim of what was to become the Yorkist line, descendants of Richard's brother Lionel, duke of Clarence. In a letter written in 1404 or 1405, probably to Owyn Glyn Dwr, Jean de Montreuil referred to Edmund, earl of March, as 'the heir of England' and later explained that March was the closest heir descending from Edward III.[80] In 1435 and 1444 Jean Juvénal also explained that, 'If there are any closer than Henry of Lancaster, it is those of the line of March, Percy and Northumberland, the issue of Lionel who was the son of Edward III and the older brother of the duke of Lancaster.'[81] Yet Louis XI was unwilling simply to acknowledge Edward IV as rightful king of England after he had usurped the throne in 1461, whether he was the rightful heir of Richard II or not. It is perhaps not surprising that a diplomatic manual written in 1464, *Pour ce que plusieurs*, was the very first of its genre to ignore the events of 1399.[82] This omis-

---

78 R. C. Famiglietti, *Royal Intrigue: Crisis at the Court of Charles VI, 1392–1420* (New York, 1982), pp. 136–42.

79 Robert Blondel, *Oeuvres*, I, pp. 38 (*De complanctu*), 140 (Robinet's translation).

80 Perhaps the Mortimer claim was well known in France at this time, or alternatively Gruffudd Yonge and John Hanmer, Owain Glyn Dwr's ambassadors at the French court, were putting forward the claim of their new allies, the Mortimers and Percies. Davies, *The Revolt of Owain Glyn Dwr*, chapter 7.

81 Jean Juvénal did suggest, though, that the failure to avenge the murder of Richard II ultimately rendered all Englishmen, including the heirs of Lionel, duke of Clarence, ineligible to succeed to the throne: the widows of Edward II and Richard II, both named Isabelle, had passed the English crown to their French family, the Valois dynasty. Jean Juvénal des Ursins, *Les écrits politiques*, I, pp. 175–82; II, pp. 156, 159.

82 *Debating the Hundred Years War: 'Pour ce que plusieurs', the 'Vraie chronique dEscoce' and 'A*

sion did not correspond with a contemporary change in French interest in the fate of Richard II, because the *Traïson et mort* was included in three of the manuscripts of *Pour ce que plusieurs*. Rather, this surprising tact demonstrates Louis XI's desire to force the Yorkists to buy his recognition, and may also reflect the author's personal support for the exiled Lancastrian king.

Yet there was mounting interest in the deposition of Richard II at the Burgundian court following the alliance between Philip the Good, duke of Burgundy, and the Yorkist king, Edward IV, in 1466. Reviewing manuscripts of Book IV of Froissart's *Chroniques* produced for the Burgundian court, Le Guay has demonstrated that there was a clear effort to use miniatures to highlight the events that had culminated in the deposition of Richard II.[83] Presumably, this narrative was valuable both because it demonstrated that the Lancastrians had never had a rightful claim to the throne, but also because it encouraged parallels between Richard II and Edward IV after the Yorkist king was driven from the English throne in 1469 and Henry regained power. Certainly the marriage between Richard II and the French princess, Isabelle, echoed the marriage between the count of Charolais and Margaret of York in 1468.

Finally, a remarkable perspective on the deposition of Richard II emerged in the 1470s in the chronicles of the Norman bishop, Thomas Basin. He defended the attempt of Richard, duke of York, to seize the English crown in 1460, citing the fact that York was the rightful heir to Richard II; the Lancastrians had committed crimes not just against king Richard but also against the earl of Cambridge, York's father, who was executed by Henry V. Thus Basin happily declared that, with the coronation of Edward IV, the crown had returned to the house of Richard II.[84] Basin had personal connections with Richard, duke of York, and so it is perhaps no surprise that he gave his support to the Yorkist cause.[85] At the same time, though, Basin was quite willing to argue that subjects had a right to coerce a tyrant, and defended the recent war of the Public Weal, a magnate rebellion in which he himself had been closely involved.[86] When such a prominent commentator condones an act of usurpation, we have clearly moved on from the fragile unanimity of the first half of the fifteenth century. It should come as no surprise that in 1484, Jean de Rély, spokesman for the Estates General, again felt the need to emphasise that 'In England, they often put their kings to death, but the good and loyal people of France would never do such a thing.'[87]

---

declaracon of the trew and dewe title of . . . my most dredd soveraigne lorde Henrie [VIII]', ed. Craig Taylor (forthcoming).

[83] Laetitia Le Guay, *Les princes de Bourgogne, lecteurs de Froissart: Les rapports entre le texte et l'image dans les manuscrits enluminés du Livre IV des 'Chroniques'* (Paris, 1999), pp. 117–18.

[84] Thomas Basin, *Histoire de Charles VII*, ed. Charles Samaran (2 vols, Paris, 1933–4), I, p. 34; II, pp. 170, 256.

[85] Basin had benefited from the support of Zenone Castiglioni, bishop of Bayeux, who had been a councillor of Richard, duke of York; he had taken part in the embassy to Charles VII in 1445 to arrange a marriage between York's son Edward and a royal princess. Bernard Guenée, *Between Church and State: The Lives of Four French Prelates in the Late Middle Ages* (Chicago, 1991), pp. 290–4.

[86] Thomas Basin, *Histoire de Louis XI*, ed. Charles Samaran (3 vols, Paris, 1963–72), I, pp. 177ff.

[87] Jean Masselin, *Journal des Etats généraux*, p. 253, and also see the comments of the chancellor of France, Guillaume de Rochefort, ibid, p. 38. The limited success of Valois propaganda on regicide has been highlighted by Sanford Zale, 'The French Kill their King: The Assassination of Childeric II in Late-Medieval French Historiography', *Fifteenth-Century Studies* xxvii (2001), pp. 273–94.